Georgia State Literary Studies

3

THE CINEMATIC TEXT

Methods and Approaches

Edited by

R. Barton Palmer

AMS Press
New York

Georgia State
Literary Studies
AMS Press
Series General Editor
Victor A. Kramer
Volume One: *British Novelists Since 1900*
Volume Two: *Harlem Renaissance Re-examined*
Volume Three: *The Cinematic Text: Methods and Approaches*
Volume Four: *Coleridge's Theory of the Imagination Today*
ISSN 0884-8696.

Georgia State Literary Studies: No. 3
Other titles published in this series:
No. 1. Jack I. Biles, ed. *British Novelists Since 1900.* 1987.
No. 2. Victor A. Kramer, ed. *The Harlem Renaissance Re-examined.*
1988

Library of Congress Cataloging-in-Publication Data

The Cinematic text.
  (Georgia State literary studies, ISSN 0884-8696; v3)
  Bibliography: p.
  Includes index.
  1. Motion pictures. I. Palmer, R. Barton, 1946- II. Series.
PN1995.C535 1987   791.43'.01   87-45796
ISBN 0-404-63203-3

AMS Press, Inc.
56 East 13th Street
New York, N.Y. 10003

Manufactured in the United States of America

TABLE OF CONTENTS

NOTES ON CONTRIBUTORS

DUDLEY ANDREW directs the film program at the University of Iowa. Among his many distinguished contributions to the field are two recent books, *Concepts in Film Theory* and *Film in the Aura of Art*.

DAVID BORDWELL is head of the film department at The University of Wisconsin (Madison). He is the author of a number of books devoted to film including, recently, *Narration in the Fiction Film* and, with Janet Staiger and Kristin Thompson, *The Classic Hollywood Cinema*.

PETER BRUNETTE teaches film in the English Department of George Mason University. Author of a number of articles on Italian film and film theory, he will soon publish a book-length study of Roberto Rossellini.

NOËL CARROLL/PATRICK CARROLL are brothers who share an interest in music. Noël teaches in the philosophy department at Wesleyan University (Connecticut) and has published many influential articles on various aspects of film theory. Patrick is a professional musician.

STUART KAMINSKY is the chairperson of the Radio/Television/Film department at Northwestern University (Evanston). A much-published novelist, he has also written extensively on the American cinema, including *American Film Genres* and a study of the director John Huston.

E. ANN KAPLAN teaches film at Rutgers University. Her *Women and Film: Both Sides of the Camera*, as well her many articles on feminist criticism, have been very influential in the field.

JAMES NAREMORE teaches English and film at Indiana University. He is the author of a number of film books, including studies of Hitchcock and Welles (*The Magic World of Orson Welles*). The essay published here is part of a larger study of performance theory and film acting soon to be published by the University of California Press.

BILL NICHOLS is chairman of the cinema studies department at San Francisco State University. His works on film include the two volumes of *MOVIES AND METHODS* as well as *Ideology and the Image*.

R. BARTON PALMER teaches English and film at Georgia State University. He is the author of a number of articles on film theory and American film history, and a forthcoming book on *film noir, Apocalyptic Desire*.

RORY PALMIERI was a graduate teaching assistant at Brown University when he wrote this article, which is part of his dissertation on the films of Sam Peckinpah.

WILLIAM SIMON is chairman of the Cinema Studies department at New York University. Author of a number of articles on contemporary American film and narrative theory, he will soon publish a book-length study of film and narrative.

STANLEY J. SOLOMON is the founder and director of the Multi-Image Center at Iona College, where he is currently engaged as writer and producer in all aspects of multi-image design. He is the author of numerous essays on film and also literature, including *The Film Idea* and *The Classic Cinema*.

JANET STAIGER currently teaches film at the University of Texas (Austin). She is the author of a number of studies of American Film/film history including, with David Bordwell and Kristin Thompson, *The Classic Hollywood Cinema*.

ROBERT STAM teaches film at New York University. He has written extensively on avant-garde and Third World film, including a book on Brazilian cinema. His most recent book is *Reflexivity in Film and Literature*.

PREFACE

This volume of essays about film theory reflects the usefulness of spirited interaction between literary and cultural studies. It is also a reflection of the fact that it is no longer possible for scholars within a particular subject area to remain isolated within that discipline; in fact, it stands as an illustration that cross-fertilization provides valuable new possibilities of analysis. As English Studies have developed during the past decades, it has become increasingly clear that while from some points of view a crisis has developed because of limitations of methodology, in other areas adaptation of theoretical methods to new fields of study has opened up wider possibilities of interpretation.

The essays in this book are part of this wider field of awareness. As an editor and scholar trained first in medieval literature and in theory, R. Barton Palmer has sought in his investigation of the cinema, and in his development of this book, to extend his methodological skills to the area of cinema, the area in the humanities best known in the past decades for growth.

It is no coincidence that such growth, interaction, and adaptation should take place in and through study of the cinema. It may be an exaggeration to say that while poetry and prose remain the core of what literature scholars study, it is in the cinema that the public, and I must suspect many of our best students, come to an awareness of the complexity of culture in a post-modern age. These essays, then, are rigorously old-fashioned in that they grow out of as great a concern for works of art as the most demanding studies of literature. In some ways, however, they go beyond such concerns to raise fundamental questions about a new poetics of the cinema.

Victor A. Kramer
General Editor
Literary Studies
Georgia State University

INTRODUCTION
R. Barton Palmer

This volume contains revised essays originally published in two issues of *Studies in the Literary Imagination* devoted to film criticism and theory: "Narration in Film" (Spring 1983) and "Contemporary Methods of Film Scholarship" (Spring 1986). It also contains three articles, or, more properly, monographs, especially commissioned for the expansion of those two issues into book form, and a postscriptum.

The film numbers represented a significant departure for *Studies*, which until that time had largely limited itself to areas of strictly literary interest. In part, the editorial board was motivated by its recognition that film studies, borrowing much from literary scholarship but addressing quite different questions and concerns, had come of age; film scholars, it was felt, had something to offer to the study of fictional texts which might prove useful to those students of literature who constitute the bulk of the journal's readers. Neither issue, however, would have been possible had not a number of leading critics in the field felt that such a forum could likewise benefit cinema studies by affording it some greater visibility to those working in a more established (and institutionally influential) area. Much the same desire has motivated the subsequent contributors to this expanded book version.

And yet these essays do not address themselves only to students of literature curious about or eager to learn from developments in a related discipline. Those authors whose work is collected here are all very much involved with shaping the direction of research in a field which, unlike literary study, has yet to be colonized by a meta-approach; such an approach might determine, in natural and seemingly inevitable ways, the tasks and concerns of the area as a whole. This

1

is to say that film studies has experienced nothing comparable to the
New Criticism which, despite a decade or more of concerted and often
shrill attack, still wields an apparently unshakable influence over the
way literary scholars view "criticsm" and even the concept of "literature" itself. As William Cain, among others, has taken pains to
demonstrate, the "crisis" in criticism today is properly not the threat
posed by different methods such as deconstruction and reception aesthetics to the notion of literary scholarship, but rather the quite evident
fact that these challenges have tended to self-destruct, accommodating
their radical insights to entrenched ideas about what critics should
actually do.[1] In film studies, the situation is quite different. As a
result, the essays in this book do not exemplify a complacent pluralism
of approaches, all of which, despite superficial differences, share something essential in common like an emphasis on close analysis or the
same canon of valorized works. Indeed, David Bordwell's polemical
definition of historical poetics argues that his approach to film study
is not a "method" in the sense that other approaches are; these, he
suggests, are interested in generating certain kinds of "interpretations," while historical poetics asks questions about form—broadly
speaking—rather than meaning. For film scholars, then, the practical
analyses and methodological statements included in this volume possess an urgent timeliness because they are related to ongoing struggles
within the field itself about a consensual agenda of research concerns
and interests.

The first part of the book contains essays that grapple, in different
ways, with the question of narrative in film. A founding premise of
most structuralist/semiotic work on narrative (work that now has its
own specialized name—narratology) is that storytelling is a function
of different semiotic systems; in Hjemslev's famous definition, natural
language is the material of expression, while narrative discourse in
that language constitutes the form of expression. Narratology, therefore, assumes that different materials of expression, film and natural
language, to cite the most relevant and important examples, can be
used in essentially the same fashion to tell stories. Thus popular handbooks of structuralist work on narrative such as Seymour Chatman's
Story and Discourse argue for the basic similarities between fictional
and cinematic narration. Such research, however, raises a related question. If film and literature constitute similar forms of narration, can
the same critical methods employed in literary study be used to analyze

individual films and to generalize about cinematic narration? Or, what is the specificity of cinematic discourse and what kind of critical response should it evoke?

There is one obvious and important difference between literary and cinematic texts. As Raymond Bellour has pointed out, the filmic text is irremediably unquotable. Therefore it can be "placed" within any critical discourse, or constituted as a proper object of that discourse, only through a necessarily distorting process of transposition. While the literary critic may easily incorporate portions of the text under discussion into the analysis, there is no way the film critic may do so other than by verbalizing what is only partly verbal. The cinema, as Christian Metz has usefully suggested, consists of five separate "tracks" of meaning—language, images, printed/written materials, diegetic noise, and music; only two of these tracks are "verbal" in the ordinary sense. The result for traditional criticism, Kristin Thompson maintains, is an inevitable reduction of the complex interplay among the different sources of meaning within the film. Thus Thompson argues that mainstream literary methods should not be used by the cinema critic:

> . . . much critical methodology has been based on general New Critical approaches. That is, the critic defines a context for analysis and interpretation . . . Since this approach consists mainly of paraphrasing cinematic meanings into words, reductivism inevitably results. Often the contextualist film critic (and by now we are far from the sophistication of true New Criticism) resorts to 'literaricizing' films by basing interpretations on metaphorical descriptions of filmic techniques.[2]

Thompson and Bellour (among others within the growing academic cinema establishment) are certainly correct to recognize that literary-based methods of analysis can easily distort the different kinds of signification contained in the filmic text. In a related essay on deconstruction and film collected in this volume, Peter Brunette points out that filmic language, more obviously than natural language, is characterized by a dissemination or dispersal of meaning that must be "repressed" if accustomed paraphrases of image content are to be made. Because film is a truly synthetic medium (as Eisenstein noticed some fifty years ago), its discourses are not adequately accommodated by the "literaricizing" methods mentioned by Thompson, methods which, after all, have developed in response to quite different critical tasks. Cinematic specificity does indeed call for particular kinds of critical analysis; such critical approach must take direct (and not metaphoric) account of uniquely cinematic properties like editing, composition, and non-diegetic sound.

That said, however, we must also emphasize that, owing to its synthetic nature, film is related to literature in important ways. Indeed, Christian Metz maintains that film as *language* has developed in response to the need to tell a story; the feature film as we know is evolved through a series of complex interrelationships with different literary forms, most important, perhaps, the commercial drama and popular novel. As a result, many cinematic properties, especially those central to the definition of what has been called the "classic" film text, are analogous in their function to the devices of literary narrative. Not surprisingly, therefore, Thompson's definition of the film text stresses the similarity between films and literary narrative as well as obvious differences:

> Basically, we may consider a film a temporal flow of devices, each justified in its inclusion by a specific motivation; these are collectively shaped by a dominant structure. A proairetic chain creates a narrative, with a hermeneutic helping to provide its forward impetus; the delays in the unraveling of the enigma deflect the proairetic into a staircase construction. . . . The narrative as embodied in the film is the plot (p. 46).

As a "temporal flow of devices," the film text is similar to the literary text; Thompson's use of Barthesian terms to account for the connectedness and directionality of that flow implicitly argues for the connection between the two media as storytelling vehicles. Thompson's exhaustively formalistic analysis of *Ivan the Terrible*, of course, predictably foregrounds the film's embodiment of narrative through cinematically specific devices. She properly describes these without recourse to distorting metaphor, "quoting" from the text by means of extensive frame enlargements whose complexities are never recuperated by simplifying summaries. But, she suggests, the narrative itself—the abstract notion of the flow of the text—may be revealingly described with concepts developed by a literary theorist. Rather, we should say theorists, because the influence of the Russian formalists (e.g., the key concept of the "device") is evident in her analysis as well. Thompson, it is interesting to note, later acknowledges that

Boris Eikhenbaum's work on literature offers more to the film critic than his observations about cinematic stylistics.

The neoformalism advocated by Thompson, of course, constitutes an approach to the film text (if not a method for its interpretation) which has hardly gained universal acceptance within the field. Yet, with its insistence on the uniquely cinematic and its deep literary roots, neoformalism does quite usefully indicate how cinema studies has both emphasized its particular aims and borrowed what was needed from literary theory. In fact, it might well be true that the field of cinema studies has been more influenced by *recent* literary theory than literary criticism itself has. Having no traditional methodologies to shed, except the primitive evaluative and sociological approaches of the journalistic past, film studies has been more open to and accommodating of the new. Cinema studies, moreover, has become increasingly "politicized" (perhaps one should say "radicalized") during the last decade for a variety of institutional and disciplinary reasons; hence the various challenges to critical orthodoxy raised in the recent past have apparently found more willing converts in film than in literature departments. Furthermore, the serious study of film began in France and thus, perhaps inevitably, has been inflected by French theoretical developments—structuralism, psychoanalytic approaches, poststructuralist methods.

Concerned with the narrative aspects of film, the essays collected in this first section illustrate the applicability of a wide variety of literary concepts and approaches to film criticism. While all (with one exception) are devoted to the analysis of filmic texts or *oeuvres*, they also evidence the concern within cinema studies for questions of theory and methodology.

Robert Stam's comparative study of Buñuel and Hitchcock is largely author-centered; that is, it notes thematic/formal patterns across a director's *oeuvre* with a view toward illuminating the relation between his life and works. Cinematic auteurism can be traced to its origin in Romantic theories of the artist and his role in textual creation. Popularized in this country by the journalist Andrew Sarris (the method derives from the *Cahiers du Cinema* circle in France), auteurism provides not only an evaluative criterion (the personality of the director as revealed by thematic obsessions and stylistic signatures) but also a grounding for interpretation. Stam's study, however, goes much further than most auteurist criticism in making use of the formalistic tactic of backgrounding, or definition of a context in which the analysis offered assumes a particular value. As he demonstrates, the careers of Buñuel and Hitchcock parallel each other significantly because each director worked within the same problematic of "law and desire." The result is an interesting and nuanced analysis that speaks to a number of larger issues, including especially the "politics" of both directors and the complex relationship between the commercial and avant-garde or "art" cinemas.

Like Stam, Rory Palmieri begins his examination of *Straw Dogs* from an auteurist premise: namely that the various works of a true auteur are related to one another by common intellectual, moral, and perceptual similarities. For Palmieri, however, the initial question of how *Straw Dogs*, a non-western, connects with Sam Peckinpah's previous films, all westerns, ultimately leads to a larger issue: the nature of genres. Working with the psychoanalytical allegoresis of the western developed by Raymond Bellour, Palmieri argues that *Straw Dogs* is structured by the codes of the classic western, insofar as these can be transposed to a contemporary drama. From this perspective, the film's relationship to its novelistic source takes on an added dimension (i.e. the adaptation process is mediated by the generic structures of the film western), while Peckinpah's interest in making a non-western can be seen, in part, as prompted by his desire to view contemporary social/sexual relations from the perspective of a persistent American myth. The result is a reading that demonstrates the effect of the western genre not only on the text but within it, as a structuring presence that affects the main character's fall into unrestrained violence. The western then, as Palmieri sees it, is not only a conventional structure of popular fiction but a "time bomb in the psyche of the repressed American male" (p. 60).

Stanley J. Solomon's survey of narrative structures in recent American films reminds us that the cinema can be seen not only in relation to the artists responsible for individual texts, but as part of a complex dialectic: this dialectic is constituted by the consumption dynamics of popular culture, which involve the desire of producers to make a popular product and the desire of the public to see and hear what it wants. Solomon begins by emphasizing that films are cultural objects, products of an industry whose ultimate aim is profit. Like other students of popular cinema types, Solomon sees film genres as, at least in part, the result of an interaction between producers and their consuming public. As he convincingly demonstrates, American films in general have discarded their Aristotelian heritage, as this was modified to suit the medium by D.W. Griffith during his influential years at Biograph. While the Griffith film relies on a causally linked chain of events with a discernible beginning, middle, and end (where the climax, to generate suspense and energy, is now placed), the narrative structure of many recent films depends on the exploration of the implications of some initially established situation. Such narratives lack both causal connections and what Roland Barthes would term a hermeneutic. As Solomon points out, these structural changes may eventually bring about an alteration in audience expectations about commercial film storytelling.

Novelist and critic Stuart Kaminsky brings a unique point of view to his analysis of Sergio Leone's *Once Upon a Time in America*, because he was in part responsible for its scripting. Since George Bluestone's pioneering work on film adaptations of novels, comparative studies of the two media have emphasized cinema's limited ability to articulate temporal distinctions. Kaminsky's essay challenges the received view that film, as André Bazin put it, has only a "present tense." Kaminsky demonstrates, in fact, that *Once Upon a Time in America* is a meditation on the relationship between time and experience, on the one hand, and consciousness, on the other. In his analysis, moreover, Kaminsky makes effective use of Gérard Genette's theorizing on the relationship between story time and discourse time, showing how the work of this narratologist has important implications for those in cinema studies.

Similarly, William Simon draws on Genette (and on other literary theorists, notably Roland Barthes and Wolfgang Iser) to explain the complexity of narration in one of the most important texts of the Hollywood Renaissance of the early seventies, Francis Ford Coppola's *The Godfather, Part One*. Simon shows how complex attitudes toward the film's main characters are developed not only by the establishment of cultural contradictions drawn from Italian-American experience, but by a narration that encourages identification with, even as it formulates a subtle and pervasive critique of, the main characters, especially Michael. Simon's analysis is particularly valuable because it demonstrates the ways in which the withholding of narrative information (creating what Iser terms "gaps") or, conversely, the straightforward exposition of that information, is closely connected with thematic development—here, particularly, the manipulation of spectatorial attitudes toward the explicit violence often foregrounded in the film. He demonstrates that the text, in fact, is less ambiguous than has commonly been thought, though he acknowledges that the director's view of Michael as hopelessly corrupted by what happens to him is established in nuanced and indirect ways.

Peter Brunette's essay on Rossellini's famous neorealist film *Paisan* proceeds from auteurist premises about the "wholeness" of a directorial *oeuvre*, but quickly moves toward a rejection of such unifying desires. As Brunette suggests, "our drive for wholeness is not an entirely innocent operation, either, for we seek (and find) an organic unity only at the expense of an 'organic' diversity" (p. 136). Examining the attempts of different critics to find centers (thematic and otherwise) is this cinematic anthology of short-story-like episodes, Brunette demonstrates that even individual episodes can hardly be supposed to have an identifiable thematic point. He therefore finally rejects any New Critical understanding of the fact of diversity as a "tension of opposites." Instead he invokes Derrida's notion of "undecidability" to explain the effect of the film. Brunette's approach suggests that conventional definitions of neorealism (which posit a close "match" between history or reality and text) may need re-evaluation in the light of what poststructuralist criticism reveals about the workings of cinematic signification. Are such films in their dispersive failure to discover the "presence" of unity truly different from other kinds of texts in which such failure is more openly acknowledged?

Unlike the other essays in this section, my own study of Siegfried Kracauer's film theory is not text-centered, at least in an obvious sense. I do argue, however, for the rehabilitation of Kracauer, whose work on the cinema has been much neglected because of earlier, only partial understandings of his intentions. Usually classified a "realist," Kracauer's theories of cinematic mimeticism are heavily inflected by both the conventionalism of literary realism and the anti-realism of the modernist movement. Kracauer, in short, attempts to identify the particular value of cinematic representation as an "incorporation" of the real—at least in part—within the signifying, formal structures of the filmic text. The cinema thus fulfills the goals of traditional realist fiction even as it exceeds the capacities of mere art—which must always deal with imitation and imitation alone—to manifest the real. Intriguingly, Kracauer suggests that narrative in the fiction film is not simply a conventional artistic structure but a phenomenon which is also, to some degree, "found" in the raw material of cinematic re-presenation. Thus, like the contributors to the first part of the book, Kracauer endorses the specificity of the film medium even as he acknowledges that the cinema shares with literature both a storytelling and a representational capacity.

As I suggested earlier, one of the purposes of this volume is to provide a forum for the competing claims of various critical orientations within the field of cinema studies. While the essays in part one address this disciplinary issue in implicit terms, those in part two do so more directly. In her essay on the current state of feminist film criticism, E. Ann Kaplan observes that such work has now been going on long enough to have generated its own narrative, its own theory of development. Kaplan rightly sees this as potentially dangerous, because such an understanding would privilege later concerns/approaches over earlier ones, dividing critical work into stages and perhaps minimizing overlaps and connections. In contrast, her own essay speaks to a theoretical needs addressed in different ways by the other contributors, namely the importance of re-assessing the major developments in film criticism over the past decade with a view toward recovering what might be useful for current work. Like Kaplan's, the other essays collected here avoid seeing the *états presents* of different approaches as achieved states that have superseded other, earlier ones, but rather as moments that must look back to the recent (and sometimes not so recent) past for both guidance and enrichment.

The time is now right for such a reappraisal. Cinema studies is no longer the marginal academic specialty it was in the early seventies. But if it has achieved a more prominent place in our universities, the study of film has in no way become an "establishment" within liberal arts curricula. Unlike professors of language and literature in the early part of this century, therefore, film scholars have not been forced to justify their position by recourse to the traditional values of academic humanism. In the early seventies, of course, this more conservative course did seem a likely one. The importatation of the *politique des auteurs* from the *Cahiers* critics in France made it possible for film studies to organize itself in a literary fashion, as the study of "great authors" whose voices, according to the Leavisite model of artistic communication, could be heard speaking of significant, morally enlightening experience. As we have seen, several essays in part one of this volume are heavily indebted to auteurism (however much Stam,

Palmieri, and Brunette find other kinds of interest in the films and directors they discuss). Auteurism might have led cinema studies to adopt a conservative, Arnoldian role within the university (can it be an accident that John Ford, the American director most thoroughly studied by the auteurists, was a patriotic traditionalist who celebrated the potent myths of American civilization, especially, in his many western films, the victory of culture over anarchy?).

Historical developments, however, prevented auteurism from becoming the dominant approach in film studies. The most important of these was the radicalization of French film/literary criticism in the wake of the upheavals of 1968. Structuralist and poststructuralist theory and approaches, imports from France (though mediated in an important way by the left-wing critics writing for the British journal *Screen*), greatly influenced the work of American cinema scholars in the formative years of the early seventies, when film studies programs became established in most American universities. As a result, film scholarship became a heavily theorized enterprise, a complex intersection of Marxist, psychoanalytic, and more traditional (auteurist, genre, sociological) approaches. Such developments have in many ways been a mixed blessing; in an essay written especially for this volume, David Bordwell discusses the ways in which these "theories" have often been misapplied or misdirected, though it seems to me fairly obvious as well that some significant advances have been made, especially in connecting the cinema, as a social phenomenon, with other areas of cultural production. In any case, though literary scholarship in America was also much inflected by many of these same theoretical innovations (most issued, in fact, from literary criticism), the new methods and outlooks attained a central position in film study that they have never established in literary study (despite the influential "conversion" of key figures in establishments such as Yale, Brown, and Johns Hopkins). It is this background which the essays in Part Two of this book reassess from various perspectives and in light of current concerns, many of which are challenging "received models."

Beginning with E. Ann Kaplan's meditations on feminist theory and critical work makes a necessary political statement about gender issues. Here is a critical perspective which, for extra-disciplinary reasons, has a prior claim on our attention. We also need to acknowledge, however, as Kaplan herself suggests, that this area of inquiry has from the outset played a central role within film criticism. Kaplan treats the accomplishments of feminist critics not in terms of stages or schools, but rather insofar as they address a basic issue: is the concept of "woman" biologically derived or culturally produced? For the so-called essentialist critics biologism plays a central role; thus what matters is the kind of representation that "femaleness" receives from the dominant institutions of cinematic production. For the anti-essentialists, however, the concept of "woman" is a patriarchal construction, one with which the cinema, as a powerful area of cultural production concerned with images and their meaning, has been heavily involved. In the wake of Laura Mulvey's influential analysis of Hollywood as a cinema dominated by the "male look," much anti-essentialist work has concerned itself with the issue of subject formation (particularly from the viewpoint of Lacanian psychoanalysis). As Kaplan recognizes, such work necessarily partakes of the pessimism inherent in the manipulation model produced by current theorizing about ideology. Advocating a different, ultimately more optimistic position (one based on Foucault's concept of discourse rather than on structuralist views of the interpellated subject), Kaplan suggests that feminist approaches to dominant cinema practice might well pay more attention to the gaps in patriarchal control, to those "points of resistance which enable new articulations, which, in turn, begin to work on and to alter the dominant discourse" (p. 167). Such a view doesn't mean the abandonment of psychoanalytically based work, but, rather, as Kaplan argues, the distinguishing of historical from hypothetical subjects. She correctly reminds us that this change would reflect "a larger move within film criticism toward theorizing historical discourse and toward historical film issues."

Within hermeneutics, particularly as exemplified by the work of Paul Ricoeur, the encounter with history (or, perhaps better, the evocation of the historical) has long been a central concern. Dudley Andrew, in his discussion of this tradition, foregrounds the "issue of history," as he terms it. Though phenomenological perspectives inform the early stages of semiotic/structuralist work on the cinema (as for example in the early essays of Christian Metz), phenomenology, in general, has been somewhat ignored by film scholars during the last decade, with the notable exception of Andrew's continuing exploration of the various questions posed by hermeneutics. The 1986 meeting of the Society for Cinema Studies, however, did sponsor two full panels on phenomenology, and there are other signs, as Andrew suggests, of a revival of interest in the area. If Kaplan indeed is correct that the common denominator of current work in cinema studies is an emphasis on the "historical," then perhaps the revival of interest in phenomenology is somewhat surprising. For here is an approach that, in Andrew's terms, enshrines the "regency of the I." But, as he argues, the contemporary phenomenologist may not only, in the manner of postmodernism, "flatten the past" and thereby reduce history to a simultaneous present. S/he may also embrace hermeneutics and its "chore of being responsible to a past that exists only insofar as the present 'cares' about it." Using Ricoeur's method of proceeding from understanding to explanation and finally to comprehension, Andrew demonstrates that the task of a historical hermeneutics is to avoid the two extremes of subjectivity and objectivity. These, Andrew suggests, have been twin pitfalls for historians of the cinema. Instead this hermeneutic approach "assumes that the cinema does not exist in some timeless realm of art but neither is it a mere by-product of social history" (p. 179). In his remarks on the numerous problems involved in writing such a history of French cinema in the thirties, Andrew in fact demonstrates that the cinema may be "open to every conceivable level of cultural influence," but that it is the "obligation of the historian to determine the levels or spheres of cultural life which are most pertinent to the cinematic culture of any given era" (188).

A concern with history is also evident in James Naremore's essay on performance theory, which is a part of a larger, comprehensive study of film acting. Naremore, in fact, revives an interest in acting techniques which was an important element of classical film theory. With its basis in the work of cinema/theater theorists such as Bertolt Brecht and Vsevolod Pudovkin and its use of sociological concepts developed by Erving Goffman, Naremore's analysis first defines the borderline between the everyday "presentation of the self" and what we usually term acting. In ordinary living, he suggests, we are required to be "expressively coherent," never violating the "truth" of the role(s) we have chosen to play. For the actor, in contrast, expressive incoherence—the revelation of acting as acting—is often necessitated. In such instances "the drama becomes a type of metaperformance, imposing contrary demands on the players." This insight allows Naremore to deconstruct the theoretical (mainly Stanislavskian) claims of realist acting, to separate the notion of "realism" into two opposed aims: creating the illusion of a unified self (as we are all called upon to do in "real life") while suggesting the dissolution of that unity into a number of contradictory roles. In certain types of comedy (Naremore mentions the work of Jerry Lewis and Charlie Chaplin) such expressive incoherence breaks down into what might be termed expressive anarchy. Radical theater/film denaturalizes the contradictory elements of realism even further by utilizing techniques that deliberately prevent any impression of the unified self. By thus constructing a typology of performance styles/goals—a typology that must be seen, as Naremore suggests, in its historical context—he enables us to understand the performance embodied in a filmic text in the same way that we now, thanks to the insights furnished by narratology, are able to understand its narrative.

Peter Brunette is also concerned with a surprisingly neglected area of theoretical inquiry in cinema studies, the deconstructive philosophy/method of Jacques Derrida. Brunette begins by explaining why most poststructuralist work on film has been based on the re-reading of Freud initiated by Jacques Lacan. The Lacanian model of development, with its key concepts of the Imaginary, the Symbolic, and the Mirror Stage, makes a ready place for the apparatus of the cinema (as Christian Metz has argued at some length). A key problem with this model, Brunette notes, is its inability to locate a position for the female subject. In fact, Lacanian psychology cannot conceive of difference outside the phallocentrism which underlies it. Though it offers an obvious critique of this model, deconstruction has not found much favor with film scholars, apparently because of its identification with the apolitical. Brunette argues, however, that there is a "possibility of deconstruction providing its own kind of political analysis." One obvious object of deconstructive practice would be, as he suggests, the political/power structures of society as they are manifested in filmic texts. Furthermore, deconstruction could be brought to bear on the "naturalness" of the cinematic image, which is a sign that "necessarily represents what is not there." In this and other ways Brunette offers a rich inventory of possible theoretical and practical moves, the making of which would certainly heighten our understanding of the ways in which film, much like literature, participates in the logocentrism of Western culture. As Brunette shows, for the deconstructionist the cinema offers a conceptual apparatus whose claims on us are in need of a Derridean critique. He concludes with a suggestive analysis of recent work in this area, arguing for a balanced and sensible deconstructive approach to the individual text.

Though the cinema, as Metz suggests, signifies through five different tracks (syntagmatically speaking, emphasizing one or more at various points in the temporal flow of the text), cinema criticism has traditionally emphasized only two of these: the image and spoken dialogue. During the middle seventies semiotic and formalist critics set themselves the task of discovering ways in which the filmic image could be discussed and its signification analyzed without recourse to the unsophisticated impressionism that had characterized much previous work in the field. In the last five years, similar attention has been paid to the non-diegetic music which has been a component of cinematic meaning since the beginning. The essay by Noël and Patrick Carroll included here may be seen as an implicit response to Metz's characterization of the cinema as a "mixed" medium, a signifying chain created by the complex intersection of different codes mobilized by five separate tracks. The authors argue here, in fact, that the cinema makes use of a certain type of music to "modify" the signification/representation offered by images and diegetic sound. They thus raise the issue of the extent to which music (in general and in its use to accompany sound/images in the cinema) can be "expressive." Music, they argue, is not narration (as some have suggested) but performs a different function altogether; it "augments the expressivity of the scene, though this does not preclude the possibility that the scene already possesses many non-musical expressive devices." This essay is particularly valuable because it clears the ground for individual textual analyses which would take into account the obviously myriad ways in which such non-diegetic music could be thought of as "modifying" the images and dialogue it accompanies.

Beginning with a long and insightful meditation on two recent (and highly influential) Marxist theoretical texts, Bill Nichols demonstrates that ideological criticism must negotiate the danger of being collapsed into a "unified body . . . that threatens to suppress difference." In particular, he shows that the notions of ideology which underlie the theorizing of both Fredric Jameson and Frank Lentricchia are in some ways too simple and inflexible (this a sympton of the Althusserian structuralism and the Burkean rhetoric which supply these two thinkers, respectively, with their theoretical starting points). In contrast, Nichols proposes that "ideology addresses and constitutes split, multiple, layered subjects through representations we cannot ignore (but perhaps quite readily refuse)" (p. 257). The complexity of this argument can hardly be summarized here, but what is important is that, like E. Ann Kaplan, Nichols proposes ways in whch materialist criticism can avoid the monotonous pessimism of negative dialectic (the double heritage of Frankfurtian cultural criticism and Stalinist repression?) and move instead toward a more positive confrontation with contemporary film texts. His analysis hinges, finally, on the uncovering of the utopian impulses of popular culture which Marxist critics (especially Jameson) have characteristically privileged, following Marx's famous analysis of the social functioning of religion. As I have argued elsewhere (*Wide Angle* 8, Spring 1986), the debased utopianism of Hollywood films can often be seen as creating positive spaces outside the hegemony of dominant culture. It is such a "positive hermeneutic" that Nichols asks, Marxist critics to embrace, one which would "discover not only the perversions of ideology but also the figurations of utopia that make our negotiations with texts matters of complex urgency."

Like Marxist cultural analysts, semiotics is currently a field in whch theorists and practical analysts alike are involved in assessing a heritage that limits future inquiry even as, paradoxically, it enables it. Moving on to a psychoanalytical phase in which initial linguistic questions have often been deferred or bracketed, cinesemiotics should, Robert Stam here argues, not neglect those questions, answers to which have much to tell us about the ways in which films make meaning. In his essay "Film Language: From Metz to Bakhtin," Stam suggests Christian Metz's pre-psychoanalytic work on the cinema does not constitute a closed body of theory somehow now superseded by other areas of interest. Reviewing the early work of Metz on the ways in which codes, derived from a variety of sources, interact to produce meaning in filmic texts, Stam advocates the continuing usefulness of these notions, whose nature is just outlined by Metz but not exhaustively catalogued by him. Because it developed from Saussurean theories of the sign, this body of semiotic inquiry, however, does not connect easily to the "issue of history" (to use Andrew's term) as this is being raised, in different ways, throughout the discipline. To compensate for this disability, Stam recommends that semiotics reorganize itself along the lines suggested by the Russian theorist Mikhail Bakhtin. What Bakhtin terms "translinguistics" takes as its object of inquiry not only the systematic nature of signification (as this can be inferred by an abstracting process of conceptualization) but all those forces and conventions which enable communication to take place. As Stam argues, "Bakhtin's critique of Saussurean linguistics, therefore, allows for the possibility of reintroducing both politics and culture into the abstract model provided by Metz" (p. 296). For this reason Stam sees an essential continuity between the early theorizing which so deeply affected the real beginnings of serious cinema study in this country and the current return from structuralist models to the "messy" indeterminacies of historical institutions, particular texts, and culturally positioned spectators.

A key Bakhtinian concept is dialogism, the notion that all speech responds to something already said and orientates itself toward some kind of an answer in return. All the essays collected in this part of the book are overtly dialogical in this sense since they are, in complex ways, "answers" to what has already been written about the cinema and its texts. Nor do they conceive of themselves as "final words" beyond further discussion and dispute. But, given the current prominence of Bakhtinianism within literary study, it is perhaps particularly appropriate to set Stam's essay beside one with a somewhat different view about any accommodation of Bakhtinian theory with the developed tradition of cinesemiotics. My own discussion of translinguistics argues that Bakhtin's critique of conventional Saussurean linguistics and semiotics is more dismissive than is usually thought. This means that, from the viewpoint of translinguistics, the work done during the linguistic phase of cinesemiotics ignores some important questions. As a practical demonstration, I explore one of the most important issues raised by Bakhtin about utterances: the extent to which they are "finalized" on their "inner side" by rhetorical and other features. For Metz, the connectedness of the discrete units in a film is explained by the existence of a master code—the grande syntagmatique—which can be understood as generating individual shots. A translinguistic approach, in contrast, would understand textual connectedness as achieved by cohesion (the repetition of already utilized elements), and coherence (the evocation, by surface textual elements, of underlying concepts). Actually, Metz's grande syntagmatique may be thought of as an explanation (or systematization) of important aspects of textual coherence, especially those related to time and space. In addition, I suggest that Bakhtin's concept of the novel, because it is based on the view that this fictional form represents speech (or different ways of talking about the world) rather than actions and characters, cannot furnish cinema studies with an analogous object of critical attention. The cinema, in short, has no "natural" language of its own to represent in a necessarily self-reflexive way. But we can think of the sound cinema as extending the ways the novel functions to represent living speech; for in films speech acts are represented much more directly (in terms of the actual practice of speech and its extraverbal aspects) than is possible in literature, which, limited by inadequate systems of transcription, necessarily simplifies and conventionalizes the richness of human communication.

Within traditional critical methods, the text itself—usually conceived as self-sufficient and complete—has been the center of attention, yielding its place, at least on occasion, only to the author imagined as its authenticating source. As Janet Staiger argues in "Reception Studies: the Death of the Reader," however, the advent of poststructuralism in media theory has meant that increasing attention has been paid to the functioning of the spectator in the production of textual meaning. Staiger's definition of the emergent area of "reception studies" distinguishes it in several important ways from work devoted to the role of the reader within the American tradition of reader-response theory and the German tradition of reception aesthetics most notably represented by the work of Wolfgang Iser and Hans Robert Jauss. Echoing Roland Barthes' famous call for the "death of author," a figure seen as a misleading mystification of bourgeois literary theory, Staiger calls for the corresponding death of the reader, that ahistorical, inferential figure called into existence by the text itself. As she imagines it, then, the field of cinematic reception studies would concern itself, first, with identifying what kinds of reception films have had and, second, with explaining, through the tools of cultural analysis, the various grounds of these receptions.

Reception studies, then, constitutes part of the larger swing within research devoted to the cinema to a specifically historical orientation; its purpose is not the production of interpretations of individual texts, but rather, at least in large part, the writing of the history of such interpretations. As Staiger argues, "the reader or spectator is recognized as historical and as participating in the circulation of available meanings." It follows then that such an area of concern can benefit immensely from various "comparativist" approaches, which would analyze the existence of what we might call different "spectating formations" (adapating a term from the cultural critic Tony Bennett). Furthermore, in order to avoid the idealism of structuralist approaches to the reader (the ideal reader, the competent reader, the superreader, etc.), a cinematic reception studies should be constantly self-critical, viewing its own interests as produced (and enabled) by certain identifiable cultural pressures.

Like Janet Staiger, David Bordwell argues for an approach to research in cinema studies which would do more than produce interpretations of texts. What he calls historical poetics owes much to previous critical movements (Russian formalism, early French structuralism) but, avoiding their idealism, he asks somewhat different questions. For the student of historical poetics what matters is not only "the principles according to which films are constructed and by means of which they achieve particular effects," but also how and why these principles arose in response to "particular empirical circumstances." Such interests, Bordwell argues, do not constitute a method for approaching particular texts and producing certain, expected kinds of knowledge from them; instead, the historical poetician responds to the individual nature of the text(s) under consideration, often devising analytical concepts in response to the special qualities of the text(s). Though historical poetics does not rule out an interest in related areas of inquiry, it does not constitute part of what Bordwell terms "Grand Theory," which would assimilate cinema studies to "the theory of ideology or sexual difference" (p. 377). In the conclusion to his essay, Bordwell differentiates historical poetics from "Grand Theory" as it has become accommodated in film studies (a mixture of Saussure, Lacan, Althusser, and Barthes that Bordwell somewhat humorously designates SLAB theory). Unlike SLAB theory, historical poetics has no doctrine, only questions it asks about the specific nature of film texts and the historical conditions that produced them. Committed to systematic research, the historical poetician avoids the reliance on doctrinal abstractions of the SLAB theorist. Historical poetics is interested in "explanatory propositions"; SLAB theory concerns itself with constructing "interpretive narratives." Unlike such "methodism," historical poetics, therefore, "becomes not one method but a model of basic research into cinema," offering "the best current hope for setting high intellectual standards for film study." Whether they agree with David Bordwell's research proposal or not, the contributors to this volume are all equally concerned with setting high standards for a field in which much important work remains to be done.

NOTES

[1] *The Crisis in Criticism: Theory, Literature and Reform in English Studies* (Baltimore and London: The Johns Hopkins University Press, 1984).

[2] *Eisenstein's Ivan the Terrible: A Neoformalist Analysis* (Princeton: Princeton University Press, 1981), p. 19.

I
APPROACHES

HITCHCOCK AND BUÑUEL: DESIRE AND THE LAW

Robert Stam

At a Hollywood party in honor of Luis Buñuel, Alfred Hitchcock is reported to have called the Spanish filmmaker "the best director in the world."[1] In an interview shortly before his death, Hitchcock again expressed his admiration, specifically citing *Viridiana* and *That Obscure Object of Desire*.[2] Clear affinities between Hitchcock and Buñuel, I shall argue here, make their work especially suitable objects for comparative analysis. The two filmmakers form a pair of doubles, strangers on the train of film history, rather like the proliferating shadow-selves that haunt Hitchcock's work. The two directors "cohabit," as it were, the same universe of concern. They explore the same paradigms, posing identical questions even when their responses to those questions sharply diverge. Their superficial differences—like those of Guy and Bruno—mask submerged analogies.

Both Hitchcock and Buñuel display instantly recognizable stylistic signatures. Each creates an idiosyncratic universe crowded with self-referential icons: stairs, birds, and lamps in Hitchcock; churches, bells, and insects in Buñuel. Both have spent a professional lifetime working out their personal obsessions, and one encounters fully developed in their later films what was but embryonic in their earliest work. Their mature directorial methods are remarkably similar; both are known for almost scholastic precision, efficiency, and pre-planning. For Hitchcock, the final execution is virtually anti-climactic, while Buñuel has claimed to know, before arriving on the set, "exactly how each scene will be shot and what the final montage will be."[3] Both put their highly personal stamp on a wide variety of source material, and both treat actors and actresses as a kind of blank slate

23

on which to write, showing little patience for the empathetic contortions of method acting.

Even doubles have their distinguishing features, however; we would be wrong, therefore, to ignore the many salient contrasts between the two directors. Buñuel rarely offers those virtuoso montage passages, such as the shower-sequence in *Psycho,* that dazzle in Hitchcock's work. Whereas Hitchcock fosters emotional suspense, Buñuel triggers intellectual surprise, preferring the shocks of recognition to the thrills of empathy. Hitchcock films engender anxiety; Buñuel's provoke doubt. The point, however, is that both directors work within the same "problematic" of the law and desire, authority and revolt, the rational and the irrational, even if their fundamental strategies differ dramatically. My purpose here is not to prove identity but rather complementarity within difference as manifested in a series of thematically paired films: *The Lodger* and *Chien Andalou, I Confess* and *Nazarin, Vertigo* and *Viridiana, North by Northwest* and *That Obscure Object of Desire, The Birds* and *Exterminating Angel.* The interest will be less in proving "influence" than in showing that both Buñuel and Hitchcock are indeed animated by similar obsessions, some broadly disseminated within western culture and others more particular to the two directors.

The overall career trajectories of the two directors are in some ways remarkably parallel. Born only six months apart (Hitchcock on August 13, 1899; Buñuel on February 22, 1900), both began with silent films in the twenties. Both were partially inspired to make films by seeing Fritz Lang's *Destiny.*[4] Both directed their first films outside their country of origin (Hitchcock in Germany, Buñuel in France) and both collaborated with Salvador Dali (Buñuel in *Chien Andalou* and *L'Age d'Or,* Hitchcock in *Spellbound*). And both sustained brilliant international careers into the seventies, "playing the cinema," as Godard said of Buñuel, the way Bach played the organ at the end of his life.

A simplistic dichotomy would pit Hitchcock the commercial entertainer against Buñuel the avant-garde *artiste.* In reality both filmmakers drank at the fount of the avant-garde just as both labored, generally, within the framework of the commercial film. But while Buñuel drew from French and Spanish avant-gardism (surrealism), Hitchcock drew from the Germanic (expressionism). *The Lodger* shows the traces of "Caligarism" in its expressionist play of light and shadow, while *Vertigo* reflects the anguish of space-time characteristic of surrealist painting. The art/commerce dichtomy, furthermore, tends to equate Buñuel with his "surrealist tryptych," obscuring the fact that the vast majority of his films were made within the commercial mainstream of the Spanish or Mexican industries or with large-scale producers like Serge Silberman. The real relation between Hitchcock and Buñuel is not one of contrast but of complementarity. To the gothic underside of Buñuel—witness the horrific ambulatory hand of *Exterminating Angel*—corresponds the quiet surrealism of much of Hitchcock. The extroverted Spanish surreality of *L'Age d'or* and *Exterminating Angel* is echoed by the understated "English" absurdism of *The Birds* or *The Trouble with Harry.* Hitchcock's obsession with dream, his Bretonian *humour noir*, and his love for narrative implausibilities qualify him as at least a crypto-surrealist. At the same time, his persistent questioning of conventional ways of shooting—one thinks, for example, of the ten-minute takes of *Rope,* the claustrophobic spatial restrictions of *Lifeboat* and *Rear Window,* and the "structural" use of electronically generated sound in *The Birds*—reveals a director eager for technical challenge and cinematic experimentation.

The play of correspondences between Hitchcock and Buñuel operates from their earliest films. At first glance, the surrealist short *Un Chien Andalou* (1928) and the suspense feature *The Lodger* (1926) seem wildly dissimilar, yet their affinities range from trivial coincidences to basic strategies and concerns.[5] Both films deal with doubles (literal in Buñuel, symbolic in Hitchcock), with androgyny, and with sex and violence. Both directors make self-referential cameo appearances; Buñuel as the man with the razor (the man who does the cutting) and Hitchcock as a newspaper "editor" and as a member of the lynch mob.[6] That Buñuel wields a razor and Hitchcock participates in a lynch mob betokens the aggressive thrust of their "cinema of cruelty." Buñuel called his film a "desperate appeal to murder" designed not to please but "to offend,"[7] while Hitchcock, masquerading as an entertainer, exhibits a more disguised and in some ways more insidious aggression.

The opening sequences of *The Lodger* and *Un Chien Andalou* already intimate shared themes and common strategies. Both open with a "prologue" revolving around an aggression staged against the body of a woman. The first shot in *The Lodger* communicates extraordinary violence; a blond woman, backlit and framed in decentered extreme close-up, screams in silent terror. The horror is decontextualized; we do not know where we are, who the woman is, why the woman is screaming, or whose viewpoint we share. *Un Chien Andalou* withholds its equivalent act of aggression until the tenth shot; a man razors a woman's eye. Here too the act is shorn of all context. We are given no clue as to the man's motivation and no explanation for the woman's blasé attitude toward her imminent mutilation. But already here we discern differences within complementarity, in the filmmaker's distinct approaches to analogous instances of violence. The visible horror in Hitchcock fosters empathy, while the deadpan response in Buñuel favors an almost comic distance, underlined when the woman reappears subsequently with eyes intact.

Impressed by *Un Chien Andalou*, Hitchcock asked Dali to design the dream sequence for *Spellbound*, in which, in an act of creative self-plagiarism, Dali "paraphrases" the earlier film by having an oneiric figure scissor eyeballs painted on the curtains of a gambling den. But apart from this somewhat fortuitous collaboration, we may note that Hitchcock and Buñuel often aim their aggressions at the eye, one of the most vulnerable of organs and the one most deeply implicated in cinematic process. Their films are rife with injured looks and broken glasses; they are pervaded by the sense of sight wounded or menaced. The razored eyeball of *Un Chien Andalou* and the scissored orbs of *Spellbound*, in this sense, presage the sightless face of farmer Fawcett, the hollow sockets of Mrs. Bates and the myriad blind men of Buñuel's subsequent films. Time and again, it is as if the spectators themselves were being reprimanded for looking. Ocular laceration becomes the talion punishment for what Stella in *Rear Window* calls a "race of Peeping Toms." Francisco in *El* inserts a needle through a keyhole to puncture the prying eyes of an imagined voyeur. An angry Pedro in *Los Olvidados*, tired of the condescension of his State Farm guardians, lobs an egg at the camera lens, and by extension at the complacent bourgeois spectator. The hero of *Death in the Garden* thrusts a pen into his jailor's eyes. At times the ocular references are purely verbal: "Why don't you have a look around," the car dealer tells Marion Crane, "and see if there's something that strikes your eyes." (His words anticipate the close juxtaposition of eyeball, drain and blood that ends the shower sequence). And an anonymous woman in a restaurant in *The Birds* accuses us, on whose eyes the fiction depends, as she looks at the camera and screams: "You're the cause of all this! You brought this on!"

Aggression in Hitchcock and Buñuel also takes the form of perversely misleading the audience. Both *The Lodger* and *Un Chien Andalou*, in this sense, are veritable mine-fields of miscues and false leads. Hitchcock crowds *The Lodger* with red herrings—Ivor Novello's gothic appearance, his half-scarved face, his fixation on Daisy's hair—all of which prod us to project guilt onto the wrong-man protagonist. Buñuel's red herrings, in contrast, are less narrative and characterological than spatio-temporal and linguistic. If Hitchcock is perverse in his hermeneutics, Buñuel is perverse in his syntax. The intertitles of *Un Chien Andalou*, for example, promise a temporal coherence which the film does not deliver. Outrageously jumbling the accustomed categories of narrative time, they mix the nebulous atemporality of fable ("once upon a time") with the reportorial precision of "three in the morning." Spatial coherence, meanwhile, is undercut by a plethora of calculated mismatches and *faux raccords*.

The two director's "ouverture" films already explore what is to become a kind of dominant fantasy at the very kernel of their relations to the world—the obsessive intertwining of the imagery of love and death. Buñuel's account of his childhood as marked by a "profound eroticism" and a "permanent consciousness of death" pinpoints that which most deeply fascinates both directors. Key moments in *Un Chien Andalou*—the sexual excitement triggered by the spectacle of death in the streets; the bloodied carcasses hauled toward the inaccessible object of desire; the protagonist's clutching at a nude woman during his dying fall; the final necromantic image of the half-buried lovers—highlight this lethal union of Eros and Thanatos. *The Lodger*, meanwhile, connects love and death by constantly eroticizing murder. Indeed, Detective Joe's parallelistic summary of his deepest desires—"to put a rope around the Avenger's neck and a ring around Daisy's finger"—apart from implying a sinister equation between marriage and legal execution, encapsulates the typical movement of Hitchcock's double plots; one ("the rope around the neck") involves the bringing of a killer to justice, and the other ("the ring around the finger") involves the constitution of the couple. One narrative is quickened by Eros, the other by death. Homicide and matrimony are intimately linked. The opening and closing sequences, with typical Hitchcokian circularity, stress this link in their orchestration of repetition and difference. The electric sign flashing "Tonight Golden Curls," associated with murder at the beginning of the film, evokes wedding-night consummation at the end.

The mediating term between love and death, for Buñuel at least, is religion. Whereas Hitchcock surrounds sexuality with guilt, Buñuel suffuses it with religiosity. Dialectically negating the negation, he exploits religious prohibitions in order to intensify that which the prohibitions are designed to combat—desire. Religion becomes an aphrodisiac, a trampoline for passion. Sexual pleasure, for Buñuel, often exists in a religious context: "it is an exciting, dark, sinful, diabolical experience."[8] Buñuel cites with approval Saint Thomas' idea that sex even in marriage is a venial sin: "Sin multiplies the possibilities of desire."[9] Lacan could hardly have said it better; the Law catalyzes desire. Innumerable passages in Buñuel fuse religious law and sexual desire in a kind of transcendental pornography. Francisco becomes enamored of Gloria's feet during mass; the blasphemous debauch of L'Age d'or is conducted by a Jesus Christ lookalike; the orgy and rape of Viridiana take place to the sounds of the Hallelujah chorus.

The most striking biographical bond between Hitchcock and Buñuel consists in their shared Catholic upbringing and Jesuit education. The implacable logic and inexorable punishment associated with the Jesuit order can be traced not only in the premeditated exactitude and artful symmetry characteristic of both directors' work but also in the motif of guilt which serves as a common motor of fascination. Their response to this shared cultural heritage is marked, however, by a number of paradoxes. While Hitchcock remained a practicing Catholic, and while critics such as Rohmer and Chabrol see him as a quintessentially religious director, there is biographical as well as textual evidence of emotional ambivalence, of a "kicking against the pricks." John Russell Taylor recounts Hitchcock's refusal to go through with a programmed visit with the Pope, on the pretext that the Holy Father might warn him to play down all "the sex and violence."[10] The anecdote, while not explicitly anti-clerical, at least betrays a feeling on Hitchcock's part that the impulse which drives his films is not one of which the Church would approve.

Buñuel, meanwhile, plays out the obverse side of the same paradox, mingling outspoken hostililty for religion with secret affection. The repressed anti-cleric in Hitchcock corresponds to the closet believer in Buñuel. Buñuel's public stance toward Catholicism, of course, has always been one of provocation and sacrilege. As an adolescent, he and Garcia Lorca would shave closely, powder their faces and masquerade as nuns in order to flirt with male passengers on streetcars, a piece of biographical evidence that merely confirms the ominpresent anticlericalism of the films. On another level, however, Buñuel's relation to the Church is parasitical, almost vampirish; it feeds on what it attacks. His insistent desacralization depends on Christianity as a source of imagery and fount of inspiration. In this sense Buñuel, who has often expressed a fondness for the Middle Ages, resurrects the carnivalesque irreverence of that period. Echoes of carnival laughter resound within the walls of the festive cloister which is Buñuel's oeuvre, as he deploys blasphemy as an aethetic strategy, a fond method for generating art. The religious travesties so frequent in his films—the parodistic liturgies of *Simon of the Desert*, the orgiastic Last Supper sequence of *Viridiana*—form the contemporary aesthetic counterpart of the monkish pranks and *parodia sacra* of the Middle Ages.[11]

Religion, pervasive in Buñuel, also subliminally informs much of Hitchcock. His "wrong men" recapitulate—at times comically (Roger Thornhill), at times tragically (Father Logan)—the golgotha of their exemplary prototype; Jesus Christ. The full name of the protagonist of the paradigmatically entitled *The Wrong Man*, drawn from his real-life model, "happens," in a marvelous instance of the "definitive by chance," to evoke the Incarnation: the Christ in "Christopher," the Man in "Manny," and God, etymologically present in the Hebrew roots of "Emmanuel." One celebrated moment deftly epitomizes the religious thrust of the film by having a shot of Manny, bowed in prayer before an icon of Christ, dissolve to the face of the actual thief. The dissolve figure, according to Metz, tends toward "substantial fusion, magical transmutation, mystical efficacy" and here it exhibits, almost in a pure state, the displacement of guilt mechanism operative in so many Hitchcock films. Manny, iconographically associated with Christ by juxtaposition within the frame, also takes on Christ's actantial function by atoning, if only temporarily for the guilt of others.

Both Hitchcock and Buñuel show a certain disabused affection for Christ-like figures such as Manny, Father Logan, Viridiana, Nazarin. *I Confess* and *Nazarin*, in fact, can be viewed as cinematic variations on a single premise: What would happen if Christ's teaching were strictly carried out in the contemporary world? The priest-protagonist of *Nazarin* literally follows Christ's example, while Father Logan obeys to the letter an obscure point of the canonical code—the rule of priestly silence—and responds with immaculate purity to a battery of temptations. But their *imitatio Christi* proves to be futile. Both protect murderers, and both are vilified. Father Logan's religiously sanctioned silence leads to the loss of innocent life, and Nazarin's unassuming charity is greeted with howls of execration. In both cases, strict adherence to religious principle leads to catastrophe, illustrating Buñuel's claim that "one can be relatively Christian, but the absolutely pure innocent person is condemned to failure."[12] And in both films the authors underline this failure by having antagonistic double figures deride their useless sacrifice: "I am alone . . . like you. You are alone. You have no friends," the murderer Keller tells Logan in the climactic scene. In the same way, the thief mocks Nazarin: "Look at me, I only do evil. But what use is your life really? You're on the side of good and I'm on the side of evil and neither of us is any use for anything." Both directors highlight the fearful symmetry of saint and sinner.

Both *Nazarin* and *I Confess* score the repressive anti-sexuality of the Church. Pursued by passionate women, the protagonists of both films are too spiritually absorbed to respond to them as sexual beings. The ideal of celibacy, criticized in *Nazarin* and hysterically lampooned in *Simon of the Desert*, is subtly undermined in *I Confess*. Hitchcock's pairing of Montgomery Clift and Anne Baxter as leading man and lady inevitably stimulates certain erotic expectations. Hitchcock even offers a tantalizing "bracketed" sample of a possible romance—a subjectivized idyll complete with libidinous thunderstorm and a phallic gazebo—only to withhold its culmination. The film as a whole, similarly, withholds the satisfying closure of final marriage and implied conjugal bliss. Thus Hitchcock frustrates the hopes and desires of the spectators, who must ultimately blame the Church and its rigidity for what seems a sad waste of amorous star talent and the denial of a legitimate cinematic expectation.

Love in occidental art, de Rougemont observes, thrives on obstacles. Romance comes into existence only where love is fatal, frowned upon, doomed. Buñuel's work, especially, both laments and celebrates *l'amour impossible*. Love in *Un Chien Andalou*, *L'Age d'or* and *That Obscure Object of Desire* becomes a tragicomic obstacle leading only to protracted frustration. Modot and Lya Lys' clumsy attempts at lovemaking in *L'Age d'or* are in this sense paradigmatic. Burlesque comedy and high tragedy meet as the twosome stumble over chairs, bang their heads on flowerpots, are interrupted by music and distracted by statues. The music evokes passion (etymologically "pathos," suffering, being acted upon), constantly swelling unfulfilled desire, a perpetual tumescence never reaching climax. Love and pathology become indistinguishable.

The entire oeuvres of Hitchcock and Buñuel can be seen as variations on the theme of the *Liebestod*—love and death. De Rougemont traces this occidental fixation back to the medieval myth of Tristan and Isolde, and it is significant that both directors make frequent allusion to Wagner's musical version of the myth. Wagner was one of Buñuel's favorite composers and *Tristan and Isolde* one of his favorite works. Recordings of the "Liebestod" accompanied the first screenings of *Un Chien Andalou*, and the orchestra plays it during Modot and Lys' inept trysting in *L'Age d'or*. Buñuel returned to it in the music track of *Cumbres Burrascosas* (Wuthering Heights) as commentative music for one of the classic novelistic treatments of the love-death theme. Hitchcock, for his part, also returned to this Wagnerian theme throughout his career. In *Murder*, the piece is played over the radio. Herrmann's score for *Vertigo*, similarly, consists of a variation on the "Liebestod," suggesting death as love's devoutly desired consummation. When Eva Marie Saint, double agent of murder and marriage, encounters Cary Grant on the train in *North by Northwest*, still another variation on the "Liebestod" underscores their tantalizing dangerous flirtation. And in *The Birds*, a reiterated shot frames Melanie Daniels, a record player, and a lone album cover—Wagner's *Tristan and Isolde*.

Buñuel's exalted vision of love-death, almost utopian in its religious aspiration, at times recalls the sublime pornography of Bataille's *Story of the Eye*.[13] Both capture the oxymoronic nature of love's healing cataclysms, in which "orgasms ravage faces with sobs and horrible shrieks;" for them, eroticism is apocalyptic and danger an aphrodisiac. For the narrator of *Story of the Eye*, death is the logical outcome of erection, and the goal of sexual licentiousness is "a geometric incandescence . . . the coinciding point of life and death, being and nothingness. . . ."[14] *L'Age d'Or* achieves the fulgurating cinematic equivalent of Bataille's vision by having Modot, his face bloodied, ardently embrace Lya Lys as he murmurs "mon amour, mon amour." In *The Exterminating Angel*, Beatriz and Eduardo, with a corpse at their side for inspiration, make soft-focus *amour fou*, invoking the language of death ("the rictus . . . horrible . . . my love . . . my death!") while in the throes of orgasm. Death goads sensuality and aggravates desire. The only possible next step in the amorous escalation of morbidity for the couple is mutual suicide (or is it reciprocal murder?), illustrating de Rougemont's observation: "Sometimes even, [death] aggravates desire to the point of turning into a wish to kill either the beloved or oneself, or to founder in a twin downrush."[15]

Since fetishistic love thrives on obstacles, death, as the ultimate obstacle, is the perfect spur to love. Love in Hitchcock and Buñuel, therefore, often takes on a decidedly necrophiliac cast. The male protagonists of both *Viridiana* and *Vertigo*, for example, are obsessed with deceased love objects. Don Jaime is haunted by the memory of his first wife, who expired in his arms on their wedding night. Just as the heartbroken Tristan weds a second Isolde in order to sustain the memory of the first, so Don Jaime attempts to transform Viridiana, the physical double of his spouse, into a reincarnation of his former love. He dresses her in his wife's wedding clothes, drugs and beds her, caressing her ankles and running his hands along her satin gown to the accompaniment of Mozart's *Requiem*. The intense sensuality of his unilateral caresses clearly suggests necrophilia. Viridiana resembles a corpse, and Don Jaime's clumsy gestures toward consummation remain incomplete, as they must, for he is in love with death itself. Later, he smiles enigmatically as he pens the suicide letter which binds Viridiana to him after death through the inheritance he leaves her. He thus realizes a crass and legalistic fulfillment of the courtly ideal of a love attainable only beyond the grave.[16]

The necrophiliac overtones of *Vertigo* are equally clear and insistent. The protagonist, Hitchcock told Truffaut, "wants to go to bed with a woman who's dead; he's indulging in a form of necrophilia."[17] Madeleine" and Judy, while not literally dead, enjoy what might be called a privileged relationship to death. "Madeleine" appears to be possessed by the deceased Carlotta Valdez, and is thus her "ghost," just as Judy, in turn, is the "ghost" of Madeleine. Like Don Jaime, Scottie shows a morbid predilection for the defunct; he can only respond to a flesh-and-blood woman after she has been transformed into a spectral repetition of a lost love. Like Don Jaime, he coaxes a reluctant surrogate into masquerading as a deceased beloved. He prefers "Madeleine"/Judy and the threat of the abyss to the life-affirming pragmatism of Midge. The film continually associates Madeleine with ghost-like ethereality, with tombstones and suicide, and the fascination she exerts is that of death, a drawing towards oblivion and annihilation, a yearning for final release. This yearning is cinematically realized by morbidly eroticized camera movements. The lure of the abyss is rendered by the subjective track which buries the dreaming Scottie in Carlotta's grave. And the subjective shots depicting Scottie's vertigo combine a backward track with a forward zoom, a double movement of attraction and repulsion whose kinesthetic in-and-out is analogous to the sex act itself.

In Buñuel, the sex-death nexus assumes at times a different form—in an ironic intimation that sexuality itself might either cause death or risk punishment by death. Such, at least, would be one possible reading of the phone call that suspends Modot and Lya Lys' lovemaking in *L'Age d'or*. An earlier sequence in which the authorities forcibly separate the passionately engaged couple has already installed the notion of sexual play as a censurable activity. In the garden sequence, the call is from the "Minister of the Interior," a possible code-word, as Raymond Durgnat has pointed out, for "Conscience," that internalized voice of the social Superego which once warned that masturbation led to madness and love-making to death. The Minister, in a parodic escalation *ad absurdum* of all the parental and societal admonitions against inappropriate sexplay, blames Modot for the deaths of countless men, women and children. Sexuality is portrayed, only half-mockingly, as capable of unleashing the downfall of "civilization."

In Hitchcock, the notion of sexuality as prosecutable offense takes on more dramatic tonalities. For Hitchcock, the law of illicit desire is to be castigated by the law. The murder charge against Father Logan becomes intimately linked to the question of a possible past affair with Ruth Grandfort. The presiding judge's request that the jury ignore the question of their alleged relationship paradoxically only calls attention to it. The short sequence showing the jury deliberations reveals that the jurors are indeed focusing on Logan's relationship with Ruth Grandfort, as if he were being prosecuted not for murder but rather for the crime of sexuality itself. Asked whether the two did in fact have an affair, Hitchcock once answered that he certainly hoped so, then added: "But far be it from me as a Jesuit to encourage that kind of behavior." Hitchcock's response counterpoises the desire for sexual liberation with the tongue-in-cheek disavowal of that very desire. Hitchcock the Victorian clearly infuses sexuality with a guilt that he himself finds oppressive, and much of the special poignancy of the "wrong man" theme in the film undoubtedly derives from this double attitude. Surrounded with guilt, sex remains at the same time one of the few radically innocent activities available to human beings. Hitchcock feels the guilt, and adroitly plays on our own, yet he is quietly outraged that such guilt should ever have been instilled.[18]

Both *Viridiana* and *Marnie* anatomize the psychic damage done by sexual guilt. In both films, the woman protagonist proceeds from extreme sexual reticence to "normal" sexuality. Superficially, they are polar opposites: Viridiana is a contemporary saint; Marnie is a liar and a thief. Viridiana's vocation is charity, the art of giving; Marnie's avocation is kleptomania, the crime of stealing. Yet there is a radical Genet-like innocence about Marnie's attempt to "help herself" in a desperate search for love. And both are repulsed by sexuality. Viridiana recoils in disgust from the phallic cow-udders, just as Marnie shrinks from Mark's "degrading" and "animal" touch. Both films trace the religious etiology of this sexophobia—Catholic in Viridiana's case, fundamentalist Protestant in Marnie's. The latter receives misguided sexual counsel from her mother; the former from her Mother Superior.

Both Marnie and Viridiana evolve toward a highly problematic normality. Viridiana, after rebuffing Don Jaime's advances, ultimately "plays cards" with his son Jorge. Marnie, after angrily rejecting Mark's embraces, moves toward acceptance and implied fulfillment. Both are readied for this "normality" by a process of symbolic as well as literal rape. Viridiana is first symbolically raped by Don Jaime, then literally raped by the cripple. Marnie is symbolically raped by Mark's predatory interrogation and by a coerced marriage, and literally raped on their "honeymoon." In both films, wedding-night consummations are surrounded with morbid association. Don Jaime restages the wedding-night death of his first wife with Viridiana as surrogate corpse, and her subsequent rejection of him triggers *his* suicide. Marnie's wedding-night, meanwhile, very nearly literalizes the sex-death connection evoked in their free-association word-game, in which "sex" is followed by "death." Hitchcock renders their sexual encounter as a kind of living death, with Marnie's body rigid and her face expressionless as Mark advances in menacingly outsized close shots. And sex is followed, the next morning, by near death, in the form of Marnie's attempted suicide.

In both *Marnie* and *Viridiana*, the men exercise social and patriarchal power over the women. Don Jaime by virtue of his role as Viridiana's benefactor, Mark by virtue of his wealth and his knowledge of Marnie's theft. The recognition of the female protagonists' sexophobia should not blind us to the psycho-sexual problems of their male counterparts. Don Jaime is not only a necrophiliac but also a transvestite, fetishist and voyeur. Mark's love for Marnie, similarly, is shot through with neurosis, pithily summarized by Marnie as a "pathological fix on a woman who's a thief and who can't stand for you to touch her." He belongs, along with L. B. Jeffries in *Rear Window*, Norman Bates in *Psycho*, and Bob Rusk in *Frenzy*, to Hitchcock's overcrowded gallery of sexually problematic males. His generosity, deeply involved with fantasies of domination, begins with a kind of rescue fantasy; he saves Marnie from joblessness by persuading her prospective employer to ovoerlook her lack of references. He then blackmails her with his secret knowledge in order to gain proprietary rights. His pretext for taking "legal possession" by marriage recalls the ancient rationale for slavery: the vanquished owes all to the victor who has spared his life. The same patriarchal power that "normalizes" the female protogonist also generates a humiliating dependency.[19]

The title of Buñuel's latest and perhaps last film points to the theme that so obsesses both Hitchcock and Buñuel—*That Obscure Object of Desire*. Here again, Buñuel anatomizes desire as pathology. Just as Mark is attracted to Marnie's frigidity, Mathieu fetishizes Conchita's virginity. Playing out a widely disseminated double bind, the aging protagonist (again played by Fernando Rey) cannot attain his desire without destroying it. His love of a virgin, like Humbert Humbert's adoration of nymphets, is foredoomed and ephemeral by definition. A shrewd piece of editing indicates the religious and cultural roots of Mathieu's fetish. Conchita's "annunciation" of her virgin status segues by direct cut to an entrance plaque alluding to two notorious virgins: "Chapel of the Annunciation, Joan of Arc School." Even Conchita's names fuse physicality and spirituality. Her real name is "Concepcion" as in "the immaculate conception," but "conchita," in colloquial Spanish, means "cunt." Once again, religion (the law) annoints sex with a halo of tantalizing interdiction.

That Obscure Object of Desire demonstrates a kind of Zeno's paradox of passion: the space between two lovers is infinitely divisible. While Mathieu enjoys the sterile plentitude of physical proximity—the same house, the same bed, naked together in the same bed—Conchita remains as spiritually remote as a medieval damsel locked in the castles of courtly love. The scene is partially set in Seville, historically one of the centers of the Provençal poetry often cited as the source of courtly love. Provençal love poetry drew on the Arabic culture pervasive in Andalusia, and especially on a kind of poetry which idealized love as the humble (and usually unrewarded) service of a lady worshipped from afar. The Buñuel film visualizes this inaccessibility by placing the lovers behind bars, fences, grillwork. Mathieu especially, in a chromatic version of the incarceral obsessions of film noir, is framed as the prisoner of desire. His vision is repeatedly barred as he is subjected to cruelly seductive revelations of Conchita's flesh. The bars become a metaphor of the treadmill of desire—always tantalizing, always unfulfilled, perpetually on the brink—both confronting and generating its own longed-for obstructions.

More important than Mathieu's desire *per se* is Buñuel's playful foiling of *our* desire. The title itself designates our own position as desiring (largely male) spectators. The film is a protracted joke on the spectator, a narrative striptease that refuse to strip. The film never delivers on the abstract erotic promise of the title. We too are cruelly locked out of the spectacle, subjected to an infinite regress of spectatorial frustration. Instead of stimulating desire, Buñuel holds the mirror to our own psychic fix on films themselves. He analyzes, as if on a Steenbeck, the most mystified moment in our culture—the moment of sexual surrender—and scrutinizes our phantasmatic relation to the spectacle, exposing desire as a cultural and cinematic construct.

In her excellent study of surrealist film, Linda Williams contrasts the completed phallic quest of *North-by-Northwest*, and the final train as metaphor for that quest, with the perpetually deferred quest, and the train as "teasing interruption," in *That Obscure Object of Desire*.[20] The comparison points to a fundamental difference between Hitchcock and Buñuel. The Lodger and Daisy, Roger Thornhill and Eve Kendall *do* consummate their marriage; the protagonists of *Chien Andalou*, *L'Age d'or* and *That Obscure Object of Desire* presumably do not. Hitchcock's narratives achieve organism; Buñuel's practice systematic *coitus interruptus*. If *North-by-Northwest* is shorn of its final shots, however, its narrative begins to resemble that of the Buñuel film. Both films posit picaresque itineraries—Buñuel might have entitled his film *North-by-Northeast*—in which desire's pursuit of its receding object is set against a background of international terror. In both films, middle-aged men, successful in the world but unfantile in love, pursue younger women. An Oedipal configuration, analyzed by Williams herself in relation to *That Obscure Object of Desire*, and by Raymond Bellour in relation to *North-by-Northwest*, links both narratives, with the difference that Buñuel leaves Mathieu's trajectory incomplete, while Hitchcock has Thornhill accede to civic heroism and responsible marriage. Thornhill is "cured," while Mathieu prefers the disease to the cure.

The women, in both cases, are portrayed as dangerously and mysteriously double. This doubleness is made literal, in Buñuel, by having two actresses, dubbed by a single voice, play the same role. The character Conchita, meanwhile, is a compendium of contradictions, at once passionate and frigid, modest and brazen, assertive and submissive. Hitchcock's heroine is similarly bifurcated: saint and temptress, madonna and whore. The actress's name, in another instance of aleatory good fortune, incarnates these dualities: the fallen Eve, the Virgin Mary, the canonical Saint. In both films, death is concatenated with desire. Terrorist explosions "punctuate" each of Mathieu and Conchita's erotic encounters, and Eve Kendal and Roger Thornhill speak of murder during their first kiss ("Maybe you're planning to murder me, right here, tonight. Shall I? Yes . . . please do . . . "), What else do you do," Thornhill asks, "besides lure men to their doom on the Twentieth Century Limited?" Both Conchita and Eve could, as Thornhill says, "tease a man to death without half trying." In both films desire is enhanced by inaccessibility and by conventionoal barriers of class conflict or political tension. Both women become damsels trapped in imaginary castles. In both films, finally, the desired woman participates in a subtext of prostitution. Conchita is the recipient of Mathieu's interested generosity and is kept, ironically, in every sense except the sexual, while Eve, in her role as double agent, is kept by a powerful pimp called the CIA. And if Eve wields sex as a "fly swatter" against America's enemies, Conchita wields virginity as a terrorist weapon against Mathieu and the bourgeois order he represents.

Both *North-by-Northwest* and *That Obscure Object of Desire* outrageously flaunt their fundamental implausibility. The narrative action swirls around an empty center: the conundrum of Conchita's virginity in the Buñuel film, and vague international intrigues in Hitchcock. The espionage of *North-by-Northwest* forms a Hitchcockian McGuffin, an empty signifier like *Obscure Object's* burlap bag. The purposes of the spies, like those of the CIA, remain obscure, hollow like the 'O' in Roger Thornhill's name that "stands for nothing." The film glories in fantastic coincidences and impossible situations. Narrative implausibilities—the couple's amorous badinage while clinging to the granite face of Rushmore—are mirrored by self-referential devices (Vandamm's malevolent "This matter is best disposed of from a great height" triggers an abrupt shift to a high angle), exhibitionist set-ups (the extreme high angle shot of Thornhill running from the U. N.) and audacious *faux raccords*. The splice which takes us, spatially, from Mount Rushmore to a hurtling train, and temporally from singledom to marriage, demonstrates a flair for discontinuity no less dazzling than that of Buñuel, whose splices magically substitute one actress for another.

It would be misguided, then, to pigeonhole Hitchcock as the classicist master-of-suspense and Buñuel as the disruptive avant-gardist. Both *North-by-Northwest* and *That Obscure Object of Desire* are highly reflexive films. Their authors, in both cases, appear in self-aggressive cameo roles. The credit-sequence of *North-by-Northwest* shows a bus door closing in Hitchcock's face. (Thornhill enters the tunnel, Bellour point out, but Hitchcock cannot enter the bus). Buñuel, meanwhile, plays the well-dressed man, early in the film, who asks to be driven to the bank and is promptly blown up by terrorists, a reminder that the film attacks *his* obsessions, *his* class, *his* privileges. Buñuel also inscribes the spectators within the diegesis in the form of Mathieu's listeners in the train compartment, a collective interlocutor not unlike the audience of a film. They ask Mathieu questions, prod him to continue, speculate about motivations and outcomes. Hitchcock's strategy is different; *North-by-Northwest* develops an insistent theatrical subtext, beginning with the title drawn from *Hamlet*, and sustained by constant allusions to the theatre and to theatrical language.[21]

The crucial difference between Hitchcock and Buñuel, in the final analysis, is that Hitchcock's narrative trains run on time, while Buñuel's never arrive. Although Hitchcock keeps the spectator in the dark during the first third of *North-by-Northwest*, after that the double series of enigmas—the espionage series and the romance series—proceed smoothly and finally coincide. Hitchcock ultimately does unravel his enigmas, even if reluctantly and only in the final reel. Buñuel, in contrast, frustrates our epistemophilia as well as our scopophilia. *That Obscure Object of Deisre* leaves its central enigmas as intact as Conchita's putative hymen. What drives her to act as she does? Did she actually make love to El Morenito? The film elicits hypothetical answers to these questions and then swiftly subverts them, leaving us with a core of irrationality. Indeed, the fact that Buñuel substituted filmic doubts for the certainties of the source novel tells us a good deal about the corrosive cinema which is his real object.

An excellent test case for both the parallels and contrasts between Hitchcock and Buñuel is provided by an instance when the two directors work similar themes, in comparable genres, at the same point in their careers: *The Birds* (1963) and *The Exterminating Angel* (1962).[22] The parallels begin with their titles, both of which refer to winged creatures seen as meting out justice to human beings. The scourge, in both instances, carries overtones of the apocalypse. The exterminating angel executes a mission of social justice, an apocalyptic laying low of the noble and the powerful. The characters in *The Birds*, similarly, are collectively the victims of a kind of Judgment Day, a theme sounded explicitly by the drunk in the restaurant: "The Lord said, I will devastate your high places" and "It's the end of the world."

The apocalypse, in both cases, has resonances of the absurd in that the central premise—the inexplicable entrapment of a pride of socialites, an avian mass attack on human beings—is as calculatedly implausible as those subtending many Beckett or Ionesco plays. Because of a curious critical double standard, Buñuel was never belabored for the improbabilities of *The Exterminating Angel*—one expects such things from an avant-gardist—while Hitchcock was ardently pursued by his nemesis "the plausibles." "Why didn't the school children hide in the cellar?" critics asked, and "Why didn't Melanie die of birdbite?" (Because it would be *boring* for Melanie to die of birdbite, Hitchcock presumably would have answered). Both authors, in any case, pointedly refuse coherent explanation. Hitchcock accepted Truffaut's account of the film as a "speculation or fantasy" without "specific explanation" while Buñuel's prefatory note to the first Parisian screening of *Exterminating Angel* warned that: "The only explanation is that there is no explanation."[23] This lack of explanation does not prevent certain of the characters in the films, like certain critics, from seeking plausibility where none exists. Hitchcock's policeman advances common sense explanations—the children *provoked* the birds, the birds were attracted to the *light*, the birds entered *after* Farmer Fawcett was murdered. In both films, such rationalists are discredited. Buñuel's positivist doctor pleads for scientific analysis, but his rationality leads nowhere. The ornithologist, who at first haughtily dismisses the very possibility of mass bird attacks, is left cowed and trembling. We are left with a core of mystery and the incomprehensible.

Both *The Birds* and *The Exterminating Angel* elaborate the theme of entrapment that so obsessed the theatre of the absurd. In *The Exterminating Angel*, the human characters are barred from crossing the magical threshold, while animals move about freely. Even sheep, the stereotypical emblems of passivity and conformism, show superior mobility. *The Birds*, as many critics have pointed out, operates on a similar inversion, moving from a situation in which the birds are caged and the people are free to one in which the people are caged—in houses, telephone booths, cars—and the birds are free. The situation in *The Exterminating Angel* would seem, at first glance, to be more claustrophobic, but in fact *The Birds*, apparently more spacious and airy, offers a more frightening situation of global entrapment. This theme is first sounded in the film's opening shot, in which bird cries are superimposed on the turning globe of the Universal logo. The birds aurally cover the earth like a roof, prefiguring a situation in which the whole earth will become a trap. It is touched on again in the dazzling aerial shot of Bodega Bay, clearly from the birds' perspective, and sealed by the final shot, again from the birds' point of view, showing the human beings beating a cautious automotive retreat, as the birds, the permanent residents, watch them leave.[24]

Both *The Exterminating Angel* and *The Birds* can be seen as proto-disaster films in which respectable people become "castaways" in situations of extreme pressure where ordinary social conventions no longer apply. Stripped of their advantages, the "castaways of Providence Street" revert to distinctly ungenteel behavior: Laetitia picks at her blackheads, the conductor makes unseemly advances, and Raul and Nobile scrap over petty offenses. As the social contract breaks down, the pathological politeness of bourgeois etiquette disappears. In *The Birds*, bourgeois good manners lapse only temporarily, just

enough to provide a glimpse of their essential fragility. This fragility
is imaged by broken glass and destroyed homes in both films. In *The
Exterminating Angel*, the Valkyrie lobs an ashtray through a window,
and the Nobile mansion is progressively reduced to rubble. *The Birds*
is littered with broken glass: the broken windows of Melanie's pranks,
the children's shattered glasses, the birds inscribed on Farmer Fawcett's broken panes, and the fractured glass of the phone booth. In
The Exterminating Angel, the mansion is destroyed from within, by
the residents, while in the Hitchcock film, it is destroyed from without, by the birds. In both cases, the escalating destruction triggers
a scapegoating process. "You led us into this," Raul tells Nobile,
"you should be killed!" And in *The Birds*, an anonymous mother of
two accuses Melanie: "You made this happen! I think you're evil!"

Having signalled these parallels between the two films, I should
note their salient contrasts. These contrasts have to do with the modes
of the films, and the consequences of these modes for spectatorial
positioning, and with politics. The mode of *The Exterminating Angel*
is ultimately comic, ironic, carnivalesque. The film is structured according to the comic formula of a slow descent into anarchy, and
much in *The Exterminating Angel*—the slapstick, the Chaplinesque
bear, the proliferating chaos à la Laurel and Hardy, the deadpan style
in the manner of Keaton—derives from the burlesque comedy that
Buñuel so admired. The mode of *The Birds*, meanwhile, despite its
comic underside, is ultimately tragic, in the sense that the film takes
us through pity and fear to catharsis. "Comic" and "tragic" are here
used in their Brechtian senses; the question is one of spectatorial
positioning. Hitchcock enlists all the cinematic codes—camera movement, framing, editing, color—in the service of an identificatory response. His predilection for point-of-view editing, in this sense, is but
the most clearly marked instance of a general subjectivization. Buñuel,
on the other hand, works in the opposite way. We identify with no
one in *The Exterminating Angel;* we merely observe critically. Buñuel
consistently refuses empathy-inducing techniques, eschewing point-
of-view editing, shot-counter-shot structures, eyeline matches and the
like. The camera, meanwhile, exhibits its own autonomy, exploring
walls and weaving through the party-scape without following individual characters. Even dreams offer no pretext for subjectivization, for
they are collective rather than individual, thus anticipating *Discrete*

Charm of the Bourgeoisie, where the members of the same class dream one another's dreams.

These differing modes and strategies are correlated with very distinct political impulses. Although both *The Birds* and *The Exterminating Angel* attack complacency, that attack takes strongly divergent forms. Hitchcock could perhaps subscribe to Buñuel's summary of the final sense of his films—"to repeat, over and over again . . . that we do not live in the best of all possible worlds"—but the import of this subscription would not be the same. *The Birds* makes a broad humanistic statement about human caring; its categories are moral rather than social or political. *The Exterminating Angel,* in contrast, radicalizes burlesque and avant-garde *topoi* by linking them to the carnivalesque theme of the "world turned upside down." The film's critique is structural; its categories are political. The logic of the film is to reduce its upper-class protagonists to the miserable condition of the very people they normally oppress—the forgotten ones, *los olvidados* of the slums. The Nobile mansion becomes an overcrowded mini-slum, without running water, with people sleeping on the floor in promiscuous cohabitation. The butler chops at the wall with an axe, revealing bare bricks and cement as in lower-class Mexican dwellings. As in a slum, copulation and defecation shed the privilege of privacy. The characters scramble openly for the drugs that they formerly took in secret, and Raul, like a lumpen vagabond, pokes through the rubble looking for stray cigarette butts. The same aristocrats who spilled expensive food as an amusing theatrical device are now ravaged by hunger and on the verge, it is suggested, of ritual murder and even cannibalism.

Our comparison, which has strategically downplayed certain obvious contrasts between Hitchcock and Buñuel, here touches on a critical arena of difference—politics. Buñuel, even while critiquing the bourgeoisie from within, never forgets *"los olvidados";* he consistently places in foreground the realities of class, of physical hunger and its social causes. While he never stoops to vulgar proselytizing—he is no socialist realist—his commitment is everywhere evident.[25] For Buñuel, a single social system generates the aristocrats of *The Exterminating Angel* and the slum-dwellers of *Los Olvidados,* the nobles of *L'Age d'or* and the famished peasants of *Land Without Bread.* While Hitchcock thinks in the psychological singular of the subjectivized monad, Buñuel thinks in the social plural of class. The contrasting titles of two of their documentary-style socially conscious films of the fifties—*Los Olvidados* (The Forgotten Ones) and *The Wrong Man*—are symptomatic in this regard. The slum-dwellers collectively are "wronged ones," the objects of societal abuse. And while it would be a mistake to underestimate the social critique performed by a film like *The Wrong Man*, where the ordinary workings of justice are revealed to be deeply flawed, it must also be admitted that the Buñuel's social critique is far more thoroughgoing and radical.

What is true of politics in general is true of sexual politics in particular. The verdict on the place of woman in Hitchcock is not yet in. Where some critics, such as Donald Spoto and Robin Wood, see a "therapist," putting his heroines through "humanizing" ordeals, others, such as Raymond Bellour and Jacqueline Rose, see "the rapist" punishing the "desire that speaks in woman's look," a desire that Hitchcock himself has willed into being. Whether we see Hitchcock as one or the other depends largely on our angle of vision. All agree that a character like Melanie is being punished; the disagreement concerns whether or not she *deserves* the punishment.[26] Buñuel's work, on the other hand, is fairly unambiguous on the subject of sexual politics; his films form an unending indictment of patriarchy and machismo. What spectator can compare Gloria and Francisco in *El*, Evie and Miller in *The Young One*, and Viridiana and Don Jaime in *Viridiana* and not realize that these "couples" exist in a relation of oppression and that this oppression forms part of a general configuration of power? (The indictment is less clear in *That Obscure Object of Desire* only because Conchita is nothing more than a phantasmatic "figure of desire" [Williams] enlisted in Buñuel's critique of Mathieu's masculinist vision).

The focus of Buñuel's attack has one Name—the Law—and many surnames: Patriarchal Power, Authority, God the Father, the Pope, the President, the Generalissimo, the Pater Familias, but also Certainty of Origin, the Unity of a Single Meaning, Dominant Cinema. Buñuel's frontal assaults on Authority, with their historical trail of scandal and censorship, find but faint echo in the kind of devious undermining performed by Hitchcock. Buñuel offers a profound critique of the symbolic structures of patriarchal thought, a critique at once political, economic, cultural, religious and anthropological. His politics are not collapsible with those of Hitchcock. The latter is merely uncomfortable with power, while the former assaults it, provokes it into showing its true face. If Hitchcock's world is an unending labyrinth of guilt, Buñuel's world is one of constant change and revolt. If both directors linger on the illicit pleasures of voyeurism and fetishism, Buñuel indulges them less and for a different purpose. If Hitchcock excites emotions to their paroxysm, Buñuel short-circuits them by a Brechtian "theatre of interruptions." Hitchcock concentrates on the inferno within, while Buñuel brandishes the camera-eye in order to set the world on fire.

NOTES

1 See Francisco Arando, *Luis Buñuel: A Critical Biography* (New York: Da Capo, 1976), p. 248.

2 David Freeman, "The Last Days of Alfred Hitchcock," *Esquire*, 97:4 (April 1982), p. 92.

3 Interview with Carlos Fuentes published in *The New York Times Magazine* (March 11, 1973), and anthologized in Joan Mellen, *The World of Luis Buñuel* (New York: Oxford Univ. Press, 1978).

4 See Virginia Higginbotham, *Luis Buñuel* (New York: G. K. Hall, 1979), p. 25; and Francois Truffaut, *Hitchcock* (New York: Simon and Schuster, 1967), p. 18.

5 Although *The Lodger* was not technically Hitchcock's first feature, it was, according to the director himself, the first "true Hitchcock movie!" See Truffaut's *Hitchcock*, p. 30.

6 While virtually all critics are aware of Hitchcock's cameo appearances, few have pointed out that Buñuel too "signs" his works with personal appearances which are shrewdly apt and over-determined with meaning. His brief appearance in *Belle de Jour* as a Spanish tourist pinpoints his situation as a Spaniard making films in France. In *Phantom of Liberty*, he dons a beard and monk's frock and has himself assassinated in a highly condensed expression of his own ambivalence toward Catholicism; doing violence against a symbolic representative of the Church he also does violence to himself.

7 From Buñuel's presentation of the film at the Cineclub de Madrid; quoted by Aranda, *Luis Buñuel*, p. 64.

8 From interview with Carlos Fuentes, in Mellen, pp. 69–70.

9 *Ibid.*, p. 70.

10 See John Russell Taylor, *Hitch: The Life and Times of Alfred Hitchcock* (New York: Pantheon, 1978), p. 310.

11 For the seminal discussion of carnivalesque demystification of religion,

see Mikhail Bakhtin, *Rabelais and His World* (Cambridge, Mass.: M.I.T. Press, 1968). For a dicussion of these tactics in Buñuel and other film-makers, see Robert Stam, "On the Carnivalesque," *Wedge*, No. 1 (Summer 1982), 47–55.

12 From a 1961 interview with Elena Poniatowska, published in *Revista de la Universidad de Mexico* and quoted in J. H. Matthews, *Surrealism and Film* (Ann Arbor: Univ. of Michigan Press, 1971), p. 154.

13 The Bataille novel, published shortly before the making of *Un Chien Andalou*, perhaps influenced certain sequences of the Buñuel film, as in the following passage:

> I remember that one day, when we were in a car tooling along at top speed, we crashed into a cyclist, an apparently very young and very pretty girl. Her head was almost totally ripped off by the wheels. For a long time, we were parked a few yards beyond without getting out, fully absorbed in the sight of the corpse. The horror and despair at so much bloody flesh, nauseating in part, and in part very beautiful, was fairly equivalent to our usual impression upon seeing each other.

Here, the cyclist, the automobile murder of a young girl, the emphasis on physical dismemberment, and the eroticizing effect on the spectacle of death all anticipate specific images in *Un Chien Andalou*.

14 George Bataille, *Story of the Eye* (New York: Urizen, 1977), p. 6.

15 Denis de Rougemont, *Love in the Western World* (New York: Harper and Row, 1977), p. 53.

16 Love beyond the grave at times acquires incestuous overtones in Hitchcock, notably in *The Lodger*, where Ivor Novello's potentially murderous hand is guided by his deceased mother, and in *Psycho*, in the form of Norman Bates' Oedipal relation to a mother who also has a privileged relationship to Death.

17 See Peter Bogdanovich, *The Cinema of Alfred Hitchcock* (New York: Museum of Modern Art, 1962), p. 32.

18 At times this sexual guiltiness is extended to art itself as a potentially erotic form of play. Manny in *The Wrong Man* "plays" the bass, and, in his imagination, the horses. Both activities are held against him by the police who see him, according to their cultural stereotypes, as a fast-living bohemian. It is as if playing itself were suspect in the eyes of the Law. A strong undercurrent in Hitchcock suggests a guilty love for the playing involved in his own art.

19 For a feminist analysis of this process in *The Birds*, see Jacqueline Rose, "Paranoia and the Film System," *Screen* 17 No. 4 (Winter 1976/1977), pp. 85–104.

[20] See Linda Williams, *Figures of Desire: A Theory and Analysis of Surrealist Film* (Urbana: Univ. of Illinois Press, 1981), pp. 190–191.

[21] I would like to thank Michael Vertucci for his observations on *North-by-Northwest*.

[22] *The Birds* are originally scheduled for completion in 1962, the same year as *The Exterminating Angel*, but production was delayed due to problems with the special effects.

[23] See Truffaut, *Hitchcock*, p. 216.

[24] Interestingly, Hitchcock contemplated a double-trap structure that would have been even more parallel to that of *The Exterminating Angel*. The foursome were to have driven off to San Francisco only to encounter the Golden Gate Bridge covered with birds. The endings of both films, in any case, are highly ambiguous. Buñuel leaves his characters trapped in a Church; it is for us to imagine subsequent events. In Hitchcock, the reconstituted "family" apparently makes a safe exit, yet we have no evidence that the birds will not attack again elsewhere. Hitchcock also wanted to forgo the formal closure of "The End," but audiences misinterpreted the lack of an ending as a projection breakdown. Universal, as a consequence, was obliged to overlay final titles on all the prints in circulation.

[25] It is important to stress that Buñuel's life-experience pushed him in a political direction. Born in Spain, having gone to France and living in Mexico, Buñuel is associated with countries with violent, changing political histories and with a strong tradition of political art. The civil war between fascists and republicans in Spain made for a situation where not to choose was to be a coward. Buñuel also knew the face of harsh poverty, in Spain, and later in Mexico. Buñuel's overall political position might be summed up as an anarchist-inflected critical Marxism, the position of an independent leftist rather like that of the late Sartre in philosophy. Marxism for him is a critical instrument rather than a precise program, a means to probe bourgeois institutions. It is Buñuel's political awareness, and his awareness of harsh social contrasts of wealth and poverty, it should be added, that has helped to make him, rather than Hitchcock, a model for many radical third world filmmakers.

[26] While it is true, as Jacqueline Rose points out, that Hitchcock identifies Mitch with the Law and Melanie with Transgression, it is also true that Hitchcock himself is less than fond of the Law and feels complicitous with Transgression.

STRAW DOGS
SAM PECKINPAH AND
THE CLASSICAL WESTERN
NARRATIVE

Rory Palmieri

Sam Peckinpah established his reputation as a major film-maker with a series of five Westerns in the sixties: *The Deadly Companions* (1961), *Ride the High Country* (1962), *Major Dundee* (1965), *The Wild Bunch* (1969), and *The Ballad of Cable Hogue* (1970). During the seventies he directed eight more features, but only one was a Western: *Pat Garrett and Billy the kid* (1973). Peckinpah has not abandoned the Western genre, however. In fact, he has said in regard to his non-Western films, "Every story is a Western,"[1] and one can see in these films a continuing preoccupation with various aspects of the Western.[2] Peckinpah's first feature film outside the Western genre, *Straw Dogs* (1971), is especially interesting because the film is set in contemporary times and concerns an American mathematician and his wife living in a rural village in England, but the narrative is modeled on that of the classical Hollywood Western. The first part of this paper will describe the narrative structure of the classical Hollywood Western (and illustrate this description through a brief analysis of Peckinpah's *Ride the High Country)* and then show how *Straw Dogs* and the novel on which it is based, Gordon M. Williams' *The Siege of Trencher's Farm*, have adopted this narrative structure. The second part of the paper will examine how the film, unlike the novel, renders the Western narrative problematic through the complex treatment of the hero and his aggressiveness.

In an interview conducted by Janet Bergstrom, Raymond Bellour describes the classical Western narrative as the intertwining of three actions: the establishment of a stable (white) civilization on the frontier, the formation of a heterosexual couple (a narrative action which Bellour considers to be central not only to the Western but to all classical Hollywood narratives), and the completion of the hero's Oedipal trajectory.[3] These three narrative actions are linked in the following way: the establishment of civilization depends on the formation of the couple, and the latter action in turn depends on the hero's Oedipal trajectory. Civilization depends on the formation of the couple because it is through the relationship with the heroine that the hero, whose prowess is necessary to civilization, is linked to the Law. In order for the marriage of hero and heroine to occur, however, the hero must resolve the Oedipus complex. He "must accept as his own a positive relationship between desire and the law; that means that he must accept the woman, who is the object of desire, but without eluding the threat of castration that looms doubly, in her and through the father" (p. 90).

At the conclusion of his description of the Western narrative, Bellour notes that even Westerns with unhappy endings are "complementary forms" (p. 93) of the narrative structure which he has outlined. In addition, Laura Mulvey has pointed out that the Western allows for an alternative happy ending which does not involve marriage for the hero. As the resolution in marriage "can be seen to represent the resolution of the Oedipus complex (integration into the symbolic), the rejection of marriage personifies a nostalgic celebration of phallic, narcissistic omnipotence."[4] Mulvey's example of this latter option for narrative closure in the Western is the Ranown series directed by Budd Boetticher and starring Randolph Scott.

A brief analysis of Peckinpah's *Ride the High Country* will illustrate and further clarify the above description of the Western narrative. Although this film principally concerns the friendship between two aging ex-lawmen and their attempts to cope with a changing land, these concerns intertwine with the narrative structure described by Bellour. Narrative closure in *Ride the High Country* still depends on the establishment of the Law on the frontier wilderness, the formation of the couple (Heck Longtree [Ron Starr] and Elsa Knudsen [Mariette Hartley]), and the resolution of the Oedipus complex (by Heck Longtree). The aging heroes, Steve Judd (Joel McCrea) and Gil Westrum

(Randolph Scott), are instrumental in the accomplishment of these goals and thereby regain self-respect and the respect of others and mend the friendship which Gil violates in the course of the film by attempting to steal the gold shipment that Steve has been hired to guard.

Frontier disorder, which the Law must rectify by the end of the film in order for narrative closure to be achieved, takes different forms in the three principal settings of the film. The civilized town of Hornitos is almost modern in appearance (we see an automobile and a uniformed cop in the first scene), but the bank does not receive any of the gold shipments that are sent down from the mining camp at Coarsegold. This latter setting is the prototypical lawless town ("The only law up there is too drunk to hit the ground with his hat," one of the bankers tells Steve), where drunkenness, debauchery, and casual violence are the order of the day. The Hammond brothers, the villains of the film, fully embody the subversive libidinal force of this frontier community. The third setting, the Knudsen farm, represents the polar opposite of Coarsegold. Joshua Knudsen (R. G. Armstrong) responds to the wilderness with a Puritan repressiveness, which finally drives his daughter, Elsa, away from his paternal authority to the libidinal Billy Hammond (James Drury) and his brothers. Therefore, with disorder established in these terms, the inscription of the Law on this frontier setting requires, first, that the gold shipment arrive safely in Hornitos (thus establishing the lines of capitalist production between wilderness and civilization);[5] second, that the Hammonds be defeated; and third, that Elsa be escorted safely back to her father's farm and from thence (since the Hammonds have murdered Knudsen) to Hornitos under the benevolent eye of a protective paternal figure (Steve, then Gil), who bears the moral authority of Knudsen without his tyranny.

Intertwined with the inscription of the Law on the frontier are the Oedipal trajectory of Heck Longtree and the formation of the couple. Heck's last name suggests the pre-Oedipal phallic power of his youth, who in the opening scenes is brimming with energy but lacks any legal, civilized channels for directing it. As a result of his attraction to Elsa and her refusal to accept him so long as he does not regulate his desires (at one point, he wrestles her to the ground and kisses her passionately until Steve rescues her), Heck gradually begins to align himself with Steve and the Law and proceeds toward the completion of his Oedipal trajectory. Heck's commitment to Steve, Elsa, the Law, and civilization, however, means facing the threat of castration, which "bears the transmission of culture."[6] Heck undergoes a symbolic castration: Steve ties his hands and takes away his gun. At first, Steve imposes this castration on Heck as punishment for his attempt (with Gil) to steal the gold shipment, but Heck subsequently accepts his castration voluntarily. During the first gun battle with the Hammonds, Steve entrusts Heck with a gun on condition that he give his word to return it after the battle. Later, when Steve demands the return of the gun, Heck draws on him, but then immediately apologizes and hands the gun over. Elsa plays an important role in this voluntary castration: she looks at Heck as he has his gun drawn, and it is in her eyes that he finds the image of his castration acceptable. After Heck has surrendered his gun, the group arrives back at the Knudsen farm, where Steve and Gil defend Elsa against the Hammonds. Thus, the resolution of Heck's Oedipus complex almost exactly coincides with the showdown through which the Law is inscribed on the frontier.

This Western narrative structure has been adapted to a rural village setting in contemporary England by Gordon M. Williams in his novel, *The Siege of Trencher's Farm*, and by Sam Peckinpah in his film version of the novel, *Straw Dogs* (Peckinpah wrote the screenplay with David Zelag Goodman). At first glance, though, novel and film seem to constitute reversals of the Western narrative as defined above. The hero (in the novel he is named George Magruder; in the film he is named David Sumner and is played by Dustin Hoffman), an American living on the outskirts of the half-civilized, half-savage village, is the most civilized, fully Oedipalized character imaginable. An American university professor who takes us residence at Trencher's Farm in order to complete some research, he opposes physical violence in any form (including capital punishment). Furthermore, he has a wife (named Louise in the novel, she is renamed Amy in the film, where she is portrayed by Susan George) and a daughter (there is no daughter in the film, however) and, most important, during the climactic siege he becomes as savage as the villagers who assault his home. This seeming reversal of the Western narrative is, in fact, only a variation of it, a variation that structures a large number of Westerns (e. g., revenge Westerns). In such Westerns the hero is an Oedipal figure at the beginning (or was at some point in the past), but then regresses to a pre-Oedipal stage of development, which is where we find the uncivilized hero at the beginning of the more traditional form of the classical Western described by Bellour. This pre-Oedipal stage is characterized by unrestrained phallic power and by aggressive behavior; which is not repressed and internalized but directed outward to the world. Subsequently, like the more traditional hero, the hero of the variation narrative saves civilization from the outlaw forces of the wilderness and inscribes the Law on the frontier. If he successfully resolves his Oedipus complex, he re-enters civilization with the heroine (as in *The Siege of Trencher's Farm*); if not, he retains his phallic power and rejects civilization (as in *Straw Dogs*, though the ending of this film is ambiguous).

Both *The Siege of Trencher's Farm* and *Straw Dogs* are set in an English village (called Dando in the novel, Wakley in the film), where, as in the Western frontier town, the forces of civilization (the Law and the Church) are still too weak to regulate the pre-Oedipal aggressive behavior of the unsocialized inhabitants. In adapting the novel, Peckinpah has altered the relationship between the village and the civilized world which lies beyond its precincts, so that the village more closely resembles the archetypal Western town. Although the opening chapter of the novel emphasizes the isolation of the village from civilization by virtue of its geography and poverty ("The men of Dando . . . had been apart for a thousand years and more, and when the outside world threatened them and their land they knew best the strength of their own apartness."),[7] subsequent chapters continually depict civilization intervening from outside into the life of the village. Peckinpah eliminates most of these interventions, however. For example, he eliminates the policeman from a neighboring town who arrives at the tail-end of the siege to prevent the hero from beating the last intruder to death. In addition, Henry Niles (played by David Warner), the mentally retarded villager who precipitates the climactic siege, lives with his brother in the village, whereas in the novel he is living in a nearby mental institution and escapes from an ambulance which overturns in a storm. Hence, all scenes involving the mental institution, the hospital, and the ambulance are absent from the film. *Straw Dogs* also introduces a new character to the *dramatis personae* of the novel, the village lawman, Major Scott (T. P. McKenna), the counterpart to the town sheriff in the Western. At the conclusion of the barroom brawl early in the film (this is a stock scene in the Western which indicates the level of uncontrolled aggressiveness that still exists in the Western town), Scott intervenes to order the chief brawler, Tom Hedden (Peter Vaughan), to go home. We see immediately that Scott is crippled—one arm is in a sling—and hence, that there is a serious weakness in the power of the Law in the village.

Into this unstable frontier community enter a husband and wife with an unstable marriage. In both novel and film the tensions between the villagers and the couple and between husband and wife increase until they finally come to a head when the husband attempts to protect Henry Niles from a lynching party of men from the village. The novel resolves this climactic situation in keeping with the requirements for closure in the classical Western. First, George Magruder successfully enforces the Law in the absence of the police when he defends Henry from the villains, who falsely accuse the retarded villager of murder. Secondly, George's regression to a pre-Oedipal stage proves temporary, for once the police arrive to take custody of the unconscious villagers, George internalizes his aggressiveness once again and reattains an Oedipal position. Third, in the process of enforcing the Law, George repairs his failing marriage and the couple's bond is strengthened. As in *Ride the High Country*, the heroine recognizes the need for male dominance and aggressiveness is a frontier situation, while the hero, having succeeded in defending the heroine, abandons his phallic powers for reintegration into the symbolic.

Straw Dogs, unlike *The Siege of Trencher's Farm*, renders the Western narrative problematic through the complex treatment of the hero and his aggressive behavior. On the one hand, the film manipulates the spectator to the point where he wants to see David regress to a pre-Oedipal stage and redeem himself from the humiliations he has suffered as a result of his passivity throughout the major portion of the film. On the other hand, once David does take the offensive, his unleashed aggressiveness becomes as chaotic and destructive as that of the villagers. In this way, *Straw Dogs* rejects the economic principle in the classical Western by which the pre-Oedipal aggressive behavior of the hero is fully recuperated for civilization. Previous Peckinpah films, even those that take a highly critical position toward the classical Western, depict the aggressiveness of the hero(es) being organized and channeled for the benefit of civilization (*The Deadly Companions, Ride the High Country, Major Dundee*) for some other productive end (the revolution in *The Wild Bunch*, the "cactus Eden" in *The Ballad of Cable Hogue*). In *Straw Dogs*, however, this aggressiveness accomplishes only the destruction of the home, the traumatizing of the heroine, and (probably) the dissolution of the marriage. Hence, in *Straw Dogs* the aggressiveness of the hero becomes a problem, which the film refuses to resolve in the manner of the classical Western.

At the end of the film it is questionable whether David has preserved the Law or simply escalated the scale of death and destruction. It looks as if chaos has triumphed over order. In contrast to *The Siege of Trencher's Farm*, and to the classical Western, *Straw Dogs* concludes in a state closer to anarchy than to civilization. In the novel George maintains a holding action until the police arrive to reintegrate Trencher's Farm with civilization. Moreover, George is able to safeguard Henry Niles without killing any of the members of the lynching party. In the film, however, the police do not arrive at the end to take the villagers into custody and transport them to the hospital and then to jail. Furthermore, no villagers survive to be arrested and sentenced to prison (except perhaps for Tom Hedden, who is last seen screaming in agony after having blown his foot off with his own shotgun). The lynching party arouses no more sympathy than the Hammond brothers do in *Ride the High Country*, but where the latter film focuses attention on the dignity and courage of the dying lawman and on the redeemed lives of the survivors, *Straw Dogs* focuses on the waste and destruction left by David's victory in the siege. After the siege is over, David leads Henry out of the house, and then we hear David start the car with ease (previously, he has always had trouble starting and driving the car—Amy was the driver in the family), but all we see on screen as he successfully starts the car is Amy trembling while she surveys her ruined home. As she sits on the staircase, she stares at the dead body of Chris Cawsey (Jim Norton) lying below her. Between Amy and the dead body is the phonograph on which David had played the bagpipe music that stimulated his fighting spirit as he struggled with Chris. The phonograph needle is stuck in a groove at the end of the played-out record, and we hear the endless rasping of the needle as we view the shots of Amy and the ruined home. The mood of desolation is further developed in the final shots of the film, which show David and Henry in the car surrounded by a foggy, pitch-black night, and in the closing lines of dialogue:

Henry: I don't know my way home.

David (smiling): That's okay. I don't either.

The final shot of the film is a long shot of the car, invisible except for the faint head- and taillights, which barely penetrate the darkness. As the car approaches the crest of a hill, the shot freezes, and what lies beyond the hill remains unknown.

Thus, *Straw Dogs* emphasizes the destructive nature of the hero's aggressiveness. In contrast to the classical Western, no civilized order has been clearly established at the end of *Straw Dogs*. In addition, it appears that the couple has been irrevocably sundered. During the siege David uses physical violence on Amy to force her to obey his commands. Consequently, she helps him to defend the house against the villagers, but she continues to fear and resent his behavior. Several incidents during the siege indicate the extent of Amy's alienation from her husband. When Norman Scott (Ken Hutchison) sneaks in through an upstairs window and prepares to rape her, she screams for help but does not know whom to trust—her husband or her former lover (but more recently one of her rapists), Charlie Venner (Del Henney). She calls first for David, and then she changes her mind and calls for Charlie. Later, as she watches Phil Riddaway (Donald Webster) assault David (Phil springs up suddenly just after David, exulting in his victory, exclaims, "Jesus! I got 'em all"), her face registers both horror and pleasure. David has to beg her to get the shotgun, and when she does finally have the gun in her hands, she hesitates for several moments before pulling the trigger and killing Phil. At the end of the film, when David leaves with Henry, Amy is in a state of trauma, the result not only of the villagers' siege but of her husband's behavior as well.

The film departs radically from the novel in its view of the effect of the siege on the couple. Far from feeling animosity toward George for using physical violence against her, Louise Magruder experiences a sense of relief. She feels "the way she'd always wanted to feel, like a woman. Protected" (p. 171). As she notices George begin to enjoy the physical violence of the siege, she feels alienated from him, but after the siege is over, and he has saved her and their daughter from the intruders, guilt overwhelms her, and she apologizes for not having helped him more during the siege. In the end, George's violent defense of his home stabilizes the previously shaky marriage: "George told himself that he and Louise were happier together at this moment than they'd been for years" (p. 188).

Besides emphasizing the collapse of the marriage and the general desolation that result from David's stand against the villagers, another means by which *Straw Dogs* questions the Western hero's aggressiveness is by symbolizing in the figure of Henry Niles the pre-Oedipal position to which David regresses.[8] If the hero of a classical Western rejects civilization and marriage, he usually departs at the end of the film in the company of some member of the natural world (an Indian friend, a horse). The final shots of *Straw Dogs* depict David riding off with Henry Niles—not a noble companion but the village idiot. Since Henry lacks the mental faculties that would enable him to control his drives and his physical powers, his presence beside David in the car at the end emphasizes the chaotic and destructive potential of David's phallic power. In addition, because Henry does murder (albeit accidentally) Janice Hedden (Sally Thomsett), he represents a phallic power directed against women, and thus he indicates David's barely repressed hostility toward Amy, which through the siege finally finds a means of release.

From the opening scene of the film, David and Amy are in a perpetual state of mutual antagonism, which is symbolized by the chess game they play before going to bed and by the scientific toys (e. g., the pair of magnets which continually attract and repel one another) on David's desk. Thus, when David decides at one point to accept the villagers' invitation to go duck-hunting on the moors, he does so only after he notices that Amy is upset at the prospect of being left alone in the house. In this way, David intends to take his revenge on Amy for having implied that he was a coward when he refused to ask the villagers directly about the murdered cat. During David's absence from home, Charlie Venner and Norman Scott leave the hunt, go to Trencher's Farm, and rape Amy. Of course, David does not know that Amy will be raped during his absence, and therefore, he is only indirectly responsible for what happens to her. This responsibility is emphasized, however, through the editing together of the rape scene and the hunting scene.

The series of hostilities between David and Amy in scene after scene lends a dark ambiguity to David's motivations for protecting Henry Niles from the villagers. David's motivations for taking a stand include his desire to see the Law upheld, his guilt at having accidentally run

Henry down with his car, and his desire to defend the sanctity of his home. These motivations mix with other less commendable ones. A couple of the latter motivations reveal themselves in the following argument between David and Amy, which takes place on the staircase as the siege begins.

> Amy: Give them Niles, David.
> David: They'll beat him to death.
> Amy: I don't care. Get him out!
> David: You really don't care, do you?
> Amy: No, I don't!
> David: No. I care. This is where I live. This is me.
>   I will not allow violence against this house. No way.

This passage of dialogue not only reveals David's concern for Henry and his desire to defend his home, but it also suggests that in David's mind the defense of the home is linked to the defense of his own ego, which Amy has wounded repeatedly throughout the film by criticizing his passivity. The siege gives David the opportunity to assert his moral superiority over her. Even before the villagers arrive and the siege begins, Amy begs David to throw Henry out of the house.

> Amy: David, David, do you know it's Henry Niles? I don't want him here.
> David: He's hurt.
> Amy: I don't want him in my house.
> David: Fine. You get upstairs, you go to bed. Take a bath. You just get outta here. He'll stay until the doctor comes. What do you mean you don't want him in your house?

David's assertion of moral superiority soon leads to his assertion of physical superiority, as Amy, exasperated with David's irrational decision to risk their lives to defend Henry, tries to join Charlie outside. At first, David gives her the chance to leave, to see if she actually will abandon him. Then, as she is unlocking the door to leave, he grabs her, and, with a smug, self-righteous look on his face, he slaps her and holds her by the hair. After this act of violence, he forcefully explains to her the perilous situation they are in: "Listen to me. You know what happens if they get in then? They'll kill us all. They've gone to far to back down now. Do you understand that?

[With a smile on his face:] We're dead if they get in." David's use of physical violence on Amy pulls the viewer in two directions simultaneously. On the one hand, David is probably right that the villagers will kill Amy (as a witness to Scott's murder) once she steps outside—though Charlie may possibly be able to protect her. Hence, the viewer sides with David as he, like Western heroes before him, slaps an hysterical female in order to silence her and save her from getting herself and others killed. On the other hand, David's slap recalls Charlie's slaps during the rape scene, which Charlie administered to Amy in order to make her submissive. The parallels between the two scenes are clearly established: the slap across the face, Amy's scream, and the slow-motion shot of her head recoiling from the blow carry over from one scene to the other. Furthermore, both men grab Amy by the hair after striking her. By linking David to the rapist (who also happens to be one of the men now besieging the house), Peckinpah undercuts the heroic nature of David's assertion of authority during the siege. The implication is that the Charlie Venner in David has suddenly emerged.

Elsewhere, the film associates the violent deeds of the villagers with David's repressed desires. For example, David expresses hostility toward Amy's cat ("If she's in my study, I'll kill her"), and one evening when Amy forces him to stop working, he satisfies his irritation at her by throwing fruit at the cat. In a later scene, Amy's noisy search for the missing cat so disturbs David's work that he leaves the house in a rage and drives into the village. Returning home in the evening, he taunts Amy about the missing cat: "By the way, Amy, did you find your, uh, kitty, kitty-kitty?" As he is undressing for bed that night, he discovers the cat strangled in the closet. David's previously established hostility toward the cat suggests that the strangling of the cat is both an actual fact and a projection into the real world of David's repressed desire. The rape scene can be read in a similar way. Peckinpah intercuts David's hunt on the moors with the rape at Trencher's Farm and, in addition, brackets the rape scene by the hunt, so that the entire sequence begins and ends with David. The editing together of the two scenes not only emphasizes David's responsibility for the rape but also suggests that the rape is both a real event and a projection of David's repressed desire. After all, his principal motivations for accepting the hunting invitation were hostility toward Amy and the desire to retaliate against her for humiliating him. Thus, the rapists realize David's repressed fantasies of aggression against Amy. The link between David and the rapists is further developed within the rape scene itself through the intercutting of shots of Charlie removing his shirt with shots (from an earlier scene) of David also removing his shirt. The fact that both men are shown in the same position in preparation for sexual intercourse with Amy further reinforces the link between the two men.

The above scenes indicate that David is repressing his aggressive desires and the images linked with these desires. He refuses to recognize his aggressiveness, and so he retreats from any situation that might lead to violent conflict. According to Amy, the Sumners left America because David "didn't want to take a stand." In the village, however, David encounters figures who gratify rather than repress those very desires that he represses. This suggests the possibility of viewing *Straw Dogs* as a portrayal of paranoia. There are a number of parallels between David and the paranoiac as described by Freud. In reviewing Freud's writing on the subject of paranoia, Jacqueline Rose writes: "Freud describes paranoia as the outward projection of a rejected idea—the content of a desire—which reappears as perceived reality, against which repression manifests itself anew as opposition."[9] In *Straw Dogs* "the outward projection of . . . the content of" David's repressed desires appears "as perceived reality," and then "repression manifests itself anew" in the form of hostility toward this projection, i. e., David kills the villagers who gratify rather than repress these aggressive desires. Of course, David differs from the paranoiac as defined by Freud in two significant ways: David does not hallucinate the villagers, and he does not hallucinate the hostilities that are directed against him. Nevertheless, although the villagers and the acts they commit have the status of real people and real events within the diegesis of the film, at the same time they are organized around the figure of David as projections of his repressed desires. Hence, David's entrance into the village is simultaneously his passage into his own unconscious.

In his study of Judge Schreber, Freud notes that paranoiacs frequently have delusions of the end of the world, a fact which Freud explains as follows: "The patient has withdrawn from the persons in his environment and from the external world generally the libidinal cathexis which he has hitherto directed on to them. . . . The end of the world is the projection of this internal catastrophe."[10] David Sumner has no delusions about the end of the world, but the film charts his gradual withdrawal from all contact with the external world. He retreats from urban America to a semi-isolated farm in rural England, and then he withdraws further from the world by retreating into his study. Finally, he retreats even from this last refuge. He fires the men from the village and then walks away from the house. Amy later finds him sitting alone on a hill, facing away from the house, which in the distance behind him. According to Freud, the next stage in paranoia, following the general withdrawal of the libido from "the people and things in the world" (p. 174), is the recovery process, in which the paranoiac re-establishes his relationship with the world. This relationship is now an aggressive one: the paranoiac experiences the world as a hostile object. In addition, the libido that has been detached from the external world now "becomes fixed on to the ego, and is used for the aggrandizement of the ego" (pp. 175–76). David's aggressiveness and megalomania ("Jesus! I got 'em all") during the climactic siege exemplify the recovery stage of paranoia.

Since *Straw Dogs* is modeled on the Western narrative, the implication is that it would not be uncommon to find other Westerns in which paranoia plays a significant part. In *Ride the High Country,* for example, Heck Longtree is a paranoid figure. On the way to Coarsegold, Steve intervenes to rescue Elsa from a sexual assault by Heck. Later, in Coarsegold, as Heck is beginning to align himself with the Law, he sees the Hammond brothers assaulting Elsa in much the same way as he once did. They constitute a projection of his own repressed desires, and on the return trip to civilization, Heck helps to kill the Hammonds. Paranoia is also an important element in other Westerns besides those by Peckinpah. Many Westerns focus on the attempt by the hero and a group of settlers to establish a civilized community on the frontier. The hero and settlers accomplish this project by repressing certain desires (usually sexual and aggressive ones) and sublimating the libido into socially productive directions. In their attempt to establish civilization on the frontier, the hero and settlers are terrorized by hostile figures (Indians, white outlaws), who embody the unsublimated libido, and who thus represent projections of the repressed desires of the hero and settlers. In response to hostility from these libidinal figures, the hero leads the settlers in subduing them. *Straw Dogs* differs from these classical Westerns because it makes the paranoia of the hero explicit and thereby renders problematic the Western's celebration of the heroic inscription of the Law on the frontier.

The highlighting of paranoia is one more way by which *Straw Dogs* makes the Western narrative problematic while simultaneously adapting that narrative to a contemporary English rural setting. In his first film outside the Western genre, Peckinpah takes a more critical view of the Western than he had in his previous films and maintains a colder, more distant perspective toward David Sumner than he did toward the heroes of his Westerns. This more critical perspective stems at least in part from the shift after his first five features to a contemporary setting. In an article on Peckinpah's Westerns, Roy Armes writes, "The Wild Bunch is for him [Peckinpah] a collection of stupid brutish men, but by casting his film in the Western mould, he comes automatically to endow them with a spurious glamour. . . . The violence too that Peckinpah intends to be horrifying as well as strangely fascinating becomes infused with a false romanticism in the context of the Western. . . . "[11] By adapting the Western narrative to a contemporary setting, Peckinpah is able to avoid much (though not all) of this romanticism.

The contemporary setting has another significant effect on Peckinpah's treatment of the Western narrative. In *Straw Dogs* Peckinpah is concerned with the Western narrative as a structure not only in fiction films but also in the contemporary American male psyche. In their article on *Straw Dogs*, Fedor Hagenauer and James W. Hamilton write: "It is interesting to note that David needed a rational motive to justify his stand, the protection of Henry Niles, and that he did not act when the issues involved were of a more intimate, personal nature. Men can often commit aggressive violent acts more readily in the name of some symbolic imagery or cause, to pacify their superegos."[12] The "symbolic imagery" in this case extends beyond the protection of Henry to include all the elements of the "last stand" situation, which recurs in Western after Western: savages threaten home and family, the Law is absent, etc. David only regresses and takes a stand when he finds himself in this classic situation. Unlike George Magruder, however, David is not a Western film fan. Through this alteration in the novel, Peckinpah seems to be implying that any American, simply through the unconscious influence of the national ideology of his country, may regress when he finds himself in a frontier situation as David Sumner does. Thus, in *Straw Dogs* Peckinpah not only exposes many of the simplifications of the classical Western narrative but also shows how that narrative lies like a time bomb in the psyche of the repressed American male.

NOTES

[1] Louis Garner Simmons, "The Cinema of Sam Peckinpah and the American Western: A Study of the Interrelationship Between an Auteur/Director and the Genre in Which He Works," Diss. Northwestern University 1975, p. 419.

[2] Terence Butler explores this approach to Peckinpah's non-Western films to some extent in his book, *Crucified Heroes: The Films of Sam Peckinpah* (London: Gordon Fraser, 1979). His interpretation of *Straw Dogs* is nearly opposite to my own, however. He considers the film an endorsement of brute force, and he argues that "Peckinpah seeks to accord a lofty moral righteousness to his hero's actions." CF. pages 69–74; the quotation is from page 72.

[3] Janet Bergstrom, "Alternation, Segmentation, Hypnosis: Interview with Raymond Belour," trans. Susan Suleiman, *Camera Obscura*, 3/4 (1979), 70–103. Bellour discusses the Western on pages 87–93. Future citations to this interview appear in parentheses in the text of my paper. Bellour's description of the classical Western narrative is similar in many respects to other descriptions of this narrative. For example, though Bellour approaches the Western through psychoanalysis, his definition of the terms of narrative closure resembles that of Will Wright in his analysis of "the classical plot" in *Six Guns and Society: A Structural Study of the Western* (Berkeley: Univ. of California Press, 1975): "This ending—the hero marrying and settling in the now peaceful community, becoming just like everybody else—is the most common ending throughout the classical Western" (p. 48). I have used Bellour for my analysis of *Straw Dogs* because of his emphasis on the function of the heroine, which is crucial in Peckinpah's film, and because of his psychoanalytical approach, which ties in with my discussion of David Sumner's character below.

[4] Laura Mulvey, "Afterthoughts on 'Visual Pleasure and Narrative Cinema' Inspired by 'Duel in the Sun' (King Vidor, 1946)," *Framework*, 15/16/17 (Summer 1981), 14.

[5] Paul Seydor describes the productive relationship between Hornitos and Coarsegold as follows: "The two communities share a relationship that is symbiotic, as the camp feeds the town gold (*coarse* gold) that is banked and then presumably invested or otherwise refined into supplies that in

turn are sold back to the camp." See *Peckinpah: The Western Films* (Urbana: Univ. of Illinois Press, 1980), p. 34.

6 Juliet Mitchell, *Psychoanalysis and Feminism: Freud, Reich, Laing and Women* (1974; rpt. New York: Vintage Books, 1975), p. 79.

7 Gordon M. Williams, *The Siege of Trencher's Farm* (1969; rpt. New York: Dell Publishing Co., Inc., 1972), p. 12. This paperback reprint was published under the title, *Straw Dogs*. Subsequent references to this edition appear in parentheses in the text of my paper.

8 This idea derives in part from points made by Terence Butler and Stephen Farber. Butler calls Henry "a surrogate for his [David's] phallic self" (p. 74). Farber states that Henry "most clearly embodies the irrational brutishness—unpredictable and unfathomable—present to some degree in all of the characters." See Farber's article, *"Straw Dogs,"* *Cinema* (Los Angeles), 7 (Spring 1972), 4.

9 Jacqueline Rose, "Paranoia and the Film System," *Screen*, 17 no. 4 (Winter 1976/7), 87.

10 Sigmund Freud, "Psychoanalytic Notes upon an Autobiographical Account of a Case of Paranoia *(Dementia Paranoides),*" *Three Case Histories*, ed. Philip Rieff (New York: Collier Books, 1963), p. 173. Subsequent references to this edition appear in parentheses in the text of my paper.

11 Roy Armes, "Peckinpah and the Changing West," *London Magazine*, 9 (March 1970), 106.

12 Fedor Hagenauer and James W. Hamilton, " 'Straw Dogs': Aggression and Violence in Modern Film," *American Imago*, 30 (Fall 1973), 241.

ARISTOTLE IN TWILIGHT: AMERICAN FILM NARRATIVE IN THE 1980s

Stanley J. Solomon

Now a whole is that which has beginning, middle, and end. A beginning is that which is not itself necessarily after anything else, and which has naturally something else after it; an end is that which is naturally after something itself either as its necessary or usual consequent, and with nothing else after it; and a middle, that which is by nature after one thing and has also another after it. A well-constructed Plot, therefore, cannot either begin or end at any point one likes . . . .
—Aristotle, *Poetics*, Chapter 7 (Bywater trans.)
Question: When you are doing this outline, do you break it up into a beginning, middle, and end? Are you conscious of setting up the problem, putting up obstacles, and moving toward the resolution?
Answer: Yeah. For instance in *Piranha*. . . . I decided that given a 90 to 100 minute movie, there should be a piranha attack every ten minutes. You open the picture with one and then every ten minutes you have another attack or some kind of action sequence. The basic problem with the story was, how do we get the piranha into the river? The first part of the story was about this but then I asked, why doesn't everyone just stay out of the river? They wanted the piranhas descending on the summer camp at the end so I had the end point. I drew a picture of a river and a lake and I said, okay, here's a schematic, visual thing of what happens but there's no point where the people are going to have a rest. So I drew a dam in the middle of it: the first half of this movie is getting to this dam; the second half of this movie is the piranhas getting around this dam, and then it started taking shape and incidents starting taking shape before I had any characters.
—From an Interview with Scriptwriter/Director John Sayles[1]

A state of anarchy prevails in contemporary American film narrative. Free form, open-endedness, experimentalism are some of the terms used to indicate the individualistic approaches to the depiction of those incidents which used to be referred to as the movie's plot, but this is not yet a cause of much concern. Indeed, it seems to have almost escaped notice that over the last decade or so the purpose of plot has shifted in the work of most filmmakers from a structuring function to a descriptive one, that is, to a pattern of events that might evolve out of a situation or relationship if the filmmaker were to poll the actors and technicians on the scene as to what ought to happen next. Yet Aristotle, whose name I cannot recall having seen mentioned in any study of film theory for many a year, remains a dimly perceived influence on the practice of filmmaking. Beginnings, middles, and ends in appropriate proportions are still the "formal causes" of certain kinds of film narratives, though not of most, nor necessarily of the most interesting.

The preponderance of loosely constructed narratives suggests a change in the conception and development of cinematic art: no longer an ordering of experience but—as it was in the 1890s—a recording of it, as if a film could indeed eventually break free of all the limitations implicit in having a plot in the first place. But the consequences of stories without structures may affect the way we condition ourselves to respond to film, which is often assumed to be the major artistic medium of our century.

It has been a few years now since an American film has really mattered to a thoughtful audience of some size. In that time, of course, we have had several films with "old-fashioned plots" (a new term in recent criticism which seems synonymous with "plots"); some, especially those with easily recognizable mythic analogues, in the last three years have had broad though perhaps superficial impact on young people: *The Empire Strikes Back*, *Raiders of the Lost Ark*, *Superman II*, *Rocky III*, *E.T., the Extra-Terrestrial*, among others. Even adults can appreciate certain qualities of filmmaking in these movies, and most of us are capable of enjoying them and thanking their creators for pleasant and stimulating moments of spectacle and activity. But we also know that in the larger history of culture—or that aspect of it beyond the popular vote—the intellectual or artistic history of this century, these films do not matter. They do not matter principally because their narratives do not really impose structures on the materials but rather grow out of the feelings such as love, sweetness, curiosity, and hope implanted in the materials, feelings that operate on their own logic. The narrative elements in such films are chronologically arranged incidents that, given the premises, could happen but have no tragic or comic necessity for happening—the causes stemming not from story but from an available mixed bag of general emotions, special effects, and faith in production values. So, ultimately, these films do not matter because they are rooted not in the patterns of life but in the fantasies of daydreams designed to embody a sentiment.

Considering the commercial success of several recent fantasies and the typical ten million dollar investment needed to launch even the most ordinary films, viewers should find it surprising that current production affords so much narrative diversity. The younger group of filmmakers who gained some artistic prominence in the seventies—such as Martin Scorsese, John Milius, Brian De Palma, John Sayles, Bob Rafelson, Hal Ashby, Ridley Scott—exert only superficial influence upon each other, their talents being perhaps too individualistic to establish narrative models for the next generation. In any case, they have made only a handful of films. Francis Coppola, almost alone among serious filmmakers, creates some public excitement with each new film, but in this industry an artist is still "only as good as your last picture," and his contribution to the 1980s so far has been *One from the Heart*.

Since the newer directors are neither prolific nor recognizably part of the stylistic movement and since the directors of the major commercial successes, the Steven Spielbergs and George Lucases, lack status in the critical realms of high art, we are not likely to locate any artistic center among the diversity of narrative structures in contemporary film. The sixties, from an eighties' perspective, look better; in those years both an established group of American filmmakers (some of them already thought of as classics, such as Hitchcock, Ford, and Hawks) and a brilliantly promising younger group (Frankenheimer, Hill, Penn, Nichols, for example) were perpetuating the tradition of quality, and it was a structured narrative tradition.

A short, unorthodox history of American narrative may help in explaining what is *not* happening now. Narrative practice is established for American cinema by Griffith around 1908–1910, but earlier, for five years or so after Porter's *The Great Train Robbery*, there seems to have been no strong notion of what the proper subject matter of film should be. No convention of scholars, no union meeting of camera operators (who were all the directors of the day) was called to discuss the crucial formative phase. Yet there were alternatives to the Griffith narrative in the works of both Porter and Méliès, who were the best known practitioners to American audiences before Griffith. It was not at all obvious, as it seems now to historians, that Griffith's structure was either naturally suited to film or better than anything else. Griffith's films were clearly better than his contemporaries'; but his typical melodramatic structure was not in itself necessarily better. Although the models he seems to have had in mind as a scriptwriter were novelistic and dramatic, Griffith was not forging a new medium in the image of Flaubert or Shakespeare; rather, he brought to film a heavily melodramatic narrative sense that placed much action, perhaps the bulk of the incidents, in the latter part of the script, the last third of the film (i.e., the last five minutes of his one-reelers) And he took the already well-developed linear motion toward a destination as the typical concluding action of his narrative. It was not always a chase, but it was always very active, very visual.

His genius and his stupendous output influenced everyone—every producer, technician, actor, and spectator. For sixty years, the Griffith narrative was refined into many varieties, but always dominated American production—and perhaps, too, most of the critical thinking about narrative in film. The most exciting films as well as the dullest, the most visual and the most talky, all tended toward narrative patterns that gathered momentum toward a conclusion. The structure that took hold shifted the well-made dramatic center of Sophocles, Shakespeare, and Ibsen, which was built around a climax in the middle, to a climax that was much closer to the end—thereby displacing the accompanying narrative issue (which generally could be stated as "What does this climax signify?") in favor of the question of "What will happen next?" In the theater, such a shift might have indicated the gulf between tragedy and melodrama, but it was an entirely reasonable procedure for the silent cinema, which could have no plot unraveling discussion to equal the physically portrayed action. To speak of narrative in film up to the sixties was to suggest Griffith's imposed structure, and any films that deviated from it seemed confusing, foreign, uncinematic, intended only for college audiences and festival critics: Resnais, Fellini, Antonioni, Bergman, Godard, the foreign influence. Films of the seventies obviously continued to drift away from the imposed structure, but lacking leadership or doctrine or even an articulated vision to announce in an *American Film* "dialogue" or on the Johnny Carson Show, filmmakers have not challenged the viability of the conventional. Some of the best known films of the past decade were in typical genre structures: *The Godfather, Jaws, The French Connection, The Exorcist, Close Encounters of the Third Kind*.

In the eighties, there are even fewer examples of major films committed to narrative structure. By imbuing some other aspects of film with the structuring function—which is an exercise in the impractical or the implausible—a filmmaker may even claim a virtue in producing the nebulous:

> In this film I tried to tell a story without dialogue and narration, but through mood and nuance and color and editorial motion. What I really like about *Conan* is that it achieves a sense of the surreal—a dreamlike, separate reality.[2]

Any disjointed narrative lacking reasonable continuity between episodes may be called dreamlike, but unless the viewers' dreams coincide with the filmmaker's the term we may prefer to use is self-indulgence. Where plot remains a key structuring device of a film in the science fiction genre (as in Meyer's *Star Trek II, the Wrath of Khan*) or in the horror genre (as in Kubrick's *The Shining*), the characteristic Griffith displacement of climax from middle to end is still apparent. Genres, of course, virtually by definition, are narrative structures, and the present decline of narrative form in general has much to do with the decline in genres.

Some genres with strong narrative structures such as the Western and the detective film are temporarily out of fashion; others like the horror film are being exploited in their minor modes: the maniacal mass killer, for instance. Still, because of their commercial viability, new genres develop from an almost general recognition of the value of repeating types of stories. George Lucas's *American Grafitti* (1973) led to a coming-of-age genre that remains popular in the eighties: Peter Yates' *Breaking Away*, Barry Levison's *Diner*, and Alan Parker's *Fame*. But a genre with real staying power cannot be created simply from imitation. Genre as a collection of motifs or icons related to a recognizable narrative grows out of a national sensibility that, given the premises of a situation or the implications of certain characters placed in certain settings, familiar patterns of action will occur. These patterns spring from widely perceived truths about human nature on the part of large publics, and there are very few such perceptions these days.

One type of narrative that is apparently important for our time has to do with the subject of conspiracy and the process of its investigation. Among the better known examples of the past few years are James Bridges' *The China Syndrome*, Sidney Pollack's *Absence of Malice*, John Avildsen's *The Formula*, and Alan Pakula's *All the President's Men* and *Rollover*. It might seem that if a sizeable group of films, several of them respectable, can still be produced in a recognizable form, the industry must still retain some interest in narrative structure. But such films are more obviously organized around their final cause—the unveiling of a conspiracy—rather than around meaningful shaping causes that could define them as a cohesive genre. In other words, some degree of structure, recurring from film to film, can be imposed upon the story elements without creating the conditions of a clear-cut genre in at least one common situation: that is, when the story materials are based on the outcome of a conflict—the ending of a film—instead of on the *process of* activities leading to an outcome.

Specifically, in conspiracy films the motivation is to show how a person or a small group at the top of a government, a corporation, a cult, a laboratory, etc. can control a powerful organization operating against the public interest, and how that control can be destroyed or at least publicly revealed. The subject of the conspiracy varies because each film is based on an issue of current interest in the popular press, a conspiracy that has already come unwound. Thus, the film's creators know that a solution exists prior to scripting; all that has to be done is to restate the problem so that it does not literally duplicate the actual event. The producers might buy the rights to a true-life account, but ordinarily they anticipate that a relatively cheap television film will get made before their theatrical film can be released. Besides, a fictionalized version of a conspiracy is malleable, easy to clarify for audiences, and always capable of being neatly tied up.

Another conventional source of film narrative is the expensive literary or theatrical property that is well-known enough to require the producer to stick close to the original plot. Since novels of this era are typically not much better structured than films, usually they lend no supporting structure other than a string of episodes to their screen adaptations, though most plays still provide some structure. Yet almost always, when the screenwriters and producers and directors begin to articulate the nature of the dramatic or literary plot, to analyze what contributed to its success—since it is that success that has cost the film company a million dollars—someone is forced by the sheer process of writing to reconstruct the outline of the story. From that point, the transformation of book into dramatized film narrative at least initiates a clarification and tightening of the original structure.

After that point, of course, the filmmaker might redirect his efforts toward (a) the exploitation aspects of the property, (b) the characterization (at the expense of plot), or (c) the era and decor implicit in the book but more readily emphasized in a visual medium. Thus, in spite of plot similarity, many adaptations puzzle the films' reviewers trying to match the events visualized with the events remembered in the source. Although, occasionally, the screenplay deliberately dissociates the film from its source (é. g., David Lynch's *Elephant Man* is not the stage play of the same name, though both are based on the same materials), more often a large part of the praise given the screen adaptation has to do with the filmmaker's capturing the spirit of the original narrative (Mark Rydell's *On Golden Pond;* Milos Forman's *Ragtime;* Alan Pakula's *Sophie's Choice*). With recurring frequency, the original writers are called in to work on the screenplay, typically without any experience in the medium, their main recommendation being an artistically numbing commitment to their original published version. Perhaps justifiably, the failure of an adaptation to present a coherent narrative, even when the confusion stems fromn parallel episodes in the source, leads to the condemnation of the filmmaker, not the original author, as John Irving escaped any blame for George Roy Hill's film version of *The World According to Garp*. It is not, of course, merely a problem of translating written ambiguities into cinematic ones, but of creating new obscurities. The endeavor of adaptation, after eighty years of cinema, is still going strong and remains one of the few plausible approaches to getting a narrative framework into film, though hopelessly unsuccessful.

While adaptation and genre continue to influence structure, more and more films have substituted situation for plot. By situation, I refer to the kind of action that follows from given premises or circumstances, but lacking the necessity of logical consequences in its development. It need not or cannot end: it simply finishes itself, exhausting the enthusiasm with which its principals greeted its premises at its opening. Indeed, increasingly films "open" with a situation rather than begin with an action of the sort Aristotle wrote about. This tendency to finish, to just run out of things to say, is the most apparent failing of the non-structured film.

The rare structured film of today still ends, its conclusion finalizing its narrative implications as authoritatively as the end of *Intolerance* or *Casablanca*, regardless of the quality of other cinematic elements. In Sidney Lumet's *The Verdict*, the final image of the heroic lawyer Galvin, played by Paul Newman, refusing to answer the telephone tells us decisively that he will not submit to any sentimental reconciliation with the woman who betrayed him. In contrast to this, the much more typical eighties film concludes in ambiguity—and frequently the final moments encapsulate that ambiguity as a frozen image.

Lumet's *Prince of the City* concludes with such an image: Lt. Danny Ciello, instructing a class of young detectives, is interrupted by at least one man's protest and walkout. Well, will the other detectives follow, indicating that the lecturer is totally isolated? Or will the others stay, redeeming Lt. Ciello from the condition of pariah? This would seem to be crucial, but instead of an answer, we are given a frozen image of the lecturer waiting for the response of the other detectives. What in the world was that film really about? It seemed to be a very interesting study of a policeman, corrupt himself, who volunteers to become an undercover investigator, stipulating only that he be excused from betraying his friends, who on a personal level (aside from their corrupt practices) deserve his love and respect. Lumet does a convincing job depicting Ciello's dilemma, showing how his integrity is broken down by his new role and how he gradually destroys even his friends. But what is his own final understanding of what he has accomplished? How much has he lost? If his loss consists of his career as well as those of his friends, the film is making a certain point about the penalty of betraying one's creed; but if, in fact, his career is eventually salvageable, if he loses only temporary status, then the point made by the film is quite different: in sacrificing personal relations, he achieves recognition by his peers who will remain at his lecture. He may be better or worse at the end, but who knows? What did Lumet think? The indefiniteness of conclusions is becoming a contemporary fixture, with or without the frozen image metaphor. Many such finishes stress only the incompleteness of the action. "Where do I go from here?" "Is there a future?" Any film may end posing such questions, though it is worth noting that such indecisiveness is still generally avoided in comedies. Blake Edwards' films, for instance, will end with the issues resolved (*10, Victor/Victoria, S.O.B.*), as does Sidney Pollack's *Tootsie* and Richard Benjamin's *My Favorite Year.*

But the mark of the serious film is becoming the indeterminate ending, which is essentially a non-conclusion to a narrative that did not appear unresolvable while it was occurring. One impulse behind the non-conclusion may be the attempt to parallel real life, where nothing ends short of death because there are no narrative plots, only on-going episodes. So powerful is this impulse that even those films with real endings may try to pretend to an open-endedness that we can dismiss as mere rhetoric: "Your mother is going away for a while," says the main character, Calvin, to his son at the very end of Robert Redford's *Ordinary People,* but she is not going away to think through the narrative premises. She is gone for good, because the plot demanded that resolution. Of course, in real life the option of return is always there, but to the chagrin of the producers, *Ordinary People* is merely real art and not real life.

Another artistically irrelevant but major influence on narrative endings is the potential film sequel. That possibility, because it encourages hedging, is more damaging for endings than the fact of a sequel planned during the production of the original film, as with *The Godfather, Superman,* and *Star Wars,* all of which incorporate the logic of the saga cycle in their design. Since every film released is thought by some studio optimist to have commercial viability, we can estimate the impact of that view on marketing strategy and on the ending. A film that is presented as a property rather than a product is an investment that should continue to gain in value after its initial marketing. Thus, if a potential resale (with new capital investment) of the property exists, it cannot be squandered for the sake of two minutes' artisitic truth at the end of a film. Until demolished, properties always contain value, no matter how ramshackle their structures may seem.

And demolition does not rule out resurrection. It may therefore be wise to plan ambiguity if you are a producer uncertain about the investment. Keep the maniac killer for an annual *Halloween*. After all, Hollywood learned in the 1930s that nothing stays dead forever, neither the Frankenstein monster nor Count Dracula. But at least in the 1930s the narratives of made-to-be-sequelized films were all conceived within totally resolved frameworks. It is a relatively recent phenomenon that emphasizes uncertainty in the conclusion. In *Star Trek II, the Wrath of Khan*, Mr. Spock (already a popular culture hero from the television series) very definitely dies at the end, yet all the reviewers and most of the audiences are apparently assured that he will be back among the living on the next voyage of the *Enterprise*. In fact, this preposterous belief (though we all believe it) saves the artistic implications of the ending, because the filmmakers did not have to hedge on the narrative denouement, relying instead on our imaginations.

Although inconclusive narratives are routinely turned out and have created audience expectations that are accepting if not approving, any widespread trend of popular culture must have many causes, not all of them commercial or sociological. There is also an implicit artistic criticism of old-fashioned narrative resolutions in serious contemporary films. Ever since film criticism began, the happy ending has been accused frequently of exploitation or excessive sentimentalism, even in Griffith's works. The unresolved ending in its way may be seeking a compromise between the sentiment of a happy ending and the grimness of an unhappy one, but to the extent that it suggests a failure to come to terms with the issues raised by the plot it may signify irresponsibility, since cinematic plot questions are premised on the possibility of good or bad outcomes.

Yet I do not equate the demise of the ending with artistic irresponsibility in most cases. Instead, we are observing a new narrative concept in characterization that is affecting structure: stories do not ordinarily have outcomes any more because characters do not make choices based on long-range consequences. Modern cinematic characters do not engage in thinking ahead, but rather they are to be measured by their decisiveness in moments of crisis. Usually when planning does occur, the plans will go askew, as for instance when a group of superheroes is on some rescue mission in an African country; at that point they will prove their worth by improvising new methods in the inevitable emergency. In this superficial way, films are made to resemble life as the unpredictable predictably occurs to complicate joy or to lessen sorrow. Therefore, lack of certainty, even confusion, may be a positive value in the ending of a 1980s film. In contrast, our classical narrative heritage in literature—Homer, the Greek playwrights, Shakespeare, the nineteenth-century novelists—is based on a commitment by such writers to demonstrate for their audiences that human actions inevitably have consequences at some distance from the occurrences; in other words, stories have unravelings, endings. This is not presently a requirement of narrative thinking, which is often just a study of characters who lack direction, but keep on going anyway.

It is less noticeable as a practice of scripting in the 1980s, but beginnings are also changing—though the choices for leading into a main narrative action were always broader than the paths out of that structure to a conclusion because the whole point of plot is to narrow options of choice. Nevertheless, a beginning always had some key functions: to introduce characters (and perhaps tone, setting, and theme), to supply what the theater critic still calls exposition, and most significantly to establish the storyline, committing a character to a course of action which allows him to make some choices. The Aristotelian middle of the narrative shows us those choices and the way that the series of events logically leads from one act to another.

Exposition was the area in which film originally distinguished itself as a narrative art. D. W. Griffith again, with a mind full of Dickensian narrative as enhanced by Ibsen's Hegelian structure, seems to have discovered intuitively that film can transfer the dialectic of exposition—a full act or two out of five in the theater that Griffith was preparing himself for—into a few visual images. From its earliest period of real narrative, film began to develop a style of beginning that eventually influenced the novel and the drama. It was a seemingly artless style: the film showed us Lillian Gish in a rural setting, and we knew everything essential in a couple of minutes of close-ups and farm scenes, and then on to the beginning of the action. With the introduction of the sound film, either because the technology was in itself attractive or because the new screenwriters used theatrical models, much Ibsen-style exposition was transferred to the film as an addition to the Griffith exposition—but did not replace it. Film historians have not properly addressed this development, assuming that films just became too talky. Actually, there were conceptual changes in narrative, particularly in beginnings, and only in recent years have filmmakers again attempted Griffith's visualized expositions. What happened in the early thirties led to a redundancy of verbal information and visual imagery. For example, in *Trouble in Paradise* (1932), Lubitsch introduces his hero-thief arranging for a romantic dinner, his clothes and his manner supplying us with knowledge of everything essential about him, everything needed for the beginning of the plot. A few minutes later in a longer but equally brilliant sequence, the hero and his female counterpart analyze each other while dining. No one would willingly spare a single line of this classic film moment, yet almost all of the sequence is verbal exposition, and in what is learned about the hero merely a repetition of earlier implications.[3]

In the 1980s, that is not likely to happen again, alas. But for the esthetic "improvement" in turning back from a theatrical to a more cinematic type of exposition in which the introduction of character and background is implanted in the visuals or in the visualized action, we have yet to recover the art of brevity. If the physical limitation of the one-reeler forced Griffith, who was by nature the most longwinded and bombastic of filmmakers, into becoming the master of brevity in establishing narrative beginnings, today's lack of limitations has made it difficult for filmmakers to begin to begin. (If Cole Porter seems to be invoked here, that is all to the good, for "Begin the Beguine" is indeed a depiction of a well-done movie exposition; it could be done, Porter tells us, merely by locating the emotion of the characters in the movie's scenery, complete with "orchestras playing" along the shore.)

Many films of this decade seem to start up without proceeding in the direction of the middle; they have no point of departure or termination where an action can be clearly determined to have originated—in other words, where the middle is not exactly similar to the beginning. In fact, some beginnings lead only to another parallel beginning or a series of them, all making the same point about the main characters; the exclusion of any one of these parallel beginnings would not affect the plot, though it might exclude some background. Almost all films that purport to deal with biography will extend their beginnings, partly because the dramatic portion of anyone's life is such a small part of his lifespan that the filmmaker/biographer would otherwise have only a thirty-minute movie if he could not pad out the drama (as Martin Scorsese does in *Raging Bull*) or shift the emphasis to the background era (as Warren Beatty does in *Reds*). For the narrative film, the biographical subject is probably best approached through character or history because, if given a dramatic emphasis, the beginning is likely to be a long time in getting to the middle (Richard Attenborough's *Gandhi* is well over three hours). Shakespeare imposed a dramatic structure on his so-called chronicle plays, but film biographies actually prefer to use a chronicle structure, perhaps to avoid the problem of where to begin. Why not just begin at the beginning:

> *American Pop* is the most complex story ever attempted in animation. Characters grow up and get older and die. They go off to wars and get killed. They have children. They travel cross-country.[4]

Time and movement may provide the opportunity for structure, but they will not of themselves suggest a narrative form. Dramatic biography is of course feasible in film form, but perhaps modern directors will have to review the films of George Arliss to remember how it was done, how it was possible to combine biography and the start of a dramatic action in a reasonably proportionate beginning.

To bridge the non-beginning beginning to the unresolved conclusion might seem to require an equally vague middle. Although Aristotle's definition seems to preclude the possibility of a middle existing without something on each side, we find in contemporary practice films with middles that can hardly be traced to a beginning and then seem to take up the rest of the film. Middles they are in the sense that linked events occur in some order. Apparently, chronological events when close enough in time can replace cause and effect linkage and still be comprehensible to a large audience. Mystery will also, sometimes, substitute for cause and effect since our experience persuades us that we will eventually understand the connections. Filmmakers relying on our capacity to suspend our disbelief until the mystery is dispersed and cause and effect re-established occasionally neglect their obligation to reconstruct the linkage of events. But by and large, the middle of a narrative in a 1980s film is likely to be less vague about the central action than the beginning or ending is; however, if that central action lacks a climactic event, limiting the direction of the ending, then the filmmaker will probably not be able to impose any order on the episodes of that action. As a result the middle will only describe events, linked or not, and the ending will seem accidental or arbitrary.[5]

If middles are measured by clocks or rulers rather than by Aristotle's philosophical scale, on which many 1980s films register absolute weightlessness, we discover, *voilà*, that every middle does indeed project a physical reality. The question then concerns substance more than form. Films are certainly no shorter than they used to be. What fills up the space that used to be filled in pursuit of the Maltese Falcon, or in trying to get that show ready for Broadway in spite of the disastrous opening out of town, or in ridding the state of the robber-baron rancher? I seem to find a lot of detached themes circulating at the heart of many 1980s films. The big movement toward the theme film occurred in the late forties and fifties, but those films, on racial or religious tolerance, for instance, always had carefully plotted narration. Themes of this decade are not typically derived from plot, and when embodied in characterization they can arise without even much dialogue, through a gesture or an arched eyebrow. Our themes are malaise, guilt, lack of fulfillment, loneliness, matters of the psyche often manifested by generalized indolence or small acts unrelated to a central action.

Put another way, plot is being replaced by texture. By texture, I mean incident or event or conversation—as distinct from structured action that has beginning, middle, and end. An incident or conversation is not sustaining in itself, but many incidents and many conversations strung together may resemble something like a traditional narrative. Texture includes tone and spectacle, and if it is consistently applied it is another organizing principle of narrative art. Whether it is enough to provide structure even when working in collaboration with character (another possible organizing principle) depends on the audience. If the audience has relatively few preconceived notions of what films should do, then structured narrative may be just one of several options for ordering the materials of films in the eighties.

Can the structured plot eventually fall into disuse as filmmakers substitute an organizing theme, a texture, for the main action, leaving Aristotle enveloped in total darkness? I do not think it likely to happen as long as narrative itself remains of interest to filmmakers, for Aristotle's theory of narrative structure is only logic applied to nature. His sense of narrative was based on the observation that human action depicted in what we could call performance media (e.g., dramatic opera, dithyramb, and publicly recited poetry) progresses in time and is therefore analyzable in time-based segments of beginning, middle, and end. Where there is life, there is movement. In all the narrative arts of this century, the achievement of a structuring narrative seems to have been intuitively grasped rather than logically devised. Fair enough: if a film really requires a plot structure and not just a series of incidents, there may be non-Aristotelian means of devising that plot. Obviously, very few screenwriters or directors have thought through the alternatives. Although Aristotle was in fact describing a single style of structure long popular into his era, he himself was aware of a viable alternative, the old-fashioned structure of Aeschylus. For our time, we might assume that either science or technology or the freedom of artistic experimentation would yield viable new narrative structures; instead, we get primarily non-structures, inconsistent points of view, and indeterminate endings.

In 1980s American films, it seems to me that at least Woody Allen has pretty well worked out an alternative, though it is not popularly perceived as one. Audiences may feel uneasy with Allen's recent avoidance of linear story development, especially when the mode is recognizably foreign, Fellini-esque in form, with overtones of Bergman. Allen's structure in *A Midsummer Night's Sex Comedy* and *Stardust Memories* is circular rather than linear, but it is an imposed structure with the idea of distancing the ending from the beginning not on a plane but in depth. It is not the kind of circle where one ends up close to where one began; rather, its progress can be likened to the distance between the top and bottom of a tornado. Although critics, who are accustomed to viewing Allen's comedy as a simple plot abounding with jokes and routines, have dismissed the structure as merely imitative, it works as well for Allen as for Fellini. And it is not entirely new to the American cinema: Griffith thought he was using it in *Intolerance* (and perhaps he was); Bob Fosse has used it recently in *All That Jazz*.

The formal basis of the narrative in both *A Midsummer Night's Sex Comedy* and *Stardust Memories* is the evolution of a problem embedded in a situation. The situation evolves incidents which bear on the central problem, each one expanding our understanding but not necessarily linked by time or space to each other, the unity stemming from their relationship to the center. Clearly, narrative structure must be quite arbitrarily imposed upon the story materials, though not in a progressive fashion. The point is not to detail the history of an action but to designate visually a place or a period in time to represent the basic situation. Then separable narrative actions develop from it, presumably in different directions. In fact, it is not necessary to locate the ultimate direction, to discover the ultimate interconnections of the narratives, because the structure holding things together has to do with the way the different narrative lines illuminate the unifying issue. Such a structure no doubt requires special story materials. Viewers unfamiliar with it may resent a seemingly circular or circuitous narrative, but it does make sense, a non-Aristotelian sense at that.

In *Stardust Memories*, the narratives seem so circular that audiences are hard pressed to describe any movement at all. The central problem *seems* to emanate from the main character's, Sandy Bates's, attempt to find meaning in his existence and perhaps thereby to exercise some control over the random events of his life through his commitment to his art, film directing. (Is there a doctoral thesis to be made from this theme, originating with Fellini's *8½*, as carried through in *All That Jazz*, *Stardust Memories*, and perhaps Richard Rush's *The Stunt Man*? And is it the subject matter that creates the need for this peculiarly modern narrative structure they share?)[6] Caught up in a weekend at the Stardust Hotel where eager fans, critics, and academics are supposedly watching a retrospective of his films, praising him and questioning him about his methods and ideas, Sandy is simultaneously embroiled in a controversy about the editing of his present film's ending (his producers think it terrible, but their alternatives are ludicrous). Sandy is also occupied with three women in his life and a groupie wanting to seduce him, plus a neurotic sister, a mother, and an actress who played his mother. For most of these complications, we are given a plot line that at least implies a beginning and features a middle, but without a resolution. Sandy is often worn to the edge trying to devise a resolution, yet he manages always to cope, with wit and charm, with both individuals and groups, though his quest for meaning consistently eludes him.

As each plot line develops, barraging the hero with confusing situations and meaningless information and interrogation, we begin to realize that the chaos surrounding Sandy is not entirely uncontrollable because, as the directing artist, he structures the episodes. No matter how silly a question posed, no matter how outrageous a demand made on his time or sensibility, he absorbs everything and shifts the focus of everyone else in the direction he wishes. Thus, the surprise ending—the old Hollywood plot with, say, Edward G. Robinson awakening from a dream in Fritz Lang's *Woman in the Window* (1945)—but one that does not require us to reverse our perception of the central structuring idea: everything that we have seen about Sandy, even the process of filming his Bergman-styled film, turns out to be sequences in a grand enclosing film, personal relationships and weekend film retrospective included. So the final vision—the actors walking out after the screening, a parallel to the confusion within the film *within* the film, leaving the hero isolated in the screening room—simply reaffirms the principle that only in art can the imitation of life—narrative—be structured. We do not know the name of the actor in the enclosing film who, we thought all along to be Sandy Bates, but undoubtedly he has a similar function as star/director. The entire narrative progress of the film, beginning with the director trying to finalize the ending of a film he is shooting in a garbage dump, goes from the process of redesigning chaos into an artistic whole to the achievement of that completed whole.

That achievement is the articulation of a personal vision that indeed discovers meaning by re-arranging otherwise random incidents into a narrative structure. Is this not one of the ways of stating the purpose of narrative art? Woody Allen's 1980s films suggest one structural solution to the problems of contemporary filming of materials that do not fit well into a traditional Aristotelian form. Most current films are probably not suited for either Aristotle or Allen, to judge from the meandering development of their stories. New structural modes have to be worked out, but first they have to be worked on; that is, some degree of awareness is required of contemporary filmmakers to see what is not succeeding on the narrative level. Certainly, there have been some excellent narrative films in the 1980s. What is particularly needed now is not just more good films, but narrative self-consciousness by filmmakers analyzing the posibilities for enhancing their vision through structure.

NOTES

[1] Tom Schlesinger, "Putting People Together, an Interview with John Sayles," *Film Quarterly*, 34 (Summer 1981), pp. 3–4.

[2] John Milius, as quoted by Kirk Honeycutt, "Milius the Barbarian," *American Film*, 7 (May 1982), 34.

[3] This highly influential film originated in an obscure foreign play. Although Lubitsch created truly effective expositions, less gifted contemporaries followed his lead by emphasizing the literary or dramatic origins of their screenplays through heavy exposition. As Neil D. Isaacs concludes in "Lubitsch and the Filmed-Play Syndrome," *Literature/Film Quarterly*, 3 (Fall 1975), 308: "There is still joy in what he wrought, but a curse on what he begot."

[4] Ralph Bakshi, as quoted by Rex McGee, "All That Jazz . . . Swing . . . Pop . . . and Rock," *American Film*, 5 (July–August 1980), 26.

[5] I am here distinguishing description from narration in the ordinary sense, but it is an arguable topic. For instance, Raymond Durgnat objects to the following point made by Christian Metz in *Film Language*, trans. Michael Taylor (New York: Oxford Univ. Press, 1974): "We all assume that description differs from narration, and that is a classical distinction, but on the other hand, a large number of narratives contain descriptions, and it is not even clear that descriptions exist other than as components of narratives" (p. 19). Durgnat, in "Film Theory: From Narrative to Description," *Quarterly Review of Film Studies*, 7 (Spring 1982), 122, argues that not only do film descriptions contain their own structures, but "all narrations are descriptions, but not all descriptions are narrations. Description is the larger category."

[6] In an article on reflexivity in cinema—the artist's self-conscious reflection on himself as filmmaker or on his medium—William C. Siska finds that where instances of reflexivity in the traditional narrative comprise a specialized type of subject matter, reflexiveness in the modernist film is very nearly a necessity, and one of the defining characteristics of the modern world view. "Metacinema: A Modern Necessity," *Literature/Film Quarterly*, 7 (1979), p. 287.

NARRATIVE TIME IN SERGIO LEONE'S *ONCE UPON A TIME IN AMERICA*

Stuart M. Kaminsky

ASSUMPTIONS

Before getting to the script of *Once Upon a Time in America*, which will be the central focus of this article, several assumptions need to be brought to the fore, assumptions of both the author of this article and those of assumed reader. In addition, some clarification will be given of the context in which the film script will be examined.

My basic position is relativist. I do not believe that the history of aesthetic thought has brought us one step closer to being able to differentiate qualitatively between works. That judgments will continue to be made is obvious, that they reflect anything beyond the acquired taste of an individual or culture segment is doubtful, that they can be substantiated with any kind of detachment is alchemical.

My point in making the above assertion is not to claim originality—the argument has been made by others including Northrop Frye, John Cawelti and Norman O. Brown—but to make clear that I am not trying to present an argument that *Once Upon a Time in America* is particularly elevated by my analysis. I am not claiming something unique for the film but citing it as an example of how a particular means of structural analysis can be used in aiding an understanding of both an individual work and the totality of film. Conversely, I am not concerned with any assertion that *Once Upon a Time in America* is not worth singular attention because it is neither high art nor folk art.

Gérard Genette several years ago engaged in a fine analysis of narrative time in Proust's *Remembrance of Things Past*.[1] Genette, dealing with an already canonized work, argued that the use of narrative time in it was a touchstone to Proust's genius, that a structural analysis would yield evidence of that genius. I think, as fine as Genette's essay is and as much as it has influenced me, he succeeded in doing nothing of the kind. What he wrote is as applicable to Stephen King as to Proust.

I wish also to recognize that I do not think the kind of structural analysis in which I will engage in particularly objective. It is "a" way, not "the" way. It is, as I believe all structural analysis is, not a discovery of a buried skeleton of truth, but a template created by the critic which he or she proposes will be a useful one in pursuing a particular line of inquiry. The legacy of Claude Lévi-Strauss has been that of grail seeking. If the world is, indeed, divided into good and bad, up and down, here and there, past and future, in fact if the world is actually a series of oppositions, then the structure is clearly there to be discovered. If, however, as Ken Wilbur and others have suggested,[2] the oppositions are not there but created by the human imagination to establish an order needed by the ego, such structural truths are not ultimate truths at all but revelations of the mind of the creator.

Put another way, if a critic discovers that the works of Vladimir Nabokov all reveal the same basic pattern of opposing relationships and follow the same "structure," the critic is dealing with his or her imposition on that work. The critic came looking, chose the tools, and discovered himself. I have no real quarrel with this procedure, however. Later I will indulge in it myself. What I object to is the assumption on the part of the critic that a discovery has been made that blots out other analysis, that objectifiable truth has been discovered about the work and, possibly, about literature, film or other acts of creation. I find it far more acceptable and valuable for critics to recognize that they are engaged in an essentially creative act. The critic's process is created or borrowed and then applied to a created work and, hopefully, the result is illuminating for the critic and reader. The criticism is a modification of the original work and illuminates the relation of the critic, and hopefully of the reader, to it. It is neither a justification, condemnation, nor vindication of the original creative act.

The reason so many "artists" are unhappy even with affirmative criticism is that they recognize, even if they are often unable to articulate, that another personality, another ego, in the process of converting the creative act to an analysis, has taken the original creation a step away and made it part of someone else's imagination. The novel, coupled with the criticism, becomes a new creative act, the novel/criticism. It is the critic's unwillingness to recognize this, to believe in a quasi-science called criticism, which causes difficulty.

Thus, the course I will take in dealing with the issue of time in *Once Upon a Time in America* will be to first indicate my relationship to the project, then move to a structural analysis of time transitions in the context of reservations indicated above, and conclude with a brief criticism of my own analysis.

CREATION

I was contacted in the summer of 1981 by Sergio Leone who had read some of my fiction published in Italy. He thought I might be an appropriate person to write the dialogue for *Once a Time in America*. The project had been in development for more than six years before I was contacted and ultimately hired. In 1982 the film was shot in English, using the dialogue I wrote.

Based originally on a rather little-known book, *The Hoods* by Harry Grey,[3] early scripts were attempted by various writers including Norman Mailer. When I came to the project in 1981, and subsequently worked on the script for more than six months, the principal screenwriters were Enrico Medioli, Leo Benvenute, and Piero di Bernardi. Medioli, whose best known credits are for scripts for Luchino Visconti (*The Damned, Death in Venice, Rocco and his Brothers*), was the only Italian writer who spoke English. Leone, at the time, spoke little English. The working procedure was for the Italian script to be translated into English and given to me. I would rewrite dialogue and make other suggestions for cutting, change, defining character, and the script would be retranslated into Italian. This process followed through five versions with supervision by Leone and input by the film's star Robert DeNiro. Writing took place in Los Angeles, Rome, and New York. The final session of four weeks before shooting began was a line-by-line discussion of the English dialogue. Leone supervised this session.

Various changes in the script were made during shooting. The first script I received from Leone indicated in a covering note[4] that he was quite consciously concerned with two aspects of the script: the fantasy/fairy tale nature of the story, and the importance of time as both a theme of the dialogue and the presentation. It was, in his view, to be a film dealing with the ephemeral nature of time and human interaction.

THE TALE

Recognizing that there are many ways to tell the story or give the plot, here is a summary of my version of what transpires in the final version of the script.

Noodles Aaronson, a Jewish gangster in New York in 1934, is in an opium den. Gangsters kill Eve, the woman with whom he has been living, and beat his friend Moe in order to find Noodles, who barely escapes from them in a Chinese opium den. Noddles then flees from New York.

At this point, the specific structure of which will be discussed later, we leap forward to 1968 and Noodles' return to New York City. With various leaps from 1968 to 1933–34, and 1922–24 (see graph on page 63), we discover that Noodles was the co-leader of a small gang on the Lower East Side. As a child, Noodles went to jail for killing another gang leaders. Out of prison Noodles and Max, his partner, have a disagreement about which direction to take the gang after the end of Prohibition. Noodles wants to stay small. Max wants to align the gang with the "syndicate." The gang does a few syndicate jobs, particularly backing Jimmy in his bid to move up in union leadership. When Max appears to go mad and insists that the gang tackle a Federal bank, Noodles turns himself and the gang in to the police to keep them from getting killed in what is sure to be a disastrous robbery. However, there is a shootout as the police close in and all the gang members, except for Noodles who has been left behind, are killed. The year is 1934, and the syndicate comes after Noodles to punish him for his betrayal of the gang. Noodles' 1968 return to New York is the result of having been summoned from his hiding place. Various events take place which force Noodles to deal with memory of his old friends and the woman he loved and lost. Near the end of the tale, Noodles discovers that Max was not killed in the shootout, that the entire event had been staged with syndicate help and that Max, who has summoned Noodles back to New York, is a high ranking government official under congressional investigation. Max's purpose in summoning Noodles is to give his old friend the opportunity to execute Max, who the syndicate and Jimmy have now decided must go to prevent scandal. Noodles refuses and, apparently, the mob does kill Max. The film ends back in the opium den in 1934 with a drugged Noodles who may or may not have imagined the entire core of the film as a fantasy to relieve himself of the responsibility for the death of his friends.

This summary, as I have said, is like all summaries: it is the emphasis of an individual's imagination at work on the material.

THE ANALYSIS

There are, in the final script of *Once Upon a Time in America*,[5] 5 separate sequences (presentations within a continuing time block). There are a total of 151 scenes within these 15 sequences. A scene involves, essentially, a continuing action without apparent break in time or space. The script, as most scripts are in spite of textbooks to the contrary, was written in scenes not shots. Normally, the director decides on the shots, not the writer. In other words, how the scene will be broken down into angles, duration of shots, distance of shots (long shot, medium shot, close-up) is the director's province. Normally each scene is shot in its entirety first—the master shot—and then the director breaks the scene into alternative angles and distances from which he and the editor can draw later. The writer(s) can, of course, suggest, but the final decision belongs to the director.

As a writer, it was interesting to envision a scene with the other writers and then, later, see the set not as we had imagined it, but as Leone and his long-time art director Carlo Simi, has seen it. In at least one instance, the writers had to rewrite a scene to accommodate the vision of the set.

The following graph indicates, from left to right, how the script moves between time periods. Each point on the graph indicates a change in time. So, Scene 1 begins in 1933. The tale remains in 1933 till Scene 23 when we leap forward and remain in 1968 from Scene 23 to Scene 34.

From looking at the chart, one might be tempted to suggest that the film's time orientation is bizarre indeed. In fact, a random examination of popular American film will often show leaps forward and back though the leaps will often be in hours, days and weeks rather in decades. For example, a chart of D. W. Griffith's *Broken Blossoms* (1919) would show similar leaps and, in fact, would present an additional problem at the conclusion when simultaneous time is shown in three consecutive sequences. A film such as *Halloween* presents similar leaps in time. The difference, however, between *Broken Blossoms* and *Halloween* and *Once Upon a Time in America* is that the leaps in time in the Leone film are foregrounded as they are in many more self-conscious films such as Fellini's *8½*. Each major transition is underlined by a foregrounded visual metaphor which accentuates its jump in time. The normal procedure in film for such leaps in time is to make the transition as conventionally invisible as possible, to avoid calling attention to itself. However, a breakdown of even the most transparent and seemingly simple feature film reveals the flexibility of conventional time in film terms.

SCENE

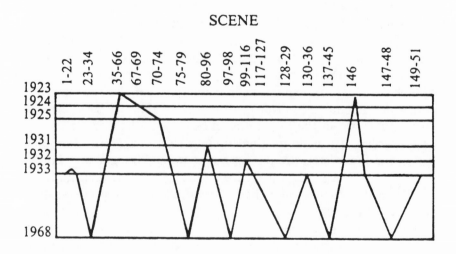

The comparison of literary time with film time is somewhat helpful but can be misleading. A continuing analytical problem in dealing seriously with film is the comparison of film to literature. Obviously, there are many points of comparison. Normally, however the reduction of the film to a narrative leaves one not with a work of literature, but an art stripped of its context. No film is its story. The tale is both the story and its telling. The artifice of leaping in time and space is and has been an accepted part of film narrative going back at least to 1903. *The Great Train Robbery* is not the simple story of a group of men who rob a train and then are gunned down in the woods as they count their loot; it is a series of moving images in which we see an action and a tale. The imaginary experience is in the viewing, not in the words to which we reduce the experience. The literary experience is quite different from that of film.

By the same token, there is much a novelist can do that a filmmaker can do only with difficulty. The novelist has ready access to interior consciousness, the thoughts of his characters. This glimpse òf interior consciousness can be achieved in film, but with difficulty.

Thus, when we return to the question of time, we see that it functions quite differently in film and literature. For example, Genette deals with Proust's use of the iterative in literature, the phrase which connotes a repeated action. Every day Miles went to town. Whenever Anne ate a sandwich, she picked up the spoon in her left hand, etc. There is no visual equivalent for this in film. Every envisioned act is an individual one for we see specific clothing, specific actions, a moment arrested in time, not a verbal comment on repeated time. Thus, the approximation of the iterative becomes quite difficult in film. Conversely, the film has no need to describe, or to consider how much to describe. The experience of reading is linear. It takes time. You cannot read thoughts, dialogue and description at the same time. In film, however, you can.

There is no suggestion of superiority of one medium over the other in the above observation. It is, on one point only, an attempt to show that each medium has its own parameters and those parameters indicate what has been done and perhaps what can be done within them. Nor am I suggesting as did Gottfried Lessing that each medium has its own destiny which cannot be violated, that vision should not be attempted in novels or that interior states of mind should not be depicted in film. It is one thing to point out the boundaries of the form and quite another to say that they are critical prisons.

Let's examine the thirteen points at which the film script of *Once Upon a Time in America* makes major leaps in time.

They are:

1—1933, Scene 22—

Noodles, after escaping from New York, hitches a ride with a truck driver. The driver asks, "Where are you going?" as Noodles gets into the truck. A long train approaches blocking our vision of the truck. The cars on the long train are 1933 Fords. When the train passes, we see Noodles, now 34 years older, returning to New York City on the same road.

2—1968, Scene 34—

Noodles is in the toilet of Fat Moe's bar. He stands on the toilet seat and looks through a vent. He is "peering into his past." We see from his point of view a young girl, Deborah, dancing. We are carried back to 1923 and a 14-year old Noodles is looking through the same vent.

3—1923, Scene 66—

The police are taking a rival gang member away in a sunlit alley. Max shouts down to the rival and there is a straight cut to 1924, one year later, and the interior of a paper plant.

4—1924, Scene 74—

Noodles is in the back of a paddy wagon being taken to jail for the murder of the rival gang leader. The prison gates clang shut leaving the four remaining gang members on the street. They do not see the inscription at the arch of the entrance reading:

"Your men will fall by the sword, your heroes in the fight."
Isaiah, 3:25

The camera moves down from the inscription which we now see at the entrance of a tombs in 1968 before which stands Noodles who has been brought here by an enigmatic message. It turns out to be the tomb of three of the gang members, the ones Noodles is supposed to have betrayed.

5—1968, Scene 79—

Noodles, carrying a suitcase full of money mysteriously given to him, is walking down the street when a frisbee hits him and flies on. "A hand reaches out of nowhere and grabs it." This is matched by a hand reaching out to take the suitcase from Noodles. As the camera pulls back we see that it is June, 1933, and the hand is that of Max who is greeting Noodles on his release from prison.

6—1934, Scene 96—

After a job in Detroit, the killing of an out-of-favor syndicate gangster, Noodles angrily tells Max that he was not "let in" on the real purpose of the job; he had been led to believe it was a jewelry robbery. Noodles drives their car off a bridge. Max emerges from underwater looking for Noodles but cannot see him. Nearby a steamshovel is dragging the river bottom lifting debris. As the debris drops into a truck, the camera reveals that it is no longer Detroit and no longer 1934, but 1968. It is Long Island and Noodles in watching a truck picking up garbage at a mansion.

7—1968, Scene 71—

Noodles is watching television at Fat Moe's bar and sees the familiar face of Jimmy Conway, the President of the Transport Union, on the screen. Jimmy, who is being badgered by the media because of alleged corruption of his union is saying, "If mistakes have been made in this situation, don't look at us." We cut to gasoline being sprayed in the face of the young Jimmy Conway in 1932. Jimmy is being threatened by hoods who want to stop a strike. Jimmy is saved by Noodles and the gang and takes his first reluctant step toward corruption.

8—1932, Scene 116—

Noodles runs toward a departing train on which the girl he loves, Deborah, is leaving New York following a violent night with Noodles. Their eyes meet. Then "she lowers the window shade and cuts him out of her life." There is a cut to 1933, one year later, as Noodles enters Fat Moe's speakeasy following, as we discover, a long period of drug-taking to forget Deborah.

9—1933, Scene 127—

At a beach in Florida after Max has announced that he want to rob a
Federal bank, Noodles looks at Carol, Max's girl, who lights a cigarette
and stretches out in the sand. A plume of smoke "issues up from the
depths of a wicker chair" and we are in 1968 looking at an old Carol
smoking in a nursing home. She then proceeds to tell Noodles, who
has found her, that Max, suffering from a brain disease, was mad when
he planned the bank robbery; that Max, in essence, committed suicide.

10—1968, Scene 128—

Carol, concluding her tale to Noodles, says, "If Max wasn't crazy, he
soon wouldda been." There is a cut back to 1933 and we see a dialogue-
less sequence in which Max and Noodles, disguised as workmen, check
out the Federal bank.

11—1933, Scene 136—

Noodles, who has just called the police so that he and the gang will be
intercepted before they can commit the bank robbery, is confronted
by Max who angrily knocks Noodles unconscious after Noodles says
Max is acting "crazy!" As the gun hits Noodles' head, there is a cut
back to 1968 and Carol in an armchair at the rest home saying, "Max
made fools of us, Noodles."

12—1968, Scene 145—

Noodles has been called to the home of U.S. Secretary of Commerce
Bailey who, he discovers, is really Max. The shootout in 1934 had been
a hoax worked out with the syndicate and crooked cops. Bailey/Max
supported by the syndicate has risen to his present position, but now
he is under siege by a Congressional committee and Jimmy has brought
word that he should shoot himself if he wants his son to live without
threat. Max has brought Noodles back to do the job. Max taunts him,
pleads, points out that Max has spent his life with Noodles' former
love, Deborah, that Max has robbed Noodles of his own life. Max gives
Noodles a gun. Noodles looks at it and "images of the past rise up."
Scene 146 consists of a series of composite images from 1923 to 1933
including Max arriving in the new neighborhood as a boy, and the
image of a disfigured corpse on the street, a corpse which is supposed
to be Max, but we now know was not. We cut back to 1968 and Noodles
looking up from the gun.

13—1968, Scene 147—

Noodles refuses to kill Max, refuses, in fact, to admit he is Max, refuses to acknowledge that his life has been wasted. He leaves Max and goes into the street where he appears to see Max being killed in the shadows behind a garbage truck. The reflectors of the truck glow "like two fiery eyes" and change into the lights of an Old Ford. The people in the car are dressed in 1930s costume. Noodles of 1968 realizes he is not back in time, but firmly in 1968 where some rich people are going to a costume party. Noodles turns a corner and steps into 1933 Chinatown. It is the night Prohibition ended, the night Max and the gang were supposedly killed. Noodles goes to the opium den and gets a pipe. According to the final line of the script, "The smoke is harsh and kind and cleansing. It wipes out memories, strife, mistakes . . . and Time."

Before moving to an examination of each of these transitions in the script, it is important to point out that within each of the narrative sections there are also jumps in time. The jumps focused on are those involving movement forward or backward of at least one year within the history of the story. Genette differentiates between historical and story time. Historical time is the actual time transpired for an action to take place. Story time is what we see of the history on the screen. Thus, in one sense, *Once upon a Time in America* takes about 45 years of historical time. In the film we see approximately three hours of that 45 years. The ratio of what is left out to what is presented is nearly astronomical. Within each narrative block of time, for example the 22 scenes in 1933 at the start of the film, there are brief movements forward in time (an hour, day, etc.) In addition, there are parallel actions, scenes which, though we see them in tandem, apparently take place at the same time. These are certainly not peculiar to this film and as techniques were well established by Griffith and others by 1912. However, those jumps of hours or even days or weeks which are unspecified are not foregrounded in the process of presenting information in *Once Upon a Time*. In other words, no narrative device, visual metaphor or optical device is used which pushes to the foreground the idea that we are seeing a leap in time which we are to recognize as such. Those smaller leaps of time are presented as part of the "invisible" process of making a film. They are non-foregrounded ellipses. They are historical time covered in zero amount of narrative time. The ellipsis is usually in the form of a cut; the historical time between two shots is not recognized until there is information given to us within the second shot to let us know that time has passed. For example, we can usually see if space has changed without dialogue to tell us.

Thus, we are going to deal only with those leaps of a year or more. As the graph shows, most of the leaps are of at least 10 years. From scene 34 to 35 there is a leap of 45 years. A similar leap occurs between Scene 145 and Scene 146. We might note that these two longest leaps are approximately twenty minutes into the film and twenty minutes before the film ends. They form part of the bookending process that begins and ends in 1934.

Now to the transitions.

Transition one, the train passing to reveal Noodles now old, establishes the motif of time change and space continuity. The cues we get to changes in time are, in most cases in the film, contextual; that is the characters look older or younger, their clothes are in keeping with the altered period as are the cultural artifacts. In this case, the automobiles are the first indication, followed by our seeing the aged Noodles. Thirty-four years have passed during the movement of that train. It is an ellipsis in Noodles' life that will not be covered in the film and only obliquely referred to. It is as if no time visually has passed in Noodles' life, but he has aged. The time has had no meaning and, indeed, at the end of the film, this is essentially what Noodles will tell Max in their final confrontation in 1968. This is a theme which will be returned to throughout the film. Noodles has, essentially, died in 1933, whether figuratively in an opium dream or lost somewhere in the vast West of the American myth. He has done nothing for 34 years but live with his guilt and memories—guilt and memories with which he has come to terms.

The first major leap, 44 years into the past comes in the second transition when the old Noodles looks down through the transom at Deborah dancing. It is the old man as voyeur. The viewer, who shares his point of view, is a vicarious voyeur. It is a nostalgic voyeurism, a voyeurism of the past and the secret spying on a young girl. This leap into the memory of the past is through the memory of the woman, the girl, the anima.

Transition three is conventional: it has no visual foregrounding of process. It is a straight cut, a leap of but one year. In transition eight there is also a straight unforegrounded cut which, we discover through dialogue, covers an ellipsis of one year. Thus the "shorter" ellipses of one year are indicated by straight cuts which require exposition. In transition three, we find immediately that the gang of boys is doing well, has taken over the small empire of their defeated rival. In transition eight, we discover that Noodles has had the first encounter with opium after losing his anima, Deborah.

Transition four involves a leap forward in time of 44 years, handled by a Biblical reference etched in stone. Both the prison and the tomb have the same inscription from Isaiah. The prison and the tomb are both, in a sense, cessations of time. The inscriptions refer to the actions of men before their time ceases. There is a possibility that the inscription on the tomb has been placed there by Max as a clue to Noodles, a further pulling in of the line which will draw Noodles to the moment when he must decide if he will acknowledge his mistake and take revenge by killing Max. The primary problem with this explanation of intentionality on Max's part is that there is no sign given in the 1924 scene that he or anyone else has seen the inscription. It is the camera which has seen the inscription, the audience which has been led to the transition which will leap 44 years of historical time. Is the image part of Noodles' fantasy? Is the whole tale, bookended by the opium scene, an opium dream by Noodles, a dream in which what he projects as a wasted life will be justified in the future, in which, in fantasy, he will discover that he did not betray his friends at all but was, himself, the tragic victim who becomes the tragic hero?

A problem with this, though it is a possibility favored by the director, Leone,[6] is that the period information in 1968 is contextually specific. In a novel, the illusion might well carry. In the film, we see television, 1968 automobiles, 1968 clothing, a frisbee, etc. The information is not a distortion alone but, if an opium fantasy, then the fantasy of a seer. Alternatively, we can, as many have suggested, assume we have moved into the realm of the imaginative projection. Thus, such questions are not reasonable, the testing of known data is not relevant. That seems to me a rather weak argument for accepting a seen future as possibly existing in the imagination of a character. We might also argue that we are dealing with a problem of convention. The fantasy of the future will lose the context of assumed naturalism of that future (which is, in this case, 1968, our past) which deviates from our experience of that world. Simply put, we have a sense of what existed in 1968. Were that to be confronted in a projection clearly seen as fantasy from 1933, it would change the genre of perception. Note, for example, the odd sensation of examining the "future" in a film which is now past. *Just Imagine, Things to Come* and *The Time Machine* all predict a future which did not come to be, but that was in the realm of science fiction. What, as in the case of *Once Upon a Time in America*, do we do if we do not want to deal with the assumption of how the future will look to someone fantasizing in 1933?

Transition five moves from the hand grasping the frisbee (1968) to Max's hand grabbing Noodles' suitcase, the same suitcase he had in 1933. An action continues from one time frame to another. Again we are reminded of an ellipsis. We see none of Noodles' time in prison as we see none of Noodles' time in exile. It is, in addition, the hand of Max bridging the time from 1968 to 1933 as we will find that it is the hand of Max which has manipulated the present. For it is always Max's function in the film to manipulate the *present*. It is Max who controls the gang in 1923–24, Max who sets Noodles up and dupes him in 1933–34, Max who recalls Noodles and brings him to be the executioner. However, it is Noodles who controls the *past*. Once the deed is done, the event over, Noodles converts it to his own nostalgia. Each period can be seen by Noodles as a nostalgic quest for family. In 1923–24, we see Noodles' real family only once. It is a scene of confrontation and rejection immediately after which Noodles makes friends with Max with both using a stolen watch as the central binding image. The watch, clearly a reference to stolen time/real time, reappears prominently in the final confrontation between Max and Noodles in 1968. The 1924 episodes end with Noodles being taken from his family/gang and imprisoned. Time is taken from him.

In 1933–34, Noodles fears absorption of the gang/pseudo family into the broader syndicate which is also referred to as "family." He fails to convince Max not to lead the gang into the broader syndicate/family, and the 1934 sequence ends with Noodles' exile in the West, alone. In the 1968 sequence, Noodles is called back and keeps meeting memories of the lost family/gang until he comes in contact with Max who tells him his entire life has been an illusion. Ironically, Noodles prefers to hold the illusion rather than engage in the reality of betrayal and waste. The 1968 sequence ends with the apparent death of Max, once again the loss of family. Also worth noting is that in their first encounter with the police in 1924 after Noodles has walked out on his real family following a fight, Noodles and Max pretend to a policeman that they are literally related, that Noodles is Max's uncle. Throughout the film, Noodles is referred to as "uncle," his familial position; he is not the leader, not at the center, but affectionately at the side in the shadow of Max the leader, father, madman, betrayer, friend, stealer of women.

Transition six comes immediately after a major argument between Max and Noodles, the one in which Noodles complains that Max did not tell him the real goal of their job, the syndicate assignment of assassination. Noodles drives the car into the water, and we pick up the image of the steamshovel and the debris, a debris in the water that carries over to 1968 and is dredged up and looked at; the debris that begins in 1934 figuatively with the betrayeal by Max is not brought out until 1968.

Transition seven involves Noodles looking at Jimmy on television. The old man in the present looks at a face from the past. As the voyeur had looked through the transom at the girl, we/he now looks at the public face on television and the memory of that face at an earlier time. Jimmy's line which leads into the jump back to 1933, "If mistakes have been made in this situation, don't look at us," is a cliché which at the same time refers to "looking" at him. The leap back gives us a look at him and how, at least to Noodles, Jimmy became corrupted.

Transition eight, discussed earlier, is a straight and not a symbolic cut in one sense. The scene cut to is not directly related by information within it to the shot before of Deborah pulling down the train window shade. However, the pulling down of the shade is a termination, a literal optical effect, a metaphoric wipe. The literariness of the image is obvious. She doesn't want to look at him and doesn't want him looking at her.

Transition nine is a specific allusion to the fantasy nature of the tale. It is a plume of smoke that carries us from 1933 to 1968 and as the smoke clears, it is Max's woman, Carol, who has aged. The shattering of time is one which comes when Max in 1933 announces that he plans to rob the bank and in 1968 when Carol tells Noodles for the first time that Max was literally mad or about to become so.

The motif of madness and fantasy is most evident in transition ten and the scene it leads into. Carol says, "If Max wasn't crazy, he soon woulda' been." We then see an essentially silent scene of disguise in which Noodles and Max check out the bank. The madness of the image is ours and Noodles' after we have been informed by Carol of Max's madness.

Transition eleven comes when Max knocks Noodles out and goes to his supposed "suicide." As the gun hits Noodles, time flies and we go back to 1968 with the blow to the head, reference to madness, and sense of his own betrayal; Noodles awakens in 1968 to Carol saying "Max made fools of us, Noodles." The transition does not relieve Noodles; the blow is not cathartic. He awakens from it to further guilt, though he is, in one sense, a man who has not only learned to live with his guilt but to accept it. The transition is ironic also. Noodles has to be hit on the head but still doesn't know that Carol's words can mean more than they seem, that she is a kind of Cassandra to whom he will not listen, cannot listen. She does not know it but Max's trick went far beyond his madness, that he was not committing suicide, but had found a way out of the family for which Noodles had sacrificed his life. The clues are there for Noodles to pick up, but he does not yet grasp them.

Transition twelve, the most elusive of the time transitions in the film, comes when Max in 1968 tells Noodles that he, Max, has stolen Noodles' past. It is at this point that Noodles "sees" and we see composite images from 1923–24 and 1933–34 which both sustained and filled Noodles with guilt and remorse. As contradictory and painful as the images are, they have given Noodles a sense of meaning in time. In a simple sense, his life (selected meaningful time experience) flashes before his eyes and he decides that the story as he has fashioned and imagined it is more important than the history that Max urges him to accept.

Transition thirteen, the final transition in the film, is in many ways the most problematic. It begins with that false move back to 1933 in which the 1968 Noodles sees the old car and people in old costumes. He seems to have leapt back in time without a direct narrative connection. He has, and we are disconcerted by the old Noodles in the fantasy of 1933–34. Is Max now dead? Did all this happen? A turn of a corner, the matching of two shots and the linking of two times without overt ellipses or devices brings Noodles back to the 1930s, back to the opium den. Past/present/future merge, and we see Noodles for the last time at the moment when his opium fantasy wiped out or transformed the painful experience of the death of his family/gang.[7]

A final point worth noting again is that the film never comes to the audience's present or an approximation of it. There is no historical present for the audience. The closest we come to the assumed "now" of the viewer is 1968. The entire film, therefore, is set in the past.

Noodles begins and ends alone, friendless, womanless, no family, only memories and time which, ultimately, may be all that any of us have.

Once Upon a Time in America, for all of its allusion to fantasy and fairy tale, suggests that the power of the fairy tale, the myth, the fantasy is to bring the viewer and Noodles to an ultimate reality, that the fairy tale beginning of "Once upon a time" really means that what we have is a truth about all tales and conclusions and the vanity of believing that we have anything beyond our imagination and mythology.

CRITICISM OF THE ANALYSIS

Any analysis that tends to focus on one aspect of a told and experienced tale is a reduction and distortion of that tale. The focus in this article on time suggests somehow that time is a more important issue than, for example, space or archetype or politics or history or psychology.

At the same time, one can argue that by focusing on one strand and unraveling it we may with patience come to the center of the ball instead of flying from loose end to loose end and never getting below the surface. That is, essentially, the structuralist argument, which I find useful, though I know a film is not a ball of string and there is no guarantee that I am actually following the string to a real center rather than imagining a journey and then like Noodles reporting it.

I realize, also, that my analysis of time is informed by my interest in archetypal criticism and Jungian analysis. Underlying my supposedly objectified analysis of what "is there" is a commitment to a tradition of understanding encompassing not only Jung, but Joseph Campbell, Heinrich Zimmer, and the rudiments of Buddhism.

I have attempted to use the tools of structural analysis to explore an interest in archetype. I have also, as I've pointed out earlier, chosen to ignore a great deal which might well be part of even an archetypal analysis. I have given little attention to the role of women in this film, have barely mentioned Eve, the potential guiding anima who runs through the film, and said little about Deborah, the idealization of the female which Noodles pursues and never attains. Even Carol the whore/witch who can lead Noodles to enlightenment is dealt with only minimally. Unmentioned is Peggy, an earth mother-figure for the gang, and the other members of the gang/family itself, Patsy, Cockeye and Fat Moe—the erratic spirit, the trickster, and the loyal brother. I have concentrated on the issue of time in relation to the traditional confrontation of male rivals, an archetypal image that draws me and, as Campbell among others has pointed out, is a dominant one in our mythological thought.

Thus, this examination of time in *Once Upon a Time in America* is not *the* meaning of the film, but *a* meaning of the film, which, to make the argument as circular as the film I have discussed, is all we can ever hope for and which, finally, may be quite enough.

NOTES

[1] Gérard Genette, *Figures* (Paris: Éditions du Seuil, 1966).

[2] Ken Wilbur, *No Boundary* (Boulder and London: Shamhala, 1979).

[3] Harry Grey, *The Hoods* (New York: Crown Publishers, 1952).

[4] "Time and the years are one other essential element in the film. In the course of them, the characters have changed, some of them rejecting their past identities and even their names—and yet in spite of themselves, they have remained bound to the past and to the people they knew and were. They have gone separate ways; some have realized their dreams, for better or worse; others have failed. But growing from the same embryo, as it were, after the careless self-confidence of youth, they are united again by the force that had made them enemies and driven them apart—Time." This quotation is taken from a note given by Leone to the author and other members of the writing and production staff in August 1981. Note the paragraph begins and ends with the word, the idea, the reference to "Time" with a capital "T."

[5] All quotations and examples are taken from the script approved by Leone in New York City in May 1982. Shooting began in Rome on June 14, 1982. There are variations and changes from that which is reported here and that which was both shot and edited.

[6] "And it is this unrealistic vein that interests me most, the vein of the fable, though a fable for our own times and told in our own terms. And, above all, the aspects of hallucination, or a dream-journey, induced by the opium with which the film begins and ends, like a haven and a

refuge." Quotation taken from the note given by Leone to the author and other members of the writing and production staff—see note 4.

[7] The film not only begins and ends in 1933–34, giving support to the importance of that time segment, but a breakdown of story time in the script shows that approximately 63 percent of the film takes place in 1933–34 while 23 percent takes place in 1923–24 and 14 percent takes place in 1968.

AN ANALYSIS OF THE STRUCTURE OF *THE GODFATHER, PART ONE*

William Simon

This essay attempts to perform several critical tasks. It is primarily an analysis of the narrative structure of *The Godfather, Part One*, directed in 1972 by Francis Ford Coppola. In these terms my aim is to explain how meaning is created in that film through an understanding of its narrative structuring and the significance of its cultural codes.

At the same time the essay is involved with the application to film of critical methods derived from several important contemporary texts in narrative theory and aesthetics. In these terms, the following constitutes a test of the efficacy and validity in applying such analyses and methods to the study of film narrative. The purpose here is not to apply any one methodology or model of analysis in a rigid fashion. Rather, several central ideas from a number of texts are absorbed into the critical analysis. Perhaps the most important notions to be tested here are derived from Wolfgang Iser's works on reader response theory, *The Implied Reader* and *The Act of Reading*.[1] I shall attempt to apply Iser's concept of the "narrative gap" and the ways in which this gap causes the spectator to retroactively reread narrative information. As well, I shall rely on the concepts of the hermeneutic and cultural codes from Roland Barthes' *S/Z*.[2] Iser's "narrative gap" and Barthes' hermeneutic code will together provide us with the tools to understand Coppola's ordering of narrative information. I shall also briefly refer to the concepts developed under the notion of "duration" by Gérard

Genette in *Narrative Discourse*.[3] The relations of narrative time to story time and the function of ellipses will prove relevant.

This essay can also be viewed as a contribution to the continuing evaluation of American narrative film in the period roughly between 1965 and 1975.[4] In this respect, I proceed from the view that this period constitutes one of the richest and least understood and appreciated periods in American film history. The collective work of Altman, Coppola, Kubrick, Scorsese, Penn and Peckinpah, and such major individual achievements as Lester's *Petulia*, Polanski's *Chinatown* and Malick's *Badlands*, are marked by an important overarching theme, the insistence that psychological and/or physical violence are at the core of American life. In addition, the films of this period are characterized by major developments in narrative form and structure, by the highly successful absorption into a mainstream popular narrativbe form of the characteristics of "open structure" associated with modernist narrative. This analysis of *The Godfather, Part One* treats the film as one of the key works of the period and as emblematic of many of its most basic characteristics and qualities.

Coppola's *The Godfather, Part One* is distinguished among other things by the number of scales or levels upon which it operates. In its combination of epic structure and highly individuated family melodrama, it is perhaps the American film which most closely approximates the nineteenth-century realist historical novel.

Three levels can be distinguished in the film's story-line. The film concentrates on the members of a single Italian-American family, the Corleones, in the period from approximately 1945 to 1955. At the same time, because the head of the family is the Don of one of the Mafia's Five Families, the film portrays the history of the Mafia during this period. On another level the life of the Corleones as an individual family and its significance as that of a Mafia Family are intimately related over the course of the film, creating an image of the Mafia Family's operations as being dialectically related to the mores and social ethos of the specific Italian-American family. A third level of meaning, one perhaps not as thoroughly interrelated to these first two levels, attempts to have the experiences of the Corleones correspond to an image of American during the decade depicted in the film. Coppola describes this large-scale ambition of the film in the following way: "The film always was a loose metaphor: Michael as America." Also, "I always wanted to use the Mafia as a metaphor for America."[5]

This metaphor presumably suggests that the experiences of Michael over the course of Part One, emerging from World War II as an innocent hero, becoming progressively corrupted as he becomes involved in the Family's "business," are to be understood as a representation of America's post-war history. Certainly the large contours of the Family's "progress" from first generation immigrants in New York's Little Italy to a home in the Long Island suburbs to total respectability on the West Coast (in this case, Nevada) corresponds to a quintessential American success story.

Aesthetically, *The Godfather* also operates on at least two levels. In its representation of the Corleone family, it is a deeply realistic work emphasizing highly individuated characterizations and the detailed observation of family mores and behavior. At the same time, the film is conceived on an epic, even operatic scale. It is divided roughly into four "acts," each building slowly to a heightened climax. Many scenes are set within family religious rituals and/or holidays (two weddings, a baptism, Christmas), thus expanding the meaning of these scenes in an epic direction as well.

There is another way of understanding the multiple levels upon which *The Godfather, Part One* operates. This has to do with what might be considered authorial attitude towards the characters and their actions. Like most gangster films, *The Godfather* treads a delicate line between valorization of its criminal characters and criticism of them. Certainly the characters in *The Godfather* conform to two of the central myths of violence described by John Cawelti in his valuable essay "Myths of Violence in American Popular Culture."[6] They conform to the "vigilante" myth in that they are positively shown as protecting the weak in the absence of an efficacious law enforcement system. And they conform to the "myth of equality through violence" in the ways in which they use their skills at violence and crime to rise from poverty to a position of wealth and power. In the rhetoric achieved by comparative characterization in the film, the principal members of the Corleone family, Don Vito Corleone and his son Michael, are infinitely more intelligent and less obviously corrupt than any of the other characters.

What is perhaps not so obvious about the film is how a critique of the Mafia and especially the central character, Michael Corleone (and accepting Coppola's intended metaphor, America), is constructed. This critique can be considered an argument which is formulated through the film's narrative structure and its treatment of certain key characters. In the following analysis I shall pay special attention to the unfolding of this critical arguments since it provides the ultimate key to the meaning of the film.

One other aspect of the following analysis should be introduced. In discussing American narrative films of the late 60s and early 70s earlier, I suggested that the representation of violence at the core of American society was the central theme of these films. The representation of violence is always a contentious issue, but one way to understand its function and significance is to try to understand its narrative and moral contexts in individual works, as Cawelti suggests.[7] Consequently, a large part of the analysis is concentrated on those violent sequences that so often constitute the dramatic climaxes in *The Godfather*. Special attention is paid to the cultural codes surrounding this violence and the specific and very complex treatment of it.

The opening sequence of *The Godfather, Part One* portrays the marriage of Don Vito Corleone's only daughter Connie to one Carlo Rizzi. The sequence lasts some 26 minutes of the film's 175-minute running time and is by far the longest sequence in the film.[8] While obviously contracting the story time through ellipses, the sequence creates the effect of a linear continuous whole, encompassing the duration of the wedding celebration.

Despite this sense of continuity, the sequence is structured on a strong set of oppositions created by cutting alternatively between Don Vito's study and the celebration in the garden outdoors. The oppositions revolve around the cultural codes that interpenetrate both the Corleone and the Mafia levels of the family. The laying out of these codes helps set in motion the critical argument of the film. The oppositions run something like the following. The interior study is very darkly lit, the characters sitting in dark shadow. The garden is bathed in sunlight. The action in the study consists of Mafia business: a series of men pay their respects to Don Corleone and ask for a service. Contracts are assigned in response to these requests. The study is an exclusive private sanctuary; only males have access to it. It is a space where men report violent violations of their families and arrange for violent reprisal.

The garden provides strong contrasts. The basic activity is the celebration of a marriage, defined as a perpetuation of the family.

(References are made to the forthcoming children of the bride and groom.) The activity is open, social and inclusive, embracing not only men, women and children, but even rival Mafia Families. The dancing, singing, joking, and picture-taking are celebratory, privileging the family as a unifying totality.

While the activities of the two spaces contrast sharply, there are also indications that they are inextricably related. For instance, it is made clear that the head of the household cannot deny a request on his daughter's wedding day. Thus, the criminal contracts being established in the study are a direct product of a particular social code of the family. Also, while at this point in the film, the violent stories related in the study seem antithetical to the celebratory spirit of the wedding, as the film unfolds and the marriage of Connie and Carlo turns increasingly violent, it is understood that the violence suggested in this first scene is a dialectical component of that marriage. What appears initially as opposition is progressively understood as dialectical. Violence on different levels is exposed as the inescapable underside of the marriage in the film. Framed by this marriage and the subsequent baptism, the film relates the violence of organized Mafia criminality to family rituals and ethos.

The setting up of the oppositions in the interior and exterior segments of the wedding sequence establishes certain implications. The exclusiveness of the study and inclusiveness of the garden create a system by which certain characters can be understood as "insiders" and others as "outsiders." Obviously, male members of the Mafia Family are insiders while women and children are defined as outsiders. Michael, the youngest son, just returned from the war, still in uniform, educated at an Ivy League college, accompanied by a non-Italian girlfriend, is the most important outsider. He dissociates himself from the family business ("That's my family, Kay, it's not me.") and unlike his older brothers, is seen only in the garden. The over-arching plot of *The Godfather, Part One* traces the shift in Michael's position from outsider to insider and the changes such a shift produces.

The other significant outsider is Kay, Michael's girlfriend. She is an outsider by virtue of being a woman, a non-Italian and a total newcomer to such rituals as an Italian wedding. The degree to which she is an outsider is especially suggested in her dialogue with Michael. She is constantly asking questions about family customs, the wedding celebration and Don Corleone's "business," about which she is especially dismayed.

Kay's position at the beginning of the film as someone who is alien to the values and activities depicted in the opening sequence is especially important in establishing her as the character through whom the critical argument of the film will be formulated. In order to appreciate how Kay functions in this respect, it is useful to observe how she is placed in relation to one of the central cultural codes of the Italian-American ethos of the film, namely the assumption that marriage exists for the purpose of procreation, preferably of male offspring. In different ways, Kay is systematically juxtaposed to manifestations of this code. For example, in this opening sequence, the first close shots of her are immediately preceded by shots of Luca Brazzi, a brutal and almost retarded enforcer for Don Corleone, rehearsing the salutation with which he is about to greet Don Corleone: "May your first child be a masculine child." Kay's first dialogue is to ask Michael in a dismayed way who this strange creature is. In other words, she is immediately juxtaposed as alienated from this character and his statement of the absolutely central theme of the operative ethos of the film. In the next section of the film, in a scene in which she and Michael emerge from Radio City Music Hall during the Christmas season, she is juxtaposed with the words "The Nativity" on the marquee. Much later in the film, during a period when she and Michael have been separated, it is revealed that she is working as a schoolteacher, that is, as a kind of surrogate mother. Much later in the film, when she is married to Michael and has learned something of the family culture, it is she who asks Michael to stand as godfather for Connie and Carlo's son. Her partial assimilation into the family is conveyed through her newfound understanding of this code.[9]

One last point about the wedding sequence has to do with the patterns it establishes in terms of the representation of violence in the film. In several important senses, the wedding sequence functions as an introduction to the workings of the Mafia, an almost instructional exposition carried out entirely in words. The scenes of petitioners to Don Corleone establish how contracts are made and imply that violence will be part of the execution of the contract. A story that Michael tells Kay about how Don Corleone freed the singer Johnny Fontaine from his contract with a band-leader specifies how violence functions as a central aspect of the Don's "business." However, these references are all verbal; violent action is either described or related, or implied by euphemisms.

The film's next sequence is both a continuation of the series of illustrations on how the Mafia operates and the culmination of the first act of the film. It also alters in complex ways the representation of violence, concluding with the film's first violent climax. Its organization merits special attention.

The action of this sequence grows out of the wedding sequence in that it shows how Tom Hagen, Don Corleone's adopted son and "consigliore," obtains a role in a film for Johnny Fontaine, the Don's godson and one of the petitioners at the wedding. Unlike the first sequence with its strong sense of linear continuity over a protracted period, this sequence consists of three brief scenes, totalling 7½ minutes of film time and covering 12–15 hours of story time. Prominent ellipses create important narrative gaps from scene to scene.

In the first scene, Hagen confronts Jack Woltz, the studio head, demanding that Johnny be given the part. Woltz violently refuses, asks Hagan to leave, and tells a henchman to find out who Hagen works for. After the first ellipsis, we now see Woltz entertaining Hagen at his mansion later that evening. Woltz is clearly more deferential towards Hagen because, we soon learn, he now understands that Hagen works for Don Corleone. The narrative gap, created through the elision, activates the spectator to fill in missing narrative information. Presumably, in the interim, Woltz's henchman had discovered that Hagen worked for Don Corleone, a fact important enough to cause Woltz to invite Hagen for dinner.

The level of narrative information omitted in this ellipsis is not very significant. The importance of it has to do with the way in which Coppola introduces the procedure of the narrative gap as a way of structuring the spectator's apprehension of narrative information. This gap, in effect, sets the groundwork for the next one which is infinitely more significant and dramatic.

In the dinner scene between Woltz and Hagen, despite Woltz's initial deference, he concludes by stating that Johnny Fontaine will never work for his studio. After another ellipsis, the next scene commences with an exterior shot of Woltz's bedroom where he is sleeping later that night. As the music reaches a climax, Woltz stirs in his bed. He lifts the sheet and discovers the bloody, severed head of his prize racehorse which he had proudly showed off to Hagen during the evening. Woltz screams in horror, a scream which continues over the exterior shot of his mansion which ends the sequence and the first major act of *The Godfather*.

The narrative gap between the second and third scenes of the Hollywood sequence sets the stage for the sensational effect of the violence in the third scene. The audience has in no way been prepared for the action; no causation has been established. We are put in the position of retrospectively inferring that after Woltz's second refusal, Hagen had commanded someone to sever the horse's head and place it in Woltz's bed as he slept. Beyond the violence of the image itself, the power of this infamous scene derives from the fact that we have not been prepared for it, that we discover the horse's head at the same time as the victim of the violent act does. Furthermore, the mode of narrative information is virtually the opposite of all previous manifestations of violence in the film. For the first time, violence or the horrifying result of it is dramatized and visualized directly. The violent power of Don Corleone and his agents is demonstrated to us directly as we experience it through the victim.

The hermeneutic pattern of withholding narrative information and then gradually revealing enough information for the spectator to fill in the narrative gap operates on a visual as well as a narrative level. In this final scene of the Hollywood sequence, the music signals that something dramatic is to happen but the initial distance of the camera in the exterior and interior shots withholds the information. The camera's slow movements suggests an intentionality, that it is moving toward something, but it is only after some time that the camera draws close enough to reveal the crucial information and its suggestion as to the nature of the elided narrative action. The handling of the camera in relation to narrative information in the space of action in this scene is a complement to the opening shots of the film. Here, the film's action starts on a tight close-up of the first petitioner addressing an unseen and unheard character. A very gradual pulling out of the camera reveals Don Corleone as the addressee of the petition. Only subsequent shots reveal that other members of the Family are in the study. This type of visual patterning activates the sense that the spectator is not always in full possession of the necessary narrative information. It suggests that things are sometimes hidden or obscured. And more often than not, as we have seen and shall continue to see, the missing information attests to the violent power of the Corleone Family or their antagonists.

While the "horse's head" sequence is the culmination of the first act of the film, the next scenes which properly speaking initiate the second section contain two interesting additional revelations about the previous section. The first scene (which consists of the Corleone Family strategy meeting about the attempts of a rival Family to engage them in the drug business) starts with a dissolve from the end of the "horse's head" scene to a close shot of Don Corleone, presiding over the meeting. While it quickly becomes clear that the meeting concerns totally new business, the dissolve acts as a certification of agency. That is, the dissolve strongly suggests that Don Corleone is to be understood as the agent/cause of the severed horse's head. The chain of causality is suggested only after the effect has been seen.

Further, in the next scene, brief reference is made to a garland of flowers standing in the Don's office. We are told that they were sent by Johnny Fontaine on the occasion of his assuming the role in the film. We are to read in that Woltz's discovery of his prized horse's severed head led him to offer Johnny the role. Narrative closure for this episode is achieved slowly and retroactively, activating the spectator to tie together its meaning.

One of the most striking features of *The Godfather, Part One* is the way in which its four acts are arranged in strikingly different systems of structuring the narrative information, a process already observed in the differences between the wedding and Hollywood scenes in the first act. The second act is also structured according to a quite different system; this quickly becomes clear as it begins to unfold. This section deals with the conflict over the drug business between the Corleone Family and the Tattaglia Family and its partner, Virgil Salozzo. The first part of the act deals with the Tattaglias' attacks on the Corleone Family, culminating in the attempted assassination of Don Corleone. The second part deals with Michael's gradual involvement in the family business as a response to the attack on his father. Its climax is the shooting of Salozzo and the police captain McCloskey by Michael.

The first part of the act proceeds as a series of brief, quickly edited scenes—none of them more than three minutes or so in length. Several of the scenes are parallel edited, in contrast to the continuity of action in the first section. Beyond the contrast in the duration and temporal arrangement of the scenes, several other contrasting patterns operate during this section. Perhaps the most important involves the shift in terms of who is exercising violent power in the film. In the first half of this second act, the Corleones become victims to Salozzo and the Tattaglias. While the attacks on the Corleones are not presented as elaborately or dramatically as the "horse's head" scene, they share with that scene that characteristic of being totally unexpected; they are not prepared for through expository information. Only after Luca Brazzi is strangled, Tom Hagen kidnapped, and the Don shot in quick successive scenes do the characters reflect that a large-scale "war" has been initiated by Salozzo and the Tattaglias. Thus, the pattern of unexpected violence continues, though directed now at the Corleones.

The reversal of this pattern in the second act of this section commences with the scene of Michael's visit to his father in the hospital. This is the longest uninterrupted scene in a long time, lasting approximately 9 minutes, after 13 scenes, none of which exceeds 3¼ minutes. In this scene, Michael with the help of one other man, succeeds brilliantly in foiling a second attempt on his father's life. The scene is structured very largely around Michael's aural and visual point of view, one of the few scenes in the film which is so strongly focalized by the perspective of a single character. Through its duration and emphasis on point of view, the structure privileges Michael as he takes the first steps towards total involvement in the family affairs.

This section of the film culminates with another dramatic act of violence, Michael's shooting of Salozzo and McCluskey, his policeman protector. From the first, the structure is radically altered in terms of how the narrative information is revealed. Instead of creating a narrative gap through elision and presenting the violence as an unexpected outburst, this incident is set up with great care. We hear the Family members discuss Michael's suggestion that he shoot the two. When they finally decide to go along with the plan, we see Michael being tutored on how to shoot. Painstaking detail surrounds the plan. Instead of elision, detailed linear causal suspense becomes the operative narrative mode. The function of the continuity at this point is to concentrate attention on Michael's developing character, his intelligence and courage as he establishes himself as the heir apparent. The violence of Michael's shooting Salozzo and McCluskey gains its impact from the detailed concentration on his actions, rather than from its unexpectedness.

The third act of *The Godfather, Part One* is a transitional one, preparing the way for Michael's final ascendance as Godfather. This section is occupied largely with Michael's experiences in Sicily where he is waiting out the aftermath of his killing of Salozzo and McCluskey and with the elimination of Sonny, the oldest Corleone son, from contention as heir apparent.

While it is a transitional section of the film, Coppola structures it is a very interesting way in order to foreground certain aspects of the cultural ethos underlying the action of the film.[10] The section is largely organized around an alternation of scenes in Sicily and scenes in New York. In Sicily, Michael meets and marries a beautiful peasant woman. The atmosphere of the courtship and wedding is idyllic, pastoral, and old-worldy, with the threat of Mafia violence hovering for the most part at the edges of the action.

By contrast, the New York scenes trace the increasing violence in Connie and Carlo's marriage and Sonny's even more violent protectiveness of his sister. The Corleone family's enemies use this violence on the family level to eliminate Sonny, murdering him as his drives to gain revenge on Carlo for beating Connie.

In effect, the contrastive editing from Sicily to New York can be understood as being based on the comparison of marriages, of male/female relationships, of domestic situations, all within the pervasive ethos and cultural codes of this film. The specific editing of scenes in relation to each other intensifies the contrasts. From a lyrical treatment of old-worldly Sicilian courtship ritual, we cut to Sonny, hurriedly leaving his illicit mistress in order to beat Carlo to a pulp. The cut back to Sicily is to wedding bells and a romantic old world ceremony, an ironic reminder of the film's opening scene.

The New York scenes fill in details of the cultural ethos. That Mafia business is the province of males only a clearly stated in a family dinner scene when Sonny admonishes Carlo with the words "We don't discuss business at the table." Ironically, Sonny himself had earlier violated this code. This breach by both men links them and suggests that Sonny's inability to live up to the domestic family ethos disqualifies him as the potential Don. His violent overreactions in his brotherly protectiveness lead directly to his death.

If Sonny is criticized according to the family ethos, it should be added that while Michael's situation seems idyllic, the double standard of his situation is also sharply and ironically underlined by the edited juxtaposition of certain scenes. Immediately after the lyrical erotic scene of Michael and his new bride's wedding night, Kay, who has been patiently waiting for Michael's return, comes to the Corleone compound to inquire of him. This juxtaposition emphasizes the degree to which Michael ignores his relationship to Kay. His hypocrisy in relation to her establishes the cultural grounds upon which the critical appraisal of Michael will be carried out in the film's final scenes.

Two manifestations of violence in this third act require attention. The murder of Sonny as he drives to Connie's is another outbreak of violence that is totally unprepared for in the narrative. It is only over the course of the film's final hour that a detailed explanation of the murder is provided. Similarly, the Sicilian section ends with Michael's new wife killed by a bomb exploding in their car, a bomb intended for Michael. Minimal preparation is given for this sudden outburst. Only after the two murders is it clarified that they are the antagonists' response to the murders of Salozzo and McCluskey. Again, the pendulum has swing so that the Corleones are victims of unexpected attacks. The final act of the film deals with the restoration of the Corleones' power.

This final act begins with a series of scenes covering the transition in power from Don Corleone to Michael over an approximately seven-year period. Don Corleone arranges for the meeting of the Five Families in which a peace is arranged and Michael is guaranteed safe return from Sicily. Vito tutors Michael and warns him of danger from Don Barzini, a family head who was behind the Salozzo-Tattaglia opposition. The Corleone Family begins a move into Las Vagas gambling. Michael finds Kay and marries her, never telling her about his Sicilian wife. Finally, Don Corleone dies, and the stage is set for Michael's ascendance to power.

The climactic scenes of this act of the film revolve around two rituals, Don Corleone's funeral and the baptism of Connie and Carlo's son, with Michael as the child's godfather. The funeral is related to the film's opening scene in that the ritual becomes a "front" for conducting Mafia business. As Don Corleone has warned, one of the family confidantes, Tessio, attempts to arrange a meeting between Michael and Don Barzini.

The baptism scene follows immediately after the funeral and is structured in a very complex way, making it the climactic scene of violence. In effect, what happens in this scene is that Michael's elimination by assasination of his five most important rivals (including Don Barzini) is intercut with the actual baptism ritual in a very elaborate montage.

The most basic notion suggested by this intercutting is that the shooting of the rivals and the baptism are happening simultaneously. However, the complexity of the structuring goes far beyond the parallel editing principle.

First, it should be noted that the baptism scene is related to the opening wedding scene in that it involves the product of Connie and Carlo's marriage. Superficially, both the wedding and the baptism are positive procreative celebrations, but both are represented as having a dialectically related underside. They are situations for violent Mafia activity. Like the wedding scene, the baptism scene is structured on edited oppositions, the baptism ritual ceremony on the one hand and the murders of the five rivals on the other.

Beyond the similarity, there are also several significant differences. Unlike the Mafia business during the wedding and unlike the treatment of Michael's killing of Salozzo and McCluskey, but like so many other violent actions, there is no narrative preparation, no causal explanation of what is about happen. The shots of men readying themselves and the shootings themselves take place in a narrative void; only after the scene is complete do the characters gradually verbalize the significance of the action, that Michael has successfully eliminated his most serious rivals.

The preparations for the killings are shown in very brief shots cut into the early stages of the baptism. We see one man cleaning a gun, another putting on a policeman's uniform, another walking to an undisclosed location. Several of the victims are seen in everyday activities, oblivious to the impending threats. Because none of these activities has been narratively prepared for, these isolated shots remain on the level of hermeneutic enigma. Only as the sequence develops and we see the actual shooting do we understand that the first group of men was preparing to shoot the rivals. At points, the editing of the very brief shots of different activities seems to match or compare the activities. For example, at one point the movement of an assassin cleaning a machine gun is matched by similarity of movement to the priest's hand anointing the baby. The obvious reading is to see the two activities as contrasting, but the intent of the montage in its entirety is to suggest the inextricable relations between the activities, that the series of shootings is related to the baptism. The fact that the sound from the baptism ceremony continues over shots taking place in the diverse locations in New York and Las Vegas reinforces this sense of identity of the actions.

The brief shots of the actual killings of the rivals are intercut with the crucial phase of the baptism ritual when Michael affirms his faith and renounces Satan. This editing produces an extremely strong effect. Once again, interpreting the juxtaposition as highlighting the contrast between the holy ritual and the brutal violence constitutes the most obvious response to the sequence of shots. However, because we recognize the victims as Michael's enemies, it is also possible to read the shots of Michael intercut with the murders as editing on agency, as declaring that Michael is responsible for these murders. In these terms, the sacrilegious profanation of the baptism ceremony is especially striking; Michael's violent actions totally negate any serious meaning of the vows he is proclaiming.

Ultimately, this extremely complex montage can be seen as positing a double meaning of Michael's experience as Godfather. He is not simply standing as Godfather for Connie and Carlo's son. He is also being initiated as the new Mafia-level Godfather of the Corleone family. The successful slaughter of his enemies in an elaborately orchestrated plot, represented in the context of his baptism vows, testifies to his power and right to become Mafia Godfather. And the inextricable ties between family and Mafia activities are powerfully demonstrated. The profanation of family ritual and values is established as a necessary condition or attribute of the Mafia Godfather. The horrible double standard of the cultural ethos is exposed in this grand operatic scene.

Some of the implications of this great climatic scene are underlined in the film's few remaining scenes, culminating in the critical portrait of Michael with which the film ends. First, Tessio, the old family friend who had betrayed the Corleones to Barzini, is led off, presumably to his death. Then, Michael for the first time confronts Carlo with the accusation that he had betrayed Sonny to his enemies. Two points are noteworthy about this brief scene. First, it continues the profanation of the baptism. Michael exclaims to Carlo while trying to make him confess, "Do you think I'd make my sister a widow? I'm godfather to your son." This reassurance leads Carlo to confess, and Michael immediately has him strangled to death. In short, the brief invocation of family values is immediately negated by Mafia vengeance.

The other interesting factor is that the accusation of Carlo's perfidy in Sonny's assassination is mentioned in this scene for the first time, approximately 45 minutes of film time and some 7 or 8 years of story time after Sonny's death. This is one of the most extreme cases of the operation of a narrative gap in the film. It causes the spectator to think back to Carlo's actions in relation to Connie and Sonny and to reinterpret them as purposeful baiting of Sonny to leave him isolated for the assassination.

The final statement on the meaning of Michael's new status as Godfather is played out in a scene with his wife Kay. The scene begins with Connie invading the male sanctum of the study, hysterically accusing Michael of killing her husband. She is led off, but Kay remains to confront Michael about Carlo. Michael, as the modern Godfather, agrees to break the code that he had previously insisted upon, namely that Kay never ask him about his business affairs. For one of the very few times in the film, Coppola employs a direct shot-counter-shot editing pattern between Michael and Kay during the ensuing dialogue. The directness with which the two look into each other's eyes, reinforced by the editing pattern, establishes a code of privileged honesty and respect between them. Kay asks him if he had Carlo killed. Michael stares into her eyes and answers "No." Kay smiles in relief and goes to the next room to pour them drinks. In a brilliant series of shots, she pours the drinks as in the background, several of Michael's henchmen kiss his hand and address him for the first time as Don Corleone, in effect saluting him for his day's brilliant success. In a shot from inside Michael's study, Kay is seen observing this action. Then, as the door to the study is closed, she is eliminated from view. The screen goes to black and the film ends.

This final shot constitutes a gesture of utter exclusion, virtually a negation of her existence from Michael's point of view as Godfather. He has invoked their marital bond by agreeing to break the male code just this one time, then profaned that bond by lying to her. The exclusion and negation of her performed by closing the door amounts to the psychological murder of Kay. As such, it comments on Michael's situation as Godfather, negates his position at the beginning of the film. It suggests the denial of human contact and positive social ethos that he is required to assume in his new position. It shows him stone-hearted and isolated, alone with his agents of violence.

Interestingly, in discussing why he decided to film Part Two of *The Godfather,* Coppola stated that he wanted to make clear what he felt had been stated about Michael in Part One but not sufficiently under- stood. "I wanted to take Michael to what I felt was the logical con- clusion. He wins every battle; his brilliance and his resources enable him to defeat all his enemies. I didn't want Michael to die. I didn't want Michael to be put into prison. I didn't want him to be assassi- nated by his rivals. But, in a bigger sense, I wanted to destroy Michael. There's no doubt that by the end of this picture, Michael Corleone, having beaten everyone, is sitting there alone, a living corpse . . . Michael is doomed."[11]

It is my contention that a careful reading of Part One makes it clear that this critical image of Michael and the values by which he lives has already been fully achieved.

NOTES

[1] Wolfgang Iser, *The Implied Reader: Patterns of Communication in Prose and Fiction from Bunyan to Beckett* (Baltimore: Johns Hopkins Univ. Press, 1974); and *The Act of Reading: A Theory of Aesthetic Response* (Baltimore: Johns Hopkins Univ. Press, 1978).

[2] Roland Barthes, *S/Z,* trans. Richard Miller (New York: Hill and Wang, 1974).

[3] Gérard Genette, *Narrative Discourse: An Essay in Method,* trans. Jane E. Lewin (Ithaca, N.Y.: Cornell Univ. Press, 1980).

[4] The key work in this evaluation is Robert Phillip Kolker, *A Cinema of Loneliness: Penn, Kubrick, Coppola, Scorsese, Altman* (New York: Oxford Univ. Press, 1980).

[5] Coppola in Stephen Farber, "Coppola and *The Godfather,*" *Sight and Sound,* 41 no. 4 (Autumn 1972), p. 223.

[6] John Cawelti, "Myths of Violence in American Popular Culture," *Critical Inquiry,* 1 no. 3 (March 1975).

[7] Cawelti, pp. 523–24.

[8] I am indebted to the students in my course, "Seminar in Film Analysis," in New York University's Department of Cinema Studies in Spring 1981 for the timing of scenes.

[9] It is very significant that in *The Godfather, Part Two,* when Kay's and Michael's marriage is shattered, she takes her most dramatic stand

against Michael by having an abortion. She purposefully chooses to violate the codes surrounding procreation.

[10] It is important to note that the complex structuring of scenes in this section of the film, as well as the cross-cutting of the baptism scene and the elimination of the rivals in the last act, are not handled in this fashion in Mario Puzo's novel. The creation of the complex juxtapositions seems clearly to be Coppola's accomplishment, given the unimaginative linearity of the novel.

[11] Coppola, quoted in Robert K. Johnson, *Francis Ford Coppola* (Boston: Twayne Publishers, 1977), p. 148.

UNITY AND DIFFERENCE IN *PAISAN*

Peter Brunette

Ironically, Roberto Rossellini is best known for what is perhaps his least typical film. *Roma, città aperta (Open City*, 1945) remains an immensely powerful film, and can quite legitimately be considered one of the founding texts of Italian neo-realism. But its heavy reliance on conventional narrative strategies, a strong, unwavering plot line, uni-dimensional characters, Hollywood-style emotional manipulation of the audience, and professional acting (at least in the two principal roles) makes it quite unlike any of the more than forty other films of his career, with the possible exception of those films made during his short-lived, self-admittedly commercial period of 1959–1962.

Even before *Open City*, Rossellini's so-called "Fascist trilogy " (*La nave bianca, 1941*; Un pilota ritorna, 1942; L'uomo dalla croce, 1943) contained what might loosely be termed experimental elements stressing long takes, non-narrative, purposely dead time, and the aleatory in general. These elements, coupled with an obsession for representing the intricacies of modern technology, quite apart from the demands of a specific narrative context, worked against the linear, otherwise conventional plot-lines of these films. It is only with *Paisà (Paisan,* 1946) that Rossellini returns to and develops even more radically this already-existing if little-known penchant for an unconventional narrative technique. This film embodies a cinematic practice that can clearly be seen as the model for the vast majority of his later films. In what follows, I shall be concentrating principally on describing Rossellini's attempts at unity in *Paisan*, on both thematic and formal levels, and those discontinuous narrative features of the film which

ceaselessly move against this search for wholeness. It is the presence
of these very features in this and later films, in fact, which assured
that Rossellini was never again, after *Open City*, to have a popular
audience.

The idea in 1946 was to make a film that would somehow encompass
the whole of Italy and reflect honestly, in the vein of *Open City*, on
the reality that the filmmakers (Rossellini and his assistant Fellini)
found in their travels. They had a general idea of what the film would
be about before shooting began, but the script was never really fixed,
in accordance with an already emerging neo-realist aesthetic orthodoxy. Characters, plots, and locations were continuously and sometimes drastically changed to correspond more closely with the people
and the places they found in the course of their six months spent
traveling from one end of the country to the other. Even by this point,
in other words, the rhetoric of neo-realism valorizes this ongoing
dialectical encounter with "reality" above all else.

It was almost as though the world were being seen for the first
time, at least that part of the world that was Italy. Fellini relates with
obvious joy how

> we were surrounded by a whole new race of people, who seemed to be
> drawing hope from the very hopelessness of their situation. There were
> ruins, trees, scenes of disaster and loss, and everywhere a wild spirit
> of reconstruction. In the midst of which, we did our tour. The troupe
> of people working on *Paisà* travelled through an Italy they scarcely
> knew, because for twenty years, we'd been in the grip of a political
> regime which had literally blindfolded us.[1]

Allied troops were everywhere, complicating the Italians' efforts to
learn how to live with one another again after the mortal divisiveness
of the war years. The ongoing project of homogenization has always
been stoutly resisted by the hundreds of regions that have become
known in modern history as Italy but which appear, even to the most
casual visitor, as enormously diverse. This struggle for geographical
and cultural unity is itself thematized, in a minor way, in the film.
On the one hand, the constant linking presence of the map of the
Italian peninsula which appears between the film's six separate episodes, and the relentless, obviously intentional chronological movement forward (there is only one flashback in this obsessively *present
tense* movie), a temporal movement that meshes with the equally re-

lentless linear, spatial movement *upward* on the map, insist upon a sameness, a unity to the Italian experience. The film wants to be, at one level, a history of *Italy* during this period. Yet the chronological movement which seems to describe merely different temporal points in a homogeneous space (Italy), and different "aspects" of a homogeneous, single national experience, cannot disguise the fact that the spaces, the regions of Italy, insist on their heterogeneity just as strongly as ever. The clearly proclaimed regionality of the map defeats in advance its simultaneous proclamation of unity.

This regionality is more sharply depicted in some parts of the film than in others, primarily due to the contribution of landscape—the last episode, shot in the Po region, is the prime example—and the visual "thereness" of the built environment, seen most clearly in the Florence episode. There, the Duomo, the Uffizi galleries, and the entire tourist panoply of "sights" that the British officers so intensely discuss from their vantage point in the gardens of the Pitti Palace cause the city to become an active character every bit as present as any human. In Naples, it is the very fact of cityness and slum life—but meant to be taken in a generalized, abstract way, unlike the specificity of Florence—that marks the episode uniquely; Sicily, on the contrary, is the atavistic place of brute rock, stodgy towers, and primitive emotions. The Roman episode is one of the least specially marked—the ironic story of missed opportunity that unfolds there, it might be argued, could have taken place anywhere—a fact which could easily be attributed to the exhaustion of Rome's signifying capability in *Open City*. To dwell on the city's specificity, in other words, as in the Florence episode, would have constituted an unwelcome and static repetition. Nevertheless, this episode's story is linked to the *history* of Rome, albeit the most recent installment of it, the Liberation; it is this historical event, obviously seen by those who participated in it as significant and as earth-shaking as any other previous event in the city's history, that marks this particular story as possible only in that city.

Curiously enough, the only episode that seems relatively abstracted from its location is the one that takes place in the monastery, and it was in filming this sequence, and this sequence alone, in fact, that Rossellini "cheated," by fictionally placing these southern monks in the north central part of Italy. This episode—the ragged, recalcitrant difference of whose theme has resisted critical attempts at closure, as we shall see—is obviously meant to convey an abstract idea of serenity and innocence made flesh in the geography of the monks' faces. One point elaborately made in the episode is that outside reality has had no effect on their lives, and thus we quite properly see nothing that is exterior to their own interrelationships and their relationship with God. Rossellini deliberately draws a frame, the outer walls of their monastery, around them, thus highlighting what goes on inside the frame and at the same time pointing purposely to the absolute artificiality (and impossibility), however desirable it may seem to a war-weary world, of their exile from the rest of reality outside.

Perhaps it would be useful at this point to rehearse the plot details of the six episodes. The first episode, as I have mentioned, takes place in Sicily just after the Allies have landed. The sense of the confusion of war is nicely captured by showing the local residents initially convinced that the American soldiers are Germans, and then, realizing their mistake, welcoming them, though somewhat ambivalently. As the local Fascist bewails the loss of "freedom" for his country that their presence represents, the soldiers take along a young woman of the village to lead them through a minefield. Finding a ancient, abandoned tower, they leave "Joe from Jersey" there with Carmela, while they search the area. Most of the episode centers on the efforts of these two in the tower to communicate with one another, since each is innocent of the other's language. But things progress so well on this pre-verbal, gestural level that Carmela is already displaying signs of jealousy when Joe shows her a wallet-sized photo of his sister and her child, whom she takes for his wife and his own child. To demonstrate the facial resemblance between him and the woman in the picture, he holds a lighter up to his face. Suddenly, we cut to a German outpost—in a truly startling intrusion of otherness which destroys the fragile unity the couple seems to have achieved—and the soldier who, because he's seen a light, fires a single shot that instantly kills Joe. Carmela hides, and the Germans take over the tower. Deeply upset by Joe's death, Carmela kills one of them with his rifle. The Americans return, find Joe dead, and bitterly assume that Carmela, "the dirty Eye-Tie," was responsible. The next shot shows the Germans looking down from the cliff off of which they have thrown Carmela, and the last thing we see, as the irony rushes over us like the sea, is Carmela's body smashed on the rocks.

The next episode takes place amid the rubble of bombed-out Naples, as children and adults display an endlessly fertile imagination, in usually illegal ways, in order to survive. Here a shoe-shine boy (less saccharine than the boys of DeSica's *Sciuscia*), in an incredible scene, "buys" a drunk, black American soldier.[2] The boy hides his prize from the police by taking him into a puppet-show, where a white Crusader puppet is beating up a black Moor; the black soldier drunkenly enters the fray on the side of his race, and gets thrown out of the theater. Sitting on a pile of rubble, the soldier and the boy try to make themselves understood through the confusion of language and alcohol. When the soldier seems about to fall asleep, the boy warns him that he will have to rob him if he does. A few days later, the soldier, who turns out to be an MP, finds the boy again and demands that he return his boots. Intent on taking the boy home to his parents for a scolding, he discovers that the boy's parents have been killed in the bombing and that he has no home at all.

The story next moves to Rome, where another drunken G.I. encounters a prostitute who takes him to her room. Through a mixture of Italian and English, Fred bitterly recounts, in flashback,[3] the story of his first entry into the city on the day of Liberation, and the lovely, innocent girl Francesca he had met but has been unable to find ever since. The prostitute realizes that she is the one he has been looking for, but since she is ashamed to reveal herself, she asks the landlady to give him her old address when he awakes the next morning. The last shots in the episode are again in an ironic vein: she desperately waits for him in front of the building in which they had first met, once again looking like the girl next door, while he is seen at the very end throwing away a slip of paper, because, as he tells his friend, it is only "the address of a whore."

The fourth tale takes place in Florence, a city dangerously divided between the Nazis and the partisans, who are fighting street by street while the British wait outside for reinforcements. Harriet, an American nurse, and her Italian friend Massimo desperately want to get over to the other, still-occupied side of the Arno, she to find her lover "Lupo," a *capo* in the Resistance, and he to rejoin his wife and child. The story consists solely of their dangerous journey across town. When they finally arrive, Harriet learns accidentally, even casually, from a partisan who is dying in her arms that "Lupo" had been killed earlier that morning.

A monastery, ostensibly in the Emilia-Romagna area, is the setting for the fifth story. There, monks who have spent the entire war in an otherworldly peace, take in three American chaplains for the night. When they discover that one of the chaplains is a Protestant and the other, even worse, a Jew, they decide to fast to try to save these lost souls. The American priest is deeply touched by the serenity of their religious feeling, a quality he has lost in the horror of war.

The last episode (and the one most consistently touted ever since) takes place in the marshland of the Po River. The opening shots show a dead partisan floating down the river on a white lifesaver to which the Germans have attached a sign labeled "partisan." Dale, an American O.S.S. man there to give technical assistance to the Resistance, and his friend Cigolani bury the dead man; they stick the accusing sign into the freshly dug earth and the same word instantly takes on dignity and worth. The Germans have their small group completely cut off, but nevertheless British orders are to cease all activity. They all know that this means that while the Americans will be made prisoners, the partisans will be executed as common criminals. After the inevitable capture, the Germans tie up the partisans and push them one by one off a boat to drown; Dale and another American rush to protest, and are shot down. As the last two bodies splash into the water, the voice-over matter-of-factly tells us that "This happened in the winter of 1944. At the beginning of Spring, the war was over." On this ambivalent note, the film ends.

Superficially the various episodes seem to have little to do with one another, as some critics initially objected, but in fact, the connections are many and subtle. On the most mechanical level, as we have seen, they are linked by the chronological and spatial chain that the map which appears before each episode constructs for us. More important, however, is the link of emotion, or more properly, the lack of emotion caused by so much deprivation and exhaustion (a theme that will be brought to its zenith in Rossellini's next film, *Germany, Year Zero*)—a link of tone and mood, principally negative—that serves provisionally to unite the film.

The principal linkage of course is thematic, in that all the episodes, in one way or another, depict the aftermath of war and "victory."[4] The most consistently present form of this generalized theme is Rossellini's ruminations on the problem of communication. We see people struggling to understand one another in nearly every episode, through the false but troublesome divisions of language, and not always being very successful at it.[5] War creates obvious horror everywhere it goes, but its subtler and more insidious manifestation is, for Rossellini, how it prevents or distorts the normal everyday sources of pleasure which are no less important for being mundane. One of our most taken-for-granted functions of daily life, communication with one's fellow human beings, is also thoroughly disrupted in war time, where one is by necessity forced together with those with whom one does not know how to communicate. What emerges in the first episode in Sicily, where Carmela and Joe from Jersey try so hard to make themselves understood to one another, is a kind of Renoirean theme that through the *attempt,* at any rate, one can work one's way back to the basic, primitive level of cooperation that both directors obviously feel underlies the surface chaos and distrust of human relationships. This can, I think, be seen most clearly in Renoir's case in the episode near the end of *La Grande Illusion* when the escaped prisoner of war played by Jean Gabin has his own private rapprochement with the German woman, as they stumble through pidgin French and German to some kind of human community and warmth. In *Paisan,* the elementary nature of the struggle between Carmela and Joe to communicate is further underlined by the fact that most of the Sicilian episode takes place at night and in an ancient tower, whose rough texture is strongly suggestive of a cave; it is almost as though some primitive ritual of connection were here being rehearsed, as though human history were beginning all over again. (The image of the primitive cave will reappear at the final climactic moments of the next episode, where it seems to stand for a symbolic descent into Hell.) The very basicness of their encounter is further abetted by the unobtrusive long take that neutrally records from a respectful distance without ever calling attention to itself.[6] Siegfried Kracauer, in his under-appreciated *Theory of Film,* has also made some insightful remarks concerning this first episode. He points out that since whatever communication the couple does accomplish is arrived at as much by the sounds of the dialogue as the meaning of the words they use, these sounds become emphasized:

And along with the dumb show, their conspicuous presence as sounds challenges the spectator empathically to sense what the two characters may sense and to respond to undercurrents within them and between them which would, perhaps, be lost on him were the words just carriers of meaning. The theater which hinges on dialogue shuns foreign languages, while the cinema admits and even favors them for benefiting speechless action.[7]

The communication theme is also manifested in the irony of the title, which is *not*, surprisingly for American audiences, an Italian word in current usage; in fact, most Italian early reviewers were careful to define the word for their readers as referring to a friend or someone from one's original village. It was originally a word in Southern dialect that had made the passage westward across the Atlantic, while being unknown in the north, only to make the return trip when the sons of the immigrants came back across the ocean. The word is used in the first two episodes, and more or less understood after that. Ironically, it marks a site of misunderstanding and difference rather than camaraderie, as one might expect, whenever it appears, for it mockingly points to the absence of any real understanding between the "liberators" and those liberated.

Closely connected with this theme of communication is what might be called the humanity theme. It seems that life in general, but especially life during wartime, leads people to treat each other as objects. That is clearly the case in the first two episodes of this film—Carmela is simply a radar-detecting device, employed for the purpose of avoiding German land-mines; and as far as she is concerned Joe and his friends are no better than the Germans, as she clearly says at one point. Yet once they have communicated, their humanity has been revealed to one another and they can no longer treat each other as objects. In Martin Buber's terms, they have moved from an "I–It" relationship to the "I–Thou." By shooting at him, the German effectively turns Joe back into an object—literally so, of course, when he dies. It is this that Carmela is reacting against when she later shoots the German soldier, in order to revenge, suicidally, an American soldier she had barely met. In the Naples episode, the shoeshine boy is thoroughly taken in by the black soldier's singing and his incomprehensible stories; responding to his humanity the boy can no longer consider him an object to sell. This is why he warns him that if he falls asleep, the boy will rob him. Once sleep cuts off the flow of humanizing language, the soldier returns to object status, and the boy, with little choice given the exigencies of war, does what he must.

Rossellini wants to find a latent humanity existing deep down in all of his characters, uniting and making them one under all the misleading, superficial differences. A unity is found, or imposed, in the film, but at the same time this essence is continually undone by these "superficial" differences. One difference that is perhaps not consciously recognized but which seems nevertheless irreconcilable and thus constitutive for Rossellini is that of gender. As in *Open City*, the women of *Paisan* are seen as passive creatures, those upon whom history acts, and those, therefore, whom history makes to suffer. Francesca, in the Roman episode, can do nothing but be sexually used by men or wait for a man who will never come. Those women who *do* act have no political opinions and act solely from whatever their "nature" calls them to do. Thus, in the Sicilian episode, Carmela tells Joe that "You're all alike, you, the Germans, the Fascists! All you people with guns! You're all the same!" but a short while later, she shoots a German soldier because "her" Joe has been killed, even though she knows it will mean her own death. Her act is totally selfless, almost primevally ritualistic. Similarly, Harriet of the Florence episode will brave the most dangerous fighting in order to reach her man. This presumably sophisticated and educated woman will turn into a primitive, and it is unclear how we are meant to view her. Thus, when she and Massimo are told that they cannot use the Galleria passage (which runs above the Ponte Vecchio, from the Pitti Palace to the Palazzo Vecchio), for fear that the Germans might discover it and thus endanger them all, Massimo hesitates. He is just as desperate to get to his family as Harriet is to get to Lupo, but he seems on the point of giving up because of the possible danger to the others. In spite of his aroused emotions, in other words, he will listen to reason. But it is precisely at that point that Harriet impetuously plunges headlong into the Galleria, and Massimo has no choice but to join her. Rossellini clearly admires these gestures, which he sees as manifestations of a kind of direct, intuitive naturalness, in spite of the fact that Carmela's causes her death and Harriet's should actually be condemned. It must also be said in his defense that Rossellini sees women, for all their political ignorance, or perhaps *because* of it, as the inveterate enemies of war. Again, they seem to have a natural inclination against war that most men stupidly repress. And, though Harriet's act is conceived finally in rather patronizing terms, the nurse figure she enacts is quite a step beyond an earlier Rossellini nurse figure in *La nave bianca* (1941), a passive, pure, little charmer spouting nationalist slogans about duty and honor. When Rossellini begins making films with Ingrid Bergman in 1949, and when, due to the exigencies of the star system, the female figure necessarily moves to center stage, she becomes a richly complex, full human being, motivated by more than the intuitively "feminine."

Another aspect of this question raised by Rossellini's women resides on the symbolic level. Armes believes that Harriet is meant symbolically to stand for the Allies who are powerless to help the Italians sort out their internal differences,[8] but this is rather too mechanically literal a view and seems unwarranted. Yet it is possible, I think, to see Carmela as symbolically representing Italy. At the end of the Sicilian sequence we realize that she has been the victim of both the Americans and the Germans, for neither understands what she has done or why. The irony is especially bitter, of course, in terms of the Americans' lack of comprehension. In thematically representing the fate of her country, she continues, in effect, Rossellini's exculpation of Italy and Italian guilt that he began in *Open City*. Like the women in these two films, Italy is the powerless, dependent victim who, despite occasional outbursts of primordial passion, is acted upon and brutalized by others—Germany, America, and England (the men). Not a very flattering role, perhaps, but certainly better than that assigned to Italy's ally, Germany. Most Italians depicted in the film seem more to be bystanders than anything else, perhaps with the exception of the partisans in Florence and on the Po (though the latter, significantly, are led by an American); for the most part they are seen favorably or at worst, neutrally. We do see some "bad" Italians—the Fascist sympathizer in Sicily and the Fascists killed in Florence—but they are totally marginal characters, either buffoons or empty faces, who disappear from the screen in a matter of moments. The Germans, on the other hand, largely absent through most of the film (though decidedly present in terms of the havoc and misery they have wreaked), are portrayed in the final episode on the Po in the same brutally negative way (presumably justified historically) that they were in *Open City*.

More important to the great majority of European critics is Rossellini's overall depiction of history and its relation to human affairs. The terms of the debate, naturally, are similar to those of *Open City*, though perhaps less specifically anchored in events than in more generally philosophical or political attitudes.

Some Marxist critics, like Raymond Borde and André Bouissy, have been deeply attached to this film, or at least parts of it, and it has become in their view Rossellini's last important film: "Could Rossellini have done better than *Paisan*," they ask rhetorically, "deepening the reportage? Certainly not. Rallying to democracy, he has remained reactionary, incapable of analyzing Italian reality in terms of class."[9] One view which has more recently gained favor among leftist critics is to consider even these earlier films as irredeemably flawed because in them Rossellini is too intent on proving how tragic the human condition is, rather than expressing optimism about the possibility of a more just society in the future. Armando Borrelli, for example, complains that in this film the director shows "the need to express the fundamental tragicness of things, their lack of logical order, the impossibility of understanding the why of events." For him, the brusque, jumpy style of *Paisan* "signifies that for Rossellini life has no order which is knowable by the human mind, that human desires and hopes always clash against an unforeseen destiny which is imposed on us from above." Even the ending of the Po episode he reads as a mockery of the ideals of the Resistance when the voice-over, announcing the final victory, clashes ironically with the shot of the partisans being pushed into the water by the Germans.[10] Similarly, Freddy Buache complains that in spite of the film's brilliance, the facts of the case aren't presented in their political, social, and economic contexts, and Rossellini is unwilling to undertake a sociological analysis that would probe for causes or depict the class struggle. Echoing a common theme, Buache accuses Rossellini of forgetting that the Resistance was also a *social* revolt that was braked by the bourgeoisie.[11] But since Rossellini was rather unabashedly bourgeois, Buache is obviously asking for the impossible. There would have been no reason for the filmmaker to choose to highlight the class struggle, since he never considered it, as would Marxist orthodoxy, the primary motive force of history. In many ways, Rossellini is the archetype of that man that Roland Barthes depicts in "Myth Today," the brilliant essay that serves as coda to his *Mythologies*. This bourgeois has so thoroughly naturalized his contingent status that he speaks in essences; he takes himself, his opinions, and his world view as natural, and thus not particularly susceptible to being individuated. He is involved in an ex-nomination process that serves to cloak history and arbitrary conventionality in the guise of the natural. In all this, of course, Rossellini was merely acting like everyone else he knew, for this is and has been for a long time simply "the way things are."

I think it can now be clearly seen that these critics are right when they accuse Rossellini of forgetting history. As in *Open City*, it is the very specificity of event in *Paisan* that can mislead the casual spectator into thinking this film is historical in any analytic sense. For though Rossellini always deeply enmeshes his characters in the specificity of a precise environment, both temporally and spatially, what he wants to portray, for better or worse, is that which transcends this specificity, what is eternal, what is "essential" in man. What must also be pointed out, however, is that Rossellini's Marxist detractors—in spite of their emphasis on man as conditioned by history—are not attacking essentialism *per se*, but rather Rossellini's view of what man's essence is. They would simply put another essence in its place. Robert Warshow, ever the challenging critic, provides a better way into the film when he frankly describes its fascination with defeat and death (which, in terms of my argument, can be seen as extreme forms of difference and discontinuity), contrasting it favorably to American films rather than wishing that Rossellini had been more optimistic:

> American culture demands victory; every situation must somehow be made an occasion for constructive activity. The characters and events in serious American films are given a specifically "universal" or "representative" meaning in order to conceal the fact that there are situations in which victory is not possible. The idea survives—that is a victory; the man dies—that is a defeat; the "GI" is created to conceal the man's death.
>
> Rossellini neither requires nor dreams of victory; indeed, it is only defeat that has meaning for him—defeat is his "universal." . . . From this hopelessness—too inactive to be called despair—Rossellini gains his greatest virtue as an artist: the feeling for particularity. In the best parts of *Paisan*, it is always the man who dies, and no idea survives him unless it is the idea of death itself.[12]

Another way of describing this "feeling for particularity" is to see it as part of the ongoing dialectic between Rossellini's avowed search for unity and the discontinuous particulars through which this unity must always finally manifest itself, and which negate it at the same time. It might also be useful to consider the film's overwhelming realism, in these terms, at least briefly. The realism of *Paisan* is startling precisely, I would argue, because it pushes outward from commonly accepted notions of realism (which in fact are constituted by highly stylized conventions), toward the inclusion of the "real" (which itself remains to be defined). The unresolved, always self-displacing tension between these two "concepts" (named only to serve as short-hand), *as they manifest themselves in terms of the film's particulars,* is in many ways what motivates the film.

The paradoxical dynamic of the Hollywood movie is that we are meant to believe it and take it as *real* while watching it, at least on one level, but that when we consider it abstractly, as part of a generic whole, it becomes, due to its basis in conventions of representation, the very definition of unreality and artificiality. "That only happens in the movies," we tell ourselves (except in the theater). On the other hand, any film which is perceived as being in any way unconventional in its narrative is often seen, again paradoxically, to be more real. Because its disjunctures continually reveal its fictional status to us, thus preventing the Coleridgean "willing suspension of disbelief" or an easy identification with the characters, relatively sophisticated spectators can come to see the unconventional representation as somehow more like "real-life," i. e., disjointed, confused, unable to penetrate the exterior of the Other, undirected, multiple and incomplete. (This very labeling, of course, can in turn constitute another form of unity-seeking recuperation of the text's discontinuities, another, even more "natural" or more "basic" grounding.)[13]

The most obvious aspect of *Paisan* in this regard is the fact that it is composed of six episodes which are linked in various ways, as we have seen, primarily in their presentation of themselves as a unity under the guise of an revealed essence of humanity, but which also stubbornly retain their status as diverse fragments. Leo Braudy quite laudably refuses to be tempted by this humanism, and insists upon the fact of discontinuity in his description of the film:

> Since Rossellini's meaning resides principally in his effort to make connection, his own narrative is more fragmented, a mirror of the efforts to bridge gaps, to cross boundaries, and to establish relationships that preoccupy his characters. . . . Like Renoir, Rossellini searches for connection through the more associative and thematically oblique connections between episodes.[14]

What this very plausible, and, as far as it goes, "correct" reading of the film does, however, is to make a unified theme out of the fragmented difference, recuperating, in effect, its radical alterity.

André Bazin, who had a great deal to say about *Paisan*, realized that it resembles a collection of short stories, and was indeed the first film to do so. (A short story collection is by definition a unity of differences). He even goes so far as to call the Naples episode a Saroyan story, while the rest he finds reminiscent of the stories of Faulkner and Hemingway. Twentieth-century American fiction, of course, has always been considered a precursor, if not a direct source, of both Italian literary and cinematic neo-realism. What Bazin neglected to add, however, is that precisely what makes the episodes so narratively unconventional—their quick, unexpected climaxes which come at the end of the story, thus omitting the traditional denouement of both conventional film and fiction—is what links them most closely to the specifically modern form of the short story, with its accent on the sudden, climactic end, with or without the character (or the audience) coming to any moral realization or Joycean epiphany. Adding to this connection is Rossellini's strong use of irony, that staple of twentieth-century fiction. This is the pattern:

First episode: Climax comes at very end, but epiphany is denied to characters; irony reigns.

Second episode: Climax at end, epiphany achieved through irony at level of character.

Third episode: Repeats the first.

Fourth episode: Realization of fact of death is climax, but no real epiphany, because the knowledge is empty.

Fifth episode: Climax and epiphany (in lighter key) at end.

Sixth episode: Climax at end; unclear whether characters experience epiphany, or only the audience, as in first and third; closure comes from outside the story, through overview and voice of history.

The effect of this pattern is once again to de-dramatize, and thus to be more "real" and less "realistic" at the same time, primarily by putting the drama—or at least the more blatant moments of emotion—at the very end. The audience barely has time to experience an emotion even momentarily before the map of Italy and the officious newsreel voice are thrust back at them. But it would be a mistake to think of this film as *totally* de-dramatized and unemotional, for the endings, brief as they may sometimes be, are often quite moving. A key factor at work here is music, though its effects are, as usual, relatively unnoticed. On several occasions, in fact, the music indicates to us precisely what we are supposed to feel (in other words, just like any other film). In the Naples episode, for example, everything looks so completely miserable and ruined throughout the entire episode that an American audience, at any rate, would not initially know that the cave-like dwellings that the soldier enters at the end are to be taken as any more deprived than anything else that has been seen. But when he does enter, the tragic musical theme acts as an "artificial" stimulator to prepare us to read and react to the visual images that we will soon be shown. There are, of course, many long passages in which all music has been suspended and where we must make our own way, emotionally and intellectually, but to hold, as Gian Luigi Rondi does in *Cinema italiano oggi* that this film is a "dry documentary," "without tears," where Rossellini trusts the emotion of pure facts, is to miss how subtly—and conventionally—music often works to produce and guide emotion.[15] In other words, this film, like all films, cannot offer an unproblematic, transparent window onto a direct experience of reality, but remains forever a constructed, and thus "unnatural" artifact. It too participates in a conventional code of realism.

Nevertheless, the film's primary mode, especially as compared with the standard Hollywood product, is certainly de-dramatized—even if "impurely" so. And its workings are complex. One one level, the brevity of each episode effectively prevents a traditional viewer identification with the characters. Yet, at the same time, a paradoxical increase in what might be called empathy or, better, sympathy, arises. Like Hitchcock's *The Wrong Man,* the avoidance of "normal" emotional moments (in other words, moments normally played up in the classic Hollywood film) actually allows the spectator a greater sense of sympathetic involvement, but in a way that is somehow more liberating than the emotional identification that is usually fostered. Thus, while the spectator is not subjected to the roller coaster ride of predictable emotion because the narrative material has been distanced, at the same time the realization of the character's plight (seen as other, not as self) is all the more dramatic. Thus, in the Hitchcock film, the low-key style of the acting, the apparently simple *mise-en-scène,* and the editing somehow make the spectator feel even more strongly what it must be like to be wrongfully locked up; in *Paisan,* these same factors add up, say, in the Florence episode, to the overwhelming realization of how a war can turn even the simplest of tasks, like getting across town, into a monumental effort. This may have something to do with the lowering of the rhetorical aspects of the spectacle to the point that the spectator *sees* (rather than gets "inside the skin of") a common man or woman—like him or her—in a difficulty that is not played up in a movie-like fashion, and not put into the kind of emotional shorthand that eliminates everyday, lifelike details in favor of non-lifelike drama. I think Warshow is talking about much the same kind of impression, though not, of course, in terms of the dynamics of identification, when he discusses Rossellini's refusal to particularize his characters in conventional ways:

> But the reality of these figures does not depend on "characterization"; they come to the screen full-grown, and are as real in ten seconds as they could be made in half an hour—they are *visibly* real. . . . In American films, on the contrary, the characters are likely to be emphatically individualized, and precisely because they are basically abstractions: without character traits and personal histories, they would disappear.[16]

In an article in the French film periodical *Image et Son*, Pio Baldelli says that this film is exemplary, in fact, precisely because Rossellini refused to find "facts" which would fit pre-established emotions, choosing instead to examine "real facts" to see what they contained. He praises the film because the "real behavior of men" provides the adventure rather than the "novelistic." He sees also a kind of Brechtian effect arising from this "fact-gathering," which makes its appeal primarily to the audience's reason rather than its emotions.[17] While his analysis is appealing, a major difficulty is that he is assuming that the "real behavior of men" is something that is unproblematically available for the director's depiction. What lurks in this Marxist critic is the kind of essentialist, inherently anti-Marxist thinking that insists at some unconscious level that the best neo-realist films can escape mediation to arrive at the direct "truth" of actual reality. Giuseppe Ferrara is on somewhat safer ground, I think, in his view that Rossellini is actually extending the Stanislawski method acting (which Brecht rejected as illusionist) by making the actor and the character virtually one. In this way, the actor also becomes a means of reaching "objective reality," according to Ferrara. The actor is there not to wrap up the viewer in an illusionist web, but to lead him ultimately to "the documentary substance of the whole discourse." In fact, Ferrara sees this use of the actors as really only one aspect of the distancing of the image itself, which is where he links Rossellini to Brecht more closely, finding the latter's *Verfremdungseffekt* in the "objectivity, the very *extraneousness* of the image, its value as cold mirror of things, of absolute presence."[18] This incessantly invoked "presence" of reality which serves to ground *all* discourses about neo-realism—both idealist *and* materialist—is, of course, only the cinematic version of what Jacques Derrida calls the metaphysics of presence. And no film, even a neo-realist film, no matter how directly it seems to offer us reality, can give us more than a constructed (and thus mediated and thus forever partial) representation of reality. Those almost palpably physical images on the screen cannot help at the same time continuously, obsessively revealing themselves for the manufactured phantasms they are. They can never "be" something. They can only point to a forever elsewhere, mark a forever not-here.

But within the limitations of representation, *Paisan* does seem to offer the "thereness" of the world and its inhabitants in an intensely concentrated form, even more than in *Open City*, and here Rossellini's visual sense seems more highly developed. The powerful impression of reality that one receives from the earlier film is largely a function of landscape and location. In *Paisan*, however, it seems to be carried additionally by faces, bodies and gestures that swarm over the screen, seemingly directly imported from a fresh infusion of reality that flows freely all about and through the (fictional) characters and their environment, and which seem in some important way to be out of control. There are simply many more "real people" populating this film, simply *there*, jamming it more full of "reality" than the earlier film. Similarly, in several of the episodes, the constant presence of the rubble caused by the wartime bombing provides an ongoing thematized commentary (which will reach its zenith in Rossellini's next film, *Germany, Year Zero*), that functions like an unspoken but ubiquitous extra line of dialogue.

Many of the film's images seem to enjoy an efficiency that will be lost in later films. Thus, the *scugnizzo* of the Naples episode wears a soldier's cap that offers a silent but eloquent commentary on the relation between his life and the war that so thoroughly engulfs him. In the same episode, the contrast between the big American black soldier and the little white Italian shoeshine boy is constantly present before us visually, and while tending toward the symbolic (as enacted, and thus displaced, in the puppet-theater), never leaves the firm anchor of its present specificity. Besides being efficient, many of the images are so perfectly balanced compositionally and so lyrically evocative that the whole debate which has always dogged Visconti's *La terra trema*—can a "true" neo-realist film be composed of "beautiful" shots—is here finally understood as utterly irrelevant, given the assumptions about realism that it conceals.

The shots that make up the final sequence on the Po often call attention to themselves and foreground their unarguable loveliness. Phenomenologists like Henri Agel have singled out this episode for its revelation of the "essence of being," but it seems equally possible to think about this experience in more purely aesthetic terms, as one haunting composition after another presents itself for the viewer's delectation. For one thing, Rossellini has deliberately kept the camera low throughout the sequence so as to place the human participants precisely between the earth and water on the one hand and the sky on the other. The many long shots also contribute to a sense of tragedy and foreboding, even despair, for they show the men swallowed up by an environment that is neither welcoming nor actively hostile, just brutally there. In a later shot, Rossellini breaks the rules of conventional cinematography when he "shows" us the captured partisans virtually in the dark; the entire sense of the sequence comes about through the anguished conjunction of their mumbled despair and the utter blackness that surrounds and engulfs them.[19]

In this film which strives so mightily for unity (on the surface, at any rate) other, more recalcitrant elements ineluctably reveal irreconcilable differences which fragment any kind of final, univocal reading of the film. The most problematic episode, which might serve as a paradigm of how difference works in this film (or, for that matter, in any film) is in fact the one that seems the tamest—the episode which takes place in the monastery. Critics have had enormous difficulty reconciling this segment with the overall structure and themes that seem to be operating in the film, and have tried in vain to naturalize its perplexing sentiment. Thus a closer look seems warranted.

On a rhythmic or tone level, the episode acts as a kind of scherzo, or lighthearted third movement in a four movement symphony which is predominantly serious in mood. The editing has here been slowed down, after the speed and excitement of the Florence episode, in preparation for the even slower and much heavier rhythms of the final sequence on the Po. In some ways, the episode also provides a kind of thematic summing-up, a counterpoint to the harsh worldliness of the other stories, a standard by which to judge how far the rest of war-weary humanity has fallen from its ideals.

But its themes clash in "impermissible" ways, for the reading which the episode demands does not correspond with traditional views of brotherhood, kindness, or even good sense. The innocent, unworldly *fraticelli,* stunned by the presence of two lost souls in their midst—Protestant minister and a Jewish rabbi—offer up their painful fast to God for the conversion of the heathens' souls. On the one hand, this gesture of concern for one's fellow man, to the point of denying oneself, is obviously praiseworthy—and Rossellini has his American Catholic priest-spokesman end the sequence by praising it. But does it not also manifest that same lack of respect for the sovereign integrity of the other that in fact precipitates the kind of intolerance and hatred that have wreaked such physical and psychic damage on everybody else in this film?

Warshow has labelled the sequence "so outrageously vulgar that it must surely be the product of a calculated dishonesty, probably for political reasons,"[20] presenting as it does through the eyes of the American chaplains an idealized view of the monks that he thinks no serious Italian would ever hold. But this response seems excessive. For one thing, we in the 80s and the dyspeptic Warshow in the 40s may have trouble understanding the meaning of this episode because Rossellini and his friends were really *serious* about that "serenity of spirit" that seems so utterly alien to our own time, and in fact appears almost a throwback to some dim, imaginary point in the Middle Ages (a point to which he will return four years later in his *Francesco, God's Jester*). But the problem lies deeper than this. Many critics have thought that in spite of the American Catholic chaplain's praise of the selfless idealism of the "innocent" brothers at the end of the episode, the "moral" is precisely what the other American chaplains marvel at earlier, in comments almost lightly passed over—how can these monks judge real men and worldly right and wrong if they are so utterly isolated from it all? If this reading is to be accepted, however, we would have to see the episode in quite radical narrative terms. For the hermeneutically privileged position we normally assign to the main character's "speech" at the end of a narrative sequence, when all attention is solemnly focused on him or her and when the rhetoric of language and image continues to underline the moment's importance, would have to be completely overturned. A casual remark dropped half-way through the sequence would have to be privileged over the highly foregrounded, final dramatic scene toward which everything has been moving.

Pio Baldelli and other critics have struggled to decide *exactly* what the director means here, but in so doing, they have revealed that any approach which grounds itself on a presumably self-present and consistent artistic intentionality will ultimately prove fruitless. When the attempt finally breaks down, as it inevitably must, these critics find the whole episode "absurd" or "confused" because, in effect, it is not *unified*. A better reading might be to admit that irreconcilable interpretations cannot, in fact, be reconciled, despite the uncomfortable lack of closure that results.[21]

What holds for the monastery sequence also holds for the entire film. The only difference is that the chimera of an imagined wholeness cannot, ironically, be recognized for what it is, due to the sheer *number* of discontinuities in the six episodes. Unreadability always confronts us more starkly in a smaller area. Our drive for wholeness is not an entirely innocent operation, either, for we seek (and find) an organic unity only at the expense of an "organic" diversity, if such a concept can be thought. Can the notion of irreconcilability ever be "truly" held in the mind, at the same time forever displacing itself? The temptation is to make this very idea of irreconcilability the basis of another, more "fundamental" reading of the monastery episode and the entire film. From the moment the concept has been named, of course, the temptation has in effect already been yielded to.

NOTES

[1] Quoted in Suzanne Budgen, *Fellini* (London: British Film Institute, 1966), p. 88.

[2] Roy Armes suggests quite plausibly that the source for this episode is Curzio Malaparte's novel *The Skin*, which also concerns the "buying" of a black soldier long enough to get him drunk and steal his things. He also points out the utter difference between Rossellini's understated treatment of the material and Malaparte's "sensationalised and over-

written prose. . . ." Roy Armes, *Patterns of Realism* (South Brunswick and New York: A S. Barnes, 1971), p. 77.

[3] Armes complains that this is the most contrived episode in the film because the flashback is a "remove from true neo-realist practice" (*Ibid.*) This is a good example of the kind of gratuitous rule-making that afflicts most critics of Italian neo-realism, more intent on establishing prescriptive categories and defending them than on describing what they see. It is even more useless when this "rule" is applied retroactively to one of the very films most often thought of as *establishing* neo-realism.

[4] It should be remembered, however, that this thematic linking is always more virtual and suggestive than precisely specific. Thus, I think that Ian Johnson is moving in an unprofitable direction when he says that the six episodes of the film correspond to the "Six Great Evils of War": "injustice, human misery, degradation, the universality of war's suffering, insensitivity through familiarity, and futility." *Films and Filming*, 12: 5 (February, 1966), p. 42. Rossellini simply does not work in this overly programmatic way.

[5] Interestingly, all of the English that American audiences hear—and it's a great deal—is also retained in the Italian version of the film; thus bereft of subtitles, since they are rare in Italy, Italian audiences are forced to re-enact the struggles of their fellow Italians to understand their American "friends."

[6] I think there is more than a little truth to the claim, currently being heard, that the long take is basically *illusion-breaking*, but in this instance, at least, it is clear that something like Bazin's notion of the long-take as inherently more "natural" is what Rossellini had in mind.

[7] Siegfried Kracauer, *Theory of Film: The Redemption of Physical Reality* (New York: Oxford Univ. Press, 1960), p. 110. Ben Lawton has argued that the primary theme is not this difficulty in communicating between people, but rather the alienation that is found throughout a film in which the characters are much more bent on their own personal concerns rather than the communal ones of *Open City*. In his view, this theme is appropriately underlined by the very fragmentariness of the episodes. "Italian Neo-Realism: A Mirror Construction of Reality," *Film Criticism*, 3: 2 (Winter, 1979), p. 11. It seems to me, however, more useful to think of the alienation and lack of communication as not being opposed, but as being two interrelated manifestations of the same problem—war. A more telling critique of this theme is offered by Robert Warshow in his brilliant, if eccentric essay on *Paisan*. Warshow complains that the existential truth of this sequence is ruined by the failed communication between Joe and Carmela, which attempts "to draw vague populist sentiment out of a purely accidental limitation, as if there

were some great truth still to be discovered in the fact that one person speaks English and another Italian, and yet both are human beings." *The Immediate Experience*, 2nd ed. (New York: Atheneum, 1971), p. 252. In this formulation, at least, his characterization of Rossellini's theme seems reductive, fashioned primarily to score rhetorical points.

[8] Armes, p. 78.

[9] Raymond Borde and André Bouissy, *Le Néo-réalisme italien: une expérience de cinéma social* (Lausanne: La cinémathèque suisse, 1960), p. 30. All translations in this essay are mine.

[10] Armando Borrelli, *Neorealismo e Marxismo* (Avellino: Edizioni di Cinemasud, 1966), pp. 81, 85. Henri Agel has argued persuasively, from a phenomenologist point of view, against an overly tragic and depressed reading of the final sequence, especially in terms of the last images that come before us. Mario Verdone, for example, though not taking the political exception of the Marxists, echoes the common critical view of the ending as thoroughly down-beat. Agel instead makes the point that the ending must be read in terms of Rossellini's other films as well, in a deeper and fuller context. In support of this view, he quotes Gaston Bachelard's *L'Eau et les rêves* in which the philosopher says that water is "the essential ontological metamorphosis between fire and earth." Water can also be seen as the source of fecundity, in other words, as the location of a possible physical and spiritual rebirth, and Rossellini in fact uses this association, according to Agel, in the opening sequence of the film he made four years later on the life of Saint Francis of Assisi in which the monks are bathed in a wonderfully insistent and life-giving rain. Thus, when the partisans are pushed into the water at the very end of *Paisan*, it can be seen as a birth and death at the same time. The voice-over announcing the allied victory in the Spring, in this reading, would not be the horribly bitter and ironic counterpoint that most critics have seen in it, but rather a kind of cause-and-effect analysis. It is in fact the men's sacrifice, says Agel, that *causes* the liberation of Italy that the voiceover is announcing as about to take place in the future. Theirs is a martyr's death, in other words, and the last image expresses "the springing up of freedom." *Poétique du cinéma: manifeste essentialiste* (Paris: Éditions du Signe, 1973), p. 81.

[11] Freddy Buache, *Le cinéma italien d'Antonioni à Rosi* (Yverdon, Switzerland: Le Thiele, 1969), pp. 24–25.

[12] Warshow, p. 256.

[13] See my article "Rossellini and Cinematic Realism," *Cinema Journal*, 25, no. 1 (Fall 1985), for a fuller discussion of this dynamic between realism and the "real."

[14] Leo Braudy, *The World in a Frame: What We See in Films* (Garden City, N.Y.: Doubleday, 1975), p. 78.

[15] Gian Luigi Rondi, *Cinema italiano oggi* (Roma: Carlo Bestetti, 1966), p. 39.

[16] Warshow, p. 257.

[17] Pio Baldelli, "Résistance, néo-réalisme et leçons des anciens," *Image et Son*, #195 (June 1966).

[18] Giuseppe Ferrara, "L'Opera di Rossellini," in *Rossellini, Antonioni, Buñuel*, eds. Piero Mechini and Roberto Salvatore (Venice: Marsilio Editore, 1973), p. 34.

[19] Related to the film's visual aesthetic is the sense of space it creates. Leo Braudy has convincingly delineated Rossellini's various creations of different spaces in each episode, making of them what he calls "a kinetic and psychological equivalent" to the themes at work. "Rossellini: From *Open City* to *General della Rovere*," in *Great Film Directors: A Critical Anthology*, ed. Leo Braudy and Morris Dickstein (New York: Oxford Univ. Press, 1978), p. 663.

[20] Warshow, p. 257.

[21] Similar to the unresolvability of the monastery sequence is a point of undecidability that Ben Lawton has noticed concerning the Naples episode. In his view, the puppet show battle (between the Moor and the Saracen, into which the drunken G.I. wades feet first to "help out" his fellow black man) offers us a key as to how to read the whole film: "the distinction between oppressor and oppressed is tenuous at best. Although present throughout the film, this concept is perhaps most perfectly synthesized in the G.I. in the second episode: Joe is Black (and as such oppressed), a member of the American occupation forces (and, as such, as oppressor), drunk (and, as such, oppressed), and an M.P. (and, as such, an oppressor). Which is he ultimately? The alternation of roles is interrupted, briefly, by an instant of communication, dependent on his perception that the *scugnizzo* 'knows the troubles (he has) seen' " (Lawton, p. 16).

MYTHOS AND MIMESIS IN *THEORY OF FILM:* KRACAUER'S REALISM RE-EXAMINED

R. Barton Palmer

In *Theory of Film: The Redemption of Physical Reality*, Siegfried Kracauer attempts to develop a consistent view of cinema's specific properties as a medium, following Lessing's dictum that each art possesses formal qualities with affinities for particular subject matter.[1] Kracauer also surveys cinema history, especially film genres, and uses the argument advanced in the book's theoretical sections to determine the success or failure of these different types. As a result, *Theory of Film* manifests two kinds of contradictions, the first of which is the conflict between the judgment of the theorist (approaching the medium as potential communication) and the enthusiasm of the critic (situated as subject in its history).

Kracauer, for example, argues that formative and realistic tendencies in the filmmaker need not conflict as long as "all creative efforts" benefit "the medium's substantive concern with our visible world" (p. 39). The formative tendency, however, must not "overwhelm" the realistic, but rather "follow its lead." Thus living, camera reality is to be preferred, in general, to "staged" reality. Yet, in discussing the musical film, Kracauer apparently forgets what he earlier formulated as the "right balance" between opposing tendencies. At one point he insists that elements of stage reality do serve a cinematic purpose within the context of camera reality:

Stage interludes within otherwise realistic films assume a cinematic

143

function to the extent that they throw into relief the flow of life from which they detach themselves. (p. 73) Stagy fantasy supports rather than obstructs the cinematic approach . . . whenever it takes on the function of a stage interlude in realistic films. (p. 80)

His point here, I think, is clear. The artificiality of what we ordinarily consider "performance" establishes by contrast the reality of the context from which it emerges. Staginess or performance, in other words, serves the purposes of realism only in a negative way; therefore its presence in the non-integrated musical is truly "cinematic."

When treating the integrated musical, however, Kracauer has to violate his own principles in order to approve a type of film he obviously liked. After admitting that such films have a "conspicuous staginess" (p. 148), he remarks that "it is hard to understand why musicals should prove attractive as films" (p. 148). But he goes on to offer two reasons why they should be so. First, he declares that "musicals invariably capitalize on everyday incidents to launch their diverse production numbers." Kracauer here calls attention to the tendency of such films to utilize their narrative/dramatic frames to justify their stage numbers. But this violates his principle that formative elements (and how else can we classify production numbers?) must be subordinated to the realistic principle. Furthermore, the musical hardly makes use of narrative/dramatic frames that could in any meaningful sense be said to consist of "every-day incidents." Kracauer's second argument is even weaker, even more transparent a rationalization. He declares: "musicals reflect tensions at the core of the cinema . . . between the realistic and the formative tendency" (p. 148). This simply says that integrated musicals are films, as Kracauer defines them. Actually, the genre subverts those tensions instead of reflecting them. In musicals the barrier between performance and life (symbolized by the stage and enforced by the distinction between performers and audience) is eliminated.[2] The narrative/dramatic frames of such films, in other words, present a world in which emotions lead naturally and directly to their expression in song and dance, where the characters communicate in "numbers" not words. There is no "camera reality" in such a genre, and therein lies its charm, its aesthetic power.

Like others in the book, this inconsistency reflects Kracauer's difficulty in applying his theoretical concepts clearly to a complex and varied film practice. As I mentioned above, his double perspective as historian and theoretician leads as well to a second kind of contradiction, one which lies at the heart of his conception of the essence of cinema: the notion of realism. For Kracauer the primary meaning of realism is attitudinal or intentional, what, as we have seen, is "the medium's substantive concern with our visible world." For a historian of cinema and of culture in general, however, realism inevitably also means the specific embodiment of these intentions in the artistic-literary movement beginning in the nineteenth century but having, as Erich Auerbach has shown, its roots in an unbroken tradition within the corpus of Western literature.[3] My point is this. Kracauer's theoretical realism often conflicts with his attraction toward (and sometimes rejection of) historical realisms. Before exploring this issue, I would like to point out that my purpose in so doing is not to discredit Kracauer's ideas. As I mentioned above, inconsistencies are what we should expect in an ambitious work like *Theory of Film;* they are not indices of the book's failure or the uselessness of its ideas. Aristotle's *Poetics,* for example, also displays the ultimate irreconcilability of theoretical and historical approaches. Because he defines tragedy as an imitation of an action realized in words, Aristotle must discount the effect of spectacle *(opsis).* When examining tragedy pragmatically, however, Aristotle maintains that spectacle indeed plays an important role in achieving the effects of pity and fear.[4] Often, as in this instance from the *Poetics,* textual contradictions are themselves an important source of meaning. In fact, a consideration of Kracauer's several realisms discovers what has largely gone unnoticed about *Theory of Film:* the inflection of its ideas by both the mainstream literary tradition and cultural modernism.

As Gerald Graff has most convincingly demonstrated, the anti-realism of the modernist and postmodernist movements can be traced to romantic humanism's acceptance of a cardinal scientific principle, namely that perception yields subjective rather than objective truth.[5]

The influence of scientific relativism on the mimetic movement has been carefully spelled out by W. H. Auden: "this destroys the traditional conception of *art* as *mimesis,* for there is no longer a nature 'out there' to be truly or falsely imitated; all an artist can be *true* to are his subjective sensations and feelings."[6] As a result, modernism manifests two stylistic extremes: formalism, which rejects the principle of referentiality and makes the work of art autotelic, and what Graff appropriately terms aggressive formalism, that visionariness, observable in romantic literary theory, which claims external reality for the subjective self as a world to be ordered and made significant. In both cases, of course, the opposition between the work of art and the reality it reflects is destroyed. Literature is reduced to itself, a consequence that the postmodern doctrine of "play" follows to its logical conclusion. A major justification for this position has emerged from structuralism, which, building upon linguistic theory, declares that meaning emerges from within the oppositions in literary structures, not from the work's reference to reality (regarded as impossible since it would depend on not only a fixed external nature, but also a social consensus about that nature).

Kracauer's reaction to modernism and its espousal of anti-realism is contradictory, on the one hand a reflection of his conservative belief (despite the evidence of science) in a reality "out there" and on the other of his acquiescence to the separation of art from its referential functions. Kracauer sees science as a threat to the understanding of material existence because, unlike Auden, he believes that science deals in abstractions or categories that focus perception. "Most sciences," he observes, "do not deal with the objects of ordinary experience but abstract from them certain elements which they then process in various ways" (p. 292). What science yields, in other words, are constructs that are not mentalistic but are rather reductions of reality; despite subjectivity, the possibility of true perception still exists, barring the interference of scientific abstractions. Also threatening modern man, Kracauer believes, is a relativism that prevents him from embracing moral values. Though he fails to recognize this development as a consequence, at least in part, of scientific positivism, he does suggest that relativism cannot be overcome until we can again see the world for what it is and not through the constructions of either science or ideology. Thus moral renewal depends on the re-vision of material reality. Such is the mission Kracauer assigns to cinema.

By linking the re-presentation of reality to a pragmatic purpose, Kracauer invests mimesis with a mission similar to that proposed for it by most literary realists, who rescued imitation from idealism and yoked it to the goals of social progress. George Lukács, for example, declares that fiction which is truly realistic (as opposed to naturalistic) develops historically typical characters whose "apparent form" conceals an "inner core" of meaning that allows the reader to understand the truth of their historical situation (a situation which functions as an analogy for "real world" historicity). In this way, Lukács argues, fiction avoids simply self-referentiality. While accepting the general aims of literary realism, however, Kracauer endorses the anti-realist view of literature (and of art in general):

> To the extent that painting, literature, the theater, etc., involve nature at all, they do not really represent it. Rather, they use it as raw material from which to build works which lay claim to autonomy. In the work of art nothing remains of the raw material itself, or, to be precise, all that remains of it is so molded that it implements the intentions conveyed through it. (p. 300)

Cinema, however, is an "art with a difference" because it avoids both self-containment (formalism) and the domination of raw material by artistic intention (aggressive formalism). And it can be true to nature, unlike realist fiction, because its mimetic capacity is *both* re-presentation and presentation; cinema's photographic essence guarantees the survival of camera reality. "Film," Kracauer declares, "is the only art which exhibits its raw material" (p. 302).

Kracauer's doctrine of the "special realism" of film therefore disassociates his theory from those of other cinematic realists who, by and large, accept the idea, traceable at least as far as Aristotle's *Poetics*, that living forms, transformed by the techniques proper to a representational art, can be thought of as realistic. Furthermore, because he at the same time, as we have seen, permits a stylization whose aims are the recording and revealing of nature, Kracauer's theories must likewise be distinguished from those of the so-called naive realists. Unlike the documentarists and the neo-realists like Grierson and Zavattini, Kracauer neither denies the role of style or convention nor attempts to purify film of their effects. For him formal constraints naturally pose a danger (since they have, in the arts, precluded the exhibition of nature in the raw). But stylization in the cinema can never destroy the medium's referentiality:

> The photographer . . . definitely lacks the artist's freedom to dispose of existing shapes and spatial interrelationships for the sake of his inner vision. (p. 4)

Thus the formative tendency does not have to be repressed in order to preserve the purity of cinema. The filmmaker's pictures may "record nature and at the same time reflect his attempt to assimilate and decipher it" (p. 20).

Stylization, then, if acknowledged as an integral part of the cinematic recording of reality, never becomes for Kracauer the means of actualizing that recording (since this capacity resides in the mechanical process of photography itself). Thus Kracauer avoids the tensions of aesthetic realism revealed, for example, in the theorizing of both Eisenstein and Vertov, who reflect the difficulty of harmonizing the modernist view of art (autotelism) with the pragmatic aims of a rhetorical referentiality. Kracauer's happy reconciliation of the formative and realistic tendencies, made possible by his concept of cinematic realism as, in part, the direct presentation of nature, is also eased by his blurring of the distinction between reality and the pro-filmic event. Quite early in *Theory of Film*, he does in fact raise this issue, conceding that:

> . . . it is entirely possible that a staged real-life event evokes a stronger illusion of reality on the screen that would the original event if it had been captured directly by the camera. (p. 35)

Beyond loading the issue by postulating a correspondence between "original" events and their "staged" equivalents, Kracauer avoids discussion of the problems posed by illusionism for referentiality; one searches in vain through the rest of his study for any further confrontation of the difficulty. Unlike Bazin, Kracauer steers clear of any concern for stylistic forms that make realistic effects possible. In Bazin's theorizing, the connection between the pro-filmic event, created by the director's manipulation of *mise-en-scène*, and the truth (for Bazin, already existing) "out there" remains unclear. In what does cinema's referentiality consist? Bazin's view that "realism in art can only be achieved one way—through artifice" leads logically to V. F. Perkins' resolution of the tension between reality and style.[7] "The camera," Perkins declares, "does not discriminate between real events . . . and action created specifically in order to be recorded." Thus, for Perkins, realism in the traditional sense becomes impossible. Cinema, instead, becomes capable only of credible illusion, of constructing a coherent imaginary world: as Perkins states, "it is absurd to claim that movies are like life." Ultimately, of course, he himself takes refuge in an idealistic mimeticism (rather like those of both Aristotle and Sir Philip Sidney) that implies a connection between the fictional film world and our own: "the world is shaped by the film-maker to reveal an order beyond chronology . . . a world more concentrated and more shaped than that of our usual experience."[8] But his resolution of the problem of stylization points toward a cinematic self-reflexivity, opening the door to a structuralist-semiotic approach that would short-circuit referentiality altogether. Seen in this light, Kracauer's rejection of traditional mimesis (i. e. his sidestepping of the problems posed by stylization) becomes an effective means for preserving the goals of realism in an age that stresses the constructing powers of convention. Kracauer neatly avoids the indefensible position of the naive realists, who insist either that style does not exist or must be avoided, and the difficulties of the aesthetic realists, for whom stylization leads ultimately to cinematic self-containment.

For Aristotle, of course, mimesis involves more than the creation of a fictional world somehow analogous to our own; the poet's task is largely dynamization, the devising of a story or mythos that presents the subject as becoming, not being.[9] The central role of narrative in traditional realism has likewise been maintained by Colin MacCabe in an influential study of the connections between the classic realist novel and the classic realist film. MacCabe suggests, as Bazin would have it, that the effect of truth derives in the classic realist novel from artifice, from the juxtaposition of various discourses (the *orationes rectae* of characters) with the unspoken and unwritten commentary of the narrator:

> No discourse is allowed to speak for itself but rather it must be placed in a context which will reduce it to a simple explicable content. And in the claim that narrative prose has direct access to a final reality we can find the claim of the classic realist novel to present us with the truths of human nature.[10]

Lacking a narrator, the classic realist film has developed another way of controlling and explicating the different discourses it contains: narrative itself. As MacCabe says, "the unquestioned nature of the narrative discourse entails that the only problem that reality poses is to go and look and see what *Things* there *are*." Kracauer's view is limited in suggesting that both omniscient narration and film narrative preclude the necessity of reader/spectator interpretation. His ideas are nonetheless important as indices of the modernist attitude toward mythos and its relationship to mimesis.

While modernism has rejected mimesis on the grounds that objective reality does not exist to be imitated and that literary structures, in any case, are self-referential, the movement has dismissed the coherent narrative of traditional literary realism for quite another reason: namely, as MacCabe suggests, that it is ideological, in Althusserian terms, one of those "perceived—accepted—suffered cultural objects" that stand between us and material experience. As formalist analysis has suggested, the narrative functions as a means of organizing reading/spectating experience. By establishing an initial setting and characters whose equilibrium is somehow disrupted, the classic narrative fosters reader/spectator identification with the trajectory created as well as with the characters involved. The resolution of the disrupting force produces a sense of closure for these feelings of identification. For the formalist the transparency of such traditional narratives must be demystified if literary structures are to become truly self-reflexive. For the aggressive formalist the narrative as such represents another convention to be subverted and re-accommodated to a subjective vision. Even within the various branches of cinematic realism, the narrative has sometimes been seen as an impediment to referentiality. For example, Rossellini affirms that "the realist film has the 'world' as its living object, not the telling of a story."[11]

Kracauer, however, does not accept this simple notion of the opposition of narrative to reality. Once again, his reaction to modernist anti-realism is contradictory, the product both of his desire to tie cinema to realist goals and of his acceptance of the view that narrative is indeed an impediment to the presentation of the flow of life. Thus Kracauer maintains that the documentary as a form is capable of only a limited realism:

> . . . it misses those aspects of potentially visible reality which only personal involvement is apt to summon. Their appearance is inseparable from human drama, as conveyed by an intrigue. (p. 212)

In his discussions of both theatrical and novelistic stories, however, Kracauer finds that their narratives are often obstructions to the cinematic presentation of living flux. For example, he objects strongly to the functioning of closure in novels, calling the device an "arbitrary invention" that cuts short "developments that might, or indeed should, be carried on and on" (p. 233). Not surprisingly, Kracauer suggests that most films based on plays and novels fail to achieve truly cinematic ends.

How to reconcile, as Kracauer puts it, "the two conflicting principles according to which the story both obstructs and stimulates camera explorations" (p. 213) ? His answer is to postulate a special category or narrative which is not ideological, which owes nothing to the formative, shaping tendency, which is, in short, part of nature itself:

> The term "found story" covers all stories found in the material of actual physical reality. . . . since the found story is part and parcel of the raw material in which it lies dormant, it cannot possibly develop into a self-contained whole—which means that it is almost the opposite of the theatrical story. (pp. 245–6)

In examining Kracauer's treatment of mimesis, we noticed that he is able to avoid the problems posed by stylization to realist theory only by ignoring an important element of the filmmaking process—the director's manipulation of *mise-en-scène*. Similarly, in discussing narrative, Kracauer is able to justify his Aristotelian view that through narrative the relationship between man and environment is dynamized only by denying the status of narrative as a formative element. This position leads him to absurd views of the filmmaking process. For example, his enthusiastic discussion of the neorealist *Paisan* ends with the following comment:

> . . . scenes and images, found in the world around the story proper, are singled out with unrivaled precision. Selected from among the many incidents with which the environment teems, they are very special samples indeed. (p. 257)

But surely *Paisan*, despite its documentary stylization, is a fiction film, not a simple record of events. Its various episodes, each of which, with one exception, Kracauer praises for randomness and lack of closure, are in fact tightly organized narratives, which climax on ironic reversals or discoveries. However they may differ from mainstream narratives in theme and subject matter, the episodes in *Paisan* consist of causally linked sequences with clear beginnings, middles, and ends. They are no more open-ended or "natural" than Maupassant short stories, which in their spare structures and cynical worldweariness they greatly resemble.

In *History: The Last Things Before the Last,* his posthumously published essay on historiography, Kracauer compares the filmmaker with the historian: each is "passive and active, a recorder and a creator."[12] Like the cineaste, the historian likewise "lacks the novelist's or dramatist's freedom to alter or shape his material as he pleases" (p. 55). In this later book, however, perhaps because he was dealing with an activity that could in no sense be considered a mechanical recording, Kracauer acknowledges, in a way he never does in *Theory of Film,* the shaping power of the imagination. "Historical ideas," he says, "are generalizations to the extent that they are derived from, and refer back to, a hard core of discovered data." But they are much more:

> . . . at the same time they must be considered products of informed intuition which as such go beyond generalizations because they quiver with connotations and meanings not found in the material occasioning them. (p. 98)

In this passage (and in others throughout the book) we find Kracauer espousing a view much closer to that of classical mimesis (for it goes without saying that history is a mimetic art). His rather different treatment of both mimesis and mythos in *Theory of Film,* I believe, stems to a great extent from his reaction to the modernist movement. Moved by the reproduction of living reality in the cinema, Kracauer was forced to postulate its "special realism" since he accepted both the formalist and aggressive formalist views of literary presentation and autonomy. Reacting against the abstractions of science in the spirit of romantic humanism, Kracauer likewise rejected traditional narrative as an imposition on nature but, in the spirit of traditional realism, located storyness in the raw material of cinema. His theories, finally, are Aristotelian in intent if not in form. And this fact distinguishes his work from that of all other cinematic realists, who either retreat from modernist views about representation and stylization or accept an aestheticism that leads logically to structuralist-semiotic conclusions.[13]

NOTES

[1] (London: Oxford Univ. Press, 1960). All quotations will be to this edition and will be noted in the text.

[2] In *The Hollywood Musical* (Bloomington: Indiana Univ. Press, 1982), Jane Feuer remarks: "the ultimate synthesis of the musical consists in unifying what initially was imaginary with what initially was real. . . . in the film's unfolding, the boundary between real and imaginary may be blurred. Musicals may project the dream into the narrative, implying a similar relationship between film and viewer" (p. 77).

[3] See *Mimesis: The Representation of Reality in Western Literature*, trans. William Trask (Princeton: Princeton Univ. Press, 1953).

[4] See the discussion of this matter in Roselyne Dupont-Roc and Jean Lallot, eds. and trans., *Aristote: La Poétique* (Paris: Éditions du Seuil, 1980), pp. 20–22.

[5] *Literature Against Itself: Literary Ideas in Modern Society* (Chicago: The Univ. of Chicago Press, 1979). See especially pp. 1–62.

[6] *The Dyer's Hand and Other Essays* (New York: Vintage Books, 1968), pp. 78–79.

[7] Quoted in Christopher Williams, ed., *Realism and the Cinema* (London: Routledge & Kegan Paul, 1980), p. 35.

[8] *Film as Film: Understanding and Judging Movies* (Harmondsworth, Middlesex: Penguin Books Ltd., 1972), p. 69.

[9] See the classic discussion of this aspect of Aristotle's theory in S. H. Butcher, ed. and trans., *Aristotle's Theory of Poetry and Fine Art* (New York: Dover Publications, Inc., 1951), pp. 113–197.

[10] Quoted in Williams, *op. cit.*, pp. 152–62. The original essay, entitled "The Classic Realist Text," appeared in *Screen*, 15 (1974).

[11] Quoted in Williams, *op. cit.*, p. 32.

[12] (New York: Oxford Univ. Press, 1969), p. 47. Subsequent references will be to this edition and will be noted in that text.

[13] Note the resemblance between the positions adopted by both Bazin and Perkins and the following remarks by Tzvetan Todorov in *Littérature et Réalité* (Paris: Éditions du Seuil, 1982): "Pour les théoriciens de la littérature de la seconde moitié du xxe siècle, le réalisme est un style littéraire ni plus ni moins valorisé qu'un autre, dont il est possible de décrire les règles, comme pour n'importe quel discours, mais dont une des caractéristiques est un peu particulière: en lisant les oeuvres réalistes, le lecteur doit avoir l'*impression* qu'il a affaire à un discours sans autre règle que celle de transcrire scrupuleusement le réel, de nous mettre en contact immédiat avec le monde tel qu'il est" (p. 7).

II
METHODS

FEMINIST FILM CRITICISM: CURRENT ISSUES AND PROBLEMS*

E. Ann Kaplan

Feminist film criticism is approximately fifteen years old—old enough to already have its own set of historical discourses, its inevitable teleological narrative about its development. Although feminist criticism is only now becoming known outside of film studies, it has been a central area within recent cinema scholarship (some may even say *the* central area, the one that has produced the most challenging and influential recent work).

While reflections on the development of feminist film criticism began as early as 1976,[1] the early 80s have seen a number of books including critical overviews of the work. A new survey article has just appeared in *Signs*.[2] Reviews of the new books on women in film have also provided an occasion for an assessment of developments.[3] Most accounts view the chronological development of feminist film criticism as having certain stages, and they also discuss the leapfrogging American-British-American phases. (For reasons too complex to raise here, France, Germany and Italy were slower to produce feminist film theory, and are now largely building on work done in America and England.)[4]

Since these review accounts are readily available, there is no need for me to rehearse them here. Let me merely indicate the main movements in the narrative which all accounts address, albeit in various ways, before suggesting that a less teleological conception of things may now be more useful. I will isolate certain tensions/dichotomies/polarities within current debates about feminist film theory, focusing particularly on what we have been calling "essentialist" versus "anti-essentialist" perspectives.

Most overview accounts agree on the following series of developments: (a) That feminist film criticism arose in America in the context of the activist Women's Liberation movement of the late 60s/early 70s; (b) That the activist context lent work in America a sociological/Marxist bent reflected generally in 60s theories across many disciplines; (c) That Kate Millett's groundbreaking text, *Sexual Politics* (1969), influenced early approaches to the female image on film; (d) That the short but densely packed articles by Claire Johnston in 1973 and Laura Mulvey in 1975 (both from Britain) had a dramatic impact on the field on both sides of the Atlantic in their use of Althusserian Marxism, Saussurean semiotics as applied by Lévi-Strauss and, perhaps most importantly, both Freudian and Lacanian psychoanalysis; these essays shaped much of the ensuing work; (e) That Mulvey's work (itself first focused on the male spectator) provoked an exploration of the position of the female spectator, which, in turn, initiated a good deal of work on the text–spectator relationship; it also led to an examination of the melodrama form addressing women, i.e. the so-called "woman's film"; (f) That particularly through the influence of the feminist film journal, *Camera Obscura*, work by Christian Metz and Raymond Bellour began to be taken up in America. In the 80s, semiotics and psychoanalytic theory have been more strongly developed in America than in England largely because of the transformation of the influential British journal, *Screen*.

As usual, the problem with such a "developmental" narrative is that it assumes that one "stage" replaced another (whereas in reality elements were "added in" to an ongoing stream of work containing earlier "stages"). The narrative also cannot help appearing to valorize later stages as "higher" or "better," although this is not necessarily the case. I obviously have my own theoretical predilections which will no doubt become clear, but I do not think that placing different kinds of work in feminist film criticism in some kind of hierarchy is at all useful. What we need at this point is a clear understanding of the various issues that are up for debate—the issues that we need to be thinking through carefully, and trying to understand if not to "resolve" (they may be unresolvable).

The chronological development hides the fact that we have now reached a certain theoretical impasse, which is partly the result of a failure to theorize clearly the differences among approaches in feminist film criticism; each of the main tendencies has failed to formulate a theoretical position that solves the dilemmas that it raises.

Let me briefly outline the two main feminist theories underlying work that produce one of the tensions/polarities within the field. Exploring this polarity paradigmatically rather than syntagmatically will enable me to provide examples of kinds of work done for people not familiar with the field while avoiding the sort of survey already available. I will then conclude with brief discussion of directions that the impasse has provoked scholars into exploring and which I think promise fruitful new work.

The tension masked by the neat chronological account of theoretical developments is that between what we have been (loosely) calling "essentialist" and "anti-essentialist" perspectives. This debate is important because it determines the kinds of questions one asks about the representations of women in film and the sorts of knowledge one uses in analyzing a particular text. Essentialist feminism assumes a basic "truth" about woman that patriarchal society has kept hidden. It assumes that there is a particular group, "women," who can be separated from another group, "men," in terms of an essence that precedes (or is outside of) culture and ultimately has to have biological origins. The essential aspects of woman, repressed in patriarchy, are often assumed to embody a more humane, moral mode of being, which, once brought to light, could help change society in a beneficial direction. Female values become a means for critiquing the harsh, competitive and individualistic "male" values that govern society and offer an alternative way, not only of *seeing* but of *being*, that threatens patriarchy; just because of this, essentialist feminists believe that female values should be resurrected, celebrated, revitalized, and used as a weapon to dig ourselves out from under our oppression.

This kind of feminist perspective, starting out as it does from the premise of pre-existing sex difference, is interested in how films illuminate socially constructed gender roles, and the ways in which patriarchy has manipulated these roles for its own ends. Feminist film critics of this persuasion believe that we can abandon/reject socially constructed roles, adopt other, more truly female ones, and confront the existing order in this way. Let me briefly discuss a well-known essay by Ruby Rich, now seen as "classical," that represents a good example of a work in this tendency. It appears in a recent (and useful) collection of articles representing different kinds of work in feminist film theory that I will draw upon later in discussing the second main perspective.[5]

The essay by Rich[6] assumes a given sex difference and an essential (but repressed) "feminine." Working from these premises, Ruby Rich elegantly rereads Leontine Sagan's film *Maedchen in Uniform* (Germany, 1932) as having lesbianism, not fascism, as its central theme, while still remaining a "profoundly antifascist drama" (p.102). A "dual coming-out story," the film shows Manuel daring to act on her desire, and Fraulein von Bernburg repudiating her own role as an agent of suppression and thereby winning "her freedom by accepting her attraction to another woman" (p.102). Rich further sees the homosexuality of the period as a form of dissent from the staid and morally bankrupt older generation. This idea leads her to move from the study of the representation of lesbianism in *Maedcchen in Uniform* to look at the historical lives of the women involved in its production; she suggests a direct relationship between the two spheres (i.e. history/representation) that other kinds of work to be discussed below have cast doubt on.

What Rich seems to be doing here is showing how "woman" as constituted in patriarchy can manoeuver within given constraints. This is important work, and we need more of it, but only within an essentialist position can we conceive of such "manoeuverings" as in and of themselves bringing woman a "freedom" that is completely outside of the system.

Rich's work is important in theorizing ways in which woman, as given in patriarchy, can work within her constraints to renegotiate her place and thereby achieve a modicum of control. Rich uses the category of gender as determining a certain product: the fact that a filmmaker is a woman will necessarily provide her with different ways of seeing, a different "look" evident in narrative structures. Following a similar line of thought, other essentialist feminists advocate films like Lizzie Borden's *Born in Flames* that show women taking control of the social order, defining themselves outside of men, abandoning all the familiar feminine qualities, etc. If such images appear utopian, I think critics would argue that it is only through such new female depictions that we can begin to bring women to see themselves differently.

Anti-essentialist feminist film critics take a rather different, if not absolutely incompatible tack (I will deal with the issue of how the two theories interrelate later on). They are concerned to understand the processes through which female subjectivity is constituted in patriarchal culture, and do not find any "essential" feminine behind the socially constructed subject. The "feminine" now is not something outside of, or untouched by patriarchy, but integral to it. Theorists are interested in the links between a given sex identity and the patriarchal order, analyzing the processes through which sexuality and subjectivity are constituted at the same time. I think we are all agreed that we can change *sex roles*—many Western cultures are in the process of enacting such changes. But anti-essentialists argue that for such changes to take a firm hold—to represent more than a merely local, fashionable and temporary change—we have to understand more about how we arrive at sex identity in the first place. If the goal is to get beyond socially constructed definitions of "man"/"woman," "masculine"/"feminine," anti-essentialists would argue that we need to know precisely how these social constructions are inscribed in the processes of becoming "human."

Anti-essentialist feminist theory obviously leads to a different kind of feminist film criticism than does essentialist feminism, and also to a different conception of feminist film practice. It was anti-essentialist feminists who found resonances in the work of Mulvey and Johnston that was central in the formulation of the anti-essentialist position. Heavily influenced themselves by European theories (from Russian Formalism, to Benjamin, to Bertold Brecht, to Barthes, Althusser, Foucault, Lacan, Kristeva and Derrida), these authors contributed several elements central to later work from this perspective, namely (1) the notion, relying on work by Comolli and Narboni of *Cahiers du Cinéma*, that, to be feminist, a cinema has to be a counter-cinema (the polarity Classical Hollywood Cinema versus the Avant-garde has been a dominant category in feminist film criticism—see attached chart); (2) the idea, building on Althusser's work, that the realist strategy inevitably embodied oppressive dominant ideology, and thus was not useful as a feminist cinematic strategy; (3) the notion, relying on Freud's twin concepts of voyeurism and fetishism, that the dominant Classical Hollywood cinema is built on a series of three basic "looks," all of which satisfy desires in the male unconscious.

CHART I

Polarized Filmic Categories in Recent Film Theory

The Classical Text (Hollywood)	The Avant-garde Text
Realism/Narrative	Non-realist anti-Narrative
History	Discourse
Complicit Ideology	Rupture of Dominant Ideology

Mulvey's introduction of the three looks in cinema was taken up by anti-essentialist feminist film critics, and produced a great deal of work on the structure of the "male" gaze in film. Critics' interest in dominant classical cinema involved Hollywood's apparent inscription of the male, as against any possible "female," unconscious. Critics, that is, found in dominant cinema an articulation of the structures of desire through which subjects are created as they enter the realm of language/the Symbolic/representation. Hollywood films appear to lay out for our contemplation and analysis unconscious processes difficult to gain access to outside of the psychoanalytic session.

Let me take as an example work by Mary Ann Doane and Kaja Silverman readily available in the collection alredy mentioned. Building on Mulvey's work on the structure of the gaze, Doane and Silverman investigate the constraints imposed on woman's look and voice (respectively) within the diegesis of the Hollywood film. Theirs is a specifically *textual* analysis, refusing to generalize to any "feminine" outside of the film. In such analyses, as against the essentialist ones, a director's gender will not be seen in itself as having any particular significance, since it is not one's biological maleness or femaleness that determines one's "look" so much as one's social construction. Both men and women within patriarchy will accept the phallus as signifier because of the nature of the Symbolic in that system. However, as feminist theorists able to "read against the grain" of classical patriarchal texts, we may perceive ways in which certain directors, not only female, manage to expose women's constraints within the system. Or our own theoretical framework may permit us to analyze the way patriarchal representational systems oppress women figures.

Doane explores the "trouble" caused in the film melodrama by the address to the female spectator. She argues that the female gaze does not utilize the usual (male) mechanisms of voyeurism and fetishism, and that thus the female look is not invested with desire in the same way as the male look. Scopophilic energy is directed away from the female body, and "the very process of seeing is now invested with fear, anxiety, horror, precisely because it is object-less, free-floating" (p.70). In order to overcome this horror, Doane argues that the medical gaze is inserted in place of the erotic one. The female body is now "an element in the discourse of medicine, a manuscript to be read for the symptoms which betray her story, her identity" (p.74).

Doane concludes that in having to de-eroticize the gaze, the woman's film melodrama effectively disembodies the female spectator. While the cinema generally denies woman that imaginary identification with discursive mastery available to the male spectator, the woman's film makes imposssible even woman's narcissistic identification with the woman as spectacle, permitting only identification with woman as victim: "masochistic fantasy *instead* of sexuality," as Doane puts it.

Turning from analysis of woman's relationship to the gaze, Kaja Silverman explores the neglected terrain of woman's link to the voice. Silverman notes that "the rule of synchronization is imposed much more strictly on the female than on the male voice within dominant cinema" (p.133). Since the male voice can be represented in disembodied form (a form denied woman), he is aligned with "transcendence, authoritative knowledge, potency and the law, in short with the Symbolic Father." While often *heard* in film, woman is usually associated "with unreliable, thwarted or acquiescent speech," Silverman notes, and her forms of speech are synchronized with the visual image of her body, confining her within the range of male sight and hearing.

Silverman thus shows that dominant cinema refuses woman access to the control of filmic discourse, just as it refuses to allow woman access to the gaze, except with the awesome consequences outlined by Doane. To allow woman to be heard and not seen would "put her beyond the control of the male gaze, release her voice from the signifying obligations which the gaze sustains" (p. 135).[7]

Both the Doane and Silverman essays ultimately bring us to what is a basic impasse familiar within the anti-essentialist position. For Doane, the very form (the woman's film) that addresses the historical female spectator, ends up, through desexualizing the female body, denying its very existence. Doane concludes that any specifically "female" form is impossible within Hollywood, although she has elsewhere argued for the possibility of a new female syntax within avant-garde film.[8]

Silverman's anti-essentialist position reaches a similar impasse, since she has to reject Mulvey's attempt to recover a pre-Symbolic female language (in, for instance, her film *Riddles of the Sphinx*, made with Peter Wollen)—repressed by patriarchy but somehow remaining intact over centuries—because of its implicit essentialism. Silverman is interested in recent feminist films that begin to interrogate the issue of the female voice in the sense of examining "the place of the female voice within the existing discursive field." The one film that Silverman sees as in any way able to achieve this is Yvonne Rainer's *Journeys From Berlin*, but exactly how the film broaches "the possibility of moving beyond masochism toward externally directed action. . ." (p.147) is unclear.

It is this very impasse that already concerned Christine Gledhill in her 1977 reflections on developments in feminist film theory.[9] Gledhill here worries about "the hiatus between the feminine position as constructed in language, and woman as produced by historical, social and economic forces. . ." (p.35). Gledhill wants to know how the anti-essentialist position can "take account of the intersection of gender with class and racial differences among others," and notes the "magnitude of the task facing feminists if patriarchy can be shifted only by an assault on the structure of the subject and ideology in general" (p.35). She concludes that "the general lack in film theory of a means to conceptualize the social relations in which a specific audience is constituted can lead to severe limitations on proposals for subversive cultural activity" (p.40).

In her "Afterword" to the 1977 essay in the 1984 volume, Gledhill critiques the anti-essentialist position while not advocating a return to essentialism. She articulates the impasse that we have reached as that of at once rejecting "given social definitions of women or femininity as mere indicators of social constructions at work" and of also rejecting "constructions of our social heroines as strong and powerful" because they indicate "male identification" (p.42). She sees the problem as the "unspoken (remaining) unknown, and the speakable (reproducing) what we know, patriarchal reality"; and she concludes that it is because of this that we have found attractive "equating the feminine with difference itself, a motive force keeping everything in process, refusing the sedimentation into fixed positions of masculine and feminine" (p.42). But this conception, however attractive, has still not, for Gledhill, avoided the problem of essentialism. She goes on to argue, in what is perhaps a confusing move, that "the essence is now posited in narrative structuration (what we opposed) or projected into a future practice that is very difficult to conceptualize except in typically avant-garde terms" (p.42).

I find this move confusing in that I do not see how theorists have made narrative "the essence"; if the subject is constructed in the processes of reception, this construction can have no "essence." The narrative structuration can also have no essence since it means nothing out of the context of reception. Also confusing is Gledhill's reference to the discourses produced by, and often for, women (her examples are "Dear Abby" columns, mother/toddler groups, women's magazine fiction, soap operas) which she feels feminist film theorists have not paid sufficient attention to. It is unclear precisely how these discourses are to be used since they are themselves integral to the patriarchal society in which they emerge. If they are a means through which women "negotiate dominant institutions and their contradictions. . .", as Gledhill suggests, then we need to know more about how precisely this takes place.

Gledhill's final point, based on Tessa Perkins' work, is that the view of narrative as first deconstructing and then reforming the subject to its own ends is mistaken. She prefers to see the discursive and the extradiscursive as held together in a complex and contradictory interrelation. I will return to this point in my conclusion, since I think it moves us in the right direction.

Like Gledhill, the editors of the volume who reprinted her essay also focus on the impasse of the anti-essentialist position. They note its dangerous implications, such as woman avoiding the problem by "relinquishing not only her place, her identity, but *any* place, *any* identity, and instead espousing process, movement." They do not, however, explain *why* this is unsatisfactory (do they have in mind some of Gledhill's points?), nor dwell on the resistance to the anti-essentialist position by many feminists. It seems to me that this resistance comes partly from the way that the position opens up the spectre of non-being and non-identity for women through its theory of woman as signifying absence, lack. This makes daily functioning problematic in addition to failing to show how concrete social change might be possible. Feeling that they have been brought up against a blank wall, women reject the anti-essentialist position.

Many of us are tired of the constant rearticulation without solution of the theoretical arguments that produce an impasse, and are eager to get beyond it. The impasse is currently provoking theorists to come up with textual readings that show ways in which representations can at least begin to articulate the oppressiveness of woman's positioning. In an essay in the same volume, Linda Williams starts off from a similar position to Doane, but in the course of her investigation of the woman's look in the horror film discovers a potentially subversive element. She shows that while on the one hand "everything conspires . . . to condemn the desire and curiosity of the woman's look" in the horror film, on the other hand, the look of the woman at the monster, which Williams argues the genre emphasizes, suggests sympathy between the two; woman recognizes (and thus has articulated for her) a freakishness similar to her own difference from the "normal" male body.[10]

It is this difference that offers a threat to male power and that, according to Williams, accounts for the often vindictive destruction of the monster and for the sympathy from the heroine that this elicits. For Williams, both the female body and the monster's body are "frightening to the male precisely because (they) cannot be castrated, (have) none of his own vulnerability" (p.97). The horror film thus at once permits expression of the potency of female desire through the woman's look, but also declares this desire to be monstrous.

In a recent (and already much discussed) essay on *Stella Dallas*,[11] Williams turns from analysis of the spectatorial regime in film (of, that is, the three looks originally outlined by Laura Mulvey) to a focus on narrative identification. She moves from examining the gaze in film (identification with the camera) and the psychoanalytic construction of the subject to examining diegetic point of view. This move entails abandoning the strictly Lacanian paradigm that leads naturally to focus on the spectatorial regime, and picking up American Freudian revisionist Nancy Chodorow and French feminists who have increasingly dissented from strict Lacanian models.

Her argument is too complex to summarize here, but what is important for my purposes is Williams' use of the "new value placed on the multiple and continuous female identity capable of fluidly shifting between the identity of mother and daughter" (p.9). While Williams quotes theorists other than Chodorow, it seems that her argument relies heavily on Chodorow's questioning of "the very standards of unity and autonomy by which human identity has typically been measured" (p.9), and her implicit valuing of woman's connectedness, relatedness—intersubjectivity, we might say—something very different from the impossible choice that Mary Ann Doane has outlined between a narcissistic overidentification with the image (arising through the nearness to the mother's body in early infancy), and the adoption of the masculine place of mastery. For Williams, the female spectator is rather "in a constant state of juggling all positions at once" (p.19); like Tania Modleski, Williams sees the female spectator of *Stella Dallas* as identifying with multiple points of view, constituted (in Modlesksi's words) "as a sort of ideal mother: a person . . . whose sympathy is large enough to encompass the conflicting claims of her family (she identifies with no character exclusively)" (p.17).

Williams' essay is important in attempting a different approach to the issue of some possible "subversiveness" in the woman's melodrama in arguing for the genre providing "a recognizable picture of woman's ambivalent position under patriarchy that has been an important source of realistic reflections of women's lives" (p.23). But her text again runs the danger of essentializing women, of insufficient attention to the way discourses through which even such "mediation of the mother and daughter's look at one another" (p.20)—a mediation which Williams claims prevents the female spectator from acquiescing to the phallic visual economy of voyeurism and fetishism (p.20)—are themselves constructed.

Teresa de Lauretis' essay "Oedipus Interruptus" — written at about the same time as Williams' but only recently published[12] — also seeks to displace "the active–passive and gaze–image dichotomies in the theorization of spectatorship, and to rethink the possibilities of narrative identification as a subject-effect in female spectators. . ."

(p.38). Like Williams, de Lauretis disagrees with the theory of woman's narcissistic over-identification with the image, but instead of turning to other psychoanalytic models for a solution, de Lauretis goes rather to semiotics and narrative theory, seeing such interests as displaced in film theory by the debate on the psychoanalytic definition of the subject (p.35). De Lauretis is concerned to theorize the historical female spectator — and to *historicize* that spectator. It seems to me that it is only through such an historicizing — through, that is, theorizing the female spectator as constructed not only by textual gaze-image or multiple narrative identifications but also through social discourses existing prior to coming to the context of reception — that we can begin to develop strategies for constructing new subjects, for moving beyond the socially defined "masculine" and "feminine." "There is," says de Lauretis, "no image outside of narrative, and no filmic image outside of history, which is also to say the history of cinema including the avant-garde and mainstream, classical and contemporary cinema" (p.35). What de Lauretis ends up asking for is a feminist text which is not anti-narrative and anti-Oedipal but rather "narrative and Oedipal with a vengeance." She advocates texts that stress the contradiction of the female subject in the inevitably Oedipal narrative, her figural identification with both masculine and feminine figures rather than merely with Metz's "all-perceiving subject of the gaze" (p.39).

It may be useful here to return briefly by way of conclusion to some of the points raised by Gledhill in the essay discussed earlier. I noted Gledhill's important observation that the discursive and what she calls the "extra-discursive" (her split is really that between narrative discourse and the world outside of that discourse) are held together in a complex and contradictory relation. I also mentioned her concern with the hiatus between woman as linguistic sign and as constructed through social practices and institutions, and a related worry about a feminist theory that espouses movement, the non-fixing of the masculine and the feminine. Let me dwell on these concerns since it is with their solution that we may find a way out of the essentialist/anti-essentialist impasse.

First, I am not sure that there is a hiatus between the notion of woman as linguistic sign and woman as constructed in social practices. For the construction of subjects in society takes place through language in the form of discourses. The processes of the subject's formation within the nuclear family as he/she enters the world of the Symbolic is not distinct from the process through which subjects are constructed/positioned by social discourses outside of the family. The construction within the family is itself a social one, and is not dissimilar from woman's construction within, say, a medical or educational discourse. Woman is in all cases positioned in a signifying chain based on her representing lack, absence. But if Foucault is correct, these discourses cannot simply control/contain all within their compass, so that gaps open up through which change can take place. The gaps, that is, permit points of resistance which enable new articulations, which, in turn, begin to work on and to alter the dominant discourse.

Since all subjectivity, wherever experienced, is discursive, it is in this terrain that we must work. With regard to the social formation, Tony Bennett's discussion of Marxism as "a set of discursive interventions" not claiming any prior ontological privilege seems to apply equally to feminism. Feminist interventions, like Marxist ones, must prove their validity through their *effects* rather than through recourse to "essence." Such interventions, in Bennett's words, can help "to uncouple and disrupt the prevailing array of discourses through which subject identities are formed. . ." New discursive articulations in turn construct new subjects; and this inevitably leads to contradictions that may create historical rupture.[13]

For feminist film theorists, an important place to begin such interventions is the cinema. Once we distinguish the hypothetical spectator that a text constructs from the historical subject in the cinema, we can envisage intervention/disruption from both sides of the camera. Such intervention may consist of the narrative/Oedipal text de Lauretis advocates in the hopes both of giving women the pleasure and satisfaction that is so hard for them to come by in art or in life, and of exposing woman's contradictory place in such narratives; such texts may, in de Lauretis' words, construct the female subject "otherwise," bringing her to experience "difference as irreducible contradiction."[14] Or feminist filmmakers may still continue to create films that refuse the idealized hypothetical subject of dominant cinema, giving the spectator, if not pleasure then at least a chance to experience an alternate subjectivity, or a dislocation of her historical construction. (We can see in these new formulations an implicit critique of the classical text versus the avant-garde text mentioned earlier; that distinction is too rigid, too wedded to limited notions of the relationship between ideology and aesthetic strategy.)[15] On the other hand, by developing feminist discourses outside of the cinema, we may be able to construct historical subjects who are capable of bringing to reception of dominant film, discourses that conflict with those offered. Through such experiences of contradiction we may produce change.

This recent move by some feminist film theorists to re-insert the historical spectator displaced by attention only to the psychoanalytic definition of the subject is important. It reflects a larger move within film criticism toward theorizing historical discourse and toward historical film issues.[16] But we should beware of falling into the error of throwing out the baby (psychoanalysis) with the bath water — of repeating a one-sidedness we now see the limits of from the other direction. Issues of history must be linked to psychoanalytic theory rather than seen as *replacing* that theory, since the subject is him/herself always constructed in history (both psychic and social).

The subjective (psychic) and the social cannot be distinguished; thus, we cannot expect to develop any new (social) discursive constructions of gender without moving through the psychoanalytic process and discourse. If the aim is not to be a mere non-fixing of the masculine and the feminine, if we are to do more than espouse movement, non-identity, then we have to gain control over the psychoanalytic processes through which our subjectivity was constructed in the first place. This means moving through recognition of woman's positioning as lack, absence, moving through understanding our patriarchally produced desire for the phallus, our masochistic longing for passivity. For reasons having to do with the cultural necessity of separating from the mother (this being the only way for the child to achieve any kind of subjectivity, to enter the symbolic realm, to become human), we cannot abolish the construction of an insatiable desire. But perhaps we can learn to *desire* differently, to displace "woman" from her position in patriarchy as the lynch-pin of desire.

It is possible that women adopting one or the other set of theories outlined here do so out of their own particular psychic histories, out of the discourses through which they have come to be constructed or to construct themselves. For some women psychoanalysis is an invaluable tool for unlocking the origins of desires that are recognized, cognitively, as retrograde. Insight into that uncomfortable unconscious may offer the only way out of remaining locked into those forms of desiring. And analysis of Hollywood female representation is one way of having such "insight," since the commercial film displays, thinly veiled, the patriarchal unconscious.

Along with such analysis, we need to construct discourses through which we can learn to desire differently, since there is no essence beneath our socially given subjectivity to "uncover," no basic femaleness to find. What we may have is an original female identification (i.e. an identification with our mothers in the pre-Oedipal period) that we can strive to remember (we cannot "recover" it) in the process of learning to desire differently. This remembering of the mother on the part of both males and females may be a start toward restructuring social gender discourses. But this is a topic, too large for this context, that I am developing elsewhere.[17]

Essentialist and anti-essentialist feminists may not be as far apart as they seem, since what appears to essentialist feminists as innate female ways of being may rather reflect their success in establishing new discourses through which to construct themselves and their lives. What I have tried to outline here, all too briefly, is a theory and a terminology through which to accommodate the needs/desires/ideas of both groups. The theory of the subject's construction through a variety of discourses, be they familial, psychoanalytic, textual, institutional, educational, medicinal, etc., once agreed upon, would seem to accommodate a number of supposed disagreements. But perhaps that theory is itself still up for debate!

NOTES

* These reflections represent the particular moment of their original writing in 1986. The author's views of feminist film theory have changed in the light of recent cultural developments (postmodernism, "Third World" politics) and their theoretical paradigms. Cf. two forthcoming volumes. *Postmodernism and Its Discontents*. ed. E. Ann Kaplan (London: Verso, 1988); and *Psychoanalysis and Cinema* (New York: Routledge, 1989)

[1] Cf. in particular Christine Glledhill, "Recent Developments in Feminist Film Criticism," originally printed in *Quarterly Review of Film Studies*, 3, no. 4 (1977), pp. 458–53 and my much shorter piece, "Aspects of British Feminist Film Theory," in *Jump Cut*, nos: 12–13 (1976), pp. 52–55.

[2] Cf. Judith Mayne, "Feminist Film Theory and Criticism: A Review

Essay," *Signs: A Journal of Women and Culture*, 11 no. 1 (Autumn 1985), pp. 81–100.

[3] Cf. especially reviews by Sara Halperin, *Jump Cut* (Winter 1984); and by Diane Waldman and Janet Walker, in *Camera Obscura*, nos. 13–14 (Spring–Summer 1985), pp. 195–214.

[4] Cf. for example the German feminist film journal, *Frauen und Film*, for work being done in Germany; and a recent collection of articles by Italian feminist film theorists. *Offscreen: Women and Film in Italy*, eds. Giuliana Bruno and Maria Nadotti. (London and New York: Routledge, 1988).

[5] Cf. *Re-Vision: Essays in Feminist Film Criticism*, eds. Pat Mellencamp, Mary Ann Doane and Linda Williams (Los Angeles: The American Film Institute, 1983).

[6] B. Ruby Rich, "From Repressive Tolerance to Erotic Liberation: *Maedchen in Uniform*," *Ibid.* pp. 100–131. Page numbers in text refer to this volume.

[7] Cf. Mary Ann Doane, "The 'Woman's Film': Possession and Address," and Linda Williams, "When a Woman Looks," both in *Re-Vision*. Page numbers refer to this anthology.

[8] Cf. Mary Ann Doane, "Woman's Stake in Representation: Filming The Female Body," *October* 17 (1981), 23–36.

[9] Christine Gledhill, "Developments in Feminist Film Criticism," reprinted in *Re-Vision*, pp. 18–48. Page numbers refer to that volume.

[10] Linda Williams, "When the Woman Looks," In *Re-Vision*, pp. 83–99. Page numbers refer to this volume.

[11] Linda Williams, " 'Something Else Besides a Mother': *Stella Dallas* and the Maternal Melodrama," *Cinema Journal* 24:1 (Fall 1984): 2–27. Cf. also following debate on this film by E. Ann Kaplan, *Cinema Journal* 24:2 (Winter 1985):40–44; and by P. Petro, C. Flinn and Kaplan in *Cinema Journal* 25:1 (Fall 1985): 50–54.

[12] Teresa de Lauretis, "Oedipus Interruptus," *Wide Angle* 7, 1–2 (1985), p. 34–41. Issues raised here are further developed in de Lauretis' recent book, *Alice Doesn't: Feminism, Semiotics, Cinema* (Bloomington: Indiana University Press, 1984).

[13] Cf. Tony Bennett, "Texts in History: The Determinations of Readings and Their Texts." Paper read at the Southampton University Conference on History and Post-Structuralism, July 1983, p.11. This essay is forthcoming in a volume edited by Derek Attridge et al. and to be published by Cambridge University Press, 1986.

[14] Cf. Teresa de Lauretis, "Now and Nowhere: Roeg's *Bad Timing*," *Re-Vision*, p.166.

[15] I discuss this issue at some length in a forthcoming study of rock videos,

Rocking Around the Clock: Music Television, Postmodernism and Consumer Culture, (London and New York: Methuen, 1987).

16 Cf. in particular the work by David Bordwell, Janet Staiger and Kristin Thompson as represented in their recent book *The Classical Hollywood Film* (New York: Columbia University Press, 1984). But cf. also work by Russell Merrit, Robert C. Allen and Douglas Gomery. Allen and Gomery's recent text, *Film History: Theory and Practice* (New York: Knopf, 1985) summarizes recent film history issues.

17 Cf. *Motherhood and Representation* (London and New York: Routledge, 1988).

HERMENEUTICS AND CINEMA: THE ISSUE OF HISTORY

Dudley Andrew

I.

For forty years film studies has flirted with phenomenology, never officially adopting it as a legitimate research attitude, yet never able to dismiss its peculiar appeal. Just as cinema has often presented itself as a special mode of thinking or representing life, so phenomenology has pledged itself to come to grips with the multifarious logics by which we live. Who is not drawn to its claim to think with and through experience, and who is not likewise obsessed with precisely the experience of the movies? In an earlier summary I sketched the erratic history of phenomenology in film studies, suggesting in conclusion that there was no turning back the clock to recover a lost research paradigm.[1] How, then, to go forward inspired by a project whose original ambitions have been largely abandoned? Vivian Sobchak will soon publish a book that promises to bring Merleau-Ponty up to date and up to the cinema, confronting our dominant academic attitudes with a renewed phenomenology.[2] But even before that major book is out and is evaluated, the heritage of phenomenology can be seen, and can be pushed, in much current work, especially in post-structuralism (Jean-Louis Schefer[3] and Gilles Deleuze)[4] and more obviously in hermeneutics. Certainly both these tendencies have questioned, in quite different ways, the regency of the "I" of phenomenology. Yet both have nevertheless been willing to entertain as necessary the priority of experience over system, or at least the vulnerability of system in confrontation with the life of private and cultural history.

The real challenge to any vestige of phenomenology in film study has unquestionably come from history. This decade of the eighties has seen an important turn by theorists in the direction of history and away from the essentializing speculation of so much semiotics and psychoanalysis. Issues of a changing canon of texts to be studied, of shifting types of spectators, and of power relations in film production and dissemination dominate our journals and classrooms. What is there for phenomenology to contribute or object to in this basically Marxist thrust? How does a phenomenologist confront texts as historically constituted? How does he confront himself, or she herself, as an historically constituted being? If history is the "meaning" of the past, is there any place for the category of "experience"investing that meaning? It seems obvious to me that the trenchant phenomenologist has two choices here, either toward a postmodernism that flattens the past and makes everything simultaneous in the present, or toward a hermeneutics that would adopt the chore of being responsible to a past that exists only insofar as the present "cares" about it. It is this latter direction I choose to take in the following speculations, and I will do so with reference to a specific present (1988) and a specific past (French cinema and culture in the thirties) because I am necessarily involved in both.

The task of this essay is grand, to accommodate the situation of the subject to the apparently concrete facade of the institutions of the past. Note the theological origins of such a hermeneutics which has always been the accommodations (through interpretation) of the desires of the individual soul to that most formidable institution of all, the Bible. Just as the Bible can be taken as making a call on each subject, so also, I am arguing, can the past, particularly when the past addresses us through those artistic self-representations that, unlike proclamations or legal documents, are alive in our archives and movie theaters.[5]

II

To make explicit the link between a bygone phenomenology and a workable cultural hermeneutics let's begin in the manner of the former. As a film historian, I must be, first of all, not an historian at all. I am a natural and cultural being who has, for irrelevant biographical and psychological reasons, hardly apparent to myself, shaped a life in large part after the representation afforded me in motion pictures, or rather, in certain movies.

What does it mean to be fascinated by film history? We know what it means to the specialist: the obsession with archives, rare films, rarer documents, chance interviews; the tabulated facts worked into a thesis capable of countering some received notion or some competing thesis. If history ultimately means this to me it has only happened by virtue of a meandering journey.

What does film history mean to someone bearing the natural attitude? It means the drive to fill out and make good on the promise of encounters with films: the first experience of *Hotel du Nord*, of *L'Atalante*, and of *La Petite Lise*, experiences I count among my most formative. Equally important was my disappointment with *Une Partie du compagne*, then, later, my disappointment with myself for having ever not seen it for the brilliant film it was. What had changed? Surely not the Renoir. What had I been to have missed my first chance with it? No matter, I've found it now. Or rather I've found a history that makes it part of me now.

To be so interested in certain films, and then in a kind of film (French film), may lead to a scenario of what is, essentially, research: the viewing of as many films as possible, the reading of biographies of directors and standard film historians. Then come cultural histories, appointments made with other artworks, and perhaps even economic studies of the industry. Political and social studies put all this in their ultimate context, unless one is inclined to ruminate on the endeavor itself and to crown one's investigation through historiographic speculation.

How natural a scenario is this? At what point does a quest for knowledge replace fidelity to some original experience and the hopes it offered? One might as well ask this question of human relations. When a chance meeting develops into a friendship, one follows out the promises of that meeting, growing to understand what one expected all along was there, yet didn't fully know. One may change oneself along the way, but only so as to be faithful to that original promise of value.

History, in the natural attitude, is like this. It begins in narcissism but is open to self-denial. This explains the popular appeal of epics and family histories, as individuals and whole cultures seek themselves in their parents, hoping to expand as they explain themselves, certain of finding their origins valuable. But it also explains the hope of every psychoanalytic journey, every descent into the past striving not just to recover a truer or expanded self, but to redirect the present in relation to that past.

This "sentimental" stance toward the partial otherness of the past forces the historian to replay, in a particularly dramatic way, the give-and-take of identity and difference that makes up the hermeneutics of culture. We might classify the old and new historiography as striving in one case at sameness and in the other at difference. Every teleological history, from Hesiod to Spengler and Croce, represents what has happened as producing what now exists. For Mussolini, the Italian state of 1930 was the Roman empire. The same is true of most film histories, based as they are on the progress of the art. Jean Mitry has announced that this is the only attitude possible, that every history is a history of self, showing how what seems strange became what is so familiar, ourselves.[6] Even when such histories find our own age to be debased in certain respects, it is the identity of past and present that condemns us; we are viewed as unworthy inheritors of an heroic past, but we are inheritors all the same, called upon to change ourselves into that proper self displayed so luminously in earlier epochs.

More recent historiography, represented foremost by the Annales school, claims to forego such a narrative of identity, searching instead for structures and problems that persist beyond change. Their goal is to represent the conditions of life at play even in moments that have usually interested us only as they pointed to us. The striking difference of medieval behavior, thought, and motivation is explicable only through the intense survey of the material conditions of daily life. Why are such differences worth pursuing? Because they hold out to us the possibilities of being other than we are. In cinema, perhaps we might cite Nöel Burch as striving to write that other history against the grain, the history of cinemas that didn't become our own (the Japanese before 1945, Europe before 1912, the avant-garde of the 50's).[7] There is a humanist ethic in this approach as well. If historians represent other ways of life, isn't it to give oppositional groups today, or oppositional impulses within the dominant group, an opportunity to represent new possibilities? Hence difference exists as a possibility for us. Its name is "value."

Historians represent the values of the past for the present. Neither in the pictures of the past they give us nor in the perspective these

pictures insist upon are historians innocent of value. These are com-
monplaces of historiography.

III

Now what of the cinema or, rather, of films? The lessons recalled
above regarding history in general must keep us from extremes that
might popularly be termed subjective and objective. If we would
recover films so as to listen to their otherness, we can't allow our first
and private immersion in them to absorb all they might have to say.
On the other hand, returning them to their proper, public place in
some precise pattern of the past makes them safe, which is to say,
dead. Hermeneutics offers a productive way to avoid these traps that
lie at the end of an unenlightened phenomenology on one side and
a blind structuralism on the other. A hermeneutic historiography
would be attentive to textual possibilities and their historical actual-
ization in those works that call to us. It would recognize the specifically
cultural life of films, where culture implies both institutions and sensibility.

What do the films that capture us bring, or drag, with them onto
the the screen? If we are truly interested not in our own experience
but in the possible significance of that which we have experienced,
we must recover the full discourse these films advance. Effectively the
film historian must move from close analysis to cultural politics by
noting and explicating the textual strategies at play in the cinematic
discourse. In this way one can aim not to recreate things as they were
but to construct a picture of life from a perspective one is led to adopt
by the films themselves.

IV

The basic problematic of phenomenology, when turned toward
history, and specifically toward the French cinema of the thirties,
permits us to recognize the existence of two fully opposed ways of
writing film history: a chronicle of masterworks on the one side and
a social, even economic approach to the situations of cinema on the
other. The chronicle approach, best represented internationally by

Lotte Eisner,[8] is upheld in French cinema by Georges Sadoul,[9] despite his self-proclaimed social orientation. To such historicans the cinema is an institution capable at all times of permitting artistic expression of the highest order. At certain times, the momentum of good films raises the quality of every film produced in that period. These are the highpoints of a national cinema. Sadoul identifies the impressionist period as one of these and the poetic realist cinema 1937–39 as another. Between these luminous periods French cinema as an institution struggled; nevertheless even in the doldrums of 1929–35 certain great works appeared and lent respectability to the history of French cinema: Jean Vigo and René Clair were responsible for these. To Sadoul the poetic realist school developed out of this tradition. He offers no explanation for the production of good movies other than the precedent of other films that increased the quality of every production. Sadoul's goal is to describe the trajectory of the most important trends in French cinema, trends epitomized by masterworks.

This method derives from a venerable heritage in art history. Material and social determinations, such as changes in technology or in the social function of art, are mentioned only to the degree that they directly cultivate the terrain propitious for the emergence of new schools of art, new masterworks. Eisner, and perhaps Sadoul, believe that what remains of history are not the social situations that films were made within but the films themselves, the best films, as testimony both to their times and to the timeless artistic spirit. These can inspire us today to ever greater visions of cinematic art. And they remind us of the specifically French contribution to what the cinema can express.

Such a humanist vision is all too familiar, its problems well understood. The collaborative nature of film production, its status as a popular entertainment, its sensitivity to censorship, to economic vicissitudes, and technological revolutions . . . all these factors would seem to demand a social history of the institution of cinema rather than an art history of a few of its products. In the past decade we have had such social histories, specifically in the work of Francis Courtade, Jean-Pierre Jeancolas and more recently François Garçon.[10] Jeancolas, who addresses the period that concerns me, the 1930's, freely admits that his primary interest is social history rather than aesthetic history. As he points out, fewer than 10% of the 1200 films produced in this decade were films by auteurs. More than 1000 films would be forgotten by Sadoul, yet by their very number they must reveal the times they lived and died within. Jeancolas characterizes this as an "ostriche" cinema,[11] hiding from current political crises by looking back to the belle epoque. The majority of these films take place in high-class settings, with large living rooms, divans, lacquered floors, always the same. The films demonstrate that the country as a whole refused political reality.

Some reviews have criticized his approach for its excessively sociological focus. Marc Cherrie writing in *Cahiers du Cinéma* complained:

Il n'apprend rien sur les films eux-mêmes (sauf les oubliés et ce n'est pas son but), tout l'interêt du livre est de faire constamment le lien entre ces films et, en amont, la société et les circonstances dans lesquelles ils sont produits; en aval, les conditions dans lesquelles ils sont reçus.[12]

Even if this is not a fair critique of Jeancolas' important study, I want to use it to mark the extreme opposite of Sadoul. For a sociological history of cinema might very well dissolve the films back into the conditions that brought them into being. The cinema here is employed as a convenient conduit to the past. It is the past that interests this type of historian, so much so that he might abandon the cinema if a better index were available to him.

Between these two extremes, the masterworks approach and the sociological approach, I hope to insert a hermeneutic attitude that will pay close attention to films as forces in history. This attitude assumes that the cinema does not exist in some timeless realm of art but neither is it a mere by-product of social history. Cinema contributes to history by providing each era with the means to represent itself. To study such representations is to seek methodically to understand the possibilities envisioned by an epoch. In so doing it can only tell us about the possibilities we imagine for ourselves as we return, with nostalgia or obsession, to a former time.

V

What does the hermeneutic attitude imply in relation to film history? It invites the three-step process that Paul Ricoeur has so often written about: a movement from understanding to explanation and from explanation to comprehension.[13] In this division Sadoul practices the understanding or appreciation of French films, as do most auteur studies (Claude Beylie's affectionate essays on Renoir, for instance). Every mature culture will question the easy extension of an artist's values out into the discourse of appreciation, forcing a "hermeneutics of suspicion" that claims not to relish but to explain the existence and the attraction of these films. Here we distance ourselves from our own feelings, putting the object within those larger systems necessary for its appearance. A masterpiece like *La Grande Illusion* becomes one of 128 films made in 1937. Its themes and style, its production, exploitation, and reputation are established and explained by painstaking research.

This second phase of the hermeneutic process constitutes most of what takes place in academic study. No wonder the school of appreciation has given way to the school of sociological explanation, for books are now written primarily by scholars for other scholars and their students. Analysis and distance are required by the rhetoric of the academy, whereas enthusiasm and appreciation properly constitute discussion at cine-clubs.

Ricoeur sees a third approach possible after our enthusiasm has been tempered by suspicion. This is the moment of comprehension, when we return to the work and use it to elaborate a vision of life in its terms. Comprehension differs from innocent and spontaneous understanding by submitting to the otherness of what it comprehends, whereas our initial understanding of anything always occurs in relation to ourselves. The distance gained in the analytical moment permits us to treat the work as different from ourselves, as offering possibilities not available to us. Here one can recognize the social gain hermeneutics has made over the phenomenology it is based on, recognizing as well the particular aptness of history as a subject, for history is at once personal and alien.

In turning to France in the thirties one needn't rely on masterpieces speaking timeless truths directly to us in 1988. But neither can we simply employ these films as inert indexes of their times. They are in fact discourses that can speak to us today but that spoke differently to their culture when they first appeared. They are models offered at a specific cultural moment, models that had to compete with other models just to be made, models that served social needs different from our own. In this way the film is something smaller than an "eternal truths of art" but larger than a mere fragment of 1930s culture, like some newspaper editorial or government decree.

To begin such a project requires a vision of history, of culture, and of the cinema. Here is a sketch of such a vision, beginning with a general perspectivist notion of history.

VI

How do we conceive of history in order to write it? An analogy with perceptual psychology will most quickly clarify my view. History is with us in the way perception is with us: constantly, seldom questioned, required for orientation, occasionally tested. It is a construction, but one that is fed by indisputable cues. It varies somewhat from culture to culture but it always results in real consequences for us as we negotiate our environment with varied projects. We scrutinize our historical field only when a discrepancy arises between what we and others make of a specific case, or when someone points to a case. We may also toy with the past experimentally, as we toy with perceptual tricks just to see what might happen if we stare at something through a filter, or a lens, or while on drugs. Artists are professionals who toy with perception; historians play the same role with the past.

E.H. Gombrich, from whom I borrow this notion of perceptual activity and its relation to art, provided the terms for a direct reflection on history in his essay "Moment and Movement."[14] How, he asks, is movement to be represented when St. Augustine and others have shown the impossibility of seeing the whole in the part or of cutting a flow into discrete units at all? Art history (and film history as conceived of by the likes of Eisner and Sadoul) has traditionally presented artworks as those privileged moments onto which condense the rest of their discourse. Between artworks flows the stream of time providing continuity to these rocks of culture, rocks we can use to ford our way to the present as we seek a proper trajectory into the future.

Our more modern view deconstructs this analogy. We sense artworks not as solid objects but as mobile bundles of tension and contradiction whose truths we can never quite get at. We have been inspired more by Monet's shimmering, multiple Cathedral at Rouen than by the rock of the Cathedral itself. Artworks, like perceptual moments, are provisional organizations of fragmentary elements that threaten to disband the next moment. All representations, whether artworks, chronicles, discourses of all sorts, seek to contain *movement* in a *moment* of understanding. Gombrich's essay examines the strategies by which moments suggest and call up the real movement of perceptual life. I consider history to be precisely a set of strategies in discourse capable of calling up and bringing to life the real movement of the past. For Gombrich perception operates by imposing a schema onto a situation and testing the adequacy of the result, adjusting the schema when necessary. I believe the same holds true for history, as we press a certain viewpoint on the myriad facts of the past.

Gombrich claims that our minds select, or filter, only certain kinds of fact, from an indefinite amount of potentially given material. Scanning a crowd we are able to pick out a friend by means of a few cues (the cock of the head, a style of hat). The same is true for the street we live on and even for unfamiliar locales in which we are led to identify likely objects and relationships on the basis of "constancies" brought forward from all our previous perceptual experience. The horizon line is one such constancy that has served us well, at least until the advent of space travel.

Artists question these constancies of perception, these habitual ways of solidifying the flow of perception. They shift the focus to a formerly nonpertinent aspect. Monet, for example, makes us take account of the particles of light reflected from the the cathedral rather than the structure of the building itself and he does so by altering his pictorial schema, the way he applies paint and interrelates color. Now a historian likewise helps us to recognize our past by indicating it with a limited number of cues. The new historian will defamiliarize the past by attending to some previously irrelevant or impertinent set of details, or some level of understanding that had always been filled in as a constant: thus psycho-history, statistical history, institutional history, and so on change the level or the focus of historical understanding, just as Monet reconceived what constituted the schema for perception.

This relativist version of history coincides with the nominalist philosophy of Nelson Goodman.[15] An artifact from the past implies a world it came from and was directed to. History books frequently assert this in their very titles: the "world" of the Cathedral, for example, or the "world" of Monet. By shifting our focus of attention, we alter the world we live in along with its substances. The chemist on vacation swims in water quite different from the water which he analyses in the lab or puts in his whiskey at night. His interest in each case is water, but water from three quite different worlds he inhabits. So it is with the past, as we attend, according to our needs or desires, to different centers of focus. Whenever we change focus, new aspects of the past come into view, just as the light reflected from the cathedral shifts minute by minute.

Unknowable in itself, the past releases knowledge to us whenever we isolate some pertinent element that forces the whole into a configuration that matters. These configurations are not true in the strict sense of the term, but they can be shown to be more or less adequate to their purposes or for the social groups who depend on them. We can check their congruence to other schemas that we rely on; we can inquire of their fertility. Floating schemas filter and interpret the shimmering energy of light that changes each instant even while it promises information. This is the state of history as I see it.

VII

Every history that treats the cinema must calculate the importance of films within a world larger than film. This larger world, defined differently by Eisner, Sadoul, Courtade, Jeancolas, etc., is nothing other than culture. From the perspective of the film scholar, culture surrounds the film like an atmosphere. The historical world around film is comprised of numerous spheres, as numerous as we want. It is generally sufficient to identify these as though they successively encompass one another from the center, the individual film, out toward the stratosphere, political structures and events. In between we find such layers as film history, the history of the arts, of culture and society. Every historian seeks what appears to be the most pertinent sphere within which to view the value of cinema.

But these spheres are also permeable, so that disturbances in one may have consequences in another. For example, a change of government may bring in a new minister of culture leading to the fostering of literary journals in the cultural sphere. These journals may, in turn, develop an aesthetic that works its views on the current theater. Ultimately film acting, which so often monitors theatrical fashion, may literally lead toward the creation of new kinds of roles and toward a new cinematic style.

The spheres are really names for kinds of constancies that make up every historical representation. If changes occur at one level, for instance the economic depression of 1934, they can be tracked in relation to the constancies in the political or cultural spheres, where they help produce new patterns within familiar territory: it is not a matter of events changing, but of our view of them changing. In the arena of film history changes tend to occur when a lost film is discovered and demands reviewing, or when a new idea such as the notion of "institution" suddenly imposes itself upon our imagination, forcing a repatterning throughout the spheres. More commonly some particular element, formerly invisible or irrelevant, gains center focus, is isolated by the historian in such a way as to produce a reconstituted representation of the past. The Annales historians have shown this over and over.

The inadequacy of every history of French film in the thirties can be blamed on an understandable but deadening fixity of focus whereby the cinema is seen within the optic of a single sphere whose importance is most often assumed. Short focus is always the major problem in the masterpiece approach, but it affects the broader studies as well. When François Courtade treats films within the atmospheres of official history (political proclamations, etc.) and official events in the film world (technological innovations like sound, economic developments like the fall of Gaumont), he takes for granted the pertinence of this context not just for France but for every national cinema in every epoch. Yet isn't the pertinence of a given context dependent on the historical moment; so that while we can choose to study films through official, public events, doing so may mask a more lively context within which the films under consideration seem to take on-life? For example, I would look to cultural subgroups, such as the surrealists or the novelists published by Gallimard, as a sphere of historical life more pertinent to the reach and importance of French cinema than the all-too-visible public life chronicled in newspapers and trade journals.

Obviously this wouldn't hold in every instance. I imagine that in revolutionary eras, such as Russia of the twenties, the film historian is right to follow closely the major events of public life, since film explicitly participated in a national reawakening. But in the interwar period of France, the daily life spheres remained relatively stable. The social disturbances that did occur led to no serious revolts nor foreign wars. Cinema, in short, was seldom enlisted to serve directly political goals. Despite the economic depression which reached its nadir in 1934 and the growing international pressures, from Hitler on the right and Stalin on the left, the cinema seldom responded to the public realities of the times. Yet the unsettled national psychology, pressured by such upheavals as a million Italian refugees arriving in southern France and the ominous events in Spain, had to spill over into the cinema, even when that cinema sought to repress such problems.

The official look of life, one promoted by the government and the cinema alike, provided the illusion of continuity. France was level-headed, while Italy, Germany, Spain, and Russia had to deal with extreme political leaderships. But breaks could be seen and felt everywhere under the surface. Terrible pressure was felt in the social fabric. It was felt most dramatically no doubt at the level of the haute bourgeoisie who lost control of national decisions. Social life seemed determined more than ever before from below, from the needs and demands of workers. By 1935 of course this situation was explicit with the rise of the Popular Front. The future was also felt to be in the hands of those outside France. Innumerable political refugees in Paris made that city, despite appearances, a capital fighting a cultural civil war.

While the cinema participated in retaining the illusion of normalcy, some films did break through this surface to glimpse the yawning cavern of a horrendous future beneath. Even most standard films mapped fault lines and danger zones despite themselves. In this, the French cinema of the thirties has much in common with the cinema of our own age, differing, for instance, from the Soviet cinema of the twenties or even the French cinema of the late fifties, called the New Wave. Most important, the cinema in the thirties must be recognized as avoiding the political sphere, making its mark somewhere between established and popular culture. This is the zone my film history would map.

Like the politics of the time, the established cultural sphere of the Third Republic in its final decade gave the appearance of immutability. The universities preached the old values in a standard way which the government fostered through its normal channels of support and benign censorship. These were the values of the haute bourgeoisie, and they appeared firmly in place within the institutions of culture.

Underneath and to the side, however, spontaneous counter-institutions arose. Worker's theater as an alternative to the Comédie Française; Sartre, Nizan, Mounier, and Kojéve as an alternative to official Sorbonne philosophy; surrealism as an alternative to everything. The cultural outlets of publishing, the stage, music and the cinema all began to turn to a more popular audience. The largest change surely resulted from audio technology, from radio and talking film. To conservatives a new, much larger audience could now be addressed patronizingly from above. To liberals, indigenous popular forms of representation, arising from below, could potentially renew a moribund culture.

We have dropped from the stratosphere of politics, through social and cultural institutions down to the artistic sphere, where a distinctive populist tone can be noted everywhere. To me this tone, and this sphere, gives the cinema of the period its particular value, that is, the value that it retains for us today. Take the social aspirations of music (with "les six" turning to radio and cinema), or the Marxist turn of writers like Eluard and Aragon who just a decade earlier had performed only for themselves or for those overripe decadents of the higher classes who fawned over Cocteau and Picabia. No doubt even in 1935 suitably reassuring concerts were performed at the Salle Pleyel and the Opera; surely the Comédie Française continued to stage Molière. Nevertheless an increasing amount of cultural energy flowed into the margins, registered in upstart journals like *Ésprit* and in the cafe round tables at Montparnasse and St. Germain. From the margins it appeared obvious that the civilization was in crisis. Would the cinema register, or even promote, this view of crisis? I believe so.

Crisis thought and the representation of a coming chaos spewed from the pens of Céline, Drieu la Rochelle, and Malraux. Former aesthetes like Gide turned to Russia for guidance or turned to the lower classes for the audience of the future. This can be felt most clearly in the popular theater and in the novel, forms of representation that grew in weight while poetry and painting declined. It was precisely these popular forms that opened most readily onto the soundstages of the cinema.

At the level of the institution of the cinema we naturally expect the most pronounced changes to be visible, for this is the site of our interest. The technological revolution of sound, for example, is an event specific to cinema history, but it had profound cultural consequences, for it provided a voice to some artists while silencing others. Who is permitted to make films in 1930 and under what conditions? We can see that the film culture of the 30s has little in common with the alternate cinema circuit of the 20s, where avant-gardists could affect high culture from the margin with their scandalous Dada and Surreal images. In the 30s one finds an ostensible homogenization of product, since the economics of production in the sound era put everyone, including the likes of Abel Gance and Jean Epstein, at the mercy of the producers. But from my point of view, this levelling is in line with a new ideology of populism, so that the most important personalities in cinema could only smile when the last of the blood of a poet had thankfully been shed and the era of the avant-garde elite had come to an end.

Intellectuals didn't abandon the cinema. Far from it. They volunteered to represent popular life for a formerly invisible working class. Of course the bulk of movies continued to convey upperclass values in drawing room comedies and sentimental melodramas. But into this constant flow of normal films was inserted a new kind of film addressed in a new way to an audience that we can sympathise with today.

Here we glimpse the dramatic consequence of the focus we have chosen. From 1930–1940 the French cinema reversed its sense of the movies: from a carefully displayed theatricalism (in sets, script, acting) to what can best be termed a novelization of the medium. The récit, not the play, became the model of the most ambitious films. The consciousness of the single character, not the public sense of savoir faire, became the criterion of truth. Poetic Realism is the name for the set of films that best exemplify this shift, which is more than a shift in genre or subject. It is a genuine change in the function, the address of the movies.

These films may be taken as still another index of the descent of values both toward the lower classes and toward the individual (we will soon be saying existential) consciousness, as a reaction against the bankruptcy of upper-class visions. But from our focus, these films are not indices but the very models of culture seen from a certain perspective. They represent possible ways of conceiving life, ways open to us today because they became available and necessary in France in the 30s.

VIII

In the section above, I tried to suggest that film history is open to every conceivable level of cultural influence. But I also tried to show that it is the obligation of the historian to determine the levels or spheres of cultural life which are most pertinent to the cinematic culture of any given era. In France of the thirties, this level floats between high and popular culture. Such a realization invites an examination of the novels of MacOrlan, or Marcel Aymé, or Beauclair, or Eugène Dabit, all of whom were noticed by, and interacted with their more famous counterparts at Gallimard, such as André Gide. Gide, through his friendship with Colette and Marc Allegret, had visible effects on the cinema.[16] Martin Du Gard prepared a script of *La Bête Humaine*. St.-Exupéry wrote several scripts. We know about Honegger's scores and Hans Eisler; Lazaare Meerson spent his free hours in Montparnasse with De Chirico, Kokoschka, and Tchelitchew. These interconnections are more than gossip, and they are meant to do more than validate a popular art. I want them to testify to the changes in the function of cinema that one can see from this cultural perspective.

Between the flat language of cinema that a purely social history of the film describes, and the personal style of a few great auteurs, described by a chronicle of masterworks, I insist on a history of cinematic "écriture" in the sense of Barthes' *Le Degré zéro de l'écriture*[17] or of "chronotope"[18] in Bakhtin's sense. Here esthetics and cultural history work together to point to the options available at a given moment for the representation of life. The particular cultural rapport that the cinema holds with established high culture (the literary, musical, artistic figures I have mentioned) permitted the cinema of the thirties to embark here and there on new forms of representation we can describe. These forms in turn had social consequences, affecting not just the films of the day, but the other arts, and the whole cultural atmosphere. To my view, films are neither reflections of society, nor creations of individuals, but discourses in dialogue with culture. Therefore it is necessary to locate first of all the most appropriate interlocutors of films (in my case looking at the casual high culture of cafe-circles, and so on), and then to measure and evaluate the discourse these films did produce.

Here we arrive at the final destination: the place and value of film within a fluctuating cultural history. From the perspective of changing chronotypes, certain films must rise into focus. Many of these are precisely the films that have addressed our own generation. They have been in focus in our ciné-clubs, revival houses, and classrooms. The reason for this should be obvious. If the thirties did produce alternate chronotopes to standard theatrical movies, some of these alternatives have led the way to the kind of cinema we are comfortable with, the kind that still addresses us. Poetic Realism, to be specific, was the most obvious achievement of this era, heralding American film noir and several styles of film that continue to be part of our current system of representation. With a "progression of styles" in mind many films, formerly unheralded, suddenly become interesting: *La Petite Lise, Gueule d'Amour, Le Grand Jeu, Amok*. They helped prepare a new sort of spectator, the kind of spectator we have become.

The prophetic works of someone like Jean Vigo are also held up in a history of cinematic "écriture," for Vigo's failure to find a public in his own day was a problem of phasure. Reviews in *Pour Vous* of *L'Atalante*[19] recognize that this will be a very difficult film for French audiences comfortable with a cinema based on dialogue. Vigo's visual density necessarily confused this audience. Jean Vidal goes so far as to compare *L'Atalante* to Céline,[20] confirming the aptness of the context we have chosen, while at the same time reminding us that the public for the cinema and the novel is by no means congruent. Céline's fiction serves as a beacon of what the cinema may become. Vigo, living densely in his epoch, is another beacon, one barely noted in his day, but brilliant to observers today.

While Vigo and Renoir surely hungered for contemporary success, they just as surely aimed to change the rules of artistic discourse so that their films could be received by a culture ready for them. If it took years for these changes to come into effect, if *Rules of the Game* is often cited today as the greatest French film, though Renoir madly recut it to help stave off the utter disdain with which it was received in 1939, we cannot say that such films are not of their times.

Despite the genius of Vigo or Renoir, the film history I have been discussing can't be understood in an heroic manner. Barthes' term "écriture" insists upon the collective struggle, rather than the privileged products of history. The very business of cinema, with its problems of distribution, censorship, limited production, and collaborative labor, makes us see it as the site of fights over the nature of representation, over the right to represent experience in such and such a way. This social struggle involves geniuses, no doubt, but ones who can hardly be termed "lone." In 1933 André Gide supported his friends Colette and Marc Allegret in their project to adapt Vicki Baum's *Lac aux Dames*. This same year he joined an association of artists against fascism, the AEAR, that many historians feel made possible the Popular Front.[21] Did his presence inspire Prévert, who next worked with Allegret on *Hotel de libre échange?* Did Prévert then inspire Renoir in the subsequent *Crime de M. Lange?* Gide's presence certainly contributed to the prestige of an emerging "écriture," one that would turn the best French films away from its theatrical heritage and toward the *récit*.

Naturally we are partial to this progression of film that points to what we think cinema should be. Doesn't the French cinema of this period intrigue us because of the continuity of the Popular Front tradition, resurrected dramatically in 1968 and again in 1980 with the election of Mitterand? Do these hopes and suspicions tie us to the projects and feelings of Vigo, Clair, Renoir, Duvivier, and Carné? But no matter what our original motivation might be, the historical attitude it provokes can take us swiftly to the arena of the thirties itself as we seek not so much the truth of what these films were trying to say, but their need to speak in such and such a way. What pressures, competitions, passions, forced these films into production? Not only can we be inspired by the drama of their creation; we can learn to listen to registers that might have escaped our ears tuned as they are to the shrill discourse of our own epoch. In sum, the interest we show in these films doubtless arose in response to the current of our contemporary situation, but that interest can be paid back by the capital invested in the past, in a situation not really like our own. In this way we acknowledge both our distance from and our proximity to texts, as we stand ready to be instructed by their rhetoric.

Thus, although we may have entered the era of the thirties attracted by the glories of Renoir and Vigo, we encounter there other chronotopes, foreign to us; the boulevard comedies of Yves Mirande, the bravado address of Sacha Guitry and, in a different way, of Abel Gance. These chronotopes did not survive, but in the thirties they did permit a particular kind of representation of experience that a cultural history can uncover.

In sum, a cultural history of cinema must proceed neither through the direct appreciation of the films of a period nor through the direct amassing of "relevant facts" about that period, but through an indirect reconstruction of the conditions of representation that permitted such films to be made, to be understood, even to be misunderstood, as controversial, or trivial. For while the cinema may point to real differences in a culture's self-image, it can also in fact produce such differences. Every film history sensitive to its subject must strive to trace the ghost of this possibility.

IX

I have determined to put into focus the address of films, the *écriture* of periods and the development of spectatorship because, as a spectator myself, it is films which seem to address me. I would maximize my rapport with them by distancing myself from myself, by attending to the event of their broadcast, the history that made them speak in the way they do. This protects me from the narcissism of teleological histories which force the past to submit to the rule of the present and which neatly suggest a single world of the movies. But it protects me as well from the professionalism which locates patterns of elements in an archive utterly cut off from us.[22]

The hermeneutic enterprise I advocate comes from a desire to pay tribute to the ground of all worlds by reaching out of my own world into that offered by the past. The films that have beckoned me are entrances to a different way of being a spectator, not totally different (else I could never intuit that they have something there for me) but different enough that I must construct the spectator to which they are addressed, must understand not their style so much as the *écriture* that makes them possible and that at the same time models a possible world for me. As an historian, I am a spectator ready to become another spectator.

NOTES

[1] Dudley Andrew, "The Neglected Tradition of Phenomenology," in Bill Nichols, ed., *Movies and Methods II* (Berkeley; University of California Press, 1985), 625–31

[2] Vivian Sobchak, *The Address of the Eye* (Princeton: Princeton University Press, forthcoming)

[3] Jean-Louis Schefer, *L'Homme ordinaire du cinéma* (Paris: Gallimard, 1981)

[4] Gilles Deleuze, *L'Image Mouvement* (Paris: Minuit, 1983)

[5] See Chapter 10, "Interpretation" in my *Concepts in Film Theory* (New York: Oxford University Press, 1984).

[6] Jean Mitry in a statement made at the August, 1985 Colloque de Cerisy-la-Salle, France.

[7] Noël Burch, *To the Distant Observer* (Berkeley: University of California Press, 1979); and "Propositions," *Afterimage 5* (Spring 1974), 40–67.

[8] Lotte Eisner, *The Haunted Screen* (Berkeley: University of California Press, 1969)

[9] Georges Sadoul, *Le Cinéma français* (Paris: Flammarion, 1962)

[10] Francis Courtade, *Les Maledictions du cinéma français* (Paris: Alain Moreau, 1978); Jean-Pierre Jeancolas, *Les 15 ans des années trentes* (Paris: Stock, 1983); Francois Garcon, *De Blum à Petain* (Paris: Cerf, 1984)

[11] Jeancolas, "Pésanteurs Sociologiques du cinéma francais," *Le Cinémathèque Quebecoise* (Montreal: June, 1976)

[13] Paul Ricoeur, *Interpretation Theory: Discourse anad the Surplus of Meaning* (Fort Worth: TCU Press, 1977).

[14] E.H.Gombrich, "Moment and Movement in Art," in *The Image and the Eye* (Ithaca, NY: Phaidon Books, 1982), 40–62

[15] Nelson Goodman, *Ways of Worldmaking* (Indianapolis: Hackett, 1978). See also Chapter 3, "Representation," in my *Concepts in Film Theory*.

[16] Denise Tual, *Le Temps devoré* (Paris: Fayard, 1980).

[17] Roland Barthes, *Le Degré zero de l'écriture* (Paris: Seuil, 1953), translated as *Writing Degree Zero* (Boston: Beacon, 1970).

[18] Mikael Bakhtin, "Forms of Time and of Chronotope in the Novel," in *The Dialogic Imagination*, edited by M. Holquist (Austin: University of Texas Press, 1981)

[19] Elie Faure, "Un Nouveau film de Jean Vigo," *Pour Vous* 283 (May 31, 1934)

[20] Jean Vidal, review of *L'Atalante* in *Pour Vous* 305 (September 20, 1934).

[21] Tual, pp. 91–98.

[22] Alexander Trauner, "Interview" in *Positif* 223 (October, 1979), p. 12.

EXPRESSIVE COHERENCE AND THE "ACTED IMAGE"

James Naremore

"I now see thinking as just a way of behaving, and behaving socially at that. It's something that the whole body takes part in, with all its senses."
—the Actor in Brecht's *Messingkauf Dialogues*, 1940

"There's an old rule in Hollywood that when your face is up there on the screen in a closeup, if you don't believe the line you're speaking, the audience will know it, and they won't believe it either."
—Ronald Reagan, quoted in *Time* magazine, 1986

I

At one level, an informal conversation between friends can allow for a good deal of incoherence, inconsistency, or irrelevance: speeches may overlap, persons may glance away from one another, insignificant movements or interruptions may occur. At another level, however, the situation is quite different. Most of the people we meet at close quarters are quick to spot affective discrepancies or inappropriate "vibes" in our behavior. The smallest signs of distraction, weariness, or irritation can stand out in the midst of an ostensibly friendly exchange, and inappropriate degrees of sympathy, interest, or amusement can easily be detected. The flicker of an eyelid, the hint of a smile, the movement of a hand—any muscular tension or minor fluctuation of tone can threaten to disrupt the emotional unity of an everyday performance. As a result intimate social behavior follows a rule of expressive coherence, a formal logic which operates just as rigorously in ordinary life as it does in professional theater.

195

When exchanges become more public, they grow increasingly theatrical, so that players are required to observe what Erving Goffmann
describes as "synecdochic responsibility", maintaining not only a coherence of manner but also a fit between setting, costume, and behavior.[1] The movies often exploit this situation for comic or dramatic
effect: princesses are not supposed to remove their shoes in court, as
Audrey Hepburn tries to do in *Roman Holiday* (1953), and the ex
British Vice-Consul in Mexico is not supposed to attend a formal
dinner without socks, as Albert Finney discovers in *Under the Volcano*
(1984). In this sense we are all actors, and our performances are judged
at nearly every moment of our lives. We prove our expertise whenever
we participate in rituals, whenever we carry off lies, or whenever we
do our jobs competently in the midst of personal grief or pain. In fact
we often employ Stanislavskian techniques on these occasions, learning emotional recall, imaginatively projecting ourselves into a role,
using the "creative *if*" to make ourselves partly believe what we do.[2]
Even when our presentation is utterly sincere we remain actors of a
sort, because the expression of "true" feeling is itself a socially conditioned behavior. As Brecht has written:

> One easily forgets that human education proceeds along theatrical lines.
> In a quite theatrical manner the child is taught how to behave; logical
> arguments only come later. When such-and-such occurs, it is told (or
> sees), one must laugh. . . . In the same way it joins in shedding tears,
> not only weeping because the grown-ups do so but also feeling genuine
> sorrow. This can be seen at funerals, whose meaning escapes children
> entirely. These are theatrical events which form the character. The
> human being copies gesture, miming, tones of voice. And weeping
> arises from sorrow, but sorrow also arises from weeping.[3]

Our manner of expression is so deeply embedded in the process of
socialization that it becomes spontaneous, instinctive, a part of thinking itself. In this regard it is ironic that various schools of psycho-
therapy (especially in America) have put so much emphasis on
emotional sincerity, using techniques of role-playing in order to make
subjects dramatize past experience. Whatever success this therapy
might have, it resembles nothing so much as a clinical version of the
Actor's Studio, and its devotion to authenticity of expression is mis-
placed. The fact is, all our feelings are wedded to a behavioral *langue*
which we have mastered and turned into an idiolect. Regression to

a childlike state of "natural" emotion would probably result in an undramatic, incoherent sort of performance, less like primal screams and more like amateur acting—for the simple reason that a child has not yet learned to theatricalize a self. We might say, with Terry Eagleton, that the child begins as a "Brechtian actor, performing what he does not truly feel, and by dint of doing so ends up as a professional or Aristotelian one, fully at home with his forms of life."[4]

In either case, we are always copying other actors, never arriving at an unacted emotional essence, even though we become increasingly adept at noticing strains or inconsistencies in the performances of others. For that reason, professional acting could be regarded as part of an unending process—a copy of everyday performances which are themselves copies. In turn, it induces members of the audience to add to the chain of representation by copying what they see, adopting mannerisms for a personal repertory. Perhaps Hollywood movies give us pleasure and a sense of "identification" simply because they enable us to recognize and adapt to the fundamentally acted quality of everyday life: they place us in a safe position outside dramatic events, from which we can observe people lying, concealing emotions, or staging performances for one another.

Notice, however, that these performances-within-performance create a major formal difference between professional acting and the presentation of self in society. Ordinary living usually requires us to maintain expressive coherence, assuring others of our sincerity; theater and movies work according to a more complex principle, frequently demanding that actors dramatize situations in which the expressive coherence of a character either breaks down or is revealed as a mere "act." As one example, consider the many occasions where characters either succeed or fail at maintaining expressive coherence in *Double Indemnity* (1944): near the beginning of the film we see Walter Neff (Fred MacMurray) violate the decorum of his role as insurance salesman by engaging in sexy *repartée* with Phyllis Dietrichson (Barbara Stanwyck), the wife of a prospective client. The wife encourages his "improper" performance, matching him in the exchange of double-entendre, showing off an ankle-braceleted leg as if she were a chorus girl instead of a lady interested in life insurance for her husband. Later, having helped Dietrichson commit murder, Neff has to behave with poker-faced calm, putting on a show of professional competence while a man who might identify him as a killer is brought to the

insurance office for questioning. Dietrichson must behave with equal
cool, acting the role of bereaved widow while under the scrutiny of
an ace investigator; in fact she is the best actor of all, because we
discover at the end of the film that her passion for Neff, concealed
so cleverly from the law, is itself a pretense, the device of a *femme
fatale*.

Sometimes we are as much taken in by these performances as the
other characters in the drama; sometimes we know that a character
is behaving falsely because the plot has given us that information; and
sometimes we can see indications of deception on a face, even when
these signs are invisible to other players in the scene. Thus Stanwyck's
work in *Double Indemnity* is somewhat different from her earlier appearance in *Stella Dallas* (1934), where she is given many opportunities
to display expressive incoherence quite openly. Phyllis Dietrichson
is a cool and skillful performer who seldom steps out of character,
but the whole point about Stella Dallas is that she never successfully
manages the roles she has chosen. Notice the crucial scene where she
offers to give up her beloved daughter to wealthy Helen Morrison.
She tries to behave with polite calm, but all the while we can see her
torment in the way she picks nervously at the arm of a chair and
twists a pair of gloves she holds in her lap.[5]

Such films give us models of human behavior, emphasizing certain
of the characters' lies or misrepresentations, meanwhile showing us
how "true" emotions are expressed. "In this exceedingly serious
sphere," Brecht wrote, "the stage is virtually functioning as a fashion
show, parading not only the latest dresses but the latest ways of
behaving: not only what is being worn but what is being done" (p.
151). As a result, the movies seldom foreground their own techniques
of representation, nor do they venture very far into philosophical
questioning of so-called natural human expression. In other words,
the rule of expressive coherence is broken only at the level of characterization, where we see persons in the drama trying to conceal or
repress their "sincere" feelings. At the level of professional acting
itself, the film requires an absolute coherence, so that everyone plays
in character, never disrupting the unified front of their job. MacMurray
can show Walter Neff concealing anxiety behind a mask of aplomb,
but he cannot deconstruct his own performance of that performance;
Stanwyck can reveal that her character is faking, but she cannot drop
the persona she has adopted for the story. All the actors must "live

the part" at the moment of its realization, in much the same way as we do in everyday life; in fact the closeness and magnification of movie images seems to require them to draw upon the very thought process of the character, creating a seamless fit between emotion and expression. Lawrence Shaffer has described the phenomenon quite accurately:

> We squirm when an actor [in a film] puts on his character's face à la Marcel Marceau. We are transfixed when he simply appears to be "economizing" by using his own face in a kind of transmigratory transference. . . . The faces of certain actors—Brando, Gielgud, Clift, March, Tracy, Bogart—seem to be acutely inner-reflective. These actors seem to be doing a good deal of thinking. Their faces look preoccupied, as if attending to some inner voice, or memory.[6]

The "inner voice" of which Shaffer speaks is a product of that roughly Stanislavskian technique we all use occasionally—an imaginative absorption which turns acting into a form of affective thinking. As I have suggested, however, it is wrong to assume that expression in films is equivalent to the way we behave in daily life. For one thing, most film actors are acutely sensitive to the purely rhetorical need to make "thought" visible for the camera. Moreover, because they *act persons who are acting*, they must sometimes put out signals which reveal this fact to the audience. In these moments where deception or repression are indicated, the drama becomes a type of metaperformance, imposing contrary demands on the players: the need to maintain a unified narrative image, a coherent persona, is matched by an equally strong need to exhibit dissonance or expressive incoherence within the characterization. Thus we could say that the work of realist acting amounts to a concentrated effort at sustaining two mutually distinct and opposing attitudes toward the self: on the one hand it tries to create the illusion of unified, individualized personality, but on the other hand it continually suggests that character is subject to division or dissolution into a variety of social roles.[7]

The two contrary demands on expressive behavior are worth examining more closely, beginning with the actor's need to maintain a consistent persona. To appreciate the virtually obsessive importance of this problem in conventional moviemaking, one need only observe that Pudovkin's classical text, *The Technique of Film Acting*, devotes more space to the "unity of the acted image" than to any other topic.[7]

Indeed Pudovkin's remarks on this and other subjects are symptomatic of mainstream practice; a Stanislavskian conservative whose attitude toward acting differed considerably from the first generation of Soviet avant-garde filmmakers, he often worked with players from the Moscow Art Theater, and his advice was addressed to them. It applies equally well to professional thespians in the Hollywood system, or to anyone who thinks in terms of traditional realism.

Pudovkin begins his study by remarking on a "basic contradiction" between the fragmentary process of shooting and the unified look of the character in the finished product (p. 22). His use of the word "contradiction," however, is misleading. It seems to establish his credentials as a Marxist/Hegelian, whereas his real concern is not to expose conflict at all; at bottom, he is a romantic idealist, and he badly wants to smooth over potential incongruities or disruptions. Thus his entire discussion is grounded in metaphors of organic unity:

> Here let us reaffirm our principal desideratum for acting on both stage and screen. *The aim and object of the technique of the actor is his struggle for unity, for an organic wholeness in the lifelike image he creates.*
>
> But the technical conditions of work on the stage and for the screen impose a number of demands on the actor that perpetually tend to destroy his unity and continuity in the role.
>
> The splitting-up of the performance on the stage into acts, scenes, episodes, the still more subdivided splitting-up of the actor's work in the shooting of a film, set up a corresponding series of obstacles through and over which the entire creative collaborative . . . must combine to carry the organic unity of line of the actor's image (p. 25).

Pudovkin knows that continuity editing can help overcome "obstacles," but he emphasizes the degree to which actors themselves contribute to the illusion of wholeness. As he suggests, the players in naturalist theater have always worked along similar lines. They need to be aware of the difference between what contemporary formalism would call "plot time" and "story time," and they need to convey the sense of *change* which is so important to classic narrative; as a result they usually try to construct a mental bridge across gaps, "living" the part at the level of the story itself, so that a soldier who has gone away to war in act one and returned in act two will seem properly and logically different. Stanislavski had been especially concerned with this effect, and had attempted to assist actors by instituting long periods of "table work" prior to rehearsal, during which everyone discussed and analyzed the full experience of the characters. When the drama itself was presented, he advised everyone to remain partly in character even while they were offstage, feeling their way into events that were elided or not shown; for example a butler who might leave a scene briefly and come back with a serving tray was encouraged to imagine the process of going to the kitchen and returning.

Pudovkin recognizes, however, that film is qualitatively different from theater—its narratives are more elliptical, and the circumstances of production pose an additional threat to actorly coherence. On stage, he notes, three minutes is a relatively short piece of performance time, but in movies it is almost the longest period a camera runs; furthermore, the temporal order of shooting is usually quite different from the temporal order of the plot, so that characterizations are not only broken but scattered, like pieces of a puzzle. As a result, even when the glances and movements of the players are fitted together perfectly in the cutting room, the "acted image" is subject to variations in expressive quality, rhythm, or intensity. (Notice the famous taxicab sequence in *On the Waterfront*, where Brando and Steiger occupy a shared, almost static position for several minutes of screen time, maintaining coherence across three or four camera setups. Here the work of matching movements from one shot to the next is minimal; the real difficulty is in the actors' attempt to sustain emotional "flow," preserving analog changes of mood despite Elia Kazan's busy camerawork. In an interview about this sequence, Steiger has claimed that his own job was made especially tough by the fact that Brando behaved like a *prima donna:* "I don't like Mr. Brando. I'll never forget, or forgive, what he did to me . . . I did the take with him, when the camera was on him, but when it came for the camera to be on me—he went home! I had speak my lines to an assistant director."[8])

Pudovkin believed that carefully shaded, intimate acting, which poses a great many potential conflicts between the rhetoric of the camera and the expression of the players, would require detailed rehearsal and close collaboration between actors and director. Ideally, he wanted the entire story to be performed first like a stage play, so that everyone concerned could bring a Stanislavskian, "organic" vision to the process of shooting; he even suggested an "actor's script" as distinct from a "shooting script," which would enable the players to study their scenes in chronological order, forming a complete mental image of the characters. Few filmmakers before or since—with the qualified exception of D. W. Griffith—have resorted to such elaborate and costly methods, but almost every narrative movie has shown a similar concern for unity, employing some kind of technique that will maintain expressive coherence across shots. Occasionally a director will photograph a scene "around the clock," using multiple cameras (Robert Rossen experimented with this device for some of the more delicate moments in *Lilith* [1963]), but generally the actors have to help, accommodating themselves to long periods of waiting between short bursts of performance, learning to render characters in no logical order.

When the continuity of the "acted image" breaks down, the results can be striking. For example in a previous essay on Lillian Gish and Griffith (*The Quarterly Review of Film Studies*, Winter, 1981), I have noted an unintentional mismatch near the beginning of *True Heart Susie* (1919), which momentarily transforms the central character from a Victorian innocent into a sophisticate. The mistake is chiefly due to a sudden, unmotivated change in Gish's posture and facial expression; in other words, she breaks expressive coherence at the level of the persona, so that Susie's entire personality threatens to fragment before our eyes. The change is only briefly visible, but it nicely illustrates how much the phenomenon of wholeness depends on the actor's emotional attitude at any given moment. The work of maintaining this wholeness is more difficult than it might appear, because neither the actor nor the character is a simple image. Both are made up of a bundle of traits, different faces and "semes" which have special functions; both tend to change over time, and all changes in appearance and manner must be kept under the control of narrative cause-and-effect. Hence the "error" in Griffith's film makes it seem as if the woman Gish plays at the end of the story—an experienced, maternal type—had suddenly been mixed up with the child she plays at the beginning.

Ironically, however, a second, quite common feature of an actor's job in realist films is to split the character visibly into different aspects. Thus the brief lapse in continuity near the beginning of *True Heart Susie* makes an interesting contrast with many occasions in the same film where Gish is actually *required* to exhibit expressive incoherence, and where the audience accepts her duality as a perfectly "natural" event. For instance an emotional scene midway through the picture shows Susie attending an engagement party to help celebrate the forthcoming marriage between the man she loves and another woman. In closeup, we see Gish seated in a parlor, fanning herself gently and smiling at the happy couple. After a moment she raises the fan to the side of her face, shielding herself from the room but giving us a privileged view; in this presumably hidden position, she lowers her glance to the floor and weeps. For a while she alternates between smiles and tears, dropping the fan to glance offscreen left at the other characters, then raising it to show her "true" feeling.

Behavior of this type has a double importance, allowing us to see the difference between Susie's public and private faces, but at the same time showing off the emotional range of the actor. A similar effect, involving a slightly different rhetoric, is achieved in a well-known scene from *Camille* (1938), when Garbo tells a lie to Robert Taylor. She pretends that she does not love him, and all the while the viewers in the theater (who already know her motives) can see clearly that she is faking, alternating between the sort of imperious, coolly amused disdain we normally associate with a figure like Dietrich, and a wilting, passionate ardor typical of Victorian melodrama. Throughout, Taylor seems completely fooled, partly because Garbo's emotional anguish is registered out of his sight—as when he briefly turns his back and she leans weakly against a table, or when she pulls him toward her and makes a tortured face over his shoulder. Even granting her skillful technique, however, the scene requires a certain suspension of disbelief. Charles Affron has written that Garbo "shifts radically from insincerity to passion, then to renunciation and grief."[9] Shouldn't we therefore expect that her lover, holding her in his arms, might notice some tremor of vulnerability, some vague alteration in tone? The answer of course is yes, but audiences in the late thirties did not mind; they were used to seeing high degrees of what Erving Goffman describes as "disclosive compensation"—a common theatrical convention whereby players are allowed to reveal information to the audience without much regard to the other characters.[10] In its oldest, "presentational" form, the convention can be seen in Shakespearian asides, but in classic Hollywood movies it has a more realistically motivated, representational quality, allowing actors to register conflicting emotions as if they were only *thinking* to themselves, outside anyone's view.

Another, somewhat more plausible form of "acting" within the diegesis can be seen in the exchanges between Bogart and Mary Astor in *The Maltese Falcon* (1941). In this case, the man recognizes that the woman is putting on a front, but the plot has made her motives ambiguous. Astor behaves like a sheltered innocent, casting demure glances down at the floor, wringing her hands and touching her brow in an appeal for sympathy. "You're good," Bogart says at one point, admiring her performance: "You're very, very good." And in fact she is good, even though she lets us see that she is slightly overplaying, registering what Lawrence Shaffer has called "appliqued" expressions; indeed the wit of the scene derives from the way she gives her ostensible innocence a somewhat knowing, flirtatious twist, as if she were acknowledging a lie in order to charm Bogart. When he calls attention to her ruse, she adopts the pose of a weary but frightened woman of the world, her head tossed back on a couch in seductive fashion, so that Bogart's amused interest gives way to a more serious, cautious study of her contradictory attitudes.

I could go on in this vein, but the examples I have already described should indicate that any film becomes a good showcase for professional acting skill if it provides moments when the characters are clearly shown to be wearing masks—in other words, if they are "bad" actors who exhibit high degrees of expressive incoherence. In such moments the player demonstrates virtuosity by sending out dual signs, and the vivid contrast between facial expressions gives the "acted image" an emotional richness, a strong sense of dramatic irony. Notice also that certain character types or fictional situations are particularly apt to foster this type of incoherence: villainy is a favorite subject for actors because it usually takes the form of an insincere or duplicitous performance; the emotional anguish of the "woman's picture" requires the central character to struggle against a spontaneous overflow of powerful feelings—thus she not only cries, but attempts to hide her tears from others; and movies about drunkenness or addiction provide excellent opportunities to show a character losing expressive control, so that many celebrated actors, from Chaplin in *One A.M.* (1916) to Jack Lemmon in *Days of Wine and Roses* (1962), have played alcoholics.[11]

Having mentioned Chaplin, I should add that broadly comic films, which often provoke alienated styles of performance, are dependent on exaggerated forms of *bodily* incoherence, often resulting in a sort of expressive anarchy. Jerry Lewis is perhaps the most obvious example, but consider a typical scene in *The Gold Rush,* when Chaplin meets Georgia Hale in a saloon. First he takes an opportunity to dance with her, establishing the "front" of a polite gentleman by tipping his hat, holding her at a slight distance, and waltzing around the floor with a finesse that contrasts nicely with the rowdy crowd in the background. Then, midway through the dance, his beltless pants start to slip, causing him to gyrate wildly with his legs and hips while desperately trying to maintain decorum with his face and arms. Steve Martin's *All of Me* (1984) creates similar chaos, casting Martin as a lawyer who has been magically possessed by the spirit of a dead woman. Through most of the film, the lawyer's body is literally at war with itself, his arm swishing out in an effeminate gesture while his face looks on with panic; the funniest scene is the one where, in the midst of a speech before a crowded courtroom, the woman inside him tries to collaborate in the manufacture of a coherent illusion, breaking into flamboyantly macho poses which leave the jurors staring in openmouthed incomprehension. Notice also the famous moment at the end of *Dr. Strangelove* (1963), when Peter Sellers tries to keep one arm from breaking into a Nazi salute. Strangelove's gloved fist, reminiscent of Rotwang's in *Metropolis,* keeps flying up in the air at a radical angle, only to be caught by the other hand and wrestled back into place; trying to keep the offensive body part out of sight, he pounds it down into his lap, but then it jumps up and grabs him by the throat.

Comic acting of this sort brings us very close to the spirit of radical deconstruction—hence *Dr. Strangelove* is able to exaggerate the melodramatic convention of the dual role, turning it into the multiple impersonations of postwar British farce; it allows Sellers to play three wildly different characters whom the audience clearly perceives as one actor, sometimes doing scenes in which he has dialog with "himself." There is of course nothing especially new in this practice. Vaudeville-style comedy has always relied on similar tactics, threatening to disrupt coherence at every level of the performance, deriving laughter not only from the foolish inconsistency of the characters, but from a split between actor and role. Hence the comedians who worked in skits during the days of live television knew they could get a big response from the studio audience if something went wrong, and a few of them began to structure "spontaneous" breakdowns into their act. Long after videotape was developed, Red Skelton tried to compensate for weak jokes by cracking up in the midst of a scene, and in its later days *The Carol Burnett Show* featured elaborate parodies of old movies in which Harvey Korman struggled to keep a straight face while playing opposite Tim Conway. (The same technique can be seen in the non-dramatic context of talk shows, where a figure like Johnny Carson can redeem a failed monologue by suddenly commenting on the writers, or where *Late Night with David Letterman* can build an entire program around the host's strategic loss of control.) As a result, comedy is usually a step removed from realist acting; it lets an incoherence in the "acted image" become almost as visible as the divisions within the character.

III

Radical theater takes the process of fragmentation even further, indicating a more complete break in the mask, or experimenting with performance styles that de-naturalize expression—for example a favorite acting exercise of the Open Theater required the ensemble to practice walking "sad" while making "happy" sounds. In cinema, however, the mechanical apparatus can disrupt continuity in another, perhaps more fundamental way. *Dr. Strangelove* suggests one possibility, but it is not nearly so unconventional as Luis Buñuel's sly, surrealist comedy, *That Obscure Object of Desire* (1977), which neatly reverses the old practice of having a single actor play multiple roles. Here is Buñuel's amusing account of how he came upon the idea:

> If I had to list all the benefits derived from alcohol, it would be endless. In 1977, in Madrid, when I was in despair after a tempestuous argument with an actress who'd brought the shooting of *That Obscure Object of Desire* to a halt, the producer, Serge Silberman, decided to abandon the film altogether. The considerable financial loss was depressing us both until one evening, when we were drowning our sorrows in a bar, I suddenly had the idea (after two dry martinis) of using two actresses in the same role, a tactic that had never been tried before. Although I made the suggestion as a joke, Silberman loved it, and the film was saved. Once again, the combination of bar and gin proved unbeatable.[12]

Buñuel chose Angelia Molina and Carole Bouquet to embody Conchita, the young temptress who makes a fool of a middle-aged businessman played by Fernando Rey. (The film is derived from Pierre Louy's *La femme et le pantin*, which Sternberg and Dietrich had used as the source for *The Devil is a Woman* in 1938.) What seems particularly important about the casting is that the two women are utterly different physical types—one of them an earthy, bosomy Spaniard, the other a tall, willowy Parisian. Buñuel takes care to make them completely interchangeable, sometimes having them play alternate sequences, occasionally substituting them for one another in the midst of a continuous action, as when Molina goes into a bathroom and a semi-nude Bouquet comes out. Furthermore, he never allows the audience to explain this inconsistency as a sign of Fernando Rey's distorted imagination; unlike the realist filmmaker, who gives every distortion or incoherence a psychological motive, he simply lays bare his technique, foregrounding the arbitrariness of his choice and making a joke of it. (Even so, as he wryly noted in his memoirs, many spectators have watched the film without ever noticing his capriciousness; accustomed to a coherence in the "acted image," they respond exactly like the central character, assuming that the two relatively unfamiliar women who play the "obscure object" are a single person.)

Buñuel's device is empty of the usual narrative significance, but it is nonetheless meaningful, commenting on the arbitrary, fetishistic structure of desire, and at the same time exposing a technique by which classical cinema usually supports that structure. The fact is, movies are the only medium in which several actors are *typically* used to play one role: a voice is dubbed, a body double represents a torso, a hand model manipulates objects in closeup, a stunt man performs dangerous action in longshot, etc. All these different figures are merged in the editing and mixing, appearing on the screen as a single characterization, an "object" of fascination which is tied together by the name of a character and the face of a star. By reminding us of such a phenomenon, Buñuel playfully attacks the very foundation of "organic," Stanislavskian aesthetics.

A similar effect, produced by Brechtian methods, may be seen in Godard's *Breathless*, where the principal actors repeatedly fracture realistic illusion with direct address to the camera—as when Belmondo turns to the lens and tells the viewer to "go hang yourself." These unpredictable shifts between representational and presentational rhetoric are in keeping with a certain "amateurish" quality of the production as a whole, which not only permits unstable camera movements, jump cuts, and 180-degree violations, but also toys with the "continuity of the acted image." At one point, for example, Godard cuts from a longshot of Belmondo to a closeup of his profile; suddenly the actor turns and glances into the camera, revealing that one eyepiece of his sunglasses is inexplicably missing, as if he had dropped half of his mask.

In other ways, however, *Breathless* is a model of naturalistic performance, and its central characters have become virtual icons of existentialist fiction, easily adapted to Hollywood. (The American remake, starring Richard Gere, was able to employ the same technique of direct address as the original, adapting it to a somewhat more symbolic mode.) It was only later, as Godard's work grew increasingly politicized, that he departed utterly from the established conventions, filming *Lehrstücke* or brief fictional skits in flat, presentational style—a technique which virtually prohibited the actors from developing psychologically "rounded" personae. Although he continued to employ famous professionals, he required them to adopt a relatively one-dimensional manner, exactly reversing the structure of bourgeois performance: in other words, the characterizations seldom involved a display of expressive incoherence, and the split between actor and role was foregrounded.

The contrast between Godard's films in the early and late sixties is in some ways so vivid that it can be used to illustrate much of what I have been saying about the formal logic of actorly expression. As an instance of the "lifelike" naturalism to which most film acting aspires, consider a shot that occurs midway through *Breathless*, when a police inspector tracks down Patricia Franchini (Jean Seberg) in the Paris offices of the *International Herald Tribune*, thrusting a newspaper in front of her face and asking, "Do you know this man?" In closeup, we see Patricia taking the newspaper and glancing down at the front page, which contains a large photo and an article announcing that her lover, Michael, is a cop killer. She is positioned in the three-quarter, "open" profile of standard movie rhetoric, with the camera looking just over the edge of the newspaper at her face. Until this point in the narrative, she has not known the full extent of Michael's criminal activity, and she tries to conceal her profound shock from the detective. Seberg's reactions seem remarkably understated compared to the ostentatious theatricality of an old-fashioned player like Lillian Gish, but they are no different in kind; in fact the edge of the newspaper functions much like the fan Gish manipulates during the engagement-party sequence in *True Heart Susie,* forming a boundary between "private" and "public" expressions. Beyond the paper, we can see a small tightening around her mouth and a deepening seriousness in her eyes, followed by subtle indications of anger and hurt as she intently scans the article; then she looks up over the edge, glancing at the offscreen detective, and her face changes, adopting the mask of a sweetly pretty, Midwestern girl. Her eyes widen slightly and her lips almost smile as she shapes them into a lie: "No," she says, shaking her head in the negative, at the same time allowing a shadow of unease to break her calm.

Seberg's performance-within-performance in this shot is dependent on a fundamental trope of realist film acting: the player assumes a representational stance, her gaze turned slightly away from the lens, and then makes at least two different faces, both clearly visible to the audience, one coded as "suppressed," the other as "ostensive." Maurice Merleau-Ponty's comments on the phenomenology of character (which Godard subsequently read) are strikingly relevant to such moments. As he suggests, there is probably no such thing as an "inner" emotion, either in life or on film: "Anger, shame, hate, and love are not psychic facts hidden at the bottom of another's consciousness: they are types of behavior or styles of conduct which are visible from the outside. They exist *on* this face or *in* those gestures, not hidden behind them".[13] The same argument could be made in semiotic terms, forcing us to abandon the notion of a Stanislavskian "subtext." The fact is, all emotion is equally manifest. Audiences have simply learned to read certain types of expressive incoherence as a sign of psychological complexity, so that the dual faces of the actor function much like irony or ambiguity in written language.

Only a few years later, Godard abandoned this style, eschewing "depth" in both staging and expression. Hence the multiple faces of Jean Seberg are quite different from those of another player near the beginning of *Two or Three Things I Know about Her* (1967). In this case we are presented with a Techniscope, color image of a woman in closeup, standing against an urban cityscape and looking directly into the lens: "This is Marina Vlady," Godard's voice whispers on the soundtrack, "she is an actress." Vlady, her expression cool and impassive, quotes Brecht: "Yes, speak as if quoting truths. Old Brecht said that. That actors should quote." She then turns her head to the right of the screen, assuming the three-quarter profile of ordinary movie acting. "But that isn't important," Godard whispers. Suddenly a jump cut takes us to another image of the same woman, framed exactly as before, the cityscape behind her seen from a slightly different angle. "This is Juliette Janson," Godard says, "She lives here." Once again the woman looks at us, her face shaped into an impassive stare. "It was two years ago in Martinique," she says, and begins describing her character in cryptic, disjointed sentences. She stops and turns her head to the left. "Now she has turned her head to the left," Godard announces, "but that isn't important."

The offscreen commentary, the speeches, and the slight mismatch of shots all serve to drive a wedge between two conceptions of the human figure on the screen. Meanwhile the performer seems alienated, distanced from both of her roles. In this respect the images are paradoxical, because we cannot make distinctions between "Vlady" and "Janson" on the basis of the player's appearance, rhetoric, or expression. Throughout, she remains essentially the same figure, with the same sweater and the same hairstyle, speaking her lines like a Brechtian actor who is "quoting the truth" rather than "living the part." As "herself," she gazes back at the lens with the compliant yet slightly cynical air of a woman who has been photographed many times, avoiding the ingratiating warmth of a typical narrator/guide, as if she were acknowledging that she speaks to an apparatus. As "Janson," she has much the same attitude—a cool, almost lobotomized manner which might be regarded as an emotional response to life in working-class Paris, but which gives the audience very little opportunity to feel empathy. Even when she turns her head to the profile position of representational theater, she indicates no special emotion, and Godard tells us that her movement is unimportant.

Notice, too, that by subordinating the expressive aspect of Vlady's performance to a rational, "epic" address, the film gives us little indication of a difference between a social mask and a private identity. Godard is less interested in the psychology of people than in how they function as workers or images, and as a result he shows us the split between actor and persona rather than the divided self of a character. Vlady's overt statements and her actions during the film's intermittent narrative take precedence over her ability to render complex emotions;

much like Brecht, who remarked that a photograph of a factory would tell us very little about its meaning, she seems almost contemptuous of the phenomenology of expression. As she says later in the film, "something can make me cry; but the cause of the tears is not to be found in . . . their traces on my cheeks; . . . one can describe everything that is produced when I do something without indicating, for all that, what makes me do it."

The technique here is exactly opposed to the closeup in *Breathless*, which uses an Iowa schoolgirl made famous by Otto Preminger to embody an American in Paris. Rather like the classic cinema to which it alludes, the early film melds a celebrity into the character she plays, making the audience feel a subtle *glissement* between star and role. Both emerge as a single, psychologically complete personality—a dangerously attractive, contemporary version of Daisy Miller, born of a union between the new wave and the *film noir*. By contrast, *Two or Three Things* disturbs the coherence of the "acted image," suggesting a different structural relationship between actor and character: both Vlady and Janson, according, to Godard, are workers, and like all workers under postindustrial capitalism, they are engaged in a type of prostitution. (At one point, Vlady/Janson removes her clothes and puts an airline bag on her head while a photographer who strongly resembles Godard "directs" her movements.)

Partly for this reason, we cannot always tell whether Vlady is addressing the camera as "herself" or as the character. In one sense, however, the problem is academic, because she is never fully merged into her role. Godard's commentary and her own somewhat flat, emotionless style make us continually aware of a double aspect to her image, as if we were always watching someone going through motions. Hence the film reverses the formal priorities of conventional cinema, becoming its dialectical opposite. It collapses private into public expression, at the same time creating divisions where we expect unity. By this means, it points to the fundamentally "two-faced" quality of most performance, revealing the process by which both theater and social life create the illusion of a unified subject. It remains a theatrical spectacle of sorts, but its players might be said to operate at the very margins of acting.

NOTES

[1] *The Presentation of Self in Everyday Life* (New York: Doubleday, 1959), p. 5.

[2] Konstantin Stanislavski, *My Life in Art*, translated by J. J. Robbins (New York: Theater Arts, 1948), p. 152.

[3] *Brecht on Theater*, translated by John Willett (New York: Hill and Wang, 1964), p. 152.

[4] "Brecht on Rhetoric," *New Literary History* 16 no. 3 (Spring 1985), p.635.

[5] Stanwyck's films often gave her the opportunity to show off acting skill by displaying two aspects of character. Besides the examples I have cited, consider her dual role in *The Lady Eve* (1941): as "Jean Harrington," she is a seductive cardsharp, leaning against a trunkful of high-heeled shoes, revealing her ribcage, and asking Henry Fonda if he sees anything he likes. As "Eve Sidwich," she is an equally seductive aristocrat, fluttering an ostrich fan, batting her eyes, and making a fool of nearly every male in sight. Only William Demarest remains skeptical; throughout, we hear him muttering, "It's gotta be the same dame!"

[6] "Reflections on the Face in Film," *Film Quarterly* 31 no. 2 (Winter 1977–88), p.6.

[7] The Italian director Elio Petri has remarked, "within us there's the possibility of having many 'I's.' . . . In a way, coherence is a word you apply to a state of madness, incoherence to a state of normality" (quoted in Ellen Oumano, *Film Forum* [New York: St. Martins, 1985], p. 143). By attempting to preserve the illusion of a unifed self, by maintaining coherence in the face of multiple possibilities, most acting on the screen (as in life) is ideologically conservative or "mad" in Petri's sense. On this point Goffmann's analysis of "role playing" has something at least tentatively in common with post-modern psychoanalytic theory. Realist types of performance might even be said to conspire in what contemporary psychoanalysis calls a fundamental "misrecognition," upon which the Ego is founded. Hence the analysis of acting can be linked to Jean-Louis Baudry's familiar argument about the paranoid structure of cinema spectatorship. Baudry, following suggestions offered by Lacan and Althusser, has described the cinema as a "mirror," in which the "fragmented body" of the viewer is brought together by a "sort of imaginary integration of the self"; the apparatus, he says, helps to foster the illusion of a "transcendental subject," and imposes meaning on "discontinuous fragments of phenomena" ("Ideological Effects of the Basic Cinematographic Apparatus," *Film Quarterly* [Winter 1973–4[, p. 45).

[7] Vsevolod Pudovkin, *Film Technique and Film Acting: The Cinema Writings*

of V. I. Pudovkin, translated by Ivor Montague (New York: Bonanza Books, 1949).

8 Quoted in Jay Leyda, *Film Makers Speak* (New York: Da Capo, 1977), pp. 440–41.

9 In "Genre and Performance: An Overview" Richard De Cordova has observed that "acting" within the diegesis occurs often in thrillers, where characters are deceptive. (*Film Genre Reader*, ed. Barry Keith Grant [Austin: University of Texas Press, 1986], pp. 129–39.) The phenomenon also seems especially apparent in "women's melodrama," where, as Laura Mulvey has noted, "there is a delicate balance between the protagonists' self-consciosness and the actresses' mastery over a self-conscious performance" ("Melodrama in and out of the Home," in *High Theory/Low Culture*, ed. Colin McCabe [New York: St. Martins, 1986], p. 97). Actually, the breakdown of repressive constraints on behavior—the "failure" of performance—is a telling moment in any sort of theater, and can have especially powerful effect in a documentary. For example in *Shoah* [1985] we see a barber, in the process of cutting a man's hair, being interviewed about the job he once had in a Nazi death camp. At first he matter-of-factly recalls how naked women were brought before him to have their heads shorn. He claims to have felt nothing, but then he remarks that some of the women were the wives, mothers, and daughters of people he knew. As he speaks, he has a good deal of difficulty maintaining his "mask"; ultimately his throat begins constricting; he rolls his tongue around in his mouth and seizes a towel, wiping sweat from his face and trying to hide his tears.

10 *Star Acting: Gish, Garbo, and Davis* (New York: Dutton, 1977), p. 199.

11 *Frame Analysis* (New York: Harper, 1974), p. 142.

12 Luis Buñuel and Jean-Claude Carriere, *My Last Sigh*, translated by Abagail Israel (New York: Vintage, 1984), p. 46.

13 *Sense and Non-Sense*, translated by Hubert and Patricia Allen Dreyfus (Evanston: Northwestern University Press, 1964), pp. 52–3.

TOWARD A DECONSTRUCTIVE THEORY OF FILM

Peter Brunette

Most post-structuralist film criticism, for better or worse, continues to be based on the strong re-reading of Freud initiated by Jacques Lacan. Despite the fact that one hears the term "deconstructive" more and more frequently (and, to my mind, incorrectly[1]) applied to certain forms of film criticism based on the Lacanian model, there have only been a few scattered attempts to apply more properly speaking deconstructive strategies, in the Derridean sense, to film. What I want to do in this essay is to consider briefly why Lacan's work has been so much more influential than Derrida's in film studies (exactly reversing the situation in literary criticism), and to indicate some of the shortcomings of the Lacanian model.[2] The bulk of the essay will be devoted to an examination—really little more than a list of suggestions—of the ways in which Derrida might help us think about film. Finally, I want to examine the work of the French critic, Marie-Claire Ropars-Wuilleumier, one of the few theorists who has attempted to apply Derrida's thought to film in a sustained and systematic fashion.

Probably the most fruitful use of Lacanian psychoanalysis has concerned the challenging of the myth of the unified, coherent, intentional self. Out of this investigation, a powerful critique of the dynamics of cinematic realism has evolved. We can now see more clearly how "subjects" are positioned and even created through the representation of reality as unproblematic and directly given, and this of course has important political implications, some of which have been spelled out by the French Marxist Louis Althusser. One can no longer doubt that at least partly because of the work of "realistic" Hollywood films, which inculcate a sense of a certain predetermined reality in the spectator, the world is seen as natural rather than constructed, and there-fore beyond the reach of political change.

Since the cinematic experience, with its apparently privileged (and therefore misleading) relationship to reality, is usually described as more "immediate" and "total" than the experience of literature, it becomes important to chart the psychological relationship of the spec-tator to the film text as accurately as possible. The illusionism that is promoted and intermittently achieved in the movie theater thus seems more crucial than the question of illusionism is in literary stud-ies. In other words, since much of Lacanian theory is based on the specular model of the mirror-stage, the illusory fullness of the ima-ginary, and the problematizing of vision as introduction to the sym-bolic, Lacan's emphasis on the visual has seemed particularly appropriate to the study of film. Unfortunately, this emphasis has led some critics to forget that the relationship between the mirror and the screen (or, in the more classically Freudian articulation, between film and dream), is analogical and suggestive rather than exactly equiva-lent. Difference is rarely figured into this equation.

Another result of this concern for investigating the spectator's psy-chological relationship to the film has been to make most film theorists *de facto* reader-response critics, focusing on the mechanics of reception rather than the autotelic text, as most formalists and even structuralists have always done. In spite of this emphasis, the reigning models of reception are surprisingly unsophisticated (at least in social, national, and racial terms) compared to those that have begun to be elaborated for literature. Perhaps because film is seen as more popular, and thus presumably connected to what is "most basic" in all of us—our "hu-manist" common denominator, I suppose—the naive assumption of most conventional film criticism, of course, has always been that all readers of film are the same. Beyond the important exception of the woman spectator, however, few Lacanian critics have bothered to make distinctions among viewers either.[3] Questions of "ideal readers" and "super-readers" have yet to trouble these assumptions about re-ception, as they have Stanley Fish and Michael Riffaterre in literary studies, but they will.

In any case, one problematic aspect of the Lacanian model has been the apparent grounding of his system in the Oedipal triangle and most especially in his founding opposition between the imaginary and the symbolic. A close reading of Lacan (if such a thing is possible) will show that these two fields are in fact complicated modes which continuously interpenetrate and displace one another, and are by no means meant to constitute some sort of developmental teleology, an engrossing narrative which has a subject "grow out" of the imaginary to live happily ever after in the symbolic. Nevertheless, some film theorists have not paid enough attention to Lacan's problematizing of these "stages" and the terms have tended to rigidify, in ordinary usage, into a grounding dualism which, with its attendant implied hierarchy, seems susceptible to a Derridean deconstruction and overturning. Derrida has himself criticized what he calls Lacan's "telos of 'full speech' in its essential tie . . . to Truth" — a concept which of course remains far from self-evident for Derrida — as well as Lacan's untheorized (and therefore unproblematized) adoption of Hegelian and Heideggerean idealist conceptuality and vocabulary.[4]

In one specific area, that of feminist film theory, Lacan's model of sexual difference has been useful, especially in showing how this difference is constitutive of linguistic difference as well. However, his grounding of the Oedipal struggle and accession to the symbolic in the exchange of the phallus and in forms of castration anxiety, no matter how vociferously his disciples insist upon the distinction between phallus and penis (constituting the former as a structural relation rather than the actual male sexual organ), has quite properly created difficulties for feminists who are trying to decenter phallocracy in *all* its forms. As Teresa de Lauretis has pointed out

> even though castration is to be understood as referring to the symbolic dimension, its signifier—the phallus—can only be conceived as an extrapolation from the real body. . . . In the psychoanalytic view of signification, subject processes are essentially phallic; that is to say, they are *subject* processes insofar as they are instituted in a fixed order of language—the symbolic—by the function of castration. Again female sexuality is negated, assimilated to the male's. . . .[5]

Trying to locate a place in which the *female* subject can constitute herself in the movie theater and elsewhere, some feminists have fruitfully posited a "pre-Oedipal" psychic space, asking, for example, why little boys and little girls do not perceive the structural differences of the symbolic as a function of having/not having *breasts* rather than having/not having a penis. This is, of course, a deconstructive strategy, for the effect is to reverse the hierarchical opposition male/female (with the first term privileged, of course). Here the penis becomes that which makes the *male* different from (and thus, by implication, inferior to) the female, who becomes the norm.

Having briefly considered a few problematic aspects of Lacanian film theory, let us now turn to an examination of how film might be conceived from a Derridean perspective. To date, there has been a surprising paucity of attempts in this direction, in spite of the fact that literary criticism—which has for better or worse historically led developments in film criticism—has increasingly turned to deconstructive strategies over the last 15 years. The reasons for this state of affairs are not complicated. For one thing, most film criticism that has sought to move beyond evaluative or formalist interpretation has, unlike literary criticism, been overtly political in nature. Post-structuralist film theory, in fact, has from the beginning been refreshingly explicit in its use of various versions of the discourse of liberation. And rightly or wrongly, and in spite of Michael Ryan's heroic attempt to bring politics and deconstructive criticism together in his *Marxism and Deconstruction,* most political film critics (including Ryan) suspect what has seemed to them the conservative streak of the so-called "Yale school" (which actually no longer exists, if it ever did) of J. Hillis Miller, Geoffrey Hartman, and the late Paul de Man. To my mind, however, most of this criticism has surfaced primarily because deconstruction does not allow *any* text to remove itself from the play of difference, including even those political texts which may "use" deconstructive techniques to analyze culture, but whose authors then characteristically want, for perhaps laudable political reasons, to privilege their own discourse. What deconstructionists have always insisted upon, to the understandable dismay of some, is that political texts as well are written in language, not in some blessed, unmediated metalanguage far above the fray.

Furthermore, as J. Hillis Miller has pointed out in a discussion of literature that seems equally relevant to film, social-minded critics who want to take language for granted will always have to come back to it, because things and ideas will always have to be represented in words.

> The most resolute attempts to . . . shift from the study of relations of word with word [in literature] to the study of the relations of words with things or with subjectivities, will only lead back in the end to the

study of language. . . . Any conceivable representation of the relations
of words to things, powers, persons, modes of production and exchange, juridical or political systems (or whatever name the presumably
non-linguistic may be given) will turn out to be one or another figure
of speech. As such, it will require a rhetorical interpretation. . . .[6]

But we must not give up so easily on the possibility of deconstruction
providing its own kind of political analysis as well. For example, it
can perhaps help us to understand how authority and power constitute
themselves through logocentric, oppositional hierarchies that a deconstructive strategy may then be able to reverse and displace. Derrida
himself has increasingly turned his attention toward the institutional
and political ramifications of such founding concepts as Reason.[7] The
work that Paul de Man was engaged upon at the time of his death
sought to understand ideology through the tradition of philosophical
aesthetics—he had already written on Hegel's *Aesthetics* and Kant's
Third Critique—by means of the insights that the latter could provide
about epistemology, and thus the way we conceptualize politics.[8] Similarly, Barbara Johnson, in her recent book, *A World of Difference*,
expressly considers "the possible political functions of undecidability," pointing out that the left's attacks on deconstruction have been
welcomed by the right because "nothing could be more comforting
to the established order than the requirement that everything be assigned a clear meaning or stand."[9] Furthermore, Johnson argues,
deconstruction can be more attentive to historically marginalized
voices (for example, the voices of the black woman writers to whom
part of her book is devoted), because it preserves the otherness in
what is written. She asks, "Isn't each radical theoretical revolution . . . a
reinvention of what reading is, such that the formerly unvoiced speaks
and is heard?" (p. 31). In a brilliant concluding essay on abortion and
the figure of apostrophe in poetry, Johnson points out that "It is often
said, in literary-theoretical circles, that to focus on undecidability is
to be apolitical. Everything I have read about the abortion controversy
in its present form in the United States leads me to suspect that, on
the contrary, the undecidable *is* the political. There is politics precisely
because there is undecidability" (pp. 193–94).

It also seems clear that film theory, especially in its more political
guises, would greatly benefit from a rethinking of our present views
concerning the nature of ideology. An important starting place in this

regard is a recent book by the Australian literary theorist John Frow called *Marxism and Literary History*. Though he complains at one point, with some justice, that the overt politics of most deconstructionists is little more than "Nietzschean romanticism," he also knows that the theoretical and, by extension, political potential of deconstruction is great. Thus, Frow criticizes Fredric Jameson's insistence, in *The Political Unconscious*, on maintaining a notion of a "real world" which is always prior to textuality (thus making history *not* a text), while at the same time admitting that we can only get to history through a process of textualization. As Frow points out, "This is surely a case of having one's referent and eating it too."[10] His larger point then becomes: "if history is accessible only through discursive or epistemological categories, is there not a real sense in which it therefore has only a discursive existence? In which its very otherness, its excess over the textual, is still a textual construct? But the really important question, I think, is why there should be any *necessity* for Marxism to ground its politics in an appeal to a transcendental realm prior to any mediation" (p. 38). In traditional Marxist thought, ideology is seen as error or false consciousness, but, as Frow points out, this view necessitates a position of authority, which is always complicitous with power. The conventional view of ideology also divides phenomena into the real and the symbolic; Frow wants rather to see the real as a "texture of symbolic systems," (a notion derived from a post-structuralist view of textuality), and, conversely, to regard the symbolic as something having real effects.

What all of these examples show, I think, is that we must not be misled by immediate and obviously important political struggles (for example, in Central America or about abortion clinics), in our attempt to rethink and perhaps recast the very basis of thought itself. Currently, too many leftists seem to combat the absolute presences of oppressive systems with other absolute presences which are really only their opposites, and therefore involved in the same constricting economy. In so doing, we inevitably and fruitlessly must adduce our own "logic of the supplement," as Derrida calls it, in order to constitute these presences. Michael Ryan, in an illuminating chapter of *Marxism and Deconstruction* called "The Metaphysics of Everyday Life," points out that "'the deconstruction of metaphysics can be integrated with the critique of ideology because metaphysics is the infrastructure of ideology, and until that infrastructure is deracinated, ideology will reappear, against the best intentions of revolutionary activists, with the regularity of weeds to a garden."[11] As Ryan describes it, capitalist ideology cannot function without such "natural" oppositions as mental/manual, public/private (which depends, like so much else, on the fundamental opposition inside/outside), and such undifferentiated, "homogeneous" presences such as "the people," or "the Third World," which deconstruction can help us to dismantle. Feminists, using deconstructive strategies, have, for example, attempted to understand the "internal" differences *within* the concepts male and female rather than passively accepting the differences *between* these supposedly stable entities. What is there of the "male" in the female and vice-versa? Other critics have examined the so-called "marginal" areas (often particularly profitable sites for deconstructive analysis) of hermaphrodism and homosexuality in order to challenge this division even further.

In addition to its political efficacy, questions have also been raised concerning the relevance of deconstruction to "practical" criticism, since much literary deconstructive writing up to the present time has concentrated principally on its own heuristic effects. Deconstructive analyses of *Billy Budd*, say, or the poetry of Wallace Stevens, have seemed more intent on demonstrating certain impasses and contradictions in the nature of language itself than on illuminating these individual texts in their own terms. But now that we understand better the ways in which the metaphysics of presence both allows and destroys our logic, our very thinking, do we need to pursue these analyses any further? If we now know that in important ways *language* doesn't really "work," at least not as we thought it did, do we need to learn that cinema doesn't work either?

I think we do. For one thing, we should remember that it is a function of the visual image, of the "directly" perceived, to appear even more originary and natural than speech itself, whose primacy, since *Of Grammatology*, most deconstruction has concentrated on decentering. How might the self-givenness of vision be deconstructed? Relevant here is a casual remark which Derrida made during the discussion period following the presentation in America, nearly twenty years ago, of his paper "Structure, Sign and Play in the Discourse of the Human Sciences":

> I don't know what perception is and I don't believe that anything

like perception exists. Perception is precisely a concept, a concept of
an intuition or of a given originating from the thing itself, present itself
in its meaning, independently from language, from the system of reference. And I believe that perception is interdependent with the concept
of origin and of center and consequently whatever strikes at the metaphysics of which I have spoken strikes also at the very concept of
perception.[12]

We might also want to concentrate attention on the film text itself,
bracketing for a moment the complexities of reception that were discussed earlier. Cinemato-graphy, after all, is also a writing. At its
most basic level of technology, of course, film is a matter of the
presence and absence of light, and thus whatever we are able to see
on the screen is constituted, finally, by a differential system of gaps
and darknesses that "create" the presences of light and make them
seem substantial. Moving from the spatial to the temporal (terms
which of course are deeply implicated in one another), the familiar
concept of persistence of vision might also be profitably reconsidered
from the perspective of the relationship between presence and absence
which deconstructive thinking can provide. At another level, film,
like all signs, necessarily represents what is *not there*. Thus, what is
particularly interesting about the cinema is that the absence or endless
chain of ungrounded signifiers which deconstruction considers to be
"inherent" to representation is both more and less blatant here than
it is in purely verbal signs. Given the very strength of the illusion
fostered in the theater, in other words, the intermittent but unavoid-
able revelation of a film's illusoriness (a process which has been well
described by Lacanian critics) will have an all the more violent effect
upon the spectator.

Another key "concept" in deconstruction is dissemination, that is,
the tendency of textual "meaning-effects" to move outward in all
directions at once, avoiding closure, always in process, always being
written and re-written. Since the notion of artistic intentionality has
historically been a crucial ingredient in the establishment of more or
less stable meanings in texts, film, as a necessarily collaborative, and
thus inherently disseminative medium, is an important place to study
the problems of intentionality that can sometimes be obscured in
literary study. It seems no accident, in other words, that film was not
taken seriously until auteurs, in whatever guise (as director, producer,

screenwriter, star, or even studio), were found. This reluctance can be accounted for in terms of the social dynamic between elite art and popular culture, of course, but a more general anxiety about representation and signification seems to be a factor here as well. The notoriously unconvincing attempts to avoid this problem of dispersed intentionality in film by relocating the missing single consciousness in the collective consciousness of an epoch or a nation might be considered a further symptom of this anxiety.

Deconstruction will also inevitably challenge much of what now passes for film history. It has shown us, for example, that film history, like any other history, is also a narrative, and thus distorted as well as enabled by the constraints of narrative technique. This history (and film theory and interpretation, for that matter) also proceeds through the largely unrecognized vehicle of metaphor and other tropes like synecdoche and metonymy, as, for example, when certain frames, shots, or sequences are taken as being "representative" of the text as a whole. Film history, like literary history, also depends on periodization, which is inevitably based upon essentializing and the repression of difference within periods, virtual sites that are barely more than conveniences. As Barbara Johnson has pointed out in her earlier book, *The Critical Difference*, what deconstruction reveals is that in the Western tradition, differences *within* are inevitably recast as differences *between*,[13] and this is nowhere more true than in our description of such self-identical "movements" as Soviet montage, German expressionism, and so on. This epistemological violence must also continue at the level of author and even individual text, scene, sequence, shot, and frame — all of which must be read for the most part univocally in order to support the essentializing demands of film history's narrative. From a deconstructive point of view, the concept of genre is, strictly speaking, similarly untenable.

What might also prove fruitful to film interpretation is Derrida's deconstruction of Kant's idea of the parergon (from the *Critique of Judgment*), an operation which directly problematizes notions of frame and framing that are ubiquitous in all aspects of aesthetic discourse.[14] What is inside and what is outside a work? Where is the frame around a painting? It is the outside which constitutes the inside (the inessential thus becoming the essential) and, less obviously, the inside which constitutes the outside. In any case, it would be a mistake to take these questions as mere philosophical conundrums with little real importance, because they have the potential, finally, to undermine the very basis of thought itself. In film, this question of the parergon becomes even more complex because the frame, considered the outside in ordinary speech, has etymologically become the entire thing, the entire inside, as well: it is both the inside and the outside at the same time. What obscure exchange is going on here? Can we employ this economy in a different, perhaps ultimately more fruitful way, to "frame" the question of the relation between film and the reality it is said to reflect? Finally, the question of inside and outside might clarify the position of the critic vis-à-vis the text, and how one is enfolded (or, to use Derrida's term, "invaginated") in the other.

Deconstruction could also help us to understand classical and modern film theory better, how Bazin and Arnheim, for example, as well as Metz and Heath, must necessarily work from exclusions and covert hierarchies in order to be able to say anything at all. What is being repressed to allow the theorist the presences (or "key terms") that he or she needs in order to theorize? We might also come to understand better the relation between the codes of realism and what might be called the codes of reality, and how the former paradoxically constitute the latter (and vice-versa); this understanding could perhaps be achieved through a deconstructive exploration of mimesis and the problematic relation between original and copy.[15] Such an investigation might tell us a great deal, for example, about the documentary and the status of its claim to re-present reality.

Similarly, in literature, understanding a text has traditionally been thought of as a function of the referentiality of its language. Even the play of figurative language is seen as coming to a halt in referentiality, no matter how long this move is delayed. How might we describe the reciprocal relation of referentiality and figurality in film, where reference seems so much more direct and undeniable because of the iconic nature of the medium? Here, de Man's tactical privileging of allegory over symbol—because the former marks a reversible, horizontal "sliding" among textual levels and individual figures, rather than a vertical relationship with an "external" reference—might also be applied in a useful way to the study of film.

The concept of figuration has itself become particularly important in film studies. Dudley Andrew, for example, has recently argued in *Concepts in Film Theory* for increased attention to this area, even echoing the deconstructive view that we must "pass from the logical clarity of linguistics to the murkier discipline of rhetoric. Henceforth the study of *figures*, not codes, must be paramount in an examination of cultural artifacts."[16] However, Andrew's definition of figure as "a direct representation of meaning" (p. 158) seems again to fall prey to an idealist definition of the sign and the relation between signifier and signified. Though he seems to celebrate the fact that figures "complicate and derail struture," (p. 158) he forgets that figures can also complicate and derail meaning of any sort. Furthermore, where deconstruction would insist on the impossibility of granting primacy to either (grammatical) structure or (figural) event (maintaining that trying to decide which came first would be to remain trapped in the myth of pure origins, another manifestation of pure presence), Andrew opts finally for the view that "the system was born and exists only as a residue of such events of figuration" (p. 170). His figures, in other words, always point to a place beyond the materiality and mediacy of the signifier, even beyond the intentional force described by psychoanalysis, to a place granted to a transcendent artistic "insight." Unfortunately, however, neither the structural analysis Andrew wants to dethrone, nor the analysis of figures he offers to replace it will ever be able to tell us, without self-contradiction, what this insight is, or, in his phrase, "what was meant."

In any case, most deconstructionists share Andrew's distaste for purely structural analyses. Derrida has even gone so far as to call structuralism a "totalitarianism" because it reduces a given textual phenomenon to a formula which attempts to govern it *totally*. Deconstructionists are more inclined to point out that every "totality" must necessarily be erected upon that which it excludes. Another problem in these structuralist analyses is that structure is also immediately metaphorized in spatial terms, and meaning becomes linked with its "geometric model." As Derrida insists, "this geometry is only metaphorical, it will be said. Certainly. But metaphor is never innocent. It orients research and fixes results."[17] What a structuralist — for example, Brian Henderson — or, for that matter, any formalist, generally wants to do is to elide the text's heterogeneity, its extension in space and time, preferring instead what Derrida calls a "theological simultaneity." When such critics complain about having to "break up" a text in having to write about it, they are, in Derrida's phrase, appealing to "the myth of a total reading or description" (p. 24). Rather, what should be remembered is that any given work can never really be present, can never really be "summarized by some absolute simultaneity or instantaneousness" (p. 14). Derrida is speaking of literary criticism here, of course, but it is easy to see how the very temporality of the film medium makes the problem even worse.

A more properly speaking deconstructive view of interpretation would give primacy to the autonomy of a film's signifiers, their resolute heterogeneity in the face of the critic's will to master them. If we think in terms of the film's sounds and visuals, for example, we can see that each frame and every millimeter of the soundtrack offer a site of continual dissemination in the construction of meaning. We know of course that verbal language harbors sediments of meaning that can never be repressed, no matter what the conscious intentions of the individual artist, yet in literature this fact can easily be forgotten in the seemingly full presence of the word, and the apparent simultaneity and "obviousness" of its meaning to its initiator and recipient. In film, however, each frame and every sound contain hundreds of signifiers or potential signifiers that we as critics must repress even more insistently (a process which is, paradoxically, easier, given film's "reality effect") in order to arrive at neat Coleridgean interpretations in which everything is "organically" related to everything else. In a a shot which occurs during Bergman's *The Seventh Seal*, for example, a very sharp eye can spot a death's head hanging on the coach in the background, behind the doomed knight's head. We take this, quite naturally, as significant. But why not the white canvas of the coach as a sign of hope? Why not the wheel as the wheel of fortune (which would make us think of the knight in a different way?) It might be said, of course, that it is repetition, patterns, and motifs which constitute individual items as significant, but this can only occur *retrospectively*. In effect, what this kind of after-the-fact sense-making involves is a version of the hermeneutic circle, in which certain signifiers are retrospectively privileged because they involve the elaboration of a certain textual signified, a signified which is achieved in its turn by repressing signifiers which don't "fit."[18] For Heidegger and for some recent phenomenological critics, of course, the hermeneutic circle is regarded positively, as the very figure of the always-incomplete interpretive process. For the deconstructionist, however, the hermeneutic circle, however richly "paradoxical," is simply another (and still unwarranted) logical ground of interpretation.

Deconstruction can also help us to see critical interpretation, in political terms, as a function of the will to power over the text's discontinuities, a dynamic which is analogous to the desire for mastery and totalization in other areas of life. Though some critics like Denis Donoghue have attacked deconstruction for its putative attitude of superiority to literature, deconstructionists in fact most often find themselves describing the critic's frustrating impotence regarding all texts. It seems to me, in other words, that deconstruction can reawaken us to the troublesome but precious individual differences within texts and help us to avoid giving in to the tyranny of the organic reading by revealing its own basis in the operation of what is really only another metaphor. We need to locate and liberate what it is in texts which resists this teleological recuperation.

With these questions in mind, it might now be useful to look more closely at the work of Marie-Claire Ropars-Wuilleumier, one of the few theorists thus far who has attempted to introduce deconstructive thinking into film studies.[19] *Le texte divisé*, published in 1981, is a complicated, provocative book, and my remarks here should be understood as little more than superficial summary of a few of its more salient ideas. Ropars' principal goal, at least in the first half of the book, is to substitute in film theory a Derridean notion of an extended writing [*écriture*] for the Saussurean concept of the sign which is based on an unproblematic relation between signifier and signified. In Derrida's system, of course, the concept of the sign is exchanged for that of the trace; if language operates solely in terms of differences and contains no positive terms, as Saussure insisted, then meaning can only be constituted through the contradictory presence/absence of the trace. Though Derrida's term *différance* has perhaps enjoyed wider circulation, at least in North America, to signify that impossible sublation of and ceaseless shuttle between opposites, Ropars wisely concentrates on another of his key terms, *espacement*. Fortuitously, the normal English translation of this word, "spacing," also carries the simultaneous sense of the act of making the space, the space itself, and the concept of spacing, a simultaneity which both uncovers and bridges the gap between structure and event. It is spacing, of course, which calls into question the so-called linearity of meaning, for only by the *breaking* of this black linearity by white spaces, as in these sentences I write, can the linearity come into being. Spacing is also privileged in Ropars' analysis because of its obvious relation to the film medium.

Ropars discusses Benveniste, Derrida, and Freud, outlining their common development of a theory of meaning which escapes the sign and in so doing, explodes it. Thus in Freud's *Interpretation of Dreams*, dreams are sometimes said to be meaningful according to a more or less fixed system of symbols, a system which models itself on the sign and a *semantic* model of meaning, while elsewhere Freud seems to favor a theory of writing which privileges the particular composition and articulation of each dreamer (in other words, a *syntactic* model of meaning). This former model presupposes the existence of the latent content of the dream, an originary meaning which the dream itself is said to translate, and in translating, distort and disfigure. A theory of *écriture*, on the contrary, would hold that an originary latent meaning can only come into existence through the dream's translation by the analyst. (The dream's "cause" paradoxically being caused by its "effect.") Meaning is thus a product of the textual process itself, rather than a process of translation of a previous signified through a collection of individuality signifying words or images, and it is here that Ropars finds important connections with Eisenstein's theories of cinematic montage.

For Eisenstein, each shot has figural meaning, of course, but he also insisted that meaning lay in the conflictual nature of montage itself, giving rise to a textual process that undoes the meaning of the individual shots by neutralizing, fragmenting, and making them conflict with one another. "Produced abstractly by the juxtaposition of images, the concept cannot in any case be linked with a particular image . . . it is the original division of shots — equally removed from representation and signification — which produces a signification not only irreducible to representation, but even, at the extreme, independent of it" (p. 39). (Ropars, in fact, interestingly maintains that it is through a notion of montage applicable to *any* text that the figurative arts can escape representation by inscribing themselves in conceptual abstraction.) The shot itself can of course be polysemous or univocal, but for Eisenstein, Ropars explains, it is still montage which provides meaning, by extracting dominant meanings from the individual shots. In shots which lack a clear dominant, however, the paradoxical situation arises of the montage depending for its functioning upon elements within the shots which its functioning produces. Another version of Eisenstein's view of montage depends on a harmonic effect in which the sum of vibrations of each frame multiplies against the sum of the following shot. Each shot is thus indeterminant because of what is produced by both the external and the interior montage. Each shot is finally dependent for its meaning on juxtaposition, and thus upon the montage itself, so an increase of semantic potential within the shot can only lead to an increase of activity in the montage.

For Ropars, what links Eisensteinian montage even more closely with Derridean *écriture* is the director's insistence on the role of rupture in the signifying process. Thus, even the so-called invisible editing of classic Hollywood cinema, as Eisenstein pointed out, must both maintain an illusion of continuity and linearity, which implies the effacing of editing, and yet at the same time each shot must be perceived as *different* enough from the preceding one to justify its inclusion in the construction of its own invisibility. Both continuity and rupture, in other words, are simultaneously foregrounded. This paradox has wide-ranging implications for our understanding of twentieth century art, for as Ropars maintains, "the cinema, as a technique of assemblage, participates in the destructuring of classical space begun by Cézanne, even if the forms utilized by montage aim to restructure it illusionistically" (p. 87).

Derrida and Eisenstein are further related in their common interest in the hieroglyph, which is both figural, i.e., dependent upon a pictorial code for its meaning, and operational within a conventional system of signs. Derrida has defined the hieroglyph as "the organized cohabitation, within the same graphic code, of figurative, symbolic, abstract, and phonetic elements" (quoted, p. 61), and written forms of Western languages as well, though basically phonetic, contain elements of opposed systems. For Ropars, the hieroglyph is both figural and conceptual and can be likened, through montage, to what she calls "the scriptive vocation of the cinema." The very heterogeneity found in both hieroglyphs and montage guarantees that the signifying complexity of the cinematic image will not be reduced by the latent sign that the individual shot is presumably aiming at. The perspective of deconstruction is always doubled, however, and though the idea of the sign is exploded by montage, this does not mean that it can be done without. Rather, the logocentric concept of the sign is always

"the desired horizon of montage and of writing. The desire for meaning thus lies in wait for writing, whose negation and motor it is."[20]

Ropars' articulation of a theory of writing within cinema seems full
of promise, but in the course of her theorizing, individual film texts
are taken up and analyzed in ways that strongly challenge current
notions of "propriety" in film criticism, especially her brilliant, excruciatingly close reading of Marguerite Duras' *India Song*, which
occupies the second half of the book. Ropars insists, of course, that
her discussions of this and other films are not meant to be *analyses*
of them, but it seems ultimately impossible to dissociate heuristics
and hermeneutics so completely. It is true that she deliberately avoids
closure, or, like a good Derridean, even a resolved dialectic — hence
the title of her book — nor does she intend to provide an organic,
totalizing reading. Far from it. But any discussion of a specific text
inevitably interprets it, if only in re-presenting it in other signs, and
thus certain hermeneutic questions concerning relevance and applicability must arise. The fundamental problem is this: in the context
of a deconstructive criticism, is it possible or desirable to establish
criteria for interpretations? Given the fact that criticism can itself only
be another form of ungrounded writing, must *every* interpretation be
considered equally valid? Are we left with any criteria which would
allow us to say what in a reading is useful or plausible, and what is
just plain silly?

In the course of her long and provocative non-analysis of *India
Song*, Ropars twists and turns, juxtaposes and rewrites the film's
textual elements in ways that are often breathtaking, and which, it
must be said, seem to *illuminate* the text (and I am fully aware of the
metaphoric basis of that verb). In one particular place, however, she
resorts to anagrammatic "evidence" to support her reading. Here is
a sample of this writing: "Repeated several times, associated with
Laos, the name *Savannakhet* sounds even stranger since it contains,
in the center the first name *Anna*, and, at either end, the two initial
letters of *St*retter; with these two letters gone, what is left is *retter*,
the reduced mark of the double infinitely turned in on
itself . . . Savannakhet, the hidden name of the point of origin, provides, while holding it back, the name of Anne-(Marie) St(retter),
which "Bir/*manie*" might complete, if *r* is substituted for *n* to make
marie. . . . *St*ein begins the same as *St*retter and also as "*st*érile"; and
the beggar, "fo*lle*," née *là*-bas, in "*La*os," multiples the letters of

Lo/la; as does the network of *l*'s built up around Bengall (E*lle les laisse, les* vend, *les* oub*lie*") and punctuated by Ca*l*cutta."[21] And so on.

In an earlier version of this essay, I questioned whether this sort of anagrammatic play was in any way even remotely available to a spectator in her or his immediate, phenomenological construction of the film. I further argued that, even though deconstruction both theoretically and practically (in Derrida's own work, especially since *Glas* [1974]), "authorizes" such interpretive play, one's immediate experience of any given film had to be privileged over what can sometimes appear to be little more than the critic's own impressionistic, free-associative romp through the elements of a text. However, my own recourse to an originary concept of "experience" can itself be deconstructed, for experience is always doubled, always constituted retrospectively, after it has "happened," and thus is forever split, internally divided between the past and the future. As Jonathan Culler has pointed out, " 'experience' is divided and deferred — already behind us as something to be recovered, yet still before us as something to be produced."[22]

What we are left with, then, is the raw evidence of the text itself, and there is no way around respecting its disseminative possibilities. For literary theorists like Gregory Ulmer and Tom Conley, this anagrammatic play is the wave of the critical future, and for Derrida as well, apparently, since all of his most recent work relies heavily on puns and anagrams, especially that work which traces what he calls the "signature-effect" through an author's proper name. Conley claims optimistically that the critic's use of anagrams in interpretation (if it still may be called that), even sliding among languages different from the one in which the text under study was originally written, "allows us to move from a passive relation with language — it usually speaks to us — to the active condition of a maker. This involves painful travel to and from all kinds of repression, the uneasiness of loosening moorings and encountering vertigo and nausea, but it has the stake of bringing a reader into a world with a new symbolic reflexivity."[23]

I remain skeptical about this critical gesture which will presumably allow, in Conley's words, "the maker, the affective subject, to pass through multiple borders that define all lived experience and, indeed, to cope with the world differently" (p. 81). Nor am I at all sure that logocentrism can be so easily jettisoned, in critical interpretation or elsewhere. Though one hardly wants to act the hermeneutic police-man, especially within a deconstructive context, what use, finally, is an interpretation that strikes one as wholly subjective and impres-sionistic? Why bother to read it unless it somehow "illuminates" the text? I am in agreement with those deconstructionists who argue that much of what passes for deconstructive criticism in literature nowa-days, especially in the form of the how-to books that have proliferated, serves merely to domesticate deconstruction's radical potential. But surely another way of defusing deconstruction is to trivialize it through the self-indulgent display of the critic's own free-play of associations.

Furthermore, even Derrida has warned that the "liberation" of the signifer, which many have called for, at one level makes no sense: "The 'primacy' or 'priority' of the signifier would be an expression untenable and absurd to formulate illogically within the very logic that it would legitimately destroy. The signifier will never by rights precede the signified, in which case it would no longer be a signifier and the 'signifying' signifier would no longer have a possible signi-fied."[24]

In any case, whatever "play" the critic may allow her- or himself must follow a kind of rigorous "deconstructive logic" of its own. As Derrida insists at the beginning of "Plato's Pharmacy,"

> One must then, in a single gesture, but doubled, read and write. And that person would have understood nothing of the game who, at this, would feel himself authorized merely to add on; that is, to add any old thing. He would add nothing: the seam wouldn't hold. Recip-rocally, he who through "methodological prudence," "norms of ob-jectivity," or "safeguards of knowledge" would refrain from committing anything of himself, would not read at all. The same foolishness, the same sterility, obtains in the "not serious" as in the "serious." The reading or writing supplement must be rigorously prescribed, but by the necessities of a game, by the logic of *play*, signs to which the system of all textual powers must be accorded and attuned.[25]

We must remember, in other words, that deconstruction is always a doubling, a double consciousness, a simultaneous presence and ab-sence, both here and there. In interpretation, as elsewhere, a logo-centric metaphysics of presence is never finally escapable into a pleasant-to-imagine but make-believe realm of the pure free play of the signifier. Nevertheless, the escape must always be attempted. In both instances, desire will always push us toward the place we are not.

NOTES

[1] In describing the processes whereby certain films, either consciously or unconsciously, manage intermittently to unstick the spectator from the lure of the screen, the term "deconstruction" has become more and more widely employed. As an aspect of the Lacanian critique of the unified self, this seems entirely appropriate, given the fact that a similar critique, albeit from a different direction, is articulated in Derrida. Unfortunately, however, the term has entered perhaps too easily into contemporary critical discourse and is thus continually used with an imprecision that makes it signify little more than Brechtian *Verfremdungseffekt* or aesthetic distanciation. It has come to stand variously for "demystification" (as we find it for example in the early Barthes) or a blocking of audience identification with the characters, a revealing of the constructed (rather than natural) nature of the film image. As such, the term has come to be associated with an old-fashioned illusion-breaking self-referentiality that is one of the hallmarks of the modernist movement of the last century, but which has only a slight connection with Derrida's use of the term. We need to stake out this term more specifically as the articulation and (self-) revelation of each text's unreadability, its advance defeat of the demands of Western logic.

[2] Of necessity, this will require to some extent the positing of a fictional "Lacan" and a fictional "Derrida." I would not want to attempt to stage a "real" encounter between these two thinkers; Barbara Johnson (see *The Critical Difference* [Baltimore, Johns Hopkins University Press, 1980], pp. 110-46) has already shown us what such a staging might begin to look like, with its attendant complexities and necessary misreadings, and I have no wish to analyze her analysis of Derrida's analysis of Lacan's analysis of Poe's short story. (For such an analysis, however, see Stephen Melville, *Philosophy Beside Itself: Deconstruction and Modernism* [Minneapolis: University of Minnesota Press, 1986], pp. 140–43.) In the present essay, I am more interested in how Lacan is actually *used* in film study, and how Derrida *might* be used. Any attempt to reconstruct the "essence" of each writer's thought would obviously be out of place (as well as foolhardy).

[3] It might be added that this matter of film's popularity — its status as aesthetic experience of the masses — has also contributed to making

deconstructive criticism seem somehow inappropriate, concerned as it
has been primarily with elite and/or obscure texts. The thought of a
deconstructive reading of the latest movie blockbuster is nevertheless
intriguing, even if it would have to disguise itself as parody.

4 *Positions*, trans. Alan Bass (Chicago: University of Chicago Press, 1981),
n. 44, pp. 107–109.

5 Teresa de Lauretis, *Alice Doesn't: Feminism, Semiotics, Cinema* (Bloomington: Indiana University Press, 1984), p. 23. Derrida's own "usefulness" for feminism has of course been hotly debated, but a full
examination of this question would take us too far afield from the purposes of the present essay. See Gayatri Spivak's complicated and exhil-
arating "Displacement and the Discourse of Woman," in *Displacement:
Derrida and After*, ed. Mark Krupnick (Bloomington: Indiana University
Press, 1983), pp. 169–95.

6 J. Hillis Miller, "The Search for Grounds in Literary Study," in *Rhetoric
and Form: Deconstruction at Yale*, ed. Robert Con Davis and Ronald
Schleifer (Norman: University of Oklahoma Press, 1985), p. 31.

7 See Derrida's "The Principle of Reason: The University in the Eyes of
Its Pupils," in *Diacritics* (Fall, 1983), 3–20.

8. See, for example, de Man's "Hegel on the Sublime," in *Displacement:
Derrida and After*, ed. Mark Krupnick. There de Man makes the claim
that "Aesthetic theory [in Kant] is critical philosophy to the second
degree, the critique of the critiques. It critically examines the possibility
and the modalities of political discourse and political action, the inescapable burden of any linkage between discourse and action. The treatment of the aesthetic in Kant is certainly far from conclusive, but one
thing is clear: it is epistemological as well as political through and
through" (p. 140).

9 Barbara Johnson, *A World of Difference* (Baltimore: Johns Hopkins
University Press, 1987), pp. 30–31.

10 John Frow, *Marxism and Literary History* (Cambridge: Harvard University Press, 1986), p. 38.

11 Michael Ryan, *Marxism and Deconstruction: A Critical Articulation* (Baltimore: Johns Hopkins University Press, 1982), p. 117. See also his
more recent "Deconstruction and Social Theory," in *Displacement: Derrida and After*, pp. 154–168.

12 Jacques Derrida, "Structure, Sign, and Play in the Discourse of the
Human Sciences," in *The Structuralist Controversy* (Baltimore: The Johns
Hopkins University Press, 1972), p. 272.

13 Barbara Johnson, *The Critical Difference*, pp. x–xi.

14 Jacques Derrida, "Parergon," in *La verité en peinture* (Paris: Flammarion, 1978), pp. 19–168. Part two of this four-part essay has been trans-

lated into English by Craig Owens and appears as "The Parergon" in *October* (Summer, 1979), pp. 3–40.

15 For example, if imitation (mimesis) really adds nothing and is only a "supplement," then why bother? As Derrida points out, in Western art the representation "adds" the essence of that which is represented, hence this essence comes from outside, from elsewhere. (*Of Grammatology* [Baltimore: The Johns Hopkins University Press 1974), p. 203.] For a discussion of how this process works in the writings of André Bazin, see my "Rossellini and Cinematic Realism," *Cinema Journal* (Fall, 1985), pp. 34–49.

16 Dudley Andrew, *Concepts in Film Theory* (New York: Oxford University Press, 1984), p. 161.

17 Jacques Derrida, "Force and Signification," in *Writing and Difference*, trans. Alan Bass (Chicago: University of Chicago Press, 1978), p. 17.

18 What is also at stake here is the legitimacy of the frame analysis technique, increasingly popular in film studies, since this technique causes even more potential signifiers to be "registered" by the critic. To reject this technique as invalid would seem implicitly to privilege the signified, once again, over the signifier. On what "level" of awareness does meaning finally organize itself?

19 Marie-Claire Ropars-Wuilleumier, *Le texte divisé* (Paris: Presses Universitaires de France, 1981). An earlier version of part of this book appeared as "The Disembodied Voice (*India Song*)" in *Yale French Studies*, #60 (1980), pp. 241–268. Another essay of hers in English translation, "The Graphic in Filming Writing: *A bout de souffle*, Or the Erratic Alphabet," has appeared in *enclitic* (Fall 1981/Spring 1982), pp. 147–161. Translations from *Le texte divisé* in the present essay are my own.

20 *Le texte divisé*, p. 52. Elsewhere she speaks of the simultaneous and contradictory "linguistic desire" to produce a sign, thus motivating it referentially and the "scriptive practice" of differing signs from one another purely on the basis of their signifiers (p. 73).

The economy of shot and montage which Ropars describes also has other important implications for film theory. Though she does not pursue the matter, her brief suggestion that privileging montage over the individual shot may even lead to a theory of a subject made up of gaps [*sujet lacunaire*], less interpellated by the image than *distanced* by the process of editing, seems to offer a possible alternative to Lacanian and Althusserian models of subject construction.

21 "The Disembodied Voice: *India Song*," p. 260.

22 Jonathan Culler, *On Deconstruction* (Ithaca: Cornell University Press, 1982), p. 82.

23 Tom Conley, "A Trace of Style," in *Displacement: Derrida and After*,

p. 81. See also Gregory Ulmer's *Applied Grammatology: Post(e)-Pedagogy from Jacques Derrida to Joseph Beuys* (Baltimore: Johns Hopkins University Press, 1985).

[24] *Of Grammatology*, p. 324, n. 9.

[25] *Dissemination*, trans. Barbara Johnson (Chicago: University of Chicago Press, 1981), p. 64.

NOTES ON MOVIE MUSIC
by Noël and Patrick Carroll

Movie music often fails to receive proper attention in film analyses and film theories. Perhaps one reason for this is that the highly technical language of musical analysis intimidates the film expert. The non-musically trained analyst of film realizes s/he is unable to explore a movie's music in the professionally preferred idiom, and, debarred from the *lingua franca* of music criticism, decides to say nothing at all. The purpose of this short paper is to supply a musically-nontechnical way of speaking about one use of movie music, which we call modifying music. We shall attempt to describe the structure of this sort of music, to explain how it works and how it fits into the system of popular expression called the movies.[1]

There are, of course, many different functions that music can perform in relation to movies. Aaron Copland suggested five broad functions: creating of atmosphere; underlining the psychological states of characters; providing neutral background filler; building a sense of continuity; sustaining tension and then rounding it off with a sense of closure.[2] These do not seem to be necessarily exclusive categories, nor do they exhaust the range of functions that music can perform in movies. This is not said in order to criticize Copland, for, in fact, we intend to follow his example. We shall analyze *a* function of movie music, freely admitting that there are others, and, moreover, we shall not deny that this function may also be yoked together with the performance of other functions, such as those Copland enumerates.

The type of music we have in mind is quite central in popular movies; it is a basic use of music, if not the most basic. To approach it, let us consider some examples, In *Gunga Din* (dir. by George Stevens; music by Alfred Newman), there is an early scene where the British, led by Cary Grant, Douglas Fairbanks Jr. and Victor Mc-

Laglen, enter a seemingly deserted village in search of foul doings. Indeed, the village has been raided by the nefarious Thugs, and those dastardly followers of Kali are lying in wait for the British. We have been somewhat alerted to this insofar as the scene is initiated by the use of an oboe in imitation of the sort of double-reed instrument associated with snake charmers, thereby signaling the presence of the Thugs in the deserted village. There is an ambush. During the ensuing battle, there is a recurring theme that is associated with the efforts of Grant, Maclaglen and Fairbanks. Earlier, we had heard the same theme accompanying their drunken brawl over a treasure map. In the ambush scene, an interlude of strings will be followed by horns at a scherzo-like tempo. Often this theme comes in when our soldiers of fortune gain the upper hand, but not always. The horns are bouncy, light and playful. The battle scene, full of death and danger, could be the object of high anxiety. But the use of the horns in this theme color the scene in such a way that we come to view it as a lark, as a game, as comic rather than potentially tragic. Thus, of course, from our point of view, what is important about the scene is the way in which the scherzo-like refrain directs the audience to view the mayhem as jaunty — almost comic — good fun.

In *Rebel Without a Cause* (dir. by Nicholas Ray; music by Leonard Rosenman), we find a wholly different feeling associated with the on-screen violence. Underlying the confrontation and the fight, called the "blade game," which occurs after the visit to the planetarium, is atonal music, marked by odd time signatures and dissonant blaring brass. The use of the timpani and horns, along with the timing, give the music a Stravinsky-like flavor. As well, the music is sometimes recorded low, and, then, abruptly, the recording level is raised. The dissonance imparts a brooding feeling to the scene, a sense of latent, almost muscular violence that flashes out when the brass blares or the recording level shoots up. The uneasy, unstable quality of the music serves to characterize the psychological turmoil — the play of repression and explosive release — with which the scene is concerned.

For an example not involved with violence, consider the opening of *The Yearling* (dir. by Clarence Brown; music by Herbert Stothart). The camera displays views of the Everglades, as Gregory Peck, playing a Civil War veteran, recalls how he came to make his home there. The score is dominated by strings which have strong connotations of richness and lushness reflecting, of course, the way in which the narrator feels about this place. What Peck's voice and the visuals may fail to make you realize about the landscape, the music enables you to grasp. Also, the strings have a slightly haunting flavor and a sense of pastness which coincides with the appearance this film suggests of being swathed in memory. When we are introduced to the juvenile lead, Jody (played by Claude Jarman Jr.), the music sounds somewhat pentatonic, like an elongated country melody, conveying a feeling that is both lazy and dreamy. This not only corresponds to what we immediately see of Jody — he is playing listlessly with a toy windmill — but to what we learn of Jody throughout the film, viz., that he is a dreamer. In terms of the subject matter of the film, a major source of tension between Peck and his wife, played by Jane Wyman, develops because Peck believes that youth *should* be a time when the imagination is given its head, before the hardships and responsibilities of practical life force one to turn to sterner things. Wyman resists this, and the battle between youth and imagination, on the one hand, versus adulthood and practicality, on the other, is staged over Flag, the yearling from whom the film derives its title. Throughout *The Yearling*, the use of the strings repeatedly stresses the theme of the imagination by underscoring and characterizing the various spoken reveries and gambolings of characters in terms of an undeniable, albeit very nineteen-fortyish, feeling of dreaminess.

These examples are not alike in every respect. The theme from *Gunga Din* functions narratively as a leitmotif, whereas the example from *Rebel Without a Cause* does not. However, the three examples share a very basic function, one which in fact enables the theme from *Gunga Din* to do its more specialized work so well. Namely, in each of these examples the music characterizes the scene, i.e., imbues the scene with certain expressive properties. This may be a matter of enhancing qualities that are already suggested in the imagery, but it need not be; the music may attribute an otherwise unavailable quality to the visuals. Nor does the expressive quality in question have to be grounded in the psychology of a character; in the *Gunga Din* example the *jauntiness* of the music appears to attach first and foremost to the action rather than to internal states of characters. And, lastly, the expressive qualities projected in these examples are in the music. We do not suddenly become dreamy when we hear the strings of *The Yearling*. Rather the dreaminess of the music characterizes Jody as dreamy to us. If we are pro-dreaminess, the way Gregory Peck and the film are, then we are apt to feel sympathetic (rather than dreamy) in regard to Jody. That is, by speaking of the projection of expressive qualities, we are not claiming that the music arouses in the spectator the selfsame expressive qualities that it projects.

We can call this use of movie music modifying music. The music modifies the movie. The music possesses certain expressive qualities which are introduced to modify or to characterize onscreen persons and objects, actions and events, scenes and sequences. To use a crude analogy, one which must be eventually abandoned, the visual track is to a noun as the music is to an adjective, or, alternatively, the visuals are to verbs as the music is to adverbs. Just as adjectives and adverbs characterize, modify and enrich the nouns and verbs to which they are attached, modifying music serves to add *further* characterization to the scenes it embellishes. This is a very pervasive use of movie music. Let us now turn to a discussion of its origin and its internal dynamics.

Movie music involves coordinating two different symbol systems: music and movies, the latter including not only visuals but recorded sounds, both natural and dialogic. In the case of modifying music, these two symbol systems are placed in a complementary relationship; each system supplies something that the other system standardly lacks, or, at least, does not posssess with the same degree of effectiveness that the other system possesses.

Music, for example, is a highly expressive symbol system. This is not to say that all music is expressive or that it should be expressive, but only that much music is expressive. For example, that the Prelude to *Tristan and Isolde* is expressive of yearning or that the "Great Gate of Kiev" from *Pictures at an Exhibition* is expressive of majesty are part of the incontestable data of aesthetic theorizing. To say that music is expressive is to say that it projects qualities describable in anthropomorphic, emotive terms. The symbol system of music is also sometimes thought to have more direct access to the emotive realm than any other symbol system. Nietzsche called music "the immediate language of the will."[3]

At the same time, it is often noted that nonvocal music — orchestral music —, though quite effective in expressing a broad palette of emotions, is not the ideal means for particularizing the feelings it projects. That is, a piece of nonvocal orchestral music may strike us as sorrowful or even more broadly as "down" but we generally cannot specify much further the kind of dolors or dumps the music projects. Is it melancholic, neurasthenic, suicidal, adolescent, etc.? That is, nonvocal music standardly lacks what music theorist Peter Kivy calls emotive explicitness.[4]

This lack of emotive explicitness has figured in numerous debates in the history of music. Some, like Johann Adam Hiller, took it as a limitation to be overcome, urging that if music is to become intelligible, i.e. emotively explicit, it must be combined with speech.[5] A similar view was espoused by James Beattie, who held that "the expression of music without poetry is vague and ambiguous."[6] Peter Kivy has brilliantly demonstrated that the development of the expressive arsenal of orchestral music, as we know it, was the result of solving the *perceived* problem of music's emotive inexplicitness through text setting.[7] In a different mood, Eduard Hanslick argued against the expression of emotion as a goal of music because he believed that music cannot express definite emotions,[8] while Nietzsche, staking out an altogether different position, sees the emotive inexplicitness of music as the path to some coveted form of universality: ". . . whoever gives himself up entirely to the impression of a symphony, seems to see all possible events of life and the world take place in himself."[9]

The vicissitudes of the preceding positions are less important to us than their recurring assumption, which we shall state weakly as follows: typically, nonvocal music is expressive of emotive qualities but ones that are inexplicit, ambiguous and broad. A theoretical explanation of why this should be is also readily available. Emotions are directed, directed at persons, objects, states of affairs and events. Indeed, it is in virtue of the objects to which emotions are directed that we individuate emotions.[10] I am afraid *of being run over by a train;* you are in love *with Bob;* we are angered *by apartheid.* For an emotion to be fully explicit and particularized, it must be aimed at some object. The object may be real, like South Africa, or fantasized, e.g., you may be terrified of The Green Slime. To become explicit, that is, the emotion must be referred to something. To say whether the joy in the music is hysterical or utopian, we would have to know toward what the joy was directed. And, of course, it is this sort of reference that is most commonly absent from music, that is, nonvocal music. Insofar as representation is not a primary function of standard orchestral music, most music of this sort will lack the logical machinery to secure emotive particularity. This is not to say that orchestral music cannot be representational: e.g., *Wellington's Victory*, Honegger's *Pacific 231* and the use of percussion to refer to King Kong's offscreen footsteps in the film of the same name.[11] And where the music is representational, a measure of emotive explicitness may be achievable. However, as we have said, as a matter of fact, most nonvocal music lacks the logical machinery which emotive explicitness requires.

So far we have claimed that orchestral music of the sort often employed in movies is a symbol system that makes a powerful yet broad and inexplicit emotive address. And this inexplicitness, in turn, is a result of the fact that generally such music is non-referring. Movies, on the other hand, are symbol systems with numerous overlapping referential dimensions, including the cinematographic image, dialogue, narrative and synched sound. Wedding the musical system to the movie system, then, supplies the kind of reference required to particularize the broad expressivity of the musical system. The *dreaminess* of the strings in *The Yearling* is specified as Jody's dreaminess, as the dreaminess of a young boy prior to the hard lessons of life.

The relation between the music and the movie in the case of modifying music is reciprocal. The movie — the visuals, the narrative, the dialogue and the synched sound — serve as *indicators*. At one level, these elements establish what the scene is about. They indicate the reference of the scene. The music then modifies or characterizes what the scene is about in terms of some expressive quality. In a manner of speaking, the music tells us something, of an emotive significance, about what the scene is about; the music supplies us with, so to say, a description (or presentation) of the emotive properties the film attaches to the referents of the scene.

In our *Gunga Din* example, the movie establishes the subject, the battle, and the music imbues it with a feeling, that of jauntiness. The musical element, which we call a *modifier*, *fills-in* the subject matter in terms of the feeling the filmmaker finds appropriate to the scene. However, at the same time, the movie elements, what we have called indicators, stand in an important relation of influence to the musical component. The music on its own is bouncy, light and comic. When conjoined with the movie elements those feelings become further particularized as manly, daredevil bravado. The musical system, so to speak, carves out a broad range or spectrum of feeling, in this case, one that is positive, lively and energetic. The movie elements, the indicators, then narrow down or *focus* more precisely the qualities in that range or spectrum that are relevant to the action. The music no longer signals mere energy but more precisely bravado. This focusing operation of the movie-as-indicator, in turn, enables the music-as-modifier to fill-in the action as a highly particularized feeling.

It might be initially helpful to think of the relation of the subject–predicate relation: the music says ". . . is jaunty" and the movie specifies the blank with "the battle." However, though suggestive, this analogy cannot be taken too seriously because the movie elements perform functions other than referring and focusing, and because the linguistic notion of predication seems to be strictly inapplicable to the image track in cinema (i.e., pictures lack discriminable subject–predicate elements and show objects with their properties, all-at-once, so to speak). Thus, though modifying music resembles linguistic predication loosely, it should not be taken as a literal example of it.

Another possible avenue of misunderstanding modifying music would be an oversimplification that regards music as exclusively expressive and the movie components as exclusively representational. As was earlier remarked, music can be used representationally. Similarly, movie elements have myriad means of expression — not only through acting, but through lighting, camera movement, camera angulation, cutting, etc. Indeed, the generally referential soundtrack can be "musically" arranged in order to aspire to musical expressivity, e.g., the natural sounds at the opening of *Street Scenes* and the dialogue in *Force of Evil*. Thus, it is not the case that the movie is pure representation to be supplemented by means of musical expression along with the visual, narrative and dramatic means already at its disposal. The addition of music givess the filmmaker an especially direct and immediate means for assuring that the audience is matching the correct expressive quality with the action at hand. This is not to say that music is the film's only expressive lever; rather it is a notably direct and reliable one. It enhances the filmmaker's expressive control over the action.

If adding music to the movie enhances one's expressive control over the action, it is also the case that the movie imagery intensifies the impact of the music by particularizing its affective resonance. The unnerving, shrieking strings in *Psycho* are cruel, painful and murderous when matched with Norman Bates' descending knife. Here, the reference afforded by the movie elements serves to individuate the emotive content of the music in the way that the narrative and pantomime do in ballet, and as the words do in a popular song or opera.

Modifying music is one of the major uses of music in popular movies. It may be used to embellish individual scenes and sequences, or it may be integrated into leitmotif systems, etc. Structurally, modifying music involves the use of movie elements — photography, narrative, dialogue and synched sound — as *indicators* that fix the reference of a shot, scene or sequence. The associated musical elements are *modifiers* which attribute expressive qualities to the referent, thereby characterizing it emotively as, for example, dreamy or jaunty. Functionally, the addition of musical modifiers to the scene augments the expressivity of the scene, though this does not preclude the possibility that the scene already possesses many non-musical expressive devices. Nevertheless, music is a particularly privileged means of direct, expressive augmentation. The musical modifiers function to *fill-in* the scene expressively, to set the expressive tone the filmmaker takes to be appropriate to the scene. The music "saturates" the scene expressively. At the same time that the musical modifiers influence the reception of the movie, the movie indicators also reciprocally influence the reception of the music. For music typically, sans referential machinery, projects a very broad and inexplicit range of emotive qualities. Thus, in *The African Queen*, when the boat is stuck in the canal, the slow, spaced out drum beats project a generic, plodding feeling while the movie elements specify that feeling as Bogart's effort, an effort charged with all his hopes and commitments. Thus, as the music fills-in the movie, the movie *focuses* the emotive content of the music, particularizing and intensifying its effect which, of course, also abets the filling-in work that the musical modifier does.

We have attempted to explain the way in which modifying music operates. Modifying music is not employed, of course, only in movies — it occurs in other sorts of films, such as art films, as well as in other art forms, such as ballet. As well, it is not the only use of music found in movies. Yet, though the relation between modifying music and the movies is not unique in any sense, there is a way in which modifying music serves the aims of the movie symbol system quite expeditiously. That is, there is something especially fitting about the relationship between modifying music and the movies. Thus, we will conclude by sketching the way that modifying music segues into the economy of the movies.

Movies are a means of popular expression. They are aimed at mass audiences. They aspire for means of communication that can be grasped almost immediately by untutored audiences. Another way of putting this is to say that movie makers seek devices that virtually guarantee that the audience will follow the action in the way that the filmmaker deems appropriate.[12] The movie close-up, for example, assures the filmmaker that the spectator is looking exactly where she should be looking at the appropriate moment. And, the close-up guarantees this automatically. Similarly, modifying music, given the almost direct expressive impact of music, assures that the untutored spectators of the mass movie audience will have access to the desired expressive quality and, in turn, will see the given scene or sequence under its aegis. Secondly, an important element accounting for the power of movies is the clarity that movies bestow upon the events that they depict. In contrast to our encounters in every-day life, movie events have an unaccustomed intelligibility and lucidity; movies, that is, are so much more legible than life. Modifying music contributes to the clarity of movies in several different respects. The filling-in function of the music modifier keeps the expressive quality of the scene constantly foregrounded, thereby supplying a continuous channel of information about the emotional significance of the action. Unlike our quotidian experience of events, the music constantly alerts us to the feeling that goes with what we see. Whereas in life, the affect that goes with an observation is so often unknown, in movies, we not only have some affect but also the appropriate affect tied to virtually everything we see, through modifying music. The movie-world is emotionally perspicuous through and through.

Reciprocally, the focusing function of the movie indicators render the emotive content of the music more and more explicit, again enhancing clarity in yet another way. The concerted interplay of the music and the movie yields images replete with highly clarified, virtually directly accessible, expressive qualities. Thus, though modifying music is not a unique feature of movies, its capacity for promoting immediately accessible, explicit and continuously emotive characterizations of the ongoing, onscreen action makes it *so suitable* to the presiding commitments of mass movie communication that it *would be a mystery* had movies failed to exploit it.[13]

NOTES

[1] For a discussion of what is meant by "movies" in this paper, see Noël Carroll, "The Power of Movies," in *Daedalus*, no. 114, (Autumn, 1985).

[2] Aaron Copland, "Tip to Moviegoers: Take off those Ear-Muffs," in *The New York Times*, Nov. 6, 1949, section six, p. 28. This article is discussed at length in Roy M. Prendergast's *Film Music: A Neglected Art* (New York: Norton, 1977), Chap. 6.

[3] Friedrich Nietzsche, *The Birth of Tragedy and The Case of Wagner*, translated by Walter Kaufman (New York: Random House, 1967), p. 103.

[4] Peter Kivy, *The Corded Shell* (New Jersey: Princeton University Press, 1980), p. 98.

[5] Johann Adam Hiller, "Abhandlung von der Nachahmung der Natur in der Musik," in *Historisch-Kritische Beyträge*, ed. by Friedrich Wilhelm Marpurg (Berlin, 1754), Vol. I, p. 524.

[6] James Beattie, *The Philosophical and Critical Works* (Hildesheim and New York: Georg Olms, 1975), p. 463.

[7] Kivy, *The Corded Shell*.

[8] Eduard Hanslick, *The Beautiful in Music*, translated by Gustav Cohen (New York: The Liberal Arts Press, 1957).

[9] Nietzsche, *Birth of Tragedy*, p. 102.

[10] A source for this view of the emotions is Anthony Kenny, *Action, Emotion and Will* (London: Routledge and Kegan Paul, 1963).

[11] For a thorough account of musical representation see Peter Kivy, *Sound and Semblance* (New Jersey: Princeton University Press, 1984).

[12] For an amplification of the view of the movie system asserted above see Carroll, "The Power of Movies."

[13] Though we stress a functional relation between sound and image in movies, our position should not be confused with the one propounded in *Composing for the Films* by Theodor Adorno and Hans Eisler. Our position is *closer* to that articulated by Schopenhauer when he writes in the Third Book of *The World as Will and Idea* that "Suitable music played to any scene, action, event or surrounding seems to disclose to us its most secret meaning, and appears as the most accurate and distinct commentary upon it."

IDEOLOGICAL AND MARXIST CRITICISM: TOWARDS A METAHERMENEUTICS

Bill Nichols

If we may speak of the formalists' revenge in the course of recent debates on critical methodology in film study, it can be localized in the constitution of Marxist/ideological criticism as an Imaginary Other. Five or six years ago, ideological criticism stood unnamed, its corpus distributed among diverse and sometimes divergent practices from Marxism to psychoanalysis (Lacanian) and from feminism to post-structuralism. The recognition or assignment of a unified body for these practices identifies a point of commonality that threatens to suppress difference, including different conceptualizations of ideology itself. Insight, here, aligns itself with blindness. An omnipresent solidity looms — oppressively to those who feel displaced beyond the boundaries of the very thing they have helped to name. This Imaginary configuration then becomes a pretext for misrecognition, *ressentiment*, and the rescue of aesthetics from ideological confinement. Dudley Andrew, for example, in his recent survey of film theory, lets us feel the pulse of the Imaginary homogeneity within Marxist/ideological criticism:

> The voice heard by today's theorists is the monotone of ideology, a voice to be isolated but certainly not amplified by the critic. It is ideology that fashions the ultimate sameness of all films.
>
> In asserting a total view of the cinematic complex (from the dark caverns of spectator psychology to the global network of socio-economics) modern theory has forsaken the enterprise of criticism. How can the study of an individual film be important to anyone who senses the

single voice of ideology emanating from every film? Criticism in this
context can only be redundant.[1]

Ideological approaches to culture reify into a monolith. The process
of naming and its promise of empowerment always lives with the
hazards of misnaming and the process of marginalization, just as recognition coexists not only with non-recognition (blindness) but, more
dangerously, with misrecognition. Certainly, the following description
poses severe problems of recognition when it relegates the active power
of ideology to crisis moments and to the solicitation of commitment
rather than disinterestedness:

> Thus Geertz can define ideology, for example, as a response to the
> loss of social and political orientation. The resultant confusion about
> what to make of the civic world of rights and responsibilities in the
> absence of suitable models for comprehending it sets off the frantic
> search for alternative models which will provide fresh insights through
> which the opportunities and conditions of the civic realm can be
> grasped. . . . [S]cience defines the structure of situations in such a way
> as to promote an attitude of disinterestedness toward them, whereas
> ideology, on the other hand, defines them in a manner which elicits
> an attitude of commitment.[2]

The passages cited remind us of the strongly committed nature of
the analysis of representation and of its role within an institutional
(here, academic) setting where issues of power get contested. This
point is not one I wish to pursue here in detail, having done so
elsewhere;[3] what I do wish to consider is whether ideological/Marxist
criticism does risk constituting an Imaginary discourse, to what degree
Marxist and ideological criticism are synonymous, and what specific
issues or problems provide the strongest sense of animation to contemporary debate (I am thinking of issues involving the text, desire,
essentialism, totalization, reading, utopia and, above all, ideology itself). I wish to conduct this inquiry through an extended set of re-
flections/commentaries on two recent works that propose terms and
directions for a Marxist criticism of culture: Fredric Jameson's *The
Political Unconscious* and Frank Lentricchia's *Criticism and Social
Change.*[4]

★   ★   ★

The reification of any critical method provides a means of containing its power and restricting its claims. The claim of a monolithic uniformity to its operation, of a regularity and certainty to its results—or of the only occasional pertinence of its central concepts (such as ideology)—reduce it to one more piece of analytic equipment. Within the terms of an academic pluralism that insists on open-mindedness, a free market of ideas, ideological/Marxist criticism could be thought to impoverish our understanding by restricting it to categories either known in advance or only infrequently germane. Referring to Christian Metz's efforts to ground cinematic spectatorship in a psychodynamics of primary identification where history and discourse are "factored out," Dudley Andrew raises his sword against the Imaginary dragon of those totalizing systems that suppress the particular in favor of the general: "No over-arching theory could ever be adequate to the essentially historical complexities of cinematic discourse."[5] What we must now examine, though, is precisely whether ideological/Marxist criticism sustains an essentializating or reductionist impulse or if it offers the occasion to grasp the full dimensionality of a particular text as it comes to be situated within the domains of history and discourse.[6]

From a perspective that values freedom, complexity, and open-endedness, the most debilitating quality of a Marxist criticism involves its instrumental view of culture. Such a view can be more readily accorded to culture when it is conceived as the form and pattern of everyday life, as a lived relation to the conditions of existence, or as those "webs of significance" by which we assign meaning to things within an historical field where the play of power, purpose, hierarchy and suasion can be readily acknowledged, than when we speak of Culture or Art, which, we have been assured, elude such expressly political forces. Lentricchia aptly conveys the authority of this assurance by assigning it to the names "Aristotle" and "Kant" where these names serve as "forces of literary desire" (CSC, p. 91). "Aristotle" names the desire "to free literary representations from the sort of particularity that would tie them to the specifications of history" while "Kant," "by attempting to take the aesthetic rigorously away from willing, cognition, and all *interest* . . . assures 'Aristotle' that literary representation can never be politicized by the temporal powers that operate in society" (CSC, p. 91).[7] Lentricchia refutes this tradition, arguing, by means of an extended explication of Kenneth Burke's writings, that "Art is an instrument, one of the powers that create us as sociopolitical beings" (CSC, p. 102) while Jameson, more tentatively, concedes that "the instrumentalization of culture" is a "temptation or tendency within all Marxisms" but that it need not be a "necessary and fatal consequence" (PUC, p. 293). Lentricchia, through his effort to understand the rhetorical claims of all literature (defined by Burke as "any writing with a design upon readers" rather than as solely "imaginative writing"),[8] and Jameson, through his effort to identify a Utopian or collective impulse in culture, however thoroughly it may be subsequently managed to provide support for reified commodity relationships, both insist that Marxist criticism be more than the deconstruction of texts, more than a negative dialectics of suspicion and protest, more than an instrumental view of culture that all too readily, to use Dudley Andrew's expression, reduces culture to "the monotone of ideology."

Some ideological/Marxist film criticism has proceeded in a manner that makes the "monotone" charge plausible, especially when the political becomes located in the Imaginary, or is repressed to the level of the Unconscious so that constant reference to its textual embodiment seems unnecessary or forced. The effort to identify the mechanisms governing a cinematic apparatus which is more than a technology, an industry or a set of stylistic procedures, which operates to produce the fundamental (or monotonous) "ideological effect" of the cinema—the construction of subject positions that subscribe the viewer to the terms of a patriarchal, capitalist, Imaginary discourse lends itself to a counter-critique in defense of specificity.[9] Laura Mulvey's seminal essay, "Visual Pleasure and Narrative Cinema," indicts classic Hollywood cinema for producing pleasure that can only be received from the position of the male spectator, an indictment that leaves little room for contestation at the more local level of individual texts, save through oppositional, avant-garde practices that place the production of meaning, subjectivity, and the attendant viewer positions all into question.[10] Such practices may deconstruct the apparatus and its effects but they also carry the risk of producing a new (monotonous) apparatus dedicated to heterogeneity, heteroglossia, dispersion, flux, écriture, and so on.

But ideological/Marxist criticism has not followed the agenda of a therapeutic diagnostics such as this exclusively. A strong tradition of textual analysis, refurbished with the tools of poststructuralism, has worked to isolate those moments of contradiction, tactics of resolution and possibilities of counter-reading, reading against the grain of the text, that return specificity and localized complexity to the relations between ideology and culture.[11] These two tendencies—toward something like a general field theory of ideology, on the one hand, and a materialist reading of specific texts, on the other—represent a vital dynamic within ideological/Marxist writings as a whole which is suppressed and reified by any effort to legitimize one at the expense of the other. Indeed, these tendencies give embodiment to a fundamental dialectic of Marxism that too easily collapses into the institutional struggle to dominate described by Jameson as:

> an uneasy struggle for priority between models and history, between theoretical speculation and textual analysis, in which the former seeks to transform the latter into so many mere examples, adduced to support its abstract propositions, while the latter continues insistently to imply that the theory itself was just so much methodological scaffolding . . . (PUC, p. 13).

The monotone of ideology can only reverberate in a bell jar evacuated of history, voided of what makes culture more than a single-edged instrument of control and criticism, more than a proof of an instrumentality we can presumably escape through "the taking of thought" (PUC, p. 283). The implicit essentialism that would make the "truth" of ideology a reductive one—a set of "effects" produced by an apparatus, a set of positions constructed by a text—can sometimes be disguised by a post-structural rhetoric that ostensibly rejects the essences, truths, and self-evident assumptions of Western metaphysics and humanism, a political rhetoric that may also reduce the crucial linkage between knowledge and power, discourse and purpose to an ahistorical, formal one. ("Essence," Lentricchia reminds us can be defined by the neglect of complexity: " 'Much must be forgotten if the essential is to be preserved' " CSC, p. 128). That theory arrives in history and operates "for the purpose of generating more history in a certain way: generating the history we want" (CSC, p. 12) is a basic prerequisite for the application of the formalist's bell jar.

★ ★ ★

We may continue here the separation begun earlier (footnote 6) when some projects of poststructural and deconstructive reading were distinguished from Marxist ones by their recourse to formal strategies of intervention and contestation in a timeless ether of ideological sameness and ask if ideological criticism is indeed synonymous with Marxist criticism.

Part of the recent dominance of the practice designated as "ideological criticism" within film study derives precisely from the aggregation of diverse constituencies, methodological emphases and political/cultural priorities into a perceived unity. Gay and lesbian criticism, feminist, psychoanalytic, deconstructive and avowedly Marxist criticism all speak to distinct constituencies, bear the marks of internal struggle and debate, and sustain varying degrees of commitment to basic Marxist criticism all speak to distinct constituencies, bear the marks of internal struggle and debate, and sustain varying degrees of commitment to basic Marxist concepts of class, class consciousness and history while contributing collectively to a far more fully elaborated understanding of the linkages between aesthetics and ideology, politics and art. Ideological criticism then stands as a Symbolic construct in terms of the by-play and reciprocity, the stress on methodological syncretism and relational mediation that characterize these criticisms in their internal operation and dialogue with one another (Jameson renames this reciprocity "transcoding": "the invention of a set of terms, the strategic choice of a particular code or language, such that the terminology can be used to analyze and articulate two quite distinct types of objects or 'texts,' or two very different structural levels of reality" (PUC, p. 40). But the term remains an Imaginary construct within the institutional context of the struggle for interpretive hegemony that pits this approach against others as though it were in an oppositional rather than a hierarchical relationship with them.

Jameson himself posits a clear hierarchy among critical methods that has recourse less to purpose than to processes of mental structuration à la Lévi-Strauss: "[I]t must be clear to anyone who has experimented with various approaches to a given text that the mind is not content until it puts some order in these findings and invents a hierarchical relationship among its various interpretations" (PUC, p. 31). The reification of ideological criticism then stands as a containment strategy intended to postpone a systematic overview and the "embarrassing questions" about a given approach's purchase on "the ultimate ground of narrative and textual production" (PUC, pp. 31–33).

Jameson,more than Lentricchia, regards ideological criticism as a moment within Marxist analysis, within a totalizing, historicizing imperative that precedes and subsumes it. The stress on rupture, discontinuity, *Aufhebung*, and so on that poststructuralists offer yields to an emphasis on the continuity of thought that is Marxist. At one level this reveals itself in a non-antagonistic relationship between Marxist analysis and other approaches which can be subsumed rather than attacked. (Jameson is particularly receptive to the hermeneutic tradition and its potential contribution to a Marxist "double hermeneutic" that establishes the textual figuration of both a positive-utopian and negative-ideological dialectic.) On another level, Jameson's emphasis on the conservation of a Marxist tradition prompts him to subsume currents of "ideological criticism" such as Barthes' *S/Z* as well, rather than posit any radical breaks. This occurs most forcefully in relation to the Althusserian critique of causality and traditional models of interpretation where a "lengthy digression" (PUC, pp. 23–58) allows Jameson to formulate a model of structural exegesis commensurate with Althusser's structural causality (in contrast to mechanistic and expressive causality) but also commensurate with a Lukácsian concept of totality. This model, James claims, avoids contenting itself with the almost canonical, but formalist, gesture of *S/Z* where Barthes "shatters a Balzac novella into a random operation of multiple codes" without reunifying this multiplicity at the historical level of the process of production (PUC, p. 56).

A less elaborate act of subsuming-by-showing-compatibility occurs with feminist criticism and its emphasis on patriarchal rather than class culture. By refining the concept of mode of production to allow for the overlapping of modes as elaborated by Nicos Poulantzas (PUC, pp. 94–95), Jameson can then "short-circuit the false problem of the priority of the economic over the sexual, or of sexual oppression over that of social class" (PUC, p. 99). Sexism represents a virulent residue of labor on the basis of gender. Jameson then allows:

> the affirmation of radical feminism, therefore, that to annul the patriarchal is the most *radical* political act—insofar as it includes and subsumes more partial demands, such as the liberation from the com-

modity form—is thus perfectly consistent with an expanded Marxian framework . . . (PUC, p. 100).

Consistent, perhaps, but also profoundly different. Different in emphasis, different in focus, different in form, and different in strategy. It is not simply a matter of being acknowledged as the most radical act (provided that the Marxist P's and Q's get minded) but of thereby reconstituting the ways and means of ideological criticism by bringing far greater refinement and complexity to our understanding of the politics of gender. (Jameson's concession also leaves unclear whether gay criticism would be subsumed by the same means, with the same provisos, or treated more epiphenomenally; no reference is made to it in *The Political Unconscious* although passing mention is made to gay literature as an historically suppressed and marginalized practice in need of recovery.)

Clearly, common cause exists among ideological criticisms though it does not prevail. In a less theoretical moment Jameson confronts this problem head on, noting that the French post-structural attacks on totalization situate themselves within a highly centralized political tradition only now challenged by more regional or local alternatives. In the United States, however, the predominance of fragmentary movements (from "feminism" to "neighborhood movements")requires a politics of alliance or affinity (PUC, p. 54). Jameson, though, makes the point in a footnote and does not elaborate on how a politics of affinity, either in terms of cultural interpretation or social action, would differ from classic party formations or from single issue or single event alliances. This omission offers powerful testimony from the interior of "ideological/Marxist criticism" of the very real difficulties yet to be faced before the term sustains as much force in the realms of the Symbolic and the Real as it does in the Imaginary.

The challenge of articulating a politics of affinity is a fundamental one that places the primary onus on those groups or movements that have been the most dominant—Marxists, males, whites—rather than on the alliances and movements that have been the least empowered and the most marginalized, in film criticism as elsewhere. How can ideological criticisms work, beyond the Imaginary? What, for example, can we make of concepts like totalization, ideology, desire or utopia? Are they even the most pressing ones within the terms of the "elective affinities" that bring diverse priorities and agendas together?

Purpose and persuasion take priority in Lentricchia's *Criticism and Social Change*—and belong fully to a discussion of ideology—but totalization reigns as an indispensable concept for any Marxist cultural theory in Jameson's *The Political Uunconscious*. What does Jameson's treatment of it offer us?

* * *

In accord with his "digression" on Althusser's critique of mechanistic and expressive causality, and in keeping with Poulantzas' notion of overlapping modes of production—both vestigial ones and those "potentially inconsistent with the existing system" but [so far] "without an autonomous space of their own" (PUC, p. 95), Jameson posits totalization as anything but a homogenous field or transcendent force. He distinguishes his own three-fold view of historical interpretation where history is "what hurts," what "refuses desire" and stands as "the ultimate ground as well as the untransccendable limit of our understanding" (PUC, 100, 102) from what he terms "hard" and "soft" models of totalization. "Hard" models envision some form of Weber's "iron cage," Foucault's "carceral continuum" or Burke's "bureaucratization of the imaginative" as an ineluctable destiny. Those final outposts of the subjective and objective realms—the unconscious and the Third World—await the iron fist of perpetual domination. "Soft" models envision a more "managed" or "massaged" future, not brute domination but seduction, not force but bribery, "cultural programming and penetration . . . the *société de consommation* with its consumption of images and simulacra, its free-floating signifiers and its effacement of the older structures of social class and traditional ideological hegemony" (PUC, p. 92) together with, we might add, its *self*-sustaining mechanisms. These positions—linked with Weber, Foucault and determinism in one instance, with Baudrillard, Bell and post-industrial, post-ideological society in the other—ignore the "ultimate determining instance" of the economic, even in its expanded form of overlapping modes of production. Such models foreclose the possibility of emergence and transformation as they absorb or obliterate transgression and repress or rewrite the utopian. They ultimately eliminate the need for interpretation, and contestation, inasmuch as they inexorably unfold as determinisms. ("Determinism will permit no rhetoric," Lentricchia reminds us; and in agreement with this view, hard and soft totalizations stress control and control mechanisms more than persuasion.)

Jameson departs from these tendencies quite forcefully, primarily through his persistent return to the book's first sentence, "Always historicize!" and his elaboration of a three-fold model of textual interpretation. The model is one of successively broader contextualizations: (1) the textual figuration of social contradictions as double binds or aporiae that the dynamics of the text seek to resolve. (2) The text as an instantiation or minimal unit (the "ideologeme") of class discourse itself which takes on both a conceptual outline and a narrative manifestation simultaneously (at its limit these facets lead to philosophical systems and complete texts). The example of an ideologeme which Jameson elaborates is *ressentiment* as a nineteenth-century concept that betrays "the binary opposition of good and evil as one of the fundamental forms of ideological thought in Western culture" [PUC, p. 88]. (3) The text in relation to cultural revolution conceived as perpetual, in accord with the notion of overlapping modes of production, with focal points of revolutionary upheaval standing as "the passage to the surface of a permanent process in human societies" (PUC, p. 97). At this third level, and corresponding to the symbolic resolution of contradiction at the first, and the "dialogical organization of class discourse" at the second, the final horizon of the cultural artifact becomes the locus of a dynamics called the "ideology of form" wherein the "sign systems of several distinct modes of production can be registered and apprehended . . . as content" (PUC, pp. 98–99). (Here is where Jameson allows the radical feminist act of annulling patriarchy to operate, revealing the formal persistence of the archaic structures of alienation peculiar to a mode of production grounded in a sexual division of labor [PUC, p. 100].)

As an historicizing, serial model of ever enlarging theoretical horizons, this agenda is as breathtakingly ambitious as it is impossible to schematize effectively. Even in raw outline, though, it possesses some extraordinary subtlety, one example of which is Jameson's discussion of the "reality effect," the realist achievement that makes the text appear as a reflection of or window onto the world as it is. Jameson shatters this naîveté not by invoking the poststructuralist catechism regarding the production of meaning and the work of the signifier per se (the basis for formalist deconstruction) but by calling for a reformulation of the relationship between the aesthetic and the Real in the paradoxical and active terms it deserves (the basis for a dialectical hermeneutics). Following his earlier essay, "The Symbolic Inference; or Kenneth Burke and Ideological Analysis,"[12] Jameson argues that the text does not accommodate itself to the perseverance of an external reality whose likeness it must emulate. Rather, if symbolic action "is a way of doing something to the world" (what Burke describes as art's ability to make something happen, what Lentriccchia examines in relation to the *act* of rhetoric), one manifestation of this action is the degree to which the "world" to which something is done must be taken up into the text, "must inhere within it" (PUC, p. 81).

The text generates its own referent or context even as it appears to distinguish itself from it:

> The whole paradox of what we have here called the subtext may be summed up in this, that the literary work or cultural object, as though for the first time, brings into being that very situation to which it is also, at one and the same time, a reaction. It articulates its own situation and textualizes it, thereby encouraging and perpetuating the illusion that the situation itself did not exist before it, that there is nothing but a text, that there never was any extra-or con-textual reality before the text itself generated it in the form of a mirage where this "mirage" will resolve contradictions that inflict themselves upon the social (PUC, pp. 81–82).

One way to understand this is in a personalist, affective frame where culture in-forms us of what it purports merely to reflect. In this view a text draws upon assumptions and perceptions about the world that pre-exist that world, but a specific text also convinces us that its "world" never truly or palpably existed until revealed in this peculiar aesthetic form.[13] Such revelations help cement our ties to the world as we encounter it, making it richer. But another understanding, the one appended by Jameson, would describe how this process in-forms us of and realizes (makes "real" by narrativizing) history itself, informs us of it in the same moment as it resolves, or attempts to resolve, those contradictions that it must also register as "logical scandal"(PUC, p. 82).

Jameson turns this subtle and supple consideration of the task of Marxist interpretation to the specific works of Balzac, Gissing and Conrad where the density and exactitude of the hermeneutic act dissolve any sense of the schematic and render the struggle for priority between theoretical speculation and textual analysis an open-ended, indeed dialectical, one. These discussions are more of piece with the woof and warp of contemporary "ideological/Marxist criticism" such as we find in Jane Feuer's *The Hollywood Musical*, Robin Woods' *Hollywood: From Vietnam to Reagan*, Richard Dyer's *The Stars*, E. Ann Kaplan's *Women and Film: From Both Sides of the Camera*, and Tania Modleski's *Loving with a Venegeance*, to name a few.[14] What Jameson brings to *The Political Unconscious* that distinguishes it from most Marxist cultural analysis is a virtuoso's facility with theory and a compelling sense of that global dominant to which any totalization must address itself: History.

What Jameson treats with somewhat less virtuosity is ideology. At times he speaks of texts that "emit" ideological messages (PUC, p. 88), of ideology as "abstract opinion, class value and the like"(PUC, p. 87), and of "ideological programming" (PUC, p. 281)—all strangely externalized notions of a thing with the power to affect or shape us. At other times he speaks more productively of ideology as "strategies of containment" (PUC, p. 53). Jameson's reluctance to work through the affective dimension of ideology, its rhetorical "designs" on readers/viewers who harbor designs of their own, a tendency to reject the concept of desire as a wholly personalist category incapable of transmutation into the terms of class consciousness and collective struggle, leaves him open to the kind of critique Lynn Spigel makes in her review of *Loving With A Vengeance* (which Spigel considers flawed by its reliance on Jameson's notions of ideology as utopia).[15] Ideology appears imposed on a text which retains a "latent" utopian element. By contrast, Spigel argues that the utopian element is not latent but produced by a text that "produces positions of desire through discursive strategies" (p. 223). For Jameson, she argues, ideology is a function of repressive operations "out there" in the social formation that impose themselves on a text. This perspective detaches desire and the reader/text relationship from a place of central importance (which, for Spigel, hinges on a Lacanian model where castration is the "axis of narrative desire" (p. 224)—precisely the sort of personalist category that Jameson indeed flatly rejects.[16]

Spigel's review, though, is a rhetorical act of its own, structured to reaffirm an embattled psychoanalytic model and to reencapsulate the political within the chrysalis of the formal and individual, even as the subject becomes evacuated of any abiding essence—save perhaps its perpetual desire for desire. If this leads to a certain warping in the interpretation of ideology and utopia, it also points us toward the need for a careful scrutiny of these terms, and a clear acknowledgment of the overly global, reductive, fragmentary and, finally, inadequate conception of ideology in the works of Marx with which Jameson defends a continuity.

Kenneth Burke provides a compelling vision of subject, rhetoric and history that omits a great deal (positions of class and gender, processes of valorization and sanction, hierarchies of power and tactics of empowerment/disenfranchisement), but also sets the scene for a more extended consideration of ideology:

> Imagine that you enter a parlor. You come late. When you arrive, others have long preceded you, and they are engaged in a heated discussion, a discussion too heated for them to pause and tell you exactly what it is about. In fact, the discussion had already begun long before any of them got there, so that no one present is qualified to retrace for you all the steps that had gone before. You listen for a while, until you decide that you have caught the tenor of the argument; then you put in your oar. Someone answers; you answer him; another comes to your defense; another aligns himself against you, to either the embarrassment or gratification of your opponent, depending upon the quality of your ally's assistance. However, the discussion is interminable. The hour grows late, you must depart. And you do depart, with the discussion still vigorously in progress.[17]

What holds considerable value in this little fable is the active representation of the subject who both sustains and shapes an interminable "discussion" that clearly constrains and shapes the individual far more than he or she shapes it. The scenario also proposes a social interaction but one mediated by discourse. In this sense discursive practices represent the place where history and ideology reach and, even more, affect us, producing that sensuous, gnostic awareness of who it is we are (or think we are), what it is we do, and what the world in which we live is like. This, the work of culture, rhetoric and ideology, at their points of fundamental intersection, is what we must examine further.

What I want to propose, in a nutshell, is that ideology addresses and constitutes split, multiple, layered subjects through representations we cannot ignore (but perhaps quite readily refuse). This proposal derives, as does Jameson's conception of structural causality, from the work of Louis Althusser but as modified by Goran Therborn, Hayden White, Kenneth Burke and Frank Lentricchia—or at least by my *bricoleur*-like borrowing from their works.[18] It departs from Althusser in its attempt to construct a more complex, historical concept of the subject and of the process that Althusser calls interpellation and that Burke describes as entering a parlor and putting in your oar.

Address, or the sense of being addressed, remains fundamental. Texts, social processes, address us. We feel ourselves within their grip. Here lies the terrain of verbal courtship or rhetoric which Burke describes, in describing form, as "the creation of an appetite in the mind of the auditor and the adequate satisfying of that appetite." "This is how it is, don't you agree?" or "This is what the world (the world this text or social practice has actively generated in the form of a mirage) is like, isn't it?" or "Ceci, c'est une pipe, n'est-ce pas?"—to reinvert Magritte's proposal to its usual, mimetic formulation.

The frequently tacit, altogether casual "n'est-ce pas?" draws us into the dynamics of response and the inevitable open-endedness of a system that does not (cannot) rely on force or coercion at a practical level or on determinism at a philosophical one. ("Determination will permit no rhetoric" CSC, p. 162). We might,, though, first consider the "world" that a given discourse proposes and what it consists of. One schema, for example, would identify this world as a representation (*Darstellung*) of history in which propositions about what exists, what's appropriate, and what's possible invite our agreement. We may tender our agreement without fully knowing it: an image of the world presents itself, full-blown; later, when we find ourselves in need of an "image," a picture to guide our thought or feeling about a given matter, that image of the world may provide it; our agreement then consists of not having replaced a proposed world with an alternative one.

These propositions regarding what exists, what's appropriate and what's possible can be considered protocols for naming (nomination), routinization and adaptation. Their operations populate given realm with facts of existence; with agendas, rituals, roles and the recipe knowledge to perform them; with myths, utopian visions or ideals and the motive fuel of aspiration. Such operations represent a channeling or focusing of potential, a harnessing of desire, a policing of boundaries. Strategies of encouragement or sanction, affirmation or marginalization—the rhetorical charge to otherwise "mere" proposals—attempt to channel subjects toward the maintenance of the preconditions, the ensemble of social relations, necessary for a given ideology's perpetuation. These operations—ideological in their intent, rhetorical in their form—are inevitably repressive.They name what we need to know (and leave unnamed that which we do not—given certain assumptions); they legitimate what we need to do (and invalidate what we do not); they fabricate a utopia (and juxtapose a hell). And, although one ideology may dominate, the social field remains criss-crossed and overlapped by contending ones that also vie for a never fully secured hegemony.

Naming the facts of existence, legitimating social practices, mythologizing cultural ideals—these operations range across the basic elements of social life and form the palpable texture of culture, the sensuous world of real material practices and of textual fabrication, that, by addressing us and the appetites they have so artfully induced, invite us to take "our place" in the relations of production and reproduction. Like the model of class consciousness that Jameson, after Bakhtin, posits as dialogical and relational ("the dialogue of class struggle is one in which two opposing discourses fight it out within the general unity of a shared code" [PUC, p. 84], this model of ideology suggests that specific ideologies must be defined relationally, in the figure of the Moebius strip: and the limits of one become the boundaries of another.

Ideologies do not "fight it out" on equal footing, however. A gradient of power pervades the arena and establishes a fundamental asymmetry such that the dominated are often quicker to articulate feelings of anger, rage, oppression, quicker to acknowledge their coherent collective identity (as a group- or class-for-itself rather than simply in-itself), and more fully aware of the tactics and purposes of the dominant ideologies that constrain them and against which they may actively resist. Conversely, the dominating group will face the contending ideologies with strategies for containment and for resistance to their claims for greater legitimacy.[19]

Around what basic concepts or images do ideologies "fight it out"? A possible repertoire—inclusive but perhaps too general—might include the following sets of terms common to a wide array of ideologies but valued and juxtaposed differently in each:

1. "Facts" of existence categorized as motility or curiosity, reproduction, work and aggression.
2. Social practices (the means of regulating and controlling "facts" of life within sanctioned codes) categorized according to the acquisition and use of knowledge, the organization of sexual drives, the utilization of labor, and the application of force.
3. Cultural ideals categorized in relation to wisdom, love, creativity and sacrifice.[20]

The social practices listed in (2) require regulation or management through institutional and representational apparatuses that make propositions regarding the social construction of education, sexuality, labor and force. Contending ideologies address and qualify us as subjects within a possible set of social relations (as, for example, a Catholic or Jew, a Canadian or American, a salesman or technician, a father or mother, a neighbor or tourist, a patriot or dissident, an eligible or ineligible sexual partner, an individual worker or a member of a class of workers, and so on). As Therborn notes, we can be constituted and reconstituted as an almost unlimited number of (either coherent or potentially schizoid) subjects with multiple subjectivities "although as a rule only one at a time" will apply (IOP, p. 78), a notion distinct from Althusser's conception of subjects subject to ideology-in-general, called forth and held in place perpetually.

Completing this model of ideological formations requires consideration of the possible responses to the "n'est-ce pas?" or "don't you agree?" implicit in the rhetoric of address. We will then be in a position to link more thoroughly the concept of ideology, which has extension across a wide range of social practices, and rhetoric, understood as co-extensive with ideology.

"Active reception is the site where the will of the residual and the will of the emergent interact and clash" (CSC, p. 141). Most messages do not coerce. They rely on persuasive tactics. They are vulnerable to resistance and refutation. In terms of the ideological propositions summarized here, distinctions can be made between affirmative and subversive responses and between different degrees of subversion. Full affirmation means acceptance of an ideology's proposals for what's recognizable, subscription to proposals for what's appropriate, and endorsement of proposals for what's possible. Such responses constitute the tragic or comic sensibility of the fatalistically resigned or intensely committed. Those institutional procedures that apply incentives and disincentives (practices of inclusion or exclusion such as restructions on who may speak, where, for how long, to whom, and so on, and validation procedures that establish or undermine claims to authoritative speech) appear inevitable or natural, beyond challenge. Affirmation in this sense leads to a static social system characterized by pervasive, monolithic ideological effects.

More commonly, at least in Western history, affirmation is more partial and the work of rhetoric more arduous. Resistance, though, is often partial, too, leading less to revolution than to localized struggles for the determination of things, practices, and ideals. Proposals regarding what exists may meet with accommodation, proposals for what's appropriate, with qualification, and for what's possible, with submission. For example, the subject who undergoes procedures designed to qualify him or her as a manager may also qualify those procedures to manage "against the grain" of established expectations. Similarly, the reader who encounters the proposal as embedded in the actions of a character that the religiously faithful owe a similar fidelity to the state, may qualify the proposition by reserving judgment on the behavior of the character of questioning the degree to which church and state serve similar ends. In these cases, something is held in reserve. Other alternatives become conceivable; though they lack full articulation, they serve to check acceptance, subscription and endorsement.

Carried further, this countervailing tendency may lead to contestation over the "facts" of existence, resistance to prevailing social practices, and dissent from cultural ideals. At the level of even more systematic and organized conflict, negative responses to an implicit "don't you agree?" sharpen into attempts to name the facts of existence differently, to delegitimate prevailing social practices or to legitimize alternatives, and to rebel against proposed cultural ideals.

Such contradictory tendencies may exhaust themselves fruitlessly; they may eventuate in limited victories; they need not, by any stretch of the imagination, lead automatically to their logical and tumultuous conclusion—revolution.

Revolution is the explosive eruption of dialectical processes of contestation that occur all the time in the far more unobtrusive form described above. Marxism, as a set of ideas, cannot guarantee a revolutionary outcome to processes of rhetorically negotiated agreement when simply put on display, like houseware upon an unfurled cloth, rather than actively, discursively proposed. Contestation, resistance, dissent—such actions constitute a negative dialectic but not a positive one. They sidestep the central issue addressed by both Lentricchia and Jameson—the grounding of rhetoric in the "potential for community" (CSC, p. 162) and the definition of the political unconscious as a "symbolic meditation on the destiny of community" (PUC, p. 70)—the associative, collective basis upon which a positive dialectic depends.

Therborn, in his accounts of social conflict, posits such conflict within a Newtonian realm of forces, pressures, momentum and energy that eludes the realm of discursive practice. Adhering to a traditional model of political theory, he remains highly reluctant to grant the discursive equal status with the non-discursive which is, for him, the realm of history in contrast to Jameson's claim that although history is not a text or a narrative, "master or otherwise," it is, as an absent cause, only accessible to us "in textual form. . . . Our approach to it and to the Real itself necessarily passes through its prior textualization, its narrativization in the political unconscious" (PUC, p. 35). Even so, Therborn acknowledges the significant gap poised between rebellion and revolution, between transgression and desire as the terms for an individual psyche and revolution and utopia as those of a collective consciousness. He concedes that distrust, discontent, and withdrawal are not the vital issue any more than nihilism or anarchism. "Every state in history has nearly always had its lawbreakers, bandits, smugglers, thieves, offenders against morality, dissenters, tax-evaders and deserters and every state has frequently had to face organized forms of protest and riotous crowds. The really crucial feature is organized counter-claims to legitimacy, and the effects these claims have, when put to the test, upon the loyalty and efficacy of the state apparatus" (IOP, p. 106).

Within such a perspective, ideology becomes quite a dynamic and variegated process, calling forth fundamentally *ex*centric, socially constructed subjects. These subjects are:

1. multiple, not endowed with a unitary consciousness but with "decenterred constraints and fissures" . . . "unintended consequences," and "diverse, often unnoticed temporalities"
2. split subjects subject to different sets of propositions about the

world that overlap and conflict and require a consciousness adjusted to "discontinuous, *situated* motivation" (italics mine) rather than to a single, determining one. An extreme example would be the torturer who, outside of work, subscribes to social practices regarding others radically at odds to those he applies to his work. At work he accepts the designation of victims he might otherwise regard as compatriots as alien or Other.

3. layered, constituted by sedimented apprehensions of the self that constantly change in relation to changes in the concrete, material practices of interpellation or rhetorical address.[21]

We must now ask what it means when counterclaims to legitimacy are "put to the test." The test of claims that invite our assent requires measurement of their rhetorical effectiveness, their satisfaction of an appetite. This domain of effectivity, extending across the full range of the narrative and the textual, makes of ideology more than the elaboration of ideas. It renders ideology into a compelling social force with designs upon us that we may subscribe to or resist without even being fully conscious of the dynamics in which we are engaged (particularly true of popular culture where the notion of "just entertainment" holds considerable sway).

What, then, gives ideology its force and what authorizes an ideological/Marxist criticism to consolidate its analysis of social practices and textual production? Lentricchia sets ideology and rhetoric down squarely on the fulcrum of form: "The rhetoric of aesthetic power is born in the linkage of form with ideology in its two psychosocial domains: ideology, in other words, both as overt 'culture,' however 'upside down'—a common, normalizing and socializing space, a conscious modus of beliefs, attitudes and judgments—and as a sort of unconscious that Althusser called a 'lived relation to the world' " (CSC, p. 108). Form—the materialization of content, the chain of signifiers through which material practices manifest themselves—provides the substance of persuasive (or in "iron cage" scenarios, disciplinary) intention. Substance, we should note, will mean both physical stuff (the thing in all its material actuality) and sub-stance, support, the grounding moment from which rhetoric arises. Such a proposition wields a death blow to vulgar Marxist criticism based on content analysis: bourgeois, patriarchal ideology, for example, does not subscribe an audience to its perspective by simply stating its assumptions, as though mere exposure to them could win assent and as though ideological/Marxist criticism had the sole objective of unmasking and refuting them.

Acceptance, subscription and endorsement in relation to a given ideology depend on the formal strategies that give this idea concrete embodiment and persuasive force. "In the moment of linkage, form would seize and direct ideological substance, transform it into power over the subject-audience; it would turn our ideology, in both senses [as culture and as lived experience] over to a disciplinary [or a repressive or persuasive] intention. . . . The aesthetic moment of linkage, then, is the manipulative moment at which the subject-audience is submitted to the productive force of ideology" (CSC, p. 104).[22]

The outcome, though, remains subject to doubt:

> Form can both gratify and control those needs [the needs it arouses] however, only if it properly engages and represents what readers consider desirable and only if the readers' overt ideologies are in some way 'respected.' Only then can those ideologies be manipulated in the engagement with form so that the power effect touched off by that engagement will engender two ultimate political effects of aesthetic power: the domination effect or its contrary, the effect of resistance (CSC, p. 104).

The retrograde valorization of machismo, charismatic authority and anarchism underwriting *Rambo,* for example, works (takes effect through the power of form) by establishing the conventions of heroic conduct (loner status, individualism, a sense of self-discipline and sacrifice, resistance to coercion, hints of a moral code) and extending them to include defiance of authority (constituted as sadistic, arbitrary and punitive) while eliminating any sense of broader social misssion and making conflict a matter of physical fortitude and skill to which only the most minimal overt ethic gets attached. If such a proposition works (satisfies the appetite it arouses) it does so through this extension and transmutation of previous conventions into a new set of assumptions to which we assent. It is not the abstract propositions of nihilism, anarchism or machismo (as ideologies in the classic sense) with which we must negotiate, but this particular, tacit embodiment of such qualities. In this way agreement can be won without the requirement of rational argument and formal, conscious consent.[23]

Why must ideology couple itself to rhetoric and depend on the persuasive power of form? The reasons are multiple and all of them have to do with an understanding of ideology as more than a set of ideas or principles conveyed by more or less overt propaganda. Such a conception assumes some more neutral ground from which the ideological might be surveyed and assessed, but the assumption here is that such an objective site does not exist. No design for living can claim superior ontological status to any other, including Marxism. Each ideology must fight it out, with the weapons at its disposal—signs and symbols—knowing that hegemony is always partial and never rests upon the bedrock of Truth and Certainty.

Second, but in close relation, as social beings humans exhibit a greater capacity for possible structures and systems than any one form of social organization can accommodate. Ideologies, as containing or repressive mechanisms, must channel this human capacity into specific, favored forms. Such channeling occurs more economically when motivation is positive—toward those practices and ideals given as desirable—than when it is negative. The result constrains choice, but does not require the same vigilant policing of deviation that coercion would. The dependence on rhetoric gives indirect proof of a human capacity (not an innate human nature) that remains available to history: "Only insofar as men are potentially free, must the spellbinder seek to persuade them. Insofar as they *must* do something, rhetoric is unnecessary" (from K. Burke, quoted in CSC, p. 162).

Third, subjective-practice *agreement* requires subjects who willingly, on their own, act in accordance with tacit prescriptions. Slavery proves a far less efficient system than wage-labor, and it, too, requires, at the level of the master, subjects who do not have to be forced to channel their capacity for action into those social practices necessary to the status quo.

Fourth, humans require of their guidance systems, of the designs a social structure has on—and for—them, more than information or knowledge, more than ideas, recipes and procedures. They also require a sense of the feel of such structures: (1) of what it means to belong or participate (what community is like), (2) of what conditional states pertain (what it would be like if . . . if we defy authority, if we betray our wife, or husband, if we achieve great personal success but live among others who have not; in short, of what subjective states attach to all those conditional situations that derive from a given set of ideological assumptions), (3) of what *form* these subjective states of mind that a given social structure prompts would be like (a form given to us in our cultural texts that often purport only to reflect the situations that they actually produce and whose contradictions they attempt to resolve). From such intangibles come motivation and purpose, discipline and self-control, belief and advocacy—in relation to what exists, what's appropriate and what's possible.

This necessary bond between ideology and rhetoric, thought and form, leads straight on toward a final paradox and challenge. Ideologies are relational; they must contend with one another in order to gain hegemony. In taking cognizance of an outside, they foster awareness of an inside, of shared premises or common bonds among adherents. The sense of common purpose and shared values stands as prototype for the utopian. The repressive mechanism intended to manage the utopian through its necessary link to rhetoric and persuasion also embodies "the affirmation of collective solidarity" necessary (but not sufficient) for a Utopia beyond class (PUC, p. 291). In providing a rationale that is without ontological grounding, in channeling human capacity, in conceding freedom of choice so that subjects will choose freely, in giving reasons for the heart as well as the mind, in all these tasks, an ideology must take cognizance of the very potentialities that remain beyond its powers of fulfillment. The essence of persuasion resides in this. So does the dialectic between ideology and utopia, or between culture as manipulation or liberation. Passages by Jameson and Lentricchia pose the issue clearly. First Jameson:

> In other words, if the ideological function of mass culture is understood as a process whereby otherwise dangerous and protopolitical impulses are "managed" and defused, rechanneled and offered spurious objects, then some preliminary step must also be theorized in which these same impulses—the raw material upon which the process works—are initially awakened within the very text that seeks to still them (PUC, p. 287).

And in Lentricchia:

> [] . . . the capitalist system must find a way to appropriate the monster of utopian yearning for itself and thereby block the historical shift that Marx had predicted would follow upon its dialectically necessary deterioration. . . . In its earlier stages, capitalism produces alienation; in its later, consumer, stage, it appropriates that alienation, turns its in-

ternal contradiction to advantage by projecting a perverse utopia of commodity-gratification that functions as the instrument for structuring desire as intention directed not toward the commodity per se but toward the capacity of the commodity to confer romance and wonder (CSC, p. 30).

Lentricchia's emphasis on the "bad faith" of capitalist culture that offers a perverse utopia couples with his own project of arguing for an actively forged and rhetorically compelling Marxist discourse that provides opposition from the outside: the writer may reinforce "habits of thought and feeling: that sustain the prevailing order or "he (sic) may work counter-hegemonically as a violator, in an effort to dominate and to re-educate, *in*form, to pin us to the wall, in order to assist in the birth of a critical mind by peeling off, one by one, and thus revealing to us for what they are, all bourgeois encrustations of consciousness. In the widest sense of the word, he would encourage cultural revolution" (CSC, p. 148). Pitched as it is toward those who labor in the academy, mainly in the humanities, Lentricchia's argument serves as a powerful defense of the political force of intellectual work itself. As an analysis of culture and ideology, the argument tends toward the crudeness of manipulation theory.

Jameson's analysis of mass culture itself provides a finer-grained picture of culture and ideology, but still leaves the question of whether the dangerous impulses, awakened in the very act of repressing them, retain the power and the glory of the genuinely utopian rather than the debased allure of a perversion. The classic case against popular culture holds out for perverted utopias that (mis)direct us toward spurious objects of desire. The more recent work of ideological/Marxist criticism, and much poststructuralism, rejects such monolithic readings; it reads against the grain to find the cracks, fissures, contradictions and complexity that render the "perverse utopia of commodity-gratification" semi- or dysfunctional. Certainly, a great deal of feminist criticism and genre analysis has proven the merit of this perspective, giving us a more comprehensive understanding of how the invitations to agreement of many classic Hollywood films are, in fact, riddled with contradictions that authorize diagnostic or symptomatic readings and the development of a powerful critique of ideological suasion.

But such readings tend toward a demystifying effort that remains necessarily on the defensive. This is the terrain of a negative dialectic that challenges and refuses, dissents and contests. In a period of conservative retrenchment, sustaining a negative dialectic of critique comes at a cost which is not evenly distributed across the social formation. "Ideological/Marxist criticism must not cease to practice this essentially negative hermeneutic function (which Marxism is virtually the only current critical method to assume today) but must also seek, through and beyond this demonstration of the instrumental function of a given cultural object, to project its simultaneously Utopian power as the symbolic affirmation of a specific historical and class form of collective unity" (PUC, p. 291).[24]

The call to project the symbolics of the utopian, to return from the political unconscious of our cultural texts with evidence of their "symbolic meditation on the possibility of community" enjoins us to forge a "positive hermeneutic," or, together, a double hermeneutic that will acknowledge as well as account for the power, the allure and fascination, of what philosophers since Plato have believed can be dispelled by the mere taking of thought. Why do vast numbers of people enjoy *Rambo* or view *Mildred Pierce* or *Gentlemen Prefer Blondes* with "innocent" pleasure, or, at a drastically different level accept, subscribe to, and endorse the propositions of fascism, sexism, or racism when patient analysis can put the procedures of a virulent ideology on display? Lentricchia and Jameson stand in agreement on the vital need to respond to people and situations as they are, not only as we hope for them to be, and to offer a positive hermeneutics of revelation as well as a negative hermeneutic of suspicion. As a challenge to contemporary ideological/Marxist criticism such a need is of utmost importance. What is clear is that many alterideologies—embedded in critical methods such as phenomenology, formalism, and reader-response theory that have gained greater currency in film study in the last six or seven years and that convincingly describe one or more local laws of a divided society—have gained their attractiveness by stressing a positive hermeneutic of which ideological/Marxist criticism is presumably incapable.

When Marx and Engels spoke of a spectre haunting Europe, it was not the spectre of unemployment, alienation, repression, exploitation, ideological bribery, crippling gender identities, deformed utopias or the power of capitalism generally. The spectre then was Communism. As a *spectre*, communism spoke from the political unconscious about community, it was what the utopian also is, the utopian that ideology must awaken in cultural texts when its work is once again to extinguish it: "a *figure* for the ultimate concrete collective life of an achieved Utopian or classless society" (PUC, p. 291). Ideological/Marxist criticism adopts solely the single-edged sword of a negative hermeneutic, of critique and demystification, of an ethics of good and evil, at its own peril. Better to remember the spirit of the original manifesto and to discover not only the perversions of ideology but also the figurations of utopia that make our negotiations with texts matters of such complex urgency.

NOTES

[1] Dudley Andrew, *Concepts in Film Theory* (New York: Oxford University Press, 1984), pp. 112, 115.

[2] Giles Gunn, "The Semiotics of Culture and the Interpretation of Literature: Clifford Geertz and the Moral Imagination," *Studies in the Literary Imagination*, 12 (Spring 1979), p. 118. Gunn here paraphrases Geertz; at another point he assigns to Marxist criticism the reduction of culture "to the ideas and assumptions one must share in order to operate in a manner deemed acceptable by the dominant social group of class" p. 115.

[3] See my "Introduction," Movies and Methods, Vol. II (Berkeley: University of California Press, 1985), esp. pp. 14–25.

[4] Fredric Jameson, *The Political Unconscious* (Ithaca: Cornell University Press, 1981); subsequently referred to as PUC. Frank Lentricchia, *Criticism and Social Change* (Chicago and London: University of Chicago Press, 1983); subsequently referred to as CSC.

[5] Andrew, *Concepts in Film Theory*, p. 152.

[6] Although conflation via a shared interest in ideology sometimes yokes psychoanalytic, semiotic and Marxist criticism, we can begin to discriminate among them at this point. For Jameson psychoanalytic and semiotic methods, especially in their poststructural forms, depart from a Marxist criticism by retaining immanence as a goal even as they repudiate phenomenology. Jameson here differentiates what Andrew would amalgamate: "The codification of a whole new alternative method—which explores the inscription of ideology in an ensemble of purely formal categories, such as representation, narrative closure, the organization around the centered subject, or the illusion of presence—is generally associated with the *Tel Quel* and *Screen* groups, and also, in a different way, with Jacques Derrida. . . . The unmasking of such

categories and their ideological consequences is then achieved in the name of newer aesthetic, psychoanalytic, and moral values variously termed heterogeneity, dissemination, discontinuity, schizophrenia, and *écriture*, that is, in the name of explicitly antiImmanent (but also anti-transcendent) concepts. Yet the impulse behind the critical practice thereby theorized is often precisely an immanent one, which brackets the historical situation in which texts are effective and insists that ideological positions can be identified by the identification of inner-textual or purely formal features. Such an approach is thereby able to confine its work to individual printed texts or visual ones and projects the ahistorical view that the formal features in question always and everywhere bear the same ideological charge" (PUC, p. 283n).

[7] Lentricchia concludes his story by naming a third desire, "Horace," "the forbidden desire for power (no humanist likes to admit to it). . . . In the rhetorical tradition—what could be more appropriate—the desire that I have called "Horace" is repressed, and abrasive terms like 'power' and 'domination' are sugared over with cunning words like 'utility,' 'guidance,' and 'teaching'—especially 'teaching" (CSC, p. 91).

[8] Lentricchia reminds us that the category of literature as imaginative writing arises in the 18th century alongside other "disciplinary mechanisms" that police boundaries and, here, supervise and contain the literary within a restricted space of its own making (CSC, p. 54).

[9] See Stephen Heath and Teresa de Lauretis, eds., *The Cinematic Apparatus* (London: Macmillan, 1980) for the most complete overview of this topic but also Jean-Louis Baudry, "Ideological Effects of the Basic Cinematographic Apparatus," *Film Quarterly* 28, no. 2 (Winter 1974-75) and Christian Metz, *The Imaginary Signifier* (Bloomington: Indiana University Press and London: Macmillan Press, 1981).

[10] Laura Mulvey, "Visual Pleasure and Narrative Cinema," *Screen* 16, no. 3 (August 1975).

[11] See, for example, E. Ann Kaplan, *Women and Film: Both Sides of the Camera* (New York and London: Methuen, 1983); Tania Modleski, *Loving with a Vengeance: Mass-Produced Fantasies for Women* (New York: Methuen, 1982); Stephen Heath, "Film and System: Terms of Analysis," *Screen* 16, no. 1 (Spring 1975), pp. 7–77, 16, no. 2 (Summer 1975), pp. 91–113, and 17, no. 1 (Spring 1976), pp. 115–17, and *Enclitic*, 5, no. 2/6: no. 1 (Fall 1981, Spring 1982), all devoted to textual analysis of film.

[12] In *Critical Inquiry*, 4 (Spring 1978), pp. 507–23.

[13] See also Giles Gunn, "The Semiotics of Culture," pp. 120–123.

[14] *The Hollywood Musical* (London: Macmillan Press, 1982), *Hollywood: From Vietnam to Reagan* (New York: Columbia University Press, 1986),

The Stars (London: Macmillan Press, 1983), *Women and Film* (New York and London: Methuen, 1983), *Loving With a Vengeance* (New York: Methuen, 1982).

15 Lynn Spigel, "Detours in the Search for Tomorrow," *Camera Obscura*, 13/14 (1985), pp. 215–234.

16 "The center around which the Freudian interpretive system turns is not sexual experience but rather wish-fulfillment, or its more metaphysical variant, 'desire,' posited as the very dynamic of our being as individual subjects. Is it necessary to stress the dependence of this 'discovery' on the increasing abstraction of experience in modern society?" (PUC, p. 65). Jameson concedes that Lacan overturns this center to focus on the category of the subject and its constitution to which Jameson applies Norman Holland's critique of myth criticism: "it works only if we have been told the work is mythic rewriting ahead of time, the unquestionable "resonances of the mythic presupposing not the operation of some mythic unconscious but rather our own preliminary conscious 'set' toward the reading in question" (PUC, p. 67). He also rejects desire on the grounds that it is based on notions of transgression that inevitably reconfirm the law or norm they oppose (PUC, p. 68). Though theoretically correct, this position, which Spigel misconceives, still neglects to provide the Marxist theorist with a means of tactical access to an audience made up of those who have been socially constructed to conceive of themselves, however wrongly, as "individual subjects." Lentricchia argues, speaking of "the worker" as a symbol but in terms equally applicable to "individual subject," that you can't simply deconstruct the term, painting "riveting portraits of workers under capitalism, of degradation and alienation: and still hope for people to mobilize and act in league as workers" (CSC, p. 27). Nor can you simply deconstruct the concept of the individual subject and still hope to mobilize the very subjects you have deconstructed. For Jameson, the antidote is a rhetoric of class but the move from individual motivation to class action remains undertheorized, a point Jameson himself admits.

17 Kenneth Burke, *The Philosophy of Literary Form*, ppp. 110–11.

18 Primary sources include Therborn's *The Ideology of Power and the Power of Ideology* (London: Verso and New Left Books, 1980), hereafter referred to as IOP; a lecture by Hayden White at UC Santz Cruz in Spring 1985; Burke's *The Philosophy of Literary Form* and *A Grammar of Motives* (Los Angeles: University of California Press, 1969), and Lentricchia's CSC. Perhaps the most glaring flaw in this model is its emphasis on individual vs. collective (or class) dynamics. This flaw surfaces in all of my sources as well and receives a sound rebuke from Jameson (who refers here to Paul Ricoeur's dual hermeneutic of kerygma and demys-

tification), "The limits of Ricoeur's formulation are . . . the persistence of categories of the individual subject: specifically, his conception of 'positive' meaning as a kerygma or interpellation (retained in Althusser's theory of ideology) is modelled on the act of communication between individual subjects, and cannot therefore be appropriated as such for any view of meaning as a collective process" (PUC, p. 285). Though flawed, and perhaps fatally, the individual subject remains such a powerful ideological construct that a politics and rhetoric of collective process that ignores it would seem impossible. The need for a rhetoric of collectivities remains vital, but, unfortunately, well beyond the scope of this essay.

[19] See, for example, Therborn's IOP, pp. 22–28, where he discusses the asymmetry of domination/submission and a taxonomy of ideologies in terms (inclusive/existential/histoorical/positional) that are fundamentally relational, though also overly schematic or arbitrary.

[20] This fourfold grid in the domains of fact, social practice, and cultural myth derives from a lecture by Hayden White at UC Santa Cruz, Spring 1985. In it White associated ideology with the middle category of routinization or social practices; here I treat all three domains as aspects of ideology and repression. Like White, I also regard these domains as sites of discursive activity and hence rhetoric rather than assigning some ("fact," for example) to an ontological level below the threshold of discourse and rather than distinguishing, rather sharply, as Therborn does, between the discursive and non-discursive (IOP, p. 33). This distinction, in the realm of political theory, tends to have the retrograde function of exempting "real," historical actions from the discursive or textual forms they often take, thereby establishing a hierarchy that valorizes political analysis over and above cultural, discursive or rhetorical analysis. I adopt the contrary position here and assume that actions are of paramount importance when and if they can be interpreted as messages within socially (ideologically) regulated codes and that actions that cannot be so interpreted primarily constitute noise, not meaning. Concrete, specific acts of murder or procreation, for example, are physical actions that affect the body of those to whom they are addressed in irreversible ways quite different from the textual representation of the same acts, but if they are to have importance as socially significant acts, they must be interpreted in relation to those ideologically governed codes of what's appropriate that will affirm or condemn a particular instantiation. That the same requirement for referral to the force field of social significance, compounded by that of literary (generic, formal, semiotic) significance, applies to discursive acts should require no elaboration.

[21] All quotes from IOP, p. 102.

22 Less deterministically, one might say that the aesthetic moment of linkage is also the rhetorical moment of address in which we are invited to share agreement with a proposal persuasively made. Lentricchia elsewhere stresses the vital importance of action and reaction among writers, in the broadest sense of those who inscribe significance upon events, and readers, who seek to interpret as well as engage in them. Here he seems to move toward a determination that would eliminate the very need for the rhetoric he also describes. His overall stance, however, allows for a more pliable reading in which resistance is everywhere as possible as endorsement.

23 Such an example may seem overly blatant, but the same procedures are at work in more subtle texts. Bergman's *Cries and Whispers* and Altman's *Three Women*, for example, invite our acceptance of and subscription to a world that they posit as the context for the textual operations that then refer to this "preexisting" context as a naturalized, obvious realm of entities and practices we will recognize (or misrecognize). This world is one in which women are the repositories of feeling, of blocked emotions from which they suffer, of anguish that has no transformative outlet but which instructs us on the depths and richness of the human (female) soul: it is a world populated by suffering and victims that we are presumably wiser for having fathomed. Its grain of truth becomes the substance around which form secretes the pearl that attracts and sways us.

24 Though Jameson means Marxism in an enlarged sense that would welcome the feminist critique of patriarchy, the word may not be the best choice for a politics of affinity. In Jameson, Marxism still tends to mean class analysis above all, and the history of such analysis, in cultural studies and beyond, has seldom been propelled by a spirit even as generous as Jameson's to other leftist or progressive models. I doubt that many gay, lesbian, feminist, cultural nationalist, and other progressive groupings would welcome a subsumption of their own distinct projects within the over-arching rubric of an enlarged, receptive Marxism. Just as Lentricchia reminds us that "worker" is not an ideal word for the construction of a positive collective identification due to the affective meanings assigned to it by the dominant ideology (it is not a term that enlists our ambition as much as our sympathies CSC, p. 27), so the word Marxism may not be a term around which groups with political affinities can effectively join.

FILM AND LANGUAGE:
FROM METZ TO BAKHTIN

Robert Stam

It has become a commonplace to proclaim that our century has been relentlessly language-haunted. Central to the project of thinkers as diverse as Russell, Wittgenstein, Cassirer, Heideger, Levi-Strauss, Bakhtin, and even Merleau-Ponty is a concern with the central importance of language in human life. If ours is the century of the atom and the cosmos, Julia Kristeva has suggested, it is also the century of *language*. Although an object of reflexion for millennia, it is only recently that language has come to be seen as a "key" to the mind, to artistic and social praxis, indeed to human existence in its totality. Semiotics in general, and film semiotics in particular, must be seen, then, as local manifestations of a more widespread "linguistic turn."

The process by which linguistics, as the methodological success story of the century, came to spread its influence over other disciplines is by now well known. The scientific advance represented by Saussure's *Course in General Linguistics* (1916), decisive in its area, was applied in other disciplines, such as literary study, by Jakobson and the School of Prague, after which the Saussurean method "passed" to Levi-Strauss, who used it with great intellectual audacity and thus founded structuralism as a movement. Kinship relations, for him, formed a kind of language susceptible to the kinds of analysis formerly applied by Troubetskoy and Jakobson to questions of phonology. Once this fundamental equation was made, it was an easy step to extend the same structural linguistic logic to all social, mental, and artistic structures. Other domains—fashion, comic strips, cuisine—came under the jurisdiction of structural linguistics. Even economics came to be seen in its semiotic dimension, as a symbolic system comparable to the exchance of women within kinship relations or the exchange of words in language, and with Lacan the Unconscious itself came to be seen as "structured like a language."

The point of this admittedly hasty overview of the intellectual history of our century is simply to suggest that film semiotics, far from being the "fad" denounced by its critics, actually forms part of the broad drift of contemporary thought. Our purpose here will be to outline briefly the overall trajectory of film semiotics, with emphasis not on an exhaustive survey of work performed but rather in the interest of a tentative evaluation: what has been the contribution of film semiotics, and what are its limitations? Where do we go from here, and how can Bakhtin's "translinguistics" help us get there?

In my overview, I will privilege Saussurean (Franco-Italian) film semiology and its Anglo-American prolongations, first because it is the tradition I know best, and secondly because it is the tradition which has dominated film-theoretical discourse, far outstripping its rival-collaborators, those who use transformationalist models (Chomsky) or American Pragmatist semiotics (rooted in Charles Saunders Peirce).[1] The key figure here is of course Christian Metz, who essentially proposed the terms of the debate in the first phase of film semiotics. Metz' purpose, as he himself defined it, was to "venir à bout de la metaphore linguistique," i.e. to get to the bottom of the linguistic metaphor, by testing it against the most advanced concepts of contemporary linguistics, in short, to take the metaphor seriously, but also skeptically, in order to discern its quantum of truthfulness.

Although I will stress developments in linguistics-based semiology in the sixties and after, it is important to remember that the notion of "film language" is an old one; indeed, it was the very perennial nature of the metaphor that inspired Metz to try to get at its roots. One finds the metaphor in the writings of Riccioto Canudo in Italy and Louis Delluc in France, both of whom saw the linguistic dimension as linked, paradoxically, to its non-verbal nature, its status as a "visual esperanto" transcending the barriers of national language.[2] While Canudo and Delluc were more interested in enhancing the prestige of the "seventh art" than in elaborating a full-blown theory, Bela Balazs probed the nature of film language more seriously, repeatedly returning to the subject in his work from the twenties through the late forties.[3] Also beginning in the twenties, the Russian Formalists, members of OPOIAZ (Society for the Study of Poetic Language), applied their critical methodology to the cinema in the anthology *Poetica Kino* (1927), with contributions by Eichenbaum, Shklovsky, Tynyanov and others.[4] Tynyanov spoke of the cinema as offering the visible world in the form of semantic signs, engendered by cinematic procedures such as lighting, montage and angle. Eichenbaum in "Problems of Cine-Stylistics" viewed the cinema in relation to "inner speech" and "image translations of linguistic tropes," concluding that the cinema is a "particular system of figurative language." Mikhail Bakhtin, meanwhile, as a kind of friendly "dialogical" adversary of the Formalists, never spoke of the cinema, yet developed a view of language, as I hope to show subsequently, rich in implications for film semiotics.

Subsequent to the work of the Russian Formalists, the notion of film-language came to form the implicit topos grounding and the many "Grammars" of cinema, beginning with Raymond Spottiswoode's *Grammar of Film* (1935), and later André Bertomieu's *Essai de Grammaire Cinémato-gaphique* (1946) and Robert Bataille's *Grammaire Cinégraphique* (1947) The linguistic trope was not well thought out, however, for grammar tended to imply a normative view of "correct" cinema (a view subsequently reproduced in certain transformationalist models), by which the authors would communicate to the prospective cinéaste how to transmit their ideas "grammatically." The "grammars" were subtended by an aesthetic of transparence and self-effacing technique. Implicit in them too was the word-shot analogy later deconstructed by Metz.

In other pre-semiotic discussions, the film-language metaphor became intimately linked to the cognate trope of "film writing." In postwar France, this "graphological" figure became a key structuring concept subtending film theory and criticism. Alexandre Astruc, in "The Birth of a New Avant-Garde: The Camera-Pen" (1948), suggested that the filmmaker should be able to say "I" like the novelist or poet. The Bazin-inspired "politique des auteurs" simply developed what was implicit in the root trope. It is not surprising, therefore, that in Marcel Martin's sympotmatically titled *Le Langage Cinématographique* (Paris: Cerf, 1955) and in Jean Mitry's *Esthétique et Psychologie du Cinéma* (Paris: Ed. Universitaires, 1963), the term film-language comes to seem roughly equatable with the notion of "film style" or "expressive resources."

The point of this hasty overview of linguistic and "grammatical" approaches to the cinema is to suggest that it is somewhat unfair, given the regularity with which the linguistic analogy has been touched on, to "blame" Metz for infecting film studies with the linguistic virus. Indeed, Metz, especially in his early work, "inherits" many of the conceptualizations developed by his predecessors. It was Marcel Martin, for example, who stressed the notion that cinema became a language *through* trying to tell stories, a notion developed in Metz' *Essais sur la Signification au Cinéma*. From Jean Mitry, Metz inherits the accent on the "signifying material," i.e. the image, and on the sequential placement of images as being productive of discourse.

In the background of Metz' initial discussion, in the early sixties, of cinema language, is Saussure's methodological question—what is the object of linguistic study? Thus Metz looks for the equivalent, in film theory, to the conceptual role played by *langue* in the Saussurean schema, i.e. the "object" of the filmolinguistic endeavor. And much as Saussure concluded that the rightful object of linguistic investigation was to disengage the abstract signifying system of a language—i.e. its key units and their rules of combination at a given point in time—so Metz concluded that the object of cine-semiology was to disengage the signifying procedures, the combinatory rules, of the cinema, in order to see to what extent these rules resembled the doubly-articulated diacritical systems of "natural languages." The question which orients Metz' early work, therefore, is whether the cinema is *langue* (language system) or *langage* (language), and Metz' well-known conclusion is that cinema is not a language system but that it *is* a language.

Metz' arguments for rejecting film as language system vary considerably in their persuasiveness. The idea that language involves immediate two-way communication while film allows only for deferred communication, for example, is somewhat problematic. First, nothing precludes the possibility of some future interactive form of cinema that would allow for immediate two-way communication. Second, the real analogy in terms of "deferred communication" is not natural language but rather literature, which also allows only for delayed response in the form of an answering poem, novel, or act of literary criticism. Finally, Metz' emphasis on two-way communication assumes spoken speech as a model in ways that leave him open to the Derridean charge of phonocentrism, i.e. that Metz implicitly privileges speech, relegating writing to the role of mere "supplement" or transcription of the spoken word. (In *Langage et Cinéma*, it is important to point out, Metz transcends this phonocentrism by highlighting cinema as text and *écriture*.).

Metz also argued that cinema can not be regarded as a language system because it lacks the equivalent of the linguistic sign, defined by Saussure as the union of a signifier (the sensible, material, acoustic or visual stimulus) and a signified (the mental concept triggered by the signifier). Central to the Saussurean definition of the sign is the notion of the arbitrary relationship between signifier and signified, i.e. that the linguistic sign, except for eccentric situations such as onomatopoeia, does not, through the disposition of its letters or the organization of its sounds, resemble or imitate the concept, but rather has an arbitrary, unmotivated relationship to it. The filmic image, in contrast, thanks to the camera's process of mechanical reproduction, is "motivated" by profilmic reality; it is an analogon. (Metz often slides, in his earlier work, between the restricted category of "analogical" and the broad notion of "motivation"). Under the pressure of criticisms by Eco and others, Metz later shed the implicit Bazinianism of this position by acknowledging that the filmic analogon is indeed coded. The analogy, he suggests in *Language and Cinema*, is less between filmic signifier and filmic signified than in the perceptual situation common to everyday life and the cinematic situation.

It is important to remember that Metz, while arguing that the cinema lacks the arbitrary sign of linguistics, never suggests that the concept of sign, and of signifier/signified, is irrelevant to the cinema. The emphasis on the cinematic signifier, for example, is useful in that it focuses attention away from the signifieds of the diegesis (story, character) onto the specifically cinematic "triggers" of filmic signification: camera movement, lighting, editing and so forth. The material aspect of the signifier, meanwhile, suggests a classification of different kinds of semiotics according to the nature of the "substance" of the signifier, that is to say, according to the sensorial order to which the signifier belongs.

In his later psychoanalytically inflected work, Metz insists on the higher degree of imaginariness of the cinematic signifier in relation to other arts such as the theatre. In "The Imaginary Signifier," Metz emphasized that what is characteristic of the cinema is not the imaginary that it may happen to represent; it is the imaginary that it is from the start. Here Metz virtually inverts not only his earlier (Bazanian) insistence on the cinema as the "art of reality," but also reverses the Saussurean definition of the *signified* as a lack, an absence in the perceptual object. He does this by suggesting that the cinematic *signifier* is defined by its absence. Unlike the theatre in which real actors share the space and time of the spectator, the film is a recording and what it records (at least the *visual* recording; sound is arguably present) is not there at the moment of it projection. The cinematic signifier combines presence and absence—presence by its intense playing on the perceptual registers of the spectator, and absence because it is only a replica of what is no longer there, "made" furthermore of nothing more than shifting patterns of light. For the later Metz, then, the cinematic signifier is imaginary in terms of its very constitution as signifier and also because it constitutes a "lure" which shares the characteristic structuration of what Lacan calls "the Imaginary."

In the inaugural phase of his work, however, Metz "tested" the cinema against the related concepts of "minimal units" and "double articulation," concluding that the cinema *as such* has nothing corresponding to the double articulation of natural languages. Cinema proceeds by whole blocks of reality—this early formulation remains marked by vestigial Bazinianism—rather than through discrete signifying elements. Everything in the cinema already signifies, both separately and in combination, and the linguistic analogy to film breaks down because the semiotics of film begins where linguistics ends: at the level of the sentence.

It is in this context that Metz explores the notion (familiar from the earliest days of film theory) that the shot is like a word while the sequence is like a sentence. We need not rehearse in detail Metz' well-known objections to this analogy—shots are infinite in number, unlike the finite lexicon of words; shots are the creation of the filmmaker, unlike words; shots are actualized rather than virtual units, and so forth—but we may linger on one disanalogy between the cinema in general and natural language, i.e. that film does not constitute a language which is widely available as a code. All speakers of English have mastered the code of English—they are able to produce sentences—but being able to produce filmic utterances depends on talent, access, and training. One might argue, of course, that this dependance is culturally and socially determined; one can hypothesize a society in which all citizens would be provided the opportunity to master the code of filmmaking. But in society as we know it Metz' point must stand. There is, furthermore, a fundamental difference in the diachrony of natural language and cinematic language. Cinematic language can be suddenly inflected by new aesthetic procedures—those introduced by a film such as *Citizen Kane*, for example, or those rendered possible by a new technology—while natural language shows a more powerful inertia and is less open to individual initiative and creativity. The analogy, in this case, is less between cinema and natural language, than between cinema and literature, which can be suddenly inflected by the novel aesthetic procedures of, for example, a James Joyce and his *Ulysses*.

Having insisted that cinema is not *langue* (language system), Metz then argues that it is nevertheless *langage* (language). It is language in that it is a signifying practice with recognizable ordering procedures. Metz posits two tendencies within the word "language:" (1) Systems are called languages if their formal structure resembles that of natural languages, as in the expression "the language of chess;" (2) Everything that signifies to human beings even without a formal system can be seen as reminiscent of language. (Here Metz comes close to the Peircian definition of the sign as "something which stands to somebody for something in some respect or capacity.") Thus poets speak of the language of flowers and semioticians study the language of fashion or the language of cuisine. Elsewhere, Metz places the notion of language in a more specifically Hjemslevian context: "It seems to me that one may call 'language' a unity that is defined in terms of matter of expression (a Hjelmslevian notion) or of 'typical sign' as Barthes puts it in *Elements of Semiology*. Literary language is the set of messages whose matter of expression is writing: cinematic language is the set of messages which are identical in their matter of expression, this being here fivefold: moving photographic image, recorded phonetic sound, recorded noises, recorded musical sound and writing (credits, intertitles). Thus 'language' is a technical-sensorial unity, immediately graspable in perceptual experience" (p. 208, *Essais sur la Signification au Cinéma*). This then is the double sense, for Metz, of cinema as "language"; first, as an artistic language, a discourse or signifying practice characterized by specific codifications and ordering procedures.

It has at times been suggested, unfairly, that Metz begins his work by proving that linguistics is inapplicable and then applies it anyway.

Brian Henderson, in *A Critique of Film Theory*, implies that Metz, after having proven the inapplicability of linguistic methods, invents the "grande syntagmatique" as a kind of desperate diversionary measure. In fact, however, Metz is quite explicit about his method in *Essais sur la Signification au Cinéma*, i.e. that he plans to begin by showing which linguistic principles do *not* apply and then suggesting those which *do*: "By initially casting light on what cinema is *not*, linguistics—and especially that part of it which leads to translinguistics (semiotics)—gradually allows us to glimpse what the cinema *is*" (p.84, *Film Language*).

As a signifying practice with recognizable ordering procedures, film, like language, constitutes itself as discourse rather than as an unmediated slice of life. Film became discourse, Metz argued at this phase in his work, by organizing itself as narrative: "It was precisely to the extent that the cinema confronted the problems of narration that . . . it came to produce a body of specific signifying procedures." While no image entirely resembles another image, most narrative films resemble one another in their principle syntagmatic figures, those units which organize spatial and temporal relations in various combinations. The grande syntagmatique is Metz' attempt to isolate these principal figures; it comes in response to the question: "How does film constitute itself as narrative discourse?"

The true analogy between film and language, then, does not exist at the level of basic units, but rather in their common syntagmatic nature. By moving from one image to two, film becomes language. Both language and film produce discourse through paradigmatic and syntagmatic operations. Language selects and combines phonemes (the minimal units of sound) and monemes (the minimal units of sense) to form sentences; film selects and combines images and sounds according to specific ordering procedures to form "syntagmas," i.e. units of narrative autonomy in which elements interact semantically.

The grande syntagmatique was proposed against the backdrop of the notorious imprecision of film terminology concerning the sequential arrangements of the fiction film. Much of the antecedent terminology was based on theatre rather than on the specifically cinematic signifiers of image and sound, shots and montage. Terms like "scene" and "sequence" were used interchangeably, and were at times based on a posited unity of action ("the farewell scene") or of place ("the courtroom sequence"), with little attention to the exact temporal and spatial articulation of the diegesis. By contrast, according to Metz' schema, a farewell scene such as that which concludes *Adieu Philippine* might be subdivided into a number of syntagmas.

The grande syntagmatique represents, at the level of the organization of images, a typology of the different ways that time and space can be ordered through montage, a fixed number of patterns according to which individual shots can be grouped into units. Metz uses "syntagma" as the general term for these units of narrative autonomy, reserving both "sequence" and "scene" to designate specific types of syntagmas. Exploiting the methodology based on binary oppositions inherited from the"phonological revolution," Metz works through a series of successive dichotomies: a syntagma consists of one shot or more than one shot; it is chronological or achronological; if it is chronological, it can be either consecutive or simultaneous, linear or nonlinear, continuous or discontinuous. Using this method, Metz generated at first a total of six types (in the version published in *Communications* in 1966) subsequently increased to eight (in the version included in *Essais sur la signification au cinéma* in 1968 and included in *Film Language*).

Syntagmatic analysis enables the analyst to determine how images come together in a pattern which forms the overall narrative armature of the film-text. Working from three-criteria—unity of action, punctuation devices, and syntagmatic structure—Metz hopes to show how syntagmatic units combine with other codic systems to generate the internal unfolding of events represented in the filmic chain. On this basis, Metz came up with the familiar octet of syntagmas: (1) the *autonomous shot* (an oxymoronic syntagma in the sense that it consists of a single shot), subdivided into the one-shot sequence and four kinds of "inserts"; (2) the *parallel syntagma* (two alternating motifs without clear spatial or temporal relationship); (3) the *bracket syntagma* (brief conceptual scenes given as typical samples of a certain order of reality but without temporal sequence); (4) the *descriptive syntagma* (objects shown successively, suggesting spatial co-existence, used, for example, to situate the action); (5) the *alternate syntagma* (narrative cross-cutting implying temporal simultaneity, such as in a chase, alternating shots of pursuer and pursued); (6) the *scene* (spatio-temporal continuity felt as being without flaws or breaks, in which the diegetic signified is continuous, as in the theatrical scene, but the signifier is fragmented into diverse shots; (7) the *episodic sequence* (a shorthand summary of stages in an implied chronological development); and (8) the *ordinary sequence* (action treated elliptically so as to eliminate "superfluous" detail with "jumps" in time and space carefully masked by continuity editing).

Before moving to a general evaluation of the grande syntagmatique, it would be worthwhile to comment on the analytic usefulness of the syntagmas themselves. The most problematic of the eight is the first, the "autonomous shot." The only one of the syntagmas defined uniquely in terms of its signifier, (i.e. the fact that it consists of one shot only), the very diversity of the kinds of situations to which the term might apply makes one dubious about its applicability. The "one-shot sequence," to take just one of these subtypes, might include, for example, the first Lumiere films, the one-shot sequences of innumerable New Wave films, and Hitchcock's *Rope*. When so much can happen within a single shot, such as those of *Rope*, where the equivalents of shot-changes are suggested through camera movement, disposition of actors within the frame, interventions on the sound track, one worries that the term has ceased to be meaningful. The work of any director, such as Fellini, who develops single-shot sequences which unfold their signification slowly over time, will fit only awkwardly into this category.

The four subtypes of "insert"—the non-diegetic insert, the subjective insert, the displaced diegetic insert, and the explanatory insert—are problematic in so far as they are identified with the single shot. There is no reason, for example, why the subjectivity of a memory or fear must be represented or evoked within the confines of a single shot (*Last Year at Marienbad*, in this sense, might be regarded as a single prolonged subjective "insert" composed of hundreds of single shots). A "subjective" shot, furthermore, only bears meaning in relation to the larger signified of the diegesis; it cannot be so clearly separated from its narrative context. By ghettoizing, as it were, the subjective shot, Metz elides the thorny problem of point of view, i.e. that subjectivity and point of view articulate films in their entirety. The subjective insert category, then, creates a kind of bulge, for all subjectivity in film cannot be neatly assigned as a subset of the autonomous shot. Metz' isolation of subjectivity into single subjective shots, furthermore, seems to assume a conventional kind of realism which does not allow for the possibility of extended subjective realism (perhaps that of *Red Desert*, or *Marienbad*, for example) and even less for a thoroughgoing reflexivity.

For all these reasons, the autonomous shot category, although it points to useful distinctions, is perhaps the weakest and most unwieldly feature of the grande syntagmatique. The other syntagmas proposed by Metz are considerably clearer in definition and of greater potential utility. The "parallel syntagma," interweaving two motifs without positing any clear temporal or spatial relationship, evokes such films as Griffith's *Corner in Wheat*, with its thematic counterpoint between images of wealth and poverty. Militant leftist films of the didactic kind show a special penchant for the parallel syntagma, using them, for example, to highlight class advantages and class/oppressions, contrasting, for example, images of upper-class leisure (the bourgeoisie playing golf) with images of lower-class squalor (the lumpenproletariat scrounging for food in garbage dumps).

The category of the "bracket syntagma," providing typical examples of a given order of reality without chronogical linkage, also helps us characterize cinematic styles. The fragmented shots of love-making that open *Une Femme mariée*, for example, are devoid of teleology or climax; they exist as typical samples of an order of reality known as "making love"; indeed, the sequence's lack of teleology and temporal development form part of a Brechtian strategy of de-eroticization, a "bracketing" of eroticism. The shots of the female protagonist of *Lucia* (Part III) doing agricultural work, similarly, show no chronological development; they are there merely to "signify" her return to work. Metz, somewhat problematically, calls the opening segment of *Adieu Philippine*—a series of shots showing the film's male protagonist working in a television studio—a bracket syntagma. The classification is contradicted by the music of this segment, which is diegetic, synchronous and uninterrupted. The temporality of the music, in such a case, with its unfolding temporal continuity, differs from and contradicts the temporality of the soundtrack.

The other syntagmatic types are of variable novelty and usefulness. The "descriptive syntagma," in practice, is often difficult to distinguish from the "bracket syntagma," although at times the very exercise of arguing the case for one or the other can help illuminate a film's textual functioning. The "alternating syntagma" strikes us as simply another name for classical narrative cross-cutting; Metz' contribution was to clearly distinguish it from the parallel syntagma, with its thematic, as opposed to temporal, articulation. The "scene," in which the signifier is fragmented while the signified is continuous, helps illuminate not only the conventional Hollywood handling of dialogue, when it implies a complete coincidence of screen and diegetic time, but also such extended "scenes" as *Cleo de 5 à 7* and *My Dinner with André*, where the signifier is fragmented into hundreds of shots, while the diegetic signified, apart from very minor exceptions, remains continuous.

The "episodic sequence" is, as far as I know, an original contribution by Metz. The episodic sequence brings together a series of brief episodes, often separated by optical devices such as dissolves, sometimes unified by a musical accompaniment, which succeed each other chronologically within the diegesis. The meaning of this succession of "scenelets" lies in the totality, that is in the overall progression and development, rather than in the scenelets themselves. Each scenelet constitutes a symbolic summary of a stage in a part of a larger development. In *Adieu Philippine*, for example, an episodic sequence involves three successive rendezvous between Michel and Liliane and Juliette. The idea of their increasing familiarity links the three outings, marking it with the teleology of growing friendliness. The "breakfast sequence" in *Citizen Kane* (a flashback of Leland's account of Kane's first marriage), consists of a series of episodes demarcated by a swish pan. The episodes in themselves are of little significance; it is rather the developing sense of estrangement as the couple passes from newlywed passion to bored hostility which gives the sequence its point.

The grande syntagmatique, while fairly widely disseminated and generating a number of syntagmatic analyses, also encountered considerable criticism, and Metz himself came both to express reservations about it and to redefine its status within cine-semiology. Some critiques focused on the general thrust of Metz' project as unduly privileging the mainstream narrative film. The definition of cinematic language as "first of all the literalness of a plot" excluded both documentaries and avant-garde film. Metz granted the point subsequently in *Language and Cinema* by redefining the grande syntagmatique as merely one of many cinematic codes, and more specifically as a sub-code of editing within a historically delimited body of films: the mainstream narrative tradition from the early thirties (the consolidation of the sound film) through the late fifties, which declined with the death of the studio aesthetic and the challenge of diverse "new waves."

Apart from complicated problems of applicability, Metz' schema at times falls into a naive referentialism in that it is based on the comparison between the "real time" of the diegesis and the actual temporal articulation of the filmic discourse itself. While it is true that the narrative discourse is the product of the interplay of the cinematic instance that signifies and the diegetic instance that is signified, it is also true that at times Metz underemphasizes the nature of filmic time as pure construct.

Relative to previous work, the grande syntagmatique provided a model whose cinematic (as opposed to literary) specificity offered a suggestive theoretical framework. The model, however, was faulted not only for privileging narrative denotation, but also for its vestigial positivism and theoretical underpinnings. Metz implicitly appeals to common observation and general experience as if these were unproblematic notions. Like the empiricist, he proceeds inductively as if searching for syntagmatic types in the films rather than constructing a theoretical combinatory which might both generate and account for the widest range of possible types.

Some of the "bugs" in Metz' schema emerge in the syntagmatic analysis of *Adieu Philippine*. Apart from perceptual inaccuracies—a jump-cut edited series of twelve lateral tracking shots is treated as if it were a single shot—other problems appear. The grande syntagmatique pretends to concern only the image track, yet in fact it has constant recourse to information drawn from the soundtrack. The characterization of a shot of Michel loafing at the TV studio (contradicting his exaggerated claims of importance) as a "displaced diegetic insert" depends on our knowledge of Michel's boasting, knowledge provided by the dialogue rather than the image track.

A less monolithic schema would allow for the possiblity of multiple syntagmatic analyses depending on whch track is being discussed. It would allow for the possibility of distinct and even contradictory temporalities depending on whether one is speaking of the image track, the dialogue track, the music track, the noise track, or even the written materials track. The permutations of these coordinates, systematically explored in a film such as *Numéro deux*, are anticipated in *Adieu Philippine* itself. The "episodic sequence" in which Michel accompanies Lilianne and Juliette to three distinct places (a train station, a country road, an airfield) combines flawless continuity on the dialogue track with clear spatial and temporal discontinuity on the image track. Importantly, Metz' discussion of the syntagmatic dimension in *Language and Cinema* answers those objections and allows for expanded possibilities.

Much of the hostility initially generated by the grande syntagmatique was based on the assumption that it was meant as definitive and exhaustive, as *the* master code of the cinema. After the analysis is finished, critics pointed out, virtually everything remains to be said. But Metz offered "the large syntagmatic category of the image track" in a more modest spirit than was often granted by his detractors, as a first step toward establishing the main types of image orderings. To the objection that "everything remains to be said" Metz would presumably have two answers. First, that it is in the nature of science to choose a principle of pertinence. To speak of the Grand Canyon in terms of geological strata, or *Hamlet* in terms of syntactic functions, hardly exhausts the interest or signification of those two phenomena, yet that does not mean that either geology or linguistics are useless. Secondly, the work of addressing all levels of signification in a film is the task of textual analysis, not of film theory or the grande syntagmatique. The grande syntagmatique is merely one of the sub-codes, functioning as an armature or support for the work of the codes comprising a film's textual system.

Although the grande syntagmatique formed part of a scientistic phase of the semiotic project, a phase subsequently both complemented and relativized by psychoanalytic methods before being aggressively questioned by the proponents of deconstruction, it would be wrong to underestimate the importance of Metz' achievement. In contrast to the imprecision of previous models, Metz introduces a relative rigor by focusing attention away from the narrative signified onto the cinematic signifier. Metz' schema is valuable not in the sense of being infallible but in asking an important question: What are the diverse possibilities of temporal and spatial articulation within the fiction film? In practical terms, the grande syntagmatique can serve as an attention-forcing device, of interest even when only partially applicable to the film in question. The syntagmatic types are also broadly useful in defining the spatiotemporal coordinates of specific genres, or the stylistic specificities of a given director or film. It is easier, finally, to point out flaws in a model than to construct one.

The grande syntagmatique, while flawed, offers a partially valid model for dealing with the specific image-ordering procedures of the narrative film.

Metz' most thoroughgoing exercise in filmo-linguistics is, of course, *Language and Cinema*, first published in French in 1971. The English version, published in 1974, was praised, denounced, and more often, ignored. Few seem to have read it with attention, partially because an egregiously inept translation turned what was already a somewhat arid text into a virtually unreadable monstrosity. Two of Metz' key terms—*langue* (language system) and *langage* (language)—were more or less systematically mistranslated into their opposites, thus transforming much of the book into nonsense. We are surprised at one point (p. 37), to learn that the same Metz who has just spoken of the necessary codic heterogeneity of the cinema also believes that is is "possible to treat the total ensemble of films as the diverse messages of a single code" (p. 37), a surprise eliminated when we discover that the original French said that is was "*im*possible" to do so. The translator, furthermore, seems disturbingly unfamiliar with film history and film genre: "*film noir*" is (superfluously) translated as "American Hardboiled Detective Films;" Murnau's *Sunrise*, translated back into English, becomes "*Dawn*;" and the painterly term "*clair-obscur*" (i.e. *chiarascuro*), becomes a meaningless "clear-obscure." "*Écriture*," meanwhile, is sometimes translated as "writing" and sometimes as "script," thus creating confusion with "film script." Given such a translation, it is scarcely surprising that many film students laid down the book in irritation or despair.

Even when read with attention, *Language and Cinema* was often misinterpreted as an exercise in linguistic imperialism and theoretical dogmatism, when in fact Metz was more interested in outlining areas of research and defining the *status* of such research than in laying down definitive answers. The book was received as a canonical enumeration of cinematic codes, when in fact Metz merely defined the *goal* of cinesemiology as dealing with the cinematic codes, the sum of which would form "film language," without claiming to have reached that goal himself. The inveterately modest Metz was denounced as "pretentious," a misconception based largely on the fact that Metz deployed the standard "difficult" language of linguistics, the discipline in which Metz was formed, in a domain where quasi-journalistic language had long been the norm.

Language and Cinema is Metz' most ambitious attempt to define what a semiotics of the cinema might look like. The contributions of this book, arid on the surface but exciting in its depths, are multiple. Quite apart from its larger systematic project, Metz combats, "along the way," as it were, a number of the oft-repeated doxa of film-critical discourse: the deployment of "art" as an honorific term (all films, Metz argues, are "art" in function of their socially defined status *as* art); the hackneyed notion of film as "primarily visual;" the idea that television and cinema form widely separate, even contrasting languages (the real differences concern conditions of production and reception, Metz argues, not their signifying procedures); and the notion that a film necessarily has a single hegemonic temporality rather than, potentially, a multiplicity of temporalities. Thus Metz questioned the underlying romanticism, essentialism, and dillettantism underlying much of what had passed for serious film theory.

It would be impossible to dwell here on Metz' long and complicated argument in *Language and Cinema*. I would like here to touch on only a few of Metz' terminological distinctions and methodological proposals. Metz begins *Language and Cinema* by introducing the distinction, borrowed from Gilbert Cohen-Seat, between "cinema" and "film." The cinema, for Metz, is the cinematic institution taken in its broadest sense as a multidimensional sociocultural fact which includes prefilmic events (the economic infrastructure of the studio system, for example), postfilmic (distribution, exhibition, the social impact of films), and a-filmic events (the decor of the theatre, the social ritual of moviegoing). Film, on the other hand, refers to a localizable discourse, a text. Thus Metz closes in on the object of semiotics as the study of discourses and texts rather than of the institution, seen as an entity too multiform to constitute a proper object for semiotics, much as *parole* was seen as too amorphous to constitute the proper object of the linguistic science. (It should be pointed out that Metz never argues that the cinema as institution should *not* be studied, only that such study is not an integral part of filmo-linguistics.) At the same time, Metz points out that films concentrate an intense charge of social, cultural and psychological meanings, and that all these deserve study. Indeed, in "The Imaginary Signifier," Metz returns to the question of the cinema institution in order to offer a startlingly original reformulation, positing the existence of three parallel and mutually inter-related industries: the cinema industry in the conventional material sense of the term; the mental "industry" which adapts the public to consuming films in a way beneficial to the material industry; and the critical industry as the "linguistic appendage" of the first two. In this sense, the cinema as institution also exists at the very heart of film.

In the second chapter of *Language and Cinema*, Metz also locates the cinema, in a different sense, at the heart of film. Here cinema represents not the industry but rather a kind of ideal ensemble, i.e. the totality of films and their traits. Thus Metz, building on Hjelmslev, prepares the terrain for his concept of the "specifically cinematic codes." Hjelmslev distinguishes between concrete ensembles, such as the totality of filmic messages, and systematic, more abstract ensembles or "codes." The notion of "code" has engendered considerable confusion. At times wielded like a magic wand by the superficially informed, as a shortcut for turning conventional criticism into "scientific analysis," the term was conceived in semiology as referring to a field of commutation, a system of comparabilities, constructed or used by the analyst. In sociology and anthropology, meanwhile, "code" tends to refer to transpersonal patterns of behavior and collective representations, while in ordinary speech the term crops up in phrases such as "area code" or "zip code," phrases which retain the root idea of a conventionalized system remaining constant over varied particular usages; a code is that which governs numerous messages.

In film, there exist numerous codes which remain constant across all or most films; however, film displays no "master code" shared by all films. As a heterogenous signifying system, film lacks the uniform substance of expression and diacritical structure of "natural languages." By arguing that cinema is *langage* but not *langue*, Metz had already implied that film lacks a single master code. In *Language and Cinema*, however, Metz elaborates what was implicit in *Essais sur la signification au cinéma*: the concept of cinema as a *necessarily* pluricodic medium. Filmic texts, for Metz, are formed by the interweaving of multiple codes, some of which are specific to the cinema, that is, they appear *only* in the cinema, and some of which are shared, to varying degrees, with languages other than the cinema. "Film language" is simply the ensemble of cinematic codes and sub-codes. Among the specifically cinematic codes, there exists what Metz himself calls a "hierarchy of specificity;" some cinematic codes are more cinematic than others. The codes operative in a film, then, can range from codes which are extremely specific, for example, those codes linked to film's definition as deploying moving, multiple images (e.g. codes of camera movement or continuity editing), to codes which are demonstrably non-specific because widely disseminated in the culture and in no way dependent on the specific modalities of the filmic medium. Film, then, is the point of convergence of innumerable non-specific codes and a much more restricted number of specific codes.

Examples of specifically cinematic codes might be camera movement (or lack of it), lighting, and montage. (Already, here, we notice a "hierarchy of specificity;" the motion picture camera defines cinema as a medium, while lighting is shared with sister arts such as the theatre). These codes form part of all films, in the sense that all films involve cameras, all films must be lit, and all films must have some system, even if minimal or anarchic, of montage. Within the particular code, there exist numerous sub-codes representing specific usages of the general code. Expressionist lighting, for example, might be seen as a sub-code of lighting within a paradigm which includes alternative approaches such as "naturalistic ambient lighting." "Eisensteinian" montage can be seen as a sub-code of montage, contrastable in its typical usage with a Bazinian mise-en-scène insisting on spatial and temporal integrity. For Metz, codes do not compete, but subcodes do. All films must be lit and edited, but not all films need resort to Eisensteinian montage. Metz notes, however, that certain filmmakers, such as Glauber Rocha, mingle contradictory sub-codes in a kind of "feverish anthological procedure," by which Eisensteinian montage and cinema verité inform the editing of the same sequence. The code, for Metz, is a construction of the analyst, a logical calculus of possible permutations, while the sub-code is a specific and concrete usage of these possibilities. A history of the cinema, at least in so far as the specifically cinematic is concerned, would trace the competition of the sub-codes.

It is not my purpose here to dwell on some of the problematic aspects of the distinction between codes and sub-codes, aspects well anatomized by David Bordwell and others, but rather to focus on Metz' conception of "textual systems" as the interweaving of cinematic and extra-cinematic codes.[5] First, it is wrong to see *Language and Cinema* as a definitive schema of codes or as a how-to book for textual analysis. Metz is more concerned with the theoretical status of textual analysis, with the ways codes might be constructed, than with laying down laws. Metz repeatedly emphasizes the idea of *constructing* codes, or better, of doing textual analysis in such a way that it exposes in the text codes which had not previously been recognized *as* codes. Second, Metz provided a seminal insight by suggesting that *no* film is constructed uniquely out of cinematic codes; films always speak of something, even if they speak about nothing more than the apparatus itself, the film experience itself, or out conventional expectations concerning that experience. (It is this insight, combined with Baudry's and Metz' work on the apparatus and primary indentification, that provides the founding gesture for Constance Penley's "The Avant-Garde and its Imaginary").

There exists a certain tension, in *Language and Cinema*, between a static, taxonomic first-phase "structuralist" view of textual systems, a view implicitly imbued with positivist and scientist overtones, and a dynamic, Kristevan, Derridean view of text as "productivity," "displacement," and "écriture." It is the latter pole, in my view, which constitutes the more suggestive dimension of Metz' work. In certain passages of *Language and Cinema*, Metz comes closer to the deconstructionists in arguing that the text builds itself on the perpetual destruction of its own codes. Metz' movement from a static to a dynamic semiotics, parallels, of course, that of Barthes from the scientistic *Elements of Semiology* (1964) to the more deconstructionist S/Z (1970). A film's textual system, within this more dynamic conception, is not the *list* of operative codes, but rather the labor of reconstruction and perpetual displacement of the codes. What is interesting is the way the film "writes" its text, modifies its codes, combines its codes, and especially, plays some codes *against* other codes, and in so doing constitutes its system. The system of the text is the instance which displaces the codes, so that the codes come to deform one another, contaminate one another, inflect and substitute one another. What matters is the passage from one code to another, the way in which signification is relayed from lighting, for example, to camera movement, from dialogue to music, or the way that music plays against dialogue or lighting against camera movement.

Metz' intermittent emphasis on inter-codic conflict suggests affinities with the politicized aesthetic of Bertolt Brecht, and any serious application of the Brechtian "separation of elements" to film must take Metz' analysis into account. The episodic nature of epic theatre implies a "horizontal" autonomy of syntagmatic segments, but also involves a "vertical" tension between the diverse strata or "tracks" of the text. Metz, lending semiotic precision to Eisenstein's intuitions concerning "vertical" and "horizontal" montage, argues that the syntagmatic dimension of the cinema is deployed along two axes—the axis of consecution (the succession of shots within a segment) and the axis of simultaneity (the reciprocal relations between and among the diverse tracks). The axis of consecution includes four parallel series—the image track, the linguistic series, noises and music, with written elements constituting another, generally more discontinuous, series. The axis of simultaneities, meanwhile, has itself two axes; first, the axis of spatial co-presence within the rectangle of the screen, the second, the simultaneous syntagmas which may be established between or among the diverse series.

This complex and open-ended schema helps us account, as I have argued elsewhere, for the semiotic complexity of a film such as *Numéro deux*, where multiple images play with and against each other within the rectangle of the screen, and where the distinct temporalities of different tracks are made to enter into fecund interaction and competition, pursuing simultaneous but distinct trajectories in what amounts to a dynamically spatialized, mobile tapestry of interwoven temporal threads.[6] The diverse tracks fall behind, catch up, overtake and dialogically relativize one another. The process of signification is constantly displaced from one track to another, a sentence, for example, beginning as a written title and ending as a spoken utterance. The shifting aural and visual coordinates highlight the process of textual structuration as a perpetual displacement and undermining of codes.

And how, one might ask, does Bakhtin fit into the discussion? Bakhtin's work, written long before Metz' work on film language, but disseminated concurrently or subsequent to that work, provides, I would argue, the basis of a critique of certain assumptions underlying Metz' work, but also potential complicities and a means to recuperate and reanimate that work. In *Marxism and the Philosophy of Language*, Bakhtin and Voloshinov offer a comprehensive account of what they call "translinguistics," a theory of the role of signs in human life and social practice.[7] The word "translinguistics" might seem comparable to Saussure's "semiology," were it not for the fact that it is precisely Saussure's notion of language that the authors attack. Saussure, we know, argued against the historical (diachronic) orientation of nine-teenth century linguistics in favor of a "synchronic" approach study-ing language as a functional totality at a given point in time. Within the synchronic, linguistics was to focus on *langue*—the language sys-tem with its basic units and rules of combination—rather than on *parole*, the concrete utterances made possible by that system. Bakhtin precisely inverted this emphasis, downplaying the language system as abstract model and stressing instead speech as lived and shared by human beings in social interaction.

While Bakhtin agrees with Saussure that a discipline should be created which might study the "life of signs within society," he differs in his view both of the nature of signs and of their role within society. Rejecting what he sees as Saussure's psychologism, Bakhtin sees lin-guistics as part of the study of ideologies. What Bakhtin calls "the word," i.e. language in the broadest sense, is the ideological phenom-enon par excellence, the "purest and most sensitive medium of social intercourse." The word, Bakhtin claims, anticipating Barthes, is om-nipresent in social life, whether in the form of inner speech, verbalized discourse, written or filmed text, and it has the capacity to register all the transitory phases of social process.

The real target of Bakhtin's attack is a vision of language subtended by what Bakhtin calls "abstract objectivism." The foundations of this tradition, of which Saussure is the heir, go back to European ration-alism and Leibniz' conception of a "universal grammar." Saussure, as an exponent of this tradition, emphasizes those factors—phonetic, grammatical, lexical—which remain identical, therefore normative, for all utterances. This body of norms forms the "code" of a language, a stable system within which ideological motives play little role. In-dividual and social variations of speech are fortuitous and relatively unimportant and do not affect the fundamental unity of language as system.

For Bakhtin, in contrast, language is never so neatly ordered; it is "messy" and conflictual like history itself, and therefore resists rigid systematization. The desire to see language as a static synchronic system, according to Bakhtin, is symptomatic of a kind of nostalgia for dead languages, whose systems were fixed precisely because they were dead, protected from the incessant pressure of daily utterance. A systematic approach to language such as Saussure's runs the danger of implicit conservatism, of regarding a living language as an arrested object, already perfected and ready. (It is hardly an accident, Bart Palmer has pointed out, that Saussure formulated his crucial distinction between *langue* and *parole* at a time when the French educational system was attempting to wipe out regional dialects and class usage by imposing the standard literary language on those pupils in its charge.)[8] The fundamental categories of structural linguistics in the Saussure tradition, Bakhtin observes, are phonetic (the units of sound) and morphological (the units of sense), categories which ultimately derive from the categories of Indo-Euopean comparative linguistics, precisely those categories most appropriate to a dead or alien language. Bakhtin argues for a shift of interest, therefore, to the dynamics of the utterance and of syntactic forms. The reality of language-speech, for Bakhtin, is not the abstract system of linguistic forms, not the isolated monologic utterance, but rather the social event of verbal interaction implemented in utterances, a social event inevitably imbricated with ideology and assymetrical arrangements of power.

Bakhtin's "translinguistics," then, is clearly relevant to the inaugural phase of cine-semiology. Bakhtin retains the linguistic paradigm, but opens it to the diachronic, to history and struggle. He shares with the Saussure tradition a kind of "relational thinking," but the relations in question no longer form part of a closed structural system. Like the semioticians, Bakhtin discerns language everywhere ("All manifestations of ideological creativity," he writes in *Marxism and the Philosophy of Language*," are bathed by, suspended in, and cannot be entirely segregated or divorced from the element of speech"), but he also sees language as everywhere imbricated with power. Bakhtin's critique of Saussurean linguistics, therefore, allows for the possibility of reintroducing both politics and culture into the abstract model provided by Metz. Film not only includes utterances in the form of verbal discourse; it *is* itself utterance, a socially informed communication.

Imprisoned by the Saussurean *langue/langage* schema, Metz tends to bracket questions of ideology, whole Bakhtin locates ideological struggle at the pulsating heart of all discourse. In the social life of the utterance, be that utterance a verbally enunicated phrase, a literary text, a comic strip or a film, each word is subject to rival pronunciations and intonations. Bakhtin gives the name "tact" to the ensemble of codes governing discursive interaction. "Tact" is determined by the aggregate of all the social relationships of the speakers, their ide-

ological horizons and the concrete situation involved in the interlo-
cution. This notion of tact is extremely suggestive for film analysis,
applying literally to the verbal exchanges within the diegesis, and
figuratively to the "tact" involved in the metaphorical dialogue of
codes in a textual system, as well as to the "dialogue" between film
and spectator. In terms of the diegesis, film can be seen, in part, as
the mise-en-scène of actual discursive situations, as the visual and
aural contextualization of speech. This dramaturgy has its special tact,
its way of suggesting, through camera placement, framing and acting,
such phenomena as intimacy or distance, camaraderie or domination,
in short, the social and personal dynamics operating between interlocutors. Metaphorically, "tact" evokes the power relations between
generic strands within a film, or even the implicit power relations
between film and audience. Does the film assume distance or a kind
of intimacy? Does it assume an interlocutor of a specific gender or
class or nation, and what attitude does it take toward this projected
interlocutor? What does the text assume about our cultural preparation, our knowledge or ideology?

What Bakhtin offers film theory and analysis is a unitary, trans-
disciplinary view of the human sciences and of cultural production,
based on the identity of their common materials: texts. Bakhtin's
broad definition of "text" as referring to all cultural production rooted
in language—and for Bakhtin no cultural production exists *outside* of
language—has the effect of breaking down not only the walls between
disciplines but also the wall between "text" and "hors-texte." Metz
has repeatedly insisted on the necessity of studying the economic-
political-ideological dimension of film along with its semio-psychoan-
alytic dimension; indeed, at times, as in his discussion of the "three
industries" in "The Imaginary Signifier," he brilliantly effects a synthesis of such concerns. He manages this, however, not because of
but rather despite the model of language which he has adopted. Because history and ideology are bracketed by the Saussurean model,
Metz is forced into a compartmentalized recommendation that film
scholars should *also* study history, economics, sociology and so forth.
Virtually all the Bakhtinian categories, in contrast, simultaneously
embrace the textual, the intertextual, and the contextual. Like Metz,
and like the formalists of his own time, he is sensitive to the specificity
of textual mechanisms, but unlike them, he refuses to dissociate these
mechanisms from social processes.

In methodological terms, a Bakhtinian approach would allow us, after having "discovered" cinematic specificity, to re-appreciate the links of film to other "series" or semiotic systems, to reaffirm the affinities of film studies to other disciplines, and to re-envision the relation between film history and the larger historical trajectory of narrative and discursive forms. Bakhtin's concept of intertextual dialogism, meanwhile, of language and discourse as shared territory, innoculates us from the romantic single-voiced assumptions undergirding auteurism (while still allowing us to be attuned to the specific tonalities and accents of individual voices); at the same time his emphasis on a boundless and ever-changing context as interacting with the text helps us avoid the Formalist and New Critical fetishization of the autonomous art object. His emphasis on *collective* speech—the missing term in structural linguistics—and the interpersonal generation of meaning, finally, enable a critique of the static ahistorical aspects of first-phase semiotics through a "trans-linguistics" compatible with the linguistic model, but without the positivist illusion of mastery and hypostatization of system typical of a certain structuralism.

NOTES

[1] The major American proponent of a transformationalist approach to the cinema has been John M. Carroll. In "A Program for Cinema Theory," *Journal of Aesthetics and Art Criticism*, 35 No. 3 (1977), Carroll argues that cinema does indeed have a grammar, that its "deep structure" consists of events while its "surface structure" consists of actualized film sequences, felt by ordinary viewers to be 'grammatical" or "ungrammatical." Carroll's normative view has the effect, unfortunately, of naturalizing and universalizing one historically-bound set of film practices—those of dominant cinema. Michel Colin's *Langue, film, discours: Prolégomenes a une sémiologie génerative du film* (Paris: Klincksieck, 1985), constitutes an even more ambitious attempt to construct a transformationalist model for the cinema. He too, however, keeps slipping into normative views of film grammar, and seems less interested in developing a semiotics of the cinema than in seeing how the analysis of film might contribute to a general transformationalist theory of discourse. (It should be added that Metz in *Language and Cinema* briefly evokes the possibility of a transformationalist approach and that Colin's work was performed under Metz' academic supervision).

The application of Peircian "pragmatist" semiotics to the cinema has generally been limited to a brief explication of the trichotomy of index, icon, and symbol. Of those who draw on this tradition. Peter Wollen and Umberto Eco are probably the most significant.

² Language-related citations from Canudo and Delluc can be found in a number of classical anthologies: Marcel Lapierre, *Anthologie du cinéma* (Paris: La Nouvelle Edition, 1946), Marcel L'Herbier, *Intelligence du cinématographe* (Paris: Ed. Correa, 1946), and Pierre L'Herminier, *L'Art du cinéma* (Paris: Seghers, 1960).

³ See Bela Balazs, *Theory of the Film: Character and Growth of a New Art*, trans. Edith Bone (New York: Arno Press, 1972).

⁴ For an English version, see Herbert Eagle, ed., *Russian Formalist Film Theory* (Ann Arbor: Michigan Slavic Publications, 1981).

⁵ See David Bordwell, "Textual Analysis, Etc.," *Enclitic* 5 no. 2/6 no. 1 (Fall 81/Spring 82).

⁶ See R. Stam, *Reflexivity in Film and Literaute: From Don Quixote to Jean-Luc Godard* (Ann Arbor: UMI, 1985), pp. 222-230.

⁷ See V.N. Voloshinov, *Marxism and the Philosophy of Language* (New York: Seminar Press, 1973). I will henceforth use "Bakhtin" as a synecdoche for "Bakhtin/Voloshinov."

⁸ See R. Barton Palmer, "Metz' Model of Film Syntagmatics: A Text Grammar Critique," paper presented at the Society for Cinema Studies (New Orleans, 1986).

BAKHTINIAN TRANSLINGUISTICS AND FILM CRITICISM: THE DIALOGICAL IMAGE?

R. Barton Palmer

In literary studies the last five years have witnessed the advent and flourishing of what now can be called, with little exaggeration, the "Bakhtin industry." Hailed as the greatest literary theoretician of the twentieth century by the French structuralist Tzvetan Todorov in a 1981 overview of his theorizing and practice, Mikhail Bakhtin has since become the most talked about (and fought over) critic on the contemporary American scene.[1] His "signed texts," particularly book length studies of Dostoevsky and Rabelais and a series of essays about various issues in criticism and linguistics, have been or are being translated into English, while those works by his so-called "circle" of which he is at least a partial author have been re-examined and appraised in the light of his growing prominence (these include three major book-length essays on Marxism and language, Freudianism, and Russian formalist criticism).[2] Key Bakhtinian terms such as heteroglossia, novelization, and dialogism are becoming common elements of critical discourse, while the practical application of his ideas about textuality and literary history expands at an amazing rate.[3]

It is hardly surprising, therefore, that Bakhtinian theory has begun to influence film criticism as well, for here is an area of academic inquiry that has, in recent years, been much affected by developments in literary criticism (particularly, of course, the importation and appropriation of various methods and theories from abroad) even as it has proved, for various institutional and disciplinary reasons, more accommodating to new and often radical approaches than has the literary establishment itself. During the seventies academic film criticism was heavily inflected (if not dominated) by semiotic approaches derived from French and Italian Italian theorists (especially Christian Metz and Umberto Eco), but, as the eighties began, these methods were criticized from a number of quarters for their ahistoricity and political indifference. Building on Saussure's theory of the sign, Bakhtin, however, developed a very different view of its functioning, which he sees not as centripetal (i.e., forced by its own signifying impetus into the systemicity of self-contained hierarchical paradigms) but rather as centrifugal (i.e., breaking away from its empty definition by difference into the socially transactional arena of evaluation, contestation, and reference). As Bakhtin/Volosinov remark in the opening chapter of *Marxism and the Philosophy of Language*:

> A sign does not simply exist as a part of a reality—it reflects and refracts another reality. Therefore, it may distort that reality or be true to it, or may perceive it from a special point of view, and so forth. Every sign is subject to the criteria of ideological evaluation. . . . The domain of ideology coincides with the domain of signs. They equate with one another. Where a sign is present, ideology is present, too. *Everything ideological possesses semiotic value. . . .* A sign is a phenomenon of the external world. Both the sign itself and all the effects it produces (all those actions, reactions, and new signs it elicits in the surrounding social milieu) occur in outer experience (pp. 10–11).

Ideology can exist only in signs, and signs, in turn, are always ideological because of their material role within the society that uses them. If the Saussurean emphasis on a *langue* that constitutes the system of a language in and for itself, a system which is a world apart from its actual use, engendered a semiotics which could hardly connect signs to history and multiform practices, then the Bakhtinian promotion of signs as *langage*, as inseparable from their imbrication within social praxis, could be appropriated to remedy this failing.

In an interesting examination of the *état présent* of cinesemiotics, Robert Stam makes just such a recommendation. Acknowledging that Bakhtin's theories offer "a critique of certain assumptions underlying Metz' work," Stam suggests nonetheless that these same theories also provide "potential complicities and a means to recuperate and rean-

imate that work." "Bakhtin retains the linguistic paradigm," Stam
argues, "but opens it to the diachronic, to history and struggle."[4] As
David Carroll has remarked in a persuasive analysis of Bakhtin's relevance to current critical concerns, "formalists see in Bakhtin a way
of affirming the impact of history on language and form."[5] And,
indeed, the kind of cooptation suggested by Stam is paralleled by the
program that Bakhtin/Medvedev devise for literary studies in *The
Formal Method in Literary Scholarship*, a program that, first, concentrates on a "sociological poetics" in order to "isolate the literary work
as such, to reveal its structure, to determine the possible forms and
variations of this structure, and to define its elements and their functions" (one can make a good case that this is precisely the aim of Metz
in his *Language and Cinema*). Only when the poetics of literature have
been analyzed can criticism take up the burden of writing literary
history, which is "concerned with the concrete life of the literary work
in the unity of the generating literary environment, the literary environment in the generating ideological environment, and the latter,
finally, in the generating socioeconomic environment which permeates
it" (pp. 27–33). This plan sounds rather similar to the future Stam
maps out for a semiotics revived by Bakhtinian theory:

> In methodological terms, a Bakhtinian approach would allow us, after
> having "discovered" cinematic specificity, to re-appreciate the links of
> film to other "series" or semiotic systems, to reaffirm the affinities of
> film studies to other disciplines, and to re-envision the relation between
> film history and the larger historical trajectory of narrative and dis-
> cursive forms (pp. 297-8).

The project Stam suggests is an important one for it would allow
film scholars to forge links between much of the valuable work done
in cinesemiotics and ongoing research in what is now called "cultural
studies." There is no doubt that Bakhtinian theory would assist in
the historicization of "cinematic specificity," and, conceiving the cinema as part of a larger nexus of social communication, assist us in
escaping from some of the idealist, abstractionist traps into which we
have tumbled because of the preoccupation, in both the linguistic and
psychoanalytical phases of semiotics, with an ahistorical subjectivity.
In the remainder of this essay, however, I would like to emphasize
another aspect of Bakhtin's views, one which we might term more

"radical" for it involves a thoroughgoing critique of Saussurean linguistics and thus, by implication, of traditional semiotics as well.

Bakhtinian functionalism (I borrow the term from contemporary pragmatics, a branch of linguistic inquiry whose spiritual, if not actual, father is Bakhtin himself) forces us to ask some very different questions about any signifying practice from those posed and answered by the abstract objectivist approach (his term for traditional linguistics). As a practical demonstration, I will show what a functionalist approach can tell us about the textuality of cinematic *langage*, what it reveals about the kinship between this kind of communication and natural language. In fact, a functionalist approach, I would argue, demonstrates that the cinema and natural language, viewed as discursive more than "linguistic" practices, have much more in common than a Metzian semiotics has been able to suggest. The second part of this essay deals with a different, if related, issue. Bakhtin's theory of literature as a secondary or complex speech genre has the virtue of indicating that literary practice forms part of a continuum of linguistic practices (thus controverting the Russian formalist notion of literature as a special form of language use unconnected to ordinary uses, a position debunked by Bakhtin/Medvedev in *The Formal Method*, pp. 104–128 as well as by Bakhtin himself, writing about the poetic "fetishization" of the word, in "Discourse in the Novel," collected in *The Dialogic Imagination*, especially pp. 275–295).

A consequence of this position, however, is that Bakhtin discards conventional notions of mimesis, which conceive of language as the material through which representation of what the narratologists call existents (setting and characters) and events occurs. In other words, most literary theories think of language as the vehicle of expression, as the means employed for creating a fictional world. Cinesemiotics proceeds from much the same assumptions; in *Film Language* Metz even suggests that cinematic language came into existence in order to serve narrational ends: "it is not because the cinema is language that it can tell such fine stories, but rather it has become language because it has told such fine stories."[6] Bakhtin's view is radically different; for him language is not the material but rather the object of representation. Literary texts do not "call up" a world, but rather represent, in a necessarily self-reflexive way, the languages of the world, languages which in their complex interaction evoke different attempts at fixing or defining what the world indeed might be. For Bakhtin the genre which best fulfils this object of literary "speech" is the novel. Does the cinema, however, offer texts analogous to the novel? Does cinematic practice in any important way resemble literary practice as Bakhtin defines it? These are questions I shall attempt to answer in the second half of this paper. As I shall argue, they are crucial to any decision regarding the applicability of Bakhtinian literary theory to the cinema as an institution of communication.

I. TRANSLINGUISTICS AND CINESEMIOTICS

In his thorough investigation of the language/cinema analogy, Metz discovers that although film texts cannot be conceived as generated by any underlying language system (the cinema lacks both minimal units and the process of double articulation), these texts nonetheless manifest a systemicity that is is linguistic to some degree. In *Language and Cinema* Metz develops this insight at some length, showing how the cinema depends on a complex interaction of codes drawn from different sources (some specifically cinematic, others derived from natural language, various social practices, and so on).[7] Lacking a grammar, a phonemic system, phonotactic constraints, and syntactical rules (for there are no filmic "words" to order), the cinema still constitutes a kind of linguistic practice because of the generating force of the codes which control its expressive possibilities. Initially viewed as only problematically applying to cinematic practice, the founding Saussurean binarism of *langue/parole* is thereby reinstated, if only in an altered form that must make room for a conceptual innovation—the so-called "textual system"—which in some sense subverts it. The textual system is a "unique utilization, proper to this film, of the resources provided by the cinematic language system" (p. 92), but it is not equivalent to the Saussurean concept of *parole*, which is properly the individual enactment or use of the normatively identical forms available to the speaker. Because cinematic practice is characterized by the employment of a diverse set of codes, some specifically cinematic and others not, the constitution of these codes as a system can be theorized only within the boundaries of the individual film text. This means that systemicity and enactment must be located in the same material site, thus controverting the opposition inherent in the Saussurean model. Such a difficulty is hardly crucial, however, as long as we remember what many linguists and semioticians are inclined to forget, namely that any modeling of linguistic systemicity should not be hypostatized, that is, treated as a material entity or force. As Bakhtin/Volosinov observe:

> The speaker's subjective consciousness does not in the least operate with language as a system of normatively identical forms. That system is merely an abstraction arrived at with a good deal of trouble and with a definite cognitive and practical focus (p. 67).

The true value of Metz's meditations on the cinema/language analogy is that they do point out and catalogue the ways in which film texts *can be thought of* as systematic signifying practices.

As Stam argues, Bakhtin does accept the "linguistic paradigm." But his interest in the systematic nature of language as a practice is fundamentally different from that of Saussure and the semioticians who work with his concept of the sign (i.e. a normatively identical form consisting of a phonetic signifier and a conceptual, mentalistic signified). Metz is constrained by his theoretical assumptions to focus on codes (for here is the site in which such signs assume meaning) even when these codes, because of the specific nature of cinematic communication, can be located *as systematic* only within the individual text. Bakhtin is led in quite another direction by his understanding of the sign as acquiring value and purpose only within the context of individual use; for him the object of study must be the dynamic of speech as a social practice. Interestingly, Metz occasionally identifies speech or discourse rather than codes as the proper object for further semiotic research, but the Saussurean framework finally means that he must conceive of cinematic discourse as generated by codes as well, particularly the so-called "grande syntagmatique." The passages that follow are quoted from his influential essay "The Cinema: Language or Language System?" (collected in *Film Language*):

> The case is, however, that the image (at least in the cinema) corresponds to one or more sentences, and the sequence is a complex system of discourse (p. 65).
> The image is therefore always speech, never a unit of language (p. 67).
> A rich message with a poor code, or a rich text with a poor system, the cinematographic image is primarily speech (p. 69).
> The cinema begins where ordinary language ends: at the level of the

sentence—the filmmaker's minimum unit and the highest properly linguistic unit of language (p. 81).

Only within the Saussurean concept of *langue* can ordinary language be theorized as "ending" with the sentence. In "The Problem of Speech Genres," Bakhtin demonstrates that the sentence, as a unit of analysis, is not connected with the utterance, or the form speech actually assumes in any dialogue between two speakers:

> The sentence as a language unit lacks all of these properties; it is not demarcated on either side by a change of speaking subjects; it has neither direct contact with reality (with an extra-verbal situation) nor a direct relation to others' utterances; it does not have semantic fullness of value; and it has no capacity to determine directly the responsive position of the *other* speaker, that is, it cannot evoke a response (p. 74).

Recognizing that cinematic language lacks the more hierarchalized systemicity of natural language (i.e. the functional relation of different systems, from the phonemic to the syntactic), Metz, I believe, saw clearly that cinematic discourse, because of its connectedness, was nonetheless linguistic. But, as we shall see, his description of this connectedness is derived from the Saussurean paradigm, and therefore is inadequate to its object (which "begins" where the notion of Saussurean language "ends").

Abstract objectivism of the kind practiced by Metz yields a sort of knowledge; to this Bakhtin would undoubtedly agree. But the larger question posed in both his early and later meditations on language is whether this knowledge has a real usefulness in helping us understand the nature of a "living" language. In *Marxism and the Philosophy of Language*, Bakhtin/Volosinov, in fact, make out a strong case that linguistics, like the philologism upon which it is ultimately based, finds its suitable object of analysis only in "dead, written alien language. . . . the isolated, finished, monologic utterance, divorced from its verbal and actual context and standing open not to any possible sort of actual response but to passive understanding on the part of a philologist" (p. 73). From the Bakhtinian viewpoint of the utterance as a minimal unit of a science of communication, a translinguistics (as he terms it) which would deal with language as a material practice, the Metzian research into cinematic codes appears largely irrelevant, a concern with the "forms of elements" that takes precedence over the "form of the whole" (*Marxism and the Philosophy of Language*, p. 77). In fact, the "form of the whole," or those principles which shape and regulate speech as a dynamic, living, and interpersonal kind of communication, cannot be conceived within the Saussurean framework; and their formulation makes such a framework unnecessary. Behind the Metzian idea of "textual system" lies perhaps the recognition that an overarching systemicity, even if one could be theorized for the cinema, might distortingly divert attention from the way texts actually work to produce meaning, reducing the *parole* of individual films to simply an enactment of *langue*; but Metz' formulation simply collapses the Saussurean opposition instead of transcending it and postulating its missing third term, the notion of collective *parole* which is the Bakhtinian object of inquiry.

We can see quite clearly the essential differences between cinesemiotics and Bakhtinian translinguistics in the opposed senses that to Metz and Bakhtin the existence of codes seems irrelevant when one considers their material operation. Influenced by Julia Kristeva's critique of the Saussurean paradigm (a critique which itself finds its origin in Derrida's concept of *différance*), Metz describes the moment of *parole* as the dissolution or dissemination of systemicity:

> The system of the text is the process which *displaces* codes, deforming each of them by the presence of the others, contaminating some by means of others, meanwhile replacing one by another, and finally—as a temporarily "arrested" result of this general displacement—*placing* each code in a particular position in regard to the overall structure, a displacement which thus finishes by a positioning which is itself destined to be displaced by another text (p. 103)

For Bakhtin, in contrast, the "movement of the code" (as Metz subsequently terms it) does not define the operations of individual texts as a kind of anarchy that obscures the true object of semiotic inquiry. Metz proceeds to affirm that "filmic systems themselves, as active processes of displacement, are only intelligible if one has some idea of what it is that has been displaced" (p. 104), and this statement obviously reasserts the primacy of system over enactment as an object of knowledge. In contrast, Bakhtin theorizes the utterance as not determined by any codical systemicity, but by the unique circumstance of communication that calls it into being:

Semiotics prefers to deal with the transmission of a ready-made message by means of a ready-made code, whereas, in living speech, messages are, strictly speaking, created for the first time in the process of transmission, and *ultimately there is no code* (emphasis mine).[8]

In his discussion of the displacement and deformation that characterize the phenomenon of cinematic *parole*, Metz essentially reproduces the disconnection between the two founding terms of the Saussurean view of language. For if *langue* is characterized by orderliness, paradigmatic arrangement, and rule-bounded constraints, then *parole* manifests an individual freedom—the will of the speaker to say what he wants—which can hardly be reconciled with the notion of overarching control. Unable to account for historical change, Saussureanism likewise cannot theorize the *parole* which is its basis; ignoring the social constraints on speech, Saussureanism finally validates a Vosslerian definition of the speech act as manifesting an individual, creative (and hence lawless) power. Thus the objectivism and subjectivism which Bakhtin/Volosinov discuss as the dominant theories of language actually inhabit the same universe, one whose politics are the "impossible" coincidence of an all-controlling state and individual liberty; such a universe cannot locate a coherent notion of the "social," which necessarily subverts any separation between system and individual.

For Metz (and of course Saussure) the sign possesses a stability, embodied in the fit between signifier and signified, which allows it to be placed with a code; individual texts contest this stability by a process of *displacement*, but this disturbance is secondary to (and only temporarily overpowering of) a founding *placement*. As Bakhtin sees it, such stability is a mirage, a mystification of the abstracting objectivism which characterizes mainstream linguistic inquiry. Consider, for example, his theory of the word. "Multiplicity of meanings is the constitutive feature of the word," Bakhtin/Volosinov argue. But this multiplicity is not what linguists usually designate by polysemousness or a multivalency that imbricates a particular signifier with a number of signifieds. Multiplicity takes shape in actual use; Bakhtin cites Marr's theory of a prehistoric language in which one signifier could be used to make reference to all the objects noted as important by that society. Words, of course, acquire a general "meaning" as a result of their use in numerous contexts, but Bakhtin/Volosinov distinguish between this "meaning," which is the "lower limit of linguistic significance" because "it only possesses potentiality," and "theme," "the upper, actual limit of linguistic significance," the signification "that is adequate to a given instant of generative process" (pp. 100–101). Thus a sentence such as "I am hungry" contains elements "that are *reproducible* and *self-identical* in all instances of repetition," (p. 100), but these elements only help actualize the theme which this sentence would acquire in an infinite number of different contexts. The stability of the sign (a fiction of Saussurean method) makes way for a notion of verbal interaction characterized by the answerability of individual utterances to the specific, unreproducible circumstances that generate them:

> Thus the constituent factor for the linguistic form, as for the sign, is not at all its self-identity as a signal but its specific variability; and the constituent factor for understanding the linguistic form is not recognition of 'the same thing,' but understanding in the proper sense of the word., i.e. orientation in the particular, given content and in the particular, given situation—orientation in the dynamic process of becoming and not 'orientation' in some inert state (p. 69).

It is important to emphasize, however, that abandoning the view of signs as self-identifying signals (and this does fairly characterize the theorizing of Franco-Italian semiotics) does not mean that all a student of film language can study is the unique embodiment of signs in the individual, uttering text. Such a conclusion could only be reached if we conceive of *parole* and utterance as largely synonymous terms.

In his later work on language, Bakhtin makes it quite clear that the object of translinguistics is an analysis of those factors which condition (but do not determine) the shape of particular utterances (this functionalism avoids the collapsing of the tension between *parole* and *langue* which characterizes Metz' notion of "textual system," a collapsing that simply re-locates the source of codical determination and thereby ignores the issue of "orientation" so important for Bakhtin). The functional view of language concerns itself not with the operation of a stable system of encoding, but rather with those pressures, forces, and enabling conventions which allow each utterance to take a rhetorically effective shape:

> Language is realized in the form of individual concrete utterances (oral and written) by participants in the various areas of human activity.

These utterances reflect the specific conditions and goals of each such area not only through their content (thematic) and linguistic style, that is, the selection of the lexical, phraseological, and grammatical resources of the languages, but above all through their compositional structure. All three of these aspects—thematic content, style, and compositional structure—are inseparably linked to the *whole* of the utterance and are equally determined by the specific nature of the particular sphere of communication ("The Problem of Speech Genres," p. 60).

Later in this essay Bakhtin discusses the notion of speech genres as an aspect of compositional structure, but, in identifying the key role of what he here terms "style," he points to an area of equal importance whose elucidation is of particular relevance to the issue I have been pursuing, namely, the incompatibility of semiotic and translinguistic approaches to cinematic signification. For Bakhtin, Allon White has argued, "language is . . . split, conflict-ridden, dispersed and drastically heterogeneous," even as it is "systematic, highly coded, patterned and regular." This dialectical perspective, White suggests, allows Bakhtin to "analyse a whole range of speech events in their historical specificity." Identifying the notion of an abstract *langue* with the "modern myth of a perfect monoglossia, universal and unitary only in the abstract," Bakhtin, however, demonstrates no interest in what the abstract objectivism of Saussurean language theory and semiotics can conceptualize about codes and their embodiment.[9] Thus his perspective on style in the utterance is what we might call rhetorical, that is, determined by the ways in which the particular selection of linguistic resources in an utterance reflects "the specific conditions and goals" manifest in each, different arena of verbal interaction. This view of style is radically different both from a subjectivist position (i.e. style as the index of creative individualism, the bending of language forms to the individual expressive will) and from an abstract objectivist position (i.e. style as the syntagmatic ordering of paradigmatic givens, a speaking from within the prison house of linguistic conventions, as so well described by Roland Barthes in *S/Z*). The Bakhtinian concept of style, in fact, has much more in common with the view of "discourse-as-product" adopted by linguists interested in discourse analysis and pragmatics. Gillian Brown and George Yule, for example, define their area of interest as investigating

how a recipient might come to comprehend the producer's intended message on a particular occasion, and how the requirements of the particular recipient(s), in definable circumstances, influence the organisation of the producer's discourse. This is clearly an approach which takes *the communicative function of language as its primary area of investigation* and consequently seeks to describe linguistic form, not as a static object, but as a dynamic means of expressing intended meaning (emphasis mine).[10]

The major difference between Bakhtin and these contemporary linguists is his emphasis on the ideological nature not just of the linguistic sign but of all aspects of the act of communication. Whereas discourse analysts proceed from the premise that language use can be considered apart from the ideological aspects of human interaction, Bakhtin would vigorously contest any division between "individuality" and "sociality":

> . . . the content of the 'individual' psyche is by its very nature just as social as is ideology, and the very degree of consciousness of one's individuality and its inner rights and privileges is ideological, historical, and wholly conditioned by sociological factors (*Marxism and the Philosophy of Language*, p. 34)

As can be seen, this Bakhtinian refusal to essentialize human behavior and empty it of its unique historical content importantly conditions how we would use a functionalist approach in any analysis of cinematic signification.

In "Problem of Speech Genres" Bakhtin concerns himself with a problem only touched on briefly in his speculations about language: the delimitation or segmentation of the utterance. Bakhtin/Volosinov accept as unproblematic the self-identity of the utterance, commenting only briefly on its inner division into paragraphs:

> The paragraph is something like a *vitiated dialogue worked into the body of a monologic utterance*. Behind the device of partitioning speech in units, which are termed paragraphs in their written form, lie orientation toward listener or reader and calculation of the latter's possible reactions. The weaker this orientation and calculation are, the less organized, as regards paragraphs, our speech will be (p. 111).

In his later monograph, Bakhtin goes on to identify the utterance in much the same way that he had earlier defined the paragraph, that is, as controlled essentially by the workings of verbal interaction or dialogue, which is, for him, the most significant, existential ground of language production:

> Any utterance is a link in a very complexly organized chain of other utterances. . . . The boundaries of each concrete utterance as a unit of speech communication are determined by a *change of speaking subjects*, that is, a change of speakers. Any utterance—from a short (single-word) rejoinder in everyday dialogue to the large novel or scientific treatise—has, so to speak, an absolute beginning and an absolute end; its beginning is preceded by the utterances of others, and its end is followed by the responsive utterances of others (or, although it may be silent, others' active responsive understanding, or, finally a responsive action based on this understanding) (pp. 69, 71).

But, Bakhtin argues, a speaker needs to do more than simply stop speaking in order to signal that his utterance has ended; what he says must be "finalized" on its "inner side." This means that utterances are in fact organized as an "organic whole." The "semantic exhaustiveness of the theme," or what a speaker/listener perceives as the semantic possibilities of the subject, imposes an outer limit (one which is naturally dependent on the type of interchange; a conversation about the weather between two neighbors obviously has quite different semantic parameters from a book on nuclear physics). Second, the speaker's "speech plan" as this is inferred by his interlocutor "determines both the choice of the subject itself . . . as well as its boundaries and its semantic exhaustiveness . . . (and) generic form in which the utterance will be constructed" (p. 77). Finally, what speech genre is selected will be "determined by the specific nature of the given sphere of speech communication" (p. 78).

This is an impressive description of the situational/structural factors that define the utterance, whose nature is only necessarily but not sufficiently (as it turns out) determined by a change in speaking subjects. Particularly important, I think, is Bakhtin's emphasis on speech genres, an aspect of communication to which most discourse analysts, still influenced by the individualist notions of the Saussurean *parole*, have paid insufficient attention. Bakhtin's notion of genre, it might be added, here continues the social importance accorded to it by Bakhtin/Medvedev, who theorize it as both constructing a certain vision of reality and offering particular "finalized" kinds of meaning to the addressee. Like the classical tradition of rhetoric on which it draws, however, this definition of the utterance, emphasizing notions of content (*inventio*) and arrangement (*dispositio*), does in large measure ignore the materiality of the language which composes the utterance (Bakhtin offers nothing in the way of the classical notion of "figures of speech," a conception which would provide him with some link between rhetorical intent, on the one hand, and linguistic style in the ordinary sense of the term, on the other). Does the utterance manifest what we might call a "textuality" determined by its linguistic materiality and not just the implications, intentions, points of reference, and conventional structures that assist in binding speaker to addressee and enabling a meaningful exchange?

An important area of current functionalist research is what has been termed text grammar or text linguistics; the object of this research is the description and explanation of those factors which account for "textuality," for the existence, in Bakhtinian terms, of the utterance defined on both its outer and inner sides. From the viewpoint of common sense, it does not really matter that texts can hardly be considered self-evident identities; texts are always in some sense presented or offered, and this necessarily rhetorical aspect of their ontology means that textuality (in the sense of a "command" to process the utterance as a unit demanding a response or reaction) does not depend on any inner, material connection. As Waldemar Gutwinski observes:

> . . . speakers of a language, when presented with any assembly of sentences following one another . . . will try as hard as they can to impose some interpretation on the whole. Simply by virtue of their appearing in a certain order together, the assumption is made that the collection of sentences is a text.[11]

But the view has been advanced by M.A.K. Halliday and Ihab Hassan that textuality may be better defined in material terms, by the presence of "texture" produced by "cohesive relations."[12] The notion of cohesion has had an enormous impact on the field of pragmatics, and although it is true, as Brown and Yule, for example, contend, that the meaning relations implied by cohesion do not have to be made explicit in the text (underlying semantic relations, communicated between speakers by a process of implication, can also produce a textural cohesion), the fact remains that in natural language explicit cohesive ties are often used to "bind" one sentence to another and establish interconnectedness across large units of text. Robert de Beaugrande and Wolfgang Dressler suggest that cohesion is to a text what grammatical or syntactical relations are to a sentence:

> . . . the stability of the text as system is upheld through a continuity of occurrences . . . the most obvious illustration is the language system of syntax that imposes organization patterns upon the surface text. . . . For long stretches of text, there are devices for showing how already used structures and patterns can be re-used, modified, or compacted. These devices contribute to stability and economy in respect to both materials and processing effort.[13]

Cohesive ties can be easily illustrated in the following pair of sentences:

> John went to school this morning. But he didn't take his galoshes with him then.

Two series of pronominal substitutions tie these sentences together: John/he, his, him; and this morning/then. These constitute meaning relations because the interpretation of the pronominal substitutions depends on the preceding occurrence of their referents; the interpretation of the second sentence, then, can only be accomplished retrospectively or anaphorically, thus making such interpretation dependent on what has already been said. There are other types of cohesive relations which I will discuss below.

Working with the Bakhtinian conception of the utterance and the attendant terms of "textuality" and "cohesion" developed by discourse analysts can, I would argue, offer interesting insights into the ways in which the cinematic text can be shown to have "style" in the Bakhtinian sense. In fact, this kind of approach can better demonstrate the linguistic nature of cinematic signification than Metzian semiotics. Earlier I noted several passages in which Metz records his own sense that filmic signification is "speech" or "discourse," lacking the minimal units or sentence which would be the primary Saussurean objects of inquiry. Metz's noted theory of the "grande syntagmatique" of the image track constitutes an attempt to explain cinematic discourse in linguistic terms. As Robert Stam describes it:

Language selects and combines phonemes (the minimal units of sound) and monemes (the minimal units of sense) to form sentences; film selects and combines images and sounds according to specific ordering procedures to form "syntagmas". . . . The grande syntagmatique represents, at the level of the organization of images, a typology of the different ways that time and space can be ordered through montage, a fixed number of patterns according to which individual shots can be grouped into units (pp. 282-83).

Since the theory is well known and its details not important for my present purpose, I shall not comment further on the typological aspects of the grande syntagmatique. I shall concentrate instead on the important problems raised by this theory as an explanation of the *linguistic* nature of cinematic signification. What follows, therefore, is not only a correction of Metz from the perspective of Bakhtin and his spiritual children, contemporary discourse analysts, but also at least a partial refutation of those who, like Brian Henderson, have found serious and fundamental fault with the Metzian attempt to establish an analogy between natural language and the cinema. The Bakhtinian concept of the utterance, not Metz's theory of codes, can best help us understand how the cinema is discourse.

The unexpressed center of Metz's investigation is the question of cinematic textuality. In what ways does a succession of images constitute a text? Like linguistic ones, cinematic texts are hardly self-evident identities, but, again in this case, these texts are defined as such (perhaps even more strongly because of the special nature of their presentation) by the rhetorical intentions that saturate them. Films, then, are juxtapositions of different signifying units whose co-occurrence "demands" a unifying interpretation; they constitute texts because they are offered as such. This situational definition of textuality, however, does not eliminate the possibility that the "texture" of individual films is also established in material ways, by "meaning relations" of one kind or another that would have textual presence. In fact, the presence of cohesion as such a material producer of meaning relations in natural language would lead us to expect something similar in cinematic discourse, for here too are "long-range stretches of text" which need to have a certain "stability and economy in respect to both materials and processing effort." Confining ourselves strictly to a consideration of the image track, we would expect that the montage of images might be controlled by devices of interpretational dependence (i.e. image B can be read only in terms partly enunciated by image A). If the cinema is linguistic, it too would likely make use of cohesion to create extended discourse. In fact, we shall see that the cinema does just that.

Lacking a notion of textuality or cohesion, Metz constructs a "generative" model (one formed on the principle of those mechanisms in natural language which, as Stam argues, account for the syntagmatic ordering of phonemes and monemes). This paradigm explains the "specific ordering procedures" (as Stam terms them) of filmic montage and also sets out the limited number of different types of units which can be so arranged. Insofar as it offers a paradigm which can generate an infinite number of syntagmas, this model is obviously linguistic (though the implicit analogy between phonemic/monemic generation and the development of extended passages of discourse is a very weak one because it ignores the difference, in natural language, between highly constrained processes such as those of sentence syntax and those operating under more rhetorical principles; as De Beaugrande and Dressler put it, "when we move beyond the sentence boundary, we enter a domain characterized by greater freedom of selection or variation and lesser conformity with established rules")[14]

But the real problem here is Metz's dubious, basic assumption that film is language only insofar as it is simultaneously narrative discourse. This means, in the first place, that any precise analogy between cinematic and natural languages is thereby discarded; for film, unlike language, is empowered by Metz to accomplish only one function, the telling of stories, whereas natural language can be used in a multiplicity of communicative situations. Hjemslev's useful distinction between the form and material of expression would also get discarded despite its great importance for an understanding of the interrelationship between semiotic systems. More important, however, by making the relationship between images one determined by narrative relationships, Metz locates the connection of these images outside their very materiality and in the interpretive schema which the viewer, following the different logics of narrative development, must construct for the film. Alternating syntagmas, for example, are connected to one another only through the rhetoric of parallel/converging lines of development within the narrative. More than anything else, Metz's "grande syntagmatique" resembles the models of universal narrative grammar whose creation and refinement is such a preoccupation within the later phases of French structuralism. It can be thought of as a *linguistic* code only if we accept Metz's statement that "the cinema . . . has become language because it has told such fine stories" and then make the further inference that narrational use determines the senses in which the cinema is language. Metz offers no real argument for this position, and it can easily be controverted by pointing to various types of film practice that are indeed anti-narrational (avant-gardism for example) and yet still are discursive in the Metzian sense. The "grande syntagmatique," I would suggest, is a most useful construction for the narratological analysis of filmic montage; its demonstration of the linguistic nature of cinematic discourse, however, is seriously flawed.

As De Beaugrande and Dressler see it, textuality in natural language is a function not only of what they call "cohesion" but also of "coherence." "Coherence," as they define the term, designates "the ways in which the components of the textual world, i.e. the configuration of concepts and relations which underlie the surface text, are mutually accessible and relevant"; this contrasts with "cohesion," which assures that "the components of the surface text . . . are mutually connected" (pp. 3–4). With this distinction in mind, it seems clear that what Metz describes in the "grande syntagmatique" are the semantic or ideational relations of the shots in a narrative film to one another; these relations, as critics of Metz have been quick to point out, depend on interpretation of the separate images involved (and such interpretation often must be clarified by recourse to information provided in one of the film's remaining four "tracks" of meaning). Coherence depends on relevant structures of meaning (and these, of course, can relate to many configurations other than narrative) whose ordering force is both evoked and confirmed by the surface elements in the text; coherence, in short, describes underlying areas of meaning of whose significance and content the "reader" is already aware (i.e. a spectator, for example, needs to be familiar with the convention of cross-cutting as a means for articulating narrative time/space and plot relations in order to be able to recognize alternating syntagmas as they occur). The usefulness of the "grande syntagmatique" lies in the way it identifies this aspect of coherence in the "classic" film (Barthes' analysis of the various semes in the five codes he identifies as belonging to high realist narrative includes these areas of coherence—the hermeneutic and proairetic codes—as well as others).

But, De Beaugrande and Dressler assert, "the stability of the text as system is upheld through a continuity of occurrences" (p. 48). On the level of the sentence, languages impose "organizational patterns" that create such a continuity, but syntactical rules do not extend beyond the boundaries of the sentence. Across the sentences of a text (and these, of course, are rhetorical as well as syntactical units), the re-utilization, modification, or compacting of previously used items creates continuity for the utterance. More important, this cohesion depends to a greater or lesser degree on the notion of ties, that is, on the presence of later elements in the text which can only be understood with reference to those placed earlier. The recurrence which characterizes cohesion is to some extent affected by the individual style or generic register of the communication (Gutwinski demonstrates very different patterns and densities of cohesive ties in fictional passages from Henry James and Ernest Hemingway), but recurrence is also controlled by two larger principles: efficiency and effectiveness. Efficiency means that the text can be processed with the maximum of ease; highly efficient texts (e.g. children's readers) are characterized by a great deal of recurrence. Effectiveness, in contrast, means that the text offers processing depth, or less recurrence and more new information. The specific dynamics of the speech act—what De Beaugrande and Dressler sum up as "appropriateness"—mediate between these two demands and regulate the amount of recurrence in the individual text. As we shall see, this principle is of some importance in considering the ways in which film texts of different types are cohesive.

Of the categories relating to cohesion some are clearly relevant to film language, others less obviously so or perhaps not at all. I list the latter group first:

- Partial Recurrence (the repetition of a word part or the substitution of a related vocabulary item with the same root)
- Pro-Forms (the substitution of a pronoun or similar item)

Composed strictly of iconic symbols, cinematic "vocabulary" naturally lacks anything corresponding to the linguistic category of "shifters," as Metz and others have noted; for much the same reasons, the cinema obviously lacks those word families necessary for the establishment of partial recurrent ties. But there are forms of cohesion with real analogues in cinematic practice:

- Recurrence (straightforward repetition)

- Parallelism (repetition of formal elements with change of content)
- Paraphrase (repetition of content with some change of formal elements)
- Ellipsis (partial repetition of the item)
- Surface signals (markers of tense, aspect, and juncture)

I shall discuss the specifics of each type below, particularly with reference to classic Hollywood practice (which, as it turns out, developed a series of rules and conventional practices to mark out and limit the kinds of cohesion this particular register of cinematic language permits or proscribes).

But, first, a more general point. Translinguistics, I have argued, demonstrates better than traditional semiotics the ways in which cinematic signification and natural language are similar. The reason for this is fairly simple, as we have seen. Saussurean methods privilege minimal units, words, and sentences as objects of analysis; within this framework language consists of "short stretches of text" in which generative rules make their presence felt most strongly (sentences, of course, also are rhetorical segments, but allow less freedom for individual or generic choice). Cinema lacks just those aspects of language which Saussurean linguistics takes as its object hence the methods of traditional semiotics can be applied to its various discursive "tracks" only in limited and ultimately distorting ways (e.g. the failed ingenuity of the grande syntagmatique). Like natural language, however, the cinema can produce the utterance or passages of extended text defined, both on the "inside" and "outside," by the kinds of factors elucidated by Bakhtin and contemporary discourse analysts. The analysis that here follows should not be thought of, therefore, in the same terms that Metz offers his model of filmic montage, that is, as the major proof of the cinema's linguistic nature (not the *only* proof, of course, for the concept of "textual system" developed in *Language and Cinema* extends the analogy, as we have seen). The notion of textual cohesion is only one area of contact between cinematic and natural language that a functional approach can discover and explicate; much more work remains to be done. The presence of cohesion as a vital and shaping force in the evolution of film "style" (in the Bakhtinian sense), however, should alert all students of film theory that the linguistic approach to cinematic discourse has many more insights to offer in and of itself (and not just as an element in theories of subjectivity elaborated in the second, psychoanalytically oriented phase of cine-semiotics).

In lengthy texts, cohesion is a feature of textuality which tends to characterize discrete units (which are given, quite often, a dense unity by a concentration of ties); some aspects of coherence, of course, will tend to tie together the text as a whole. The rhetorical segmentation of texts, what M.A.K. Halliday has termed "chunking," tends to be accomplished somewhat by certain forms of cohesion (and naturally coherence as well).[15] In the classic Hollywood film the units tied together by strong cohesive relations tend also to be narrative or dramatic units; here style ultimately serves the needs of the narrative discourse. Furthermore, in discussing cohesion in the film text, we need to make an analytic distinction between content (the various existents in the pro-filmic event) and form (the various elements of the image, such as camera angle, scale, lighting/photographic codes, and so on). Representationalism and realism (in its various, complex senses) are such important, traditional aspects of the ways in which—at least within the Hollywood system—images are read, that content, rather than form, tends to be privileged as the level on which most cohesive ties are established in the classic film. The recurrence of formal patterns (a category that Raymond Bellour has usefully termed "visual rhymes") is therefore less foregrounded and perceivable as a unifying factor.

Within most types of sequences, the simple recurrence of content (human figures, objects, aspects of setting) functions to create obvious and bonding types of cohesion. Lacking pro-forms, cinematic language cannot accomplish what natural language can so easily, that is, the establishment of recurrent patterns without the straightforward repetition of surface elements. As we have seen, the use of pro-forms creates particularly strong cohesive ties because pro-forms can only be interpreted anaphorically, by relating them to their previously occuring referent. Within most registers of speech, the ratio of pro-forms to "full" words is determined by the opposing forces of efficiency and effectiveness (pro-forms can be interpreted less efficienctly, but contribute to the effectiveness of discourse by not drawing too much attention to already mentioned elements, something which the overuse of simple recurrence would certainly cause). But the cinematic image track, consisting entirely of iconic signs, does not require the same kind of processing effort that natural language does because it consists almost entirely of conventional signs. Thus we might say that the cinema does not need a repertoire of pro-forms in order to avoid producing ineffective texts (i.e. texts consisting of too many already mentioned elements).

Constructing visual spaces characterized by the presence, placement, and specific character of certain existents, the cinematic image track establishes "what there is to be seen," thereby performing what we might, in linguistic terms, call deixis (i.e. the "pointing out" of objects, people, and so on); this act of initial deixis identifies what exists in the world of the film (it hardly seems an accident that in Hollywood practice such shots are called "establishing" or "master" shots). Succeeding images in the same sequence manifest the recurrence of the important "established" elements which, because they are now "pointed out" (it is no longer a question of *a* house, but *the* or *this* house), are more easily and readily processed. The cohesive tie in this instance is established by the process of deixis; for the determination or specification manifest in the subsequent occurrence of content is dependent on, "readable" only in terms of its initial placement (e.g. image 1 offers a house, while images 2-6 offer "the same" house).

Recurrence, we might say, is the most important category of cohesion in the succession of images within a sequence (and also, of course, to some degree across the image track of the film as a whole). But then recurrence is the most important category of cohesion for natural language as well; it is just that for reasons of effectiveness a number of other devices have developed within natural language to avoid an overuse of straightforward recurrence even as they preserve most of its efficiency. Two of these devices, partial recurrence and the use of pro-forms, have, as we have seen, no analogy within cinematic discourse. But the presence (and, within the register of the classic film, importance) of the remaining devices suggests that cinematic discourse also needs to avoid too much recurrence in order to produce effective texts. Within the Hollywood system, for example, paraphrase and ellipsis are used together within so-called analytic editing or "shot breakdown." The typical classic sequence of this type begins with an establishing or master shot (which gives the overall parameters of the content that organizes the sequence, typically human characters in a certain setting). Subsequent shots then "repeat" this master shot, but only by paraphrasing or ellipting its content. A change of scale (the move to a two-shot or close-up) yields the most common form of ellipsis (the actual recurrence in the image corresponds to or "stands for" the whole initially identified in the establishing shot), while paraphrase manifests itself in altered angles, different lighting setups, and so on; in fact, paraphrase and ellipsis can characterize the same shot.

Analytic editing patterns, of course, were developed in the course of cinema history. Such discursive development, however, while obviously conditioned by the use of the cinema to tell extended stories, is more a feature of cohesiveness than narration (images can be tied together in these ways for rhetorical purposes other than storytelling). As has been often pointed out, analytic editing serves well the needs of a cinematic narrational register in which coherent construction of spatial relations and dramatic, human emphasis are important elements. But analytic editing also has the advantage of avoiding the monotony (i.e., the same content given too much focus) which a one-shot, affidavit recording (to use Eisenstein's term) of a scene would often produce; this effect, I would suggest, can be best described in linguistic terms, as achieved by a recurrence across the series of shots made more effective by the uses of both paraphrase and ellipsis.

We are accustomed to discussing Hollywood editing conventions in representational and narrational terms; crosscutting, we say, articulates the existence of two ultimately converging spaces as it develops independent lines of action which, at some point, will be united. But the "rules" governing those conventions can also be understood as establishing a certain density of cohesion. Matches on action, for example, offer a dynamic form of recurrence tied to a central figure or figures. In contrast, the "180-degree rule" governs allowable forms of paraphrase—that is, the change of angle cannot, in effect, reverse the positionality of the pro-filmic content. Using the terms developed by the linguist H.A. Gleason, we might say that the Hollywood register allows a series of shots to be enate (same form with a partial or complete change of content) but not agnate (same content with a reversal of form).[16] Enate or parallel series, of course, are not common because, as I have noted, cohesion in the Hollywood cinema depends more on a recurrence of content than form; but agnate series (violations of the 180 degree rule) are proscribed because formal anti-parallels (still a kind of recurrence) are not readily perceptible for spectators used to "invisible" style (agnate series also create space in a different way).

The "30-degree rule" can be explained in terms of permissible forms of cohesion. It states that the camera angle in two edited shots of the same content with the same scale must change at least thirty degrees in order to avoid a "jump cut" (that jarring juxtaposition which results from too "close" a paraphrase).

Point-of-view editing can also be understood in terms of cohesion. The prospective type (shot 1 shows someone looking; shot 2 what was looked at) depends on what we might call a cataphoric tie. As I have said, cohesive ties are usually anaphoric, that is, the second occurrence of an item is dependent upon a previous occurrence for its interpretation. In the prospective type of point of view editing the look or glance, in contrast, identifies something not yet revealed or named whose subsequent depiction explains the glance or look. Retrospective types of point-of-view editing, in contrast, are more anaphoric. Here the sequence of something seen/someone looking means that the glance is explained or interpreted in terms of what has already been shown. Finally, we might observe that the language of classic cinema, like natural language, has developed a number of "surface signals" to indicate the relationships between segments. The straight cut is similar in its range of meanings to syndetic and asyndetic coordination (i.e. coordination with or without the conjunction "and"); it can imply simple connection (as among the items in an analytically edited series) as well as more complex types such as cause and result, whole and part, now and then. More "expressed" forms of cutting, such as fades, usually carry temporal meanings (normally indicating the passage of significant time).

Much more could be said about the workings of cinematic cohesion, but this is hardly the place to do so. I do hope, however, to have offered sufficient detail to demonstrate the remarkable similarity between natural and cinematic languages as types of *discourse*. Such similarity is best analyzed using the Bakhtinian concept of the utterance; for the utterance must be determined on both its "inner" and "outer" sides, that is to say, rhetorically and onotogically, and such determination leads us to the discovery of important principles governing language *as used*. Utterances, however, as Bakhtin argues, are always already imbricated within the network of other utterances by their "orientation," that is, by the ways, often complex, that they dialogically address themselves, responding and asking for an answer in return. The remarkable degree of cohesion in the classic Hollywood text contributes, among other factors, to its stability and unity; here is a communication similar to literary language in its astute balancing of the pressures toward efficiency and effectivity, a series of texts readily processed by a diverse audience and yet manifesting a "depth" sufficient to intrigue or captivate. Here is a language certainly worthy of the detailed attention that a modern translinguistics is so well designed to pay to it.

II. BAKHTIN'S NOVEL AND THE FICTION FILM

One of the most useful aspects of Bakhtin's theorizing about literature is the way he accounts for the similarities and differences that literary uses of language manifest vis-à-vis "ordinary uses." Literature is one among many secondary or complex speech genres that "arise in more complex and comparatively highly developed and organized cultural communication (primarily written) that is artistic, scientific, sociopolitical, and so on." As a secondary genre, literature incorporates many primary ones, but these are necessarily altered in their function and significance; ". . . rejoinders of everyday dialogue or letters found in a novel retain their form and their everyday significance only on the plane of the novel's content" ("The Problem of Speech Genres," p, 62). This formulation, of course, leaves important questions unaddressed even as it satisfactorily accounts, at least on one level, for the co-presence of language in primary and secondary genres. If, we might ask, primary genres lose their "orientation" through such a process of incorporation, then what is the different "orientation" of the literary text that subsumes them? Considering the rhetoric of the literary text necessarily opens questions relating to the social production of art, questions which Bakhtin, with his linguistic bias, never did ask. With regard to the novel at least Bakhtin was able to formulate a definition of its effects (even if such definition draws its strength from intrinsic aspects of the form itself and not from any consideration of the cultural institutions, among other mediations, that define its production and consumption).[17]

Anticipating the model of many contemporary sociolinguists, Bakhtin suggests that all languages are defined by the dialectical interplay between pressures toward standardization and conformity (monoglossia), on the one hand, and dialectal diversification and mixture (heteroglossia), on the other. For monoglossia to assert the claims of a single and correct language the existence (or value) of other varieties must be suppressed.

As Allon White has argued, "heteroglossia not only foregrounds the words of people normally excluded from the realms of the 'norm' and the 'standard,' it also relativizes the norm itself, subverting its claim to universalism."[18] Monoglossia, however, Bakhtin astutely observes, can be subverted not only from within but also from without, in situations of so-called "language contact" (the presence, in a given cultural milieu, of two or more different languages, each with a claim to some social standing and usefulness). This polyglossia defamiliarizes and demystifies the languages involved, which can hardly be thought of as natural, inevitable, or privileged forms of communication, but rather as relativized means (replete with advantages and disadvantages) of social intercourse. Polyglossia differs from heteroglossia in one important respect: the former is the result of historical accidents (such as the co-presence, in pre-Christian southern Italy, of Greek, Oscan, and Latin communities), while the latter is the natural condition of any single language which can only be transformed through cultural politics of some kind (e.g. the evolution of classical Latin as the medium for the self-definition of the ruling elite in imperial Rome).

Literature, envisioned as a series of forms (both actualized and potential), corresponds to these essential features of language. Bakhtin identifies the so-called "fixed genres" (especially the epic) with monoglossia; composed in a language that is fetishized, revered, and artificially preserved, these forms allow no contact between the world they evoke (eternally fixed as it is in an untouchable past) and the present community of writer and reader, who speak with each other in a different language altogether. Like monoglossia, these fixed forms, Bakhtin goes on to argue, are hardly the natural state of literary expression, which can be brought into contact with present reality and living, heterogeneous language whenever the claims of the fixed forms are challenged (by, for example, the advent of polyglossia):

> They become more free and flexible, their language renews itself by inforporating extraliterary heteroglossia and the 'novelistic' layers of literary language, they become dialogized, permeated with laughter, irony, humor, elements of self-parody, and finally—this is the most important thing—the novel inserts into these other genres an indeter-

minacy, a certain semantic openendedness, a living contact with unfinished, still-evolving, contemporary reality (the openended present)
(*The Dialogic Imagination*, p. 7).

Bakhtin's definition of the novel is thus highly idiosyncratic. To him,
it is not only a specific literary form arising in determinate historical
circumstances (though it is this), but also the universal form of literary
expression which would prevail, so the implication runs, if opposing
cultural forces were restrained. Just as language is inherently dialogical, so, too, would be its literary embodiment. Bakhtin's theorizing
clearly leads to these conclusions even if he was reluctant, or perhaps
unable, given the strictly linguistic basis of his approach, to draw
them. As Ken Hirschkop has perceptively pointed out, Bakhtin theorizes literary expression as both *inherently* and *preferably* dialogical,
dominated by a liberating heteroglossia.[19] Between these two aspects
of his theory lies an implicit recognition that literature is sometimes
prevented from being what it should, that the fixed forms result from
an unnatural and imprisoning attitude toward language and its social
effects. As I have already briefly indicated, however, Bakhtin does
not share the commitment to a "materialist aesthetics" as elaborated
particularly by Walter Benjamin and Bertolt Brecht. This is somewhat
strange, for occasionally Bakhtin comes close to enunciating the "author as producer" position:

> Art, too, is just as immanently social; the extraartistic social milieu,
> affecting art from outside, finds direct, intrinsic response within it.
> This is not a case of one foreign element affecting another but of one
> social formation affecting another social formation ("Discourse in Life
> and Discourse in Art" in *Freudianism*, p. 95).

We must remember that monoglossia defined literary production in
Bakhtin's own country after 1934 (i.e. the Stalinist institutionalization
of socialist realism). Therefore an advocacy of the novel as an anti-
genre which, acting on fixed forms, would insure "their liberation
from all that serves as a brake on their unique development' (*Dialogic
Imagination*, p. 39) was probably as radical a position as Bakhtin could
afford to defend.

As it stands, there are a number of problems, some more serious
than others, with Bakhtin's conception of the novel. Ignoring the
different modes of literary production/consumption which, in diver-

gent historical periods, have led to the creation and subsequent prop-
agation of quite dissimilar objects, Bakhtin tends to reduce the history
of literary forms to the dramatic interplay of a limited number of
attitudes toward language and its literary representation. This reduc-
tionism has the virtue of pointing out similarities that are certainly
worth noting (e.g. the ways in which Rabelaisian satire and Dostoev-
skyan fiction foreground heteroglossia), but, as Todorov argues, it
proves inadequate to the task of describing the "novel" as a genre
according to Bakhtin's own definition:

> The not very coherent, and ultimately irrational, character of Bakhtin's
> description of the genre of the novel is a strong indication that this
> category does not occupy its own place in the system. The intersection
> of two categories, present intertextuality and temporal continuity, does
> not provide a definition of a sufficiently specific object so that it may
> be located historically. . . . a genre appears at a certain period, and at
> no other. "Representing" or "relating" does not define a genre, but
> categories of discourse in general. . . . What he described under this
> name is not a genre, but one or two properties of discourse, whose
> occurrence is not confined to a single historical moment (pp. 90–91).

Conceived then as a related set of discursive features, the Bakhtinian
novel can be theorized as anti-generic, as more of a process—the
liberating impulses of novelization—than a product. It is logically
incoherent, therefore, for Bakhtin to offer a list, though not an exhaustive one, of what he calls novelistic subgenres, historically specific
fictional forms that, controlled by relatable formal/ideological qualities, offer the finalization/orientation that Bakhtin/Medvedev postulate
as necessary attributes of a genre. (Some of these, it might be added,
hardly foreground heteroglossia or open out to the present of the
writer and his audience, e.g. the chivalric romance, and thus can only
problematically be related to the category "novel.")

The overarching problem here seems to be Bakhtin's divergent (if
not opposed) attitudes toward the concept of "genre"; genres, on the
one hand, are the enabling categories of all speech acts, while, on the
other, they constitute an important part of the linguistic/representational
rigidification resulting from monoglossia. Genres, then, as part of a
stifling fixity, are opposed by the anti-genericism of the novel; but
genres, as an essential element of sociality, constitute, as
Bakhtin/Medvedev put it, "the aggregate of the means of collective

orientation in reality, with the orientation toward finalization" (p. 135). The most important problem, however, relates not to Bakhtin's difficulties with systematic analysis and contradiction (aspects of his *oeuvre* that do not vitiate his largely useful insights). Ignoring the series of mediations (ideological, institutional, and personal) that affect and shape the production of literary texts, Bakhtin assumes too straightforward a connection between primary and secondary speech genres. The latter are conceived as incorporating the former and, as I have noted, re-orienting their content; but Bakhtin passes over the ways in which the literary representation of certain varieties of speech is different from those speech varieties in their *primary setting*. Literary speech, as discourse analysis of actual conversation shows, is radically different from ordinary speech. The novel, therefore, cannot be conceived of as directly materializing linguistic diversity, but, rather, as Lennard Davis, for one, persuasively argues, creating models of linguistic competence whose style and purpose have conversely affected how we regard linguistic intercourse.[20] The point, I would suggest, is vital. The Bakhtinian model of representation is ultimately distortingly simplistic and thus not very useful for a materialist criticism; it lacks any focus on rhetoric (i.e., the intentionalities of novelistic production/consumption, the whys and wherefores that govern the actual writing and reading of novels) and avoids any consideration of mediation (i.e., that whole complex of often contradictory social forces/institutions which affect the shape of particular novels and the novel in general). Bakhtin celebrates the plural (and therefore populist) text, but his views on literature as an institution (and novelists as artists) are thoroughly traditional and hence problematic. It is therefore easy to see why he has attained such a quick and easy popularity with a critical establishment still controlled, despite apparent theoretical upheaval, by New Critical assumptions about textuality, the role of the author, and the object of literary study.[21]

What, then, does the Bakhtinian approach to literature (especially his views on the novel) have to offer cinema studies? In this area of academic inquiry, the moment of text-centered "art as ideology" approaches has passed, though its useful insights have been incorporated within current research, which is much more in line with "art as production" theories of various kinds. Key Bakhtinian concepts, therefore, particularly heteroglossia and novelization, are more relevant to earlier stages of thinking about both film history (conceived largely in formal rather than institutional terms) and textual content (understood as the reflection of ways of thinking, talking, and seeing, as various ideological "languages" which can be incorporated, rather directly, within the text itself). This does not mean, however, that these concepts cannot be radicalized and contextualized to make them more relevant to current concerns in film studies; Ken Hirschkop has suggested some ways that this kind of Bakhtinianism might be constituted:

> . . . if we are going to continue using "dialogism" as a theoretical term denoting a general quality of linguistic practice, then some revision of the term is needed, so that specifically monological cultural forms are understood as *forms* of the dialogical—dialogical in some profound sense—rather than as some inexplicable perversion of the dialogical. But this also means that monologism must itself be recognized as a strategy of response toward another discourse. . . . We are thus led to a very different vision of what Bakhtin means by "dialogue," one which includes not only the liberal exchange of views but also questions of cultural oppression and power (p. 75).

Such a view of heteroglossia (and its textual embodiment as dialogism) would thus lead to an essentially Foucauldian view of languages as instances or instruments of power. From this perspective the dialogic text could be understood not just as a liberating celebration of or return to essential linguistic/ideological realities (i.e. as either Rabelais or Dosteovsky), but as an intervention in that never-ending struggle over meaning which defines language for Bakhtin. Rethought in this way, the terms monoglossia/heteroglossia would provide a useful framework for theorizing the workings of classic cinema as a standard "language," dominated by a certain rhetoric, which developed from a number of divergent "dialects"; the subsequent history of this standard language would be importantly characterized by a polyglossia (the challenge to the hegemony of classic cinema posed by Italian Neorealism and the French New Wave in the postwar era) that has "novelized" its various fixed forms (producing, among other effects, the self-consciousness, generic "explosions," and parodies of the Hollywood Renaissance).

This kind of appropriation, however, runs into some formidable difficulties. Structuralism and semiotics are essentially trans-medic approaches to the study of fictional texts; that is, these methods assume language (natural or cinematic) to be the vehicle through which stories are told. In terms of their conception of representation, semiotics and structuralism are thoroughly Aristotelian and Platonic, making a distinction between mimesis and diegesis, but assuming that the imitation of speech is an imitation of an action as well. For this reason, semiotic/structural methodologies could be easily adapted to cinematic uses, and a number of early narratological "handbooks" (particularly Seymour Chatman's *Story and Discourse*) could move easily from literature to film and vice versa without troubling about differences between the two media, which were conceived as inessential. Once again, Bakhtinian theory proves radically different from semiotics. Centered as it is on the linguistic, Bakhtin's conception of literature would have a usefulness for cinema studies only insofar as fundamental analogies can be made between cinematic and natural languages. Bakhtin's view that literature represents language rather than characters, setting, and events is, of course, a characteristically modernist notion, one shared, as Patricia Waugh has shown, by many postmodern/modern writers.[22] Such a concept is also to found in the theorizing of certain critcs—Wolfgang Iser is perhaps the most notable example—whose views are highly inflected by modernist assumptions about literature. The structualist/semiotic notion of language as *vehicle*—or even as anti-vehicle, as in the theorizing of the later Roland Barthes—demonstrates the extent to which this approach is grounded in assumptions about literature derived from high realism. In any case, the connection between primary and secondary speech genres would seem, at least at first glance, irrelevant to the quite different reality of cinematic language which, for obvious technical and institutional reasons, exists only in, as it were, certain elaborated or secondary forms. The cinema, therefore, could not be understood as containing some primary material which would be "objectified" and reoriented; indeed, if the object of representation for the cinema is the constructed "real" of the pro-filmic event, then the cinema does not have the same connection to ideology as literature (which represents linguistic signs that themselves "reflect" or "refract" the real and hence are ideology in its basic, material form). In other words, literature is fundamentally ideological, in the same sense any speech genre is, because it represents (and turns into "content") various ways of talking about, conceiving, or imagining the real; turning Plato upside down, Bakhtin argues that because literature is an "imitation" of an "imitation" it has value (the more dialogical it is, the closer the literary text gets to "living speech reality," the more valuable it is as an objectification). Bakhtin, of course, does not develop a theory of the reader or of reading to account for *why* this more dialogic imitation is to be preferred over monologic, fixed forms, but he seems to be operating with what we might call a realist epistemology within which the re-creation of the social real for the reader is valorized. For some film theorists—Eisenstein is the most prominent and *engagé* example—the superiority of cinematic representation is that it can dispense with words, "directly materializing" (to use Eisenstein's phrase) reality instead of constructing it verbally.[23] For Bakhtin, in contrast, verbalization poses no Shandyean barriers to the re-creation of experience; instead, words themselves are the experience, the contested areas of meaning and significance which literature is so uniquely qualified to represent. Indeed, for Bakhtin/Volosinov, human experience as such can only be approached through its material embodiment in signs, of which language is the most important category:

> . . . not only can experience be outwardly expressed through the agency of the sign (an experience can be expressed to others variously—by word, by facial expression, or by some other means), but also, aside from the outward expression (for others), experience exists even for the person undergoing it only in the material of signs (p. 28).

Though, as Bill Nichols has usefully demonstrated, the cinematic image can hardly be conceived as ideologically neutral, as an aspect of "given" reality that can simply be individually stylized, the fact remains that the cinema, unlike literature, has no corresponding language to objectify and examine in the very process of representation.[24] And, so the implication runs, the cinema possesses nothing analogous to the Bakhtinian novel, a form which takes the natural, populist forces of heteroglossia within living language as both material and theme. Bakhtin's notion of chronotopes—those particular constructions of space/time relations, conceived as indissoluble wholes, which enable him to classify novels into various sub-groupings—does appear to possess some usefulness for the description of different film genres. Vivian Sobchack, for one, has intriguingly shown how forties *film noir* can be conceived as characterized by such a chronotope, which she names "lounge time."[25] In my opinion, however, this aspect of Bakhtin's novelistic theory is weaker (because less innovating and radical) and, as I have already said, does not connect logically to his other view of the novel as an anti-genre which liberates established forms from their fixity. The idea of chronotope is an ingenious tool for classification, rather on the lines of Northrop Frye's scheme of myths and modes, but it is not related to Bakhtin's overall conception of the intimate relationship between language and literature. This is why it can be understood as applying to an area of fictional production outside of literature itself.

The cinema, then, offers no form truly *analogous* to the novel as Bakhtin conceives it. But this does not mean that the fiction film cannot be understood as extending novelistic practice in interesting and important ways. In short, we may conceive of the cinema—or, at least, the sound cinema—as a secondary or elaborated speech genre which takes as its primary object of representation the dramatic dialogue of human communication. Though the novel depends on the transposition of speech into writing, the sound cinema can "directly materialize" speech acts, preserving more of their innate complexity. As Lennard Davis points out, in fact, written transcription makes the representation of conversation in novels essentially unrealistic—because conventional—in ways that serve the interests of a hegemonic monoglossia. The narrator's language, for example, is usually presented in realist fiction as having "no accent," as belonging, by inference, to the standard language of ascendant groups; characters represented as speaking a "dialect"—a somewhat exceptional circumstance, most speeches being assimilated to an assumed standard pronunciation—are therefore juxtaposed with a superior narration that stands outside the heteroglossia which determines the characters' places in the novel's evoked social world. Furthermore, writing is simply inadequate to the phonetic complexity of speech—with its pauses, hesitations, emphases, and tones; as an act of communication, conversation is usually ungrammatical and "unfinished" because what Bakhtin would call "orientation" (the forging of unique themes for general and abstract linguistic forms) is often accomplished extraverbally, at least in part; that is, by means of gesture, expression, body language, shared understandings, and so on.

My point is this. Linked inextricably to written transcription, the novel is capable only of suggesting certain aspects of the dialogism which characterizes living speech; actually, by "refusing" the fact that everyone speaks a dialect and ignoring the complex struggle, both verbal and extraverbal, toward meaning which is the existential ground of dialogue, the novel unwittingly takes part in the establishment or entrenchment of monoglossia. In comparison to the epic (and other traditional fixed forms), the novel, no doubt, does open out more to the contemporary linguistic reality of writer and reader, acknowledging that speech is living and hence multifarious. But it would be foolish to ignore the fact that the novel "rises" in Europe at the same time that the various national languages in which it is written "rise" as well, asserting, as part of a claim to national unity and identity, the existence of *a single* variety of speech from which others are, in some sense, deviations. During the nineteenth century, moreover, the novel becomes tied to a literary culture also conceived now as national in some sense; its language—the language of writing which it shares, essentially, with other written forms—is then used as a medium of instruction, as a means for, however gently, enforcing adherence to standard usages, for which novels become, in part, the authority (consider the use of quotations from novels as support for usage/vocabulary "rules" in prescriptive grammars and dictionaries of the modern languages). The drive toward monoglossia within the modern European languages is an indisputable fact (one which, as Bakhtin/Volosinov fail to recognize, has much to do with the abstract objectivism of linguistics, founded as it is on the concept of an underlying unitary system to which the diversity of speech may untimately be related). And indisputable as well is the role which the novel has played in the establishment of monoglossia in the major European languages.

The cinema, especially in America, has been positioned quite differently in regard to the language which it has so powerfully re-presented for its mass public millions. To begin, the sound cinema is capable of much more accurate—hence more dialogical—representation of human speech. Voices in the cinema are all marked by accents; all must be understood as relativized and socially evaluated in the ways described by Volosinov/Bakhtin. Any suppression of linguistic difference, therefore, is readily apparent (as not in the conventionalized transcriptions of the novel). Furthermore, the cinema can faithfully record those extraverbal elements of conversation so important to its social meaning. It would be naive, of course, to think that cinematic speech is the same as ordinary conversation; spoken dialogue, like the novel's written speech, is certainly conventionalized (hesitating sounds, sentences started but abandoned, phrases that lack clear meaning, for example, are eliminated; these are usually coded as "bad acting"). But cinematic speech, it seems to me, is still more dialogical, more truly representative of the heteroglossia of the living language; the films of Robert Altman, for one, testify to the capacities of the cinema to offer the difficulties and complexities of real conversation. Almost as important, however, is the fact that films, unlike novels, have never been caught up in the establishment of monoglossia; the cinema, I would argue, by virtue of its representational ability, is uniquely disqualified to perpetuate or further the illusion of a unitary, unvarying language.

The cinema, moreover, is ideally constituted in another way to represent the dialogism of human communication. Bakhtin points out that in any dialogue speech is directed not only at the interlocutors, but at an addressee who remains silent. This addressee relates to the dialogue she/he overhears in different ways. In cinematic representation the camera would be that addressee. The relationship of the camera to the speech acts it records could be theorized in terms of its function as a silent addressee. As David Patterson describes Bakhtin's view:

> The *third* represents the horizon of possibility of the multiplicity of responses that might be offered in the dialogue; as possibility—or the one for whom all things are possible—the *third* sustains the movement of the dialogue. . . . What is more, each response offered in a dialogue expands the horizon of the third, so that the dialogue bears a proliferation of possibilities.[26]

Understanding the camera as "the third" would, I suggest, provide an interesting perspective from which its movements, scale, and position could be analyzed (as opposed to conceiving the camera as an element of narration). As Robert Stam suggests, a key Bakhtinian concept is "tact," or those relations of intimacy or distance which affect the ways in which interlocutors address one another. Tact, as far as the cinematic representation of speech acts is concerned, would be a feature not only of diegetic dialogue but of the camera's relationship—as "the third"—to that dialogue.

Moreover, if, as Bakhtin argues, the author must become other to himself in order to create a protagonist speaking a voice different from his own, how much easier this act of distanciation is for the director, who literally addresses those other than himself even as they respond to him and his camera. Here too, the cinema more closely approaches this ideal of novelistic representation than the novel itself. To quote Patterson again: "Thus when novelistic discourse is viewed in dialogical terms, the notion of character takes on a dynamic quality; the character is an *event*, and not a static entity whom we can file into a predetermined category" (p. 134). But the novelistic character starts life as a collection of signs on the page, to be animated only by the reader's imagination, his filling in of the "gaps" as Wolfgang Iser would have it. Such characters can never be truly dynamic, never more than functions in the dialogue the author constructs within himself. But cinematic characters—what they look like, how they talk, what meanings stick to them—are always "events" in the sense described by Patterson, never just bundles of signs that can be manipulated absolutely by their creator. The speech of the film character then, however "written" it might be, always suggests more of living dialogue than his literary counterpart.

The cinema, we may conclude, possesses no "novel" of its own, but can readily be seen as extending novelistic dialogism in ways which exceed the necessary limitations of literary form (which uses writing to represent speech, a formal restraint whose monoglossic distortions were underestimated by Bakhtin). But is this Bakhtinian perspective of any use to film criticism? I think so. Attention to cinema's representation of natural language—viewed now in the functionalist sense of a complex verbal/non-verbal communicative act—makes us realize the liberating potentials of a form with the greater capacity to avoid a conventionalizing, reductive approach to dialogue. Bakhtinian translinguistics can help us understand the different senses in which the mixed signifying practices of the cinema are language; viewing films as utterances, moreover, helps us better see the rhetoric which controls their communicative intentions. But Bakhtinanism can also help students of the cinema balance a concentration on the image—the heritage of semiotics and formalist approaches—with some consideration of the voices that animate the image. Like the novel, the sound cinema draws on the living language for its raw material. And, again like the novel, the sound cinema is structured, in large part, by the contentious interchange of the different voices speaking that language. The image cannot be dialogical in the absolute Bakhtinian sense, but it frames the dialogical in ways which students of film have just begun to appreciate.

NOTES

[1] *Mikhail Bakhtin: The Dialogical Principle*, translated by Wlad Godzich (Minneapolis: University of Minnesota Press, 1984) The quotation runs as follows: "One could praise Mikhail Bakhtin, without too many qualms, on two counts: that he is the most important Soviet thinker in the human sciences and the greatest theoretician of literature in the twentieth century" (p. ix).

[2] In this essay I will be making reference to the following translations of this body of work: M.M. Bakhtin/P.M. Medvedev, *The Formal Method in Literary Scholarship*, translated by Albert J. Wehrle (Cambridge: Harvard University Press, 1985); V.N. Volosinov, *Marxism and the Philosophy of Language*, translated by Ladislav Matejka and I.R. Titunik (Cambridge: Harvard University Press, 1986); V.N. Volosinov, *Freudianism: a Marxist Critique*, translated by I.R. Titunik and edited in collaboration with Neal H. Bruss (New York: Academic Press, 1976); M.M. Bakhtin, *Speech Genres and Other Late Essays*, translated by Vern W. McGee, edited by Caryl Emerson and Michael Holquist (Austin: University of Texas Press, 1986); *The Dialogic Imagination: Four Essays by M.M. Bakhtin*, translated by Michael Holquist and edited by Caryl Emerson and Michael Holquist (Austin: University of Texas Press, 1981). Specific references will be noted in the text.

[3] Perusing the MLA annual bibliography, I find only sporadic examples of essays making a central or extensive use of Bakhtinian theory throughout the late seventies (despite the fact that his books on Rabelais and Dostoevsky as well as the collaborative studies with Volosinov and Medvedev had been available for some time). The 1985 edition, in contrast, lists by my count some 33 essays or book chapters dealing with the practical application of Bakhtin's ideas and approaches.

[4] "Film and Language: From Metz to Bakhtin," in this volume, p. 296.

[5] "The Alterity of Discourse: Form, History, and the Question of the Political in M.M. Bakhtin," *Diacritics* 13 no. 2 (Summer 1983), p. 67.

[6] Christian Metz, *Film Language*, translated by Michael Taylor (New York: Oxford University Press, 1974), p. 47. Future references to this book will be noted in the text.

[7] Translated by Donna Jean Umiker-Sebeok (The Hague: Mouton Publishing, 1974). Future specific references to this work will be noted in the text.

[8] Quoted in Todorov, p. 56. The passage is from Bakhtin's notebooks as these have been edited and published in a 1979 Russian language collection. The observation was made in the early seventies as the discipline of semiotics began to attract international attention.

[9] "Bakhtin, Sociolinguistics, and Deconstruction," in Frank Gloversmith, ed., *The Theory of Reading* (New Jersey: Barnes and Noble Books, 1984), p.138. Future references to this essay will be noted in the text.

[10] *Discourse Analysis* (Cambridge: Cambridge University Press,1983), p. 24.

[11] *Cohesion in Literary Texts* (The Hague: Mouton Publishing, 1976), p.54.

[12] *Cohesion in English* (London: Longman, 1976).

[13] *Introduction to Text Linguistics* (London: Longman, 1981), p. 48.

[14] *Introduction*, p. 17.

[15] Halliday's theory of "chunking" or the rhetorical segmentation of discourse within syntactical boundaries has some potential, I think, for application to cinematic discourse, where questions of segmentation (i.e. the division of the film into "shots") have always been more crucial for a variety of reasons. As I argue further below, analytic editing (among other conventional cinematic practices) manifests cohesion through a recurrence established by both paraphrase and ellipsis; the theory of chunking might help us better understand why such analysis of a unitary dramatic scene came to be preferred within classic practice. See Halliday's "Language Structure and Language function" in J. Lyons, ed., *New Horizons in Linguistics* (Harmondsworth: Penguin Books, 1970).

[16] See *Linguistics and English Grammar* (New York: Holt, Rinehart, and Winston, 1965), pp. 195–221.

[17] Janet Wolff's criticism of approaches like Bakhtin's is telling; because, she observes, "some Marxist theories of cultural intervention . . . assume artists or authors are more or less 'free,' unconstituted agents," there is a tendency to think that all such artists have to do is "engage in cultural politics in the most effective way." This assumption ignores the fact that "in the production of art, social institutions affect, amongst other things, *who* becomes an artist, *how* they become an artist, how they are then able to *practise* their art, and how they can ensure that their work is produced, performed, and *made available* to a public" (*The Social Production of Art*, New York: St. Martin's Press, 1981, p. 131, 40).

[18] White, p. 127

[19] In his most effective and critical reaction to the current trend toward a conservative recuperation of Bakhtin's theories, "A Response to the Forum on Mikhail Bakhtin," published in Gary Saul Morson, ed., *Bakhtin: Essays and Dialogues on his Work* (Chicago: University of Chicago

Press, 1986), p. 75. Hirschkop writes: dialogism "is both the natural state of being of language as such and a valorized category of certain discourses. . . . When these two senses of the term are conflated, the specific form dialogism takes in the novel is assumed to be the mani-festation of the true essence of language, an essence somehow repressed in the monological. In fact, it is the status of monologism which is the most problematic; if dialogism is the nature of all language, then what gives rise to monologism? For monologism is not merely an illusion or an error, it is a form of discourse with real, if mystifying effects."

[20] Davis's central thesis about represented speech in novels is that "nov-elists invented conversation and . . . novelistic conversation too is a defensive, ideological structure. The point is that after novelists invented conversation, readers strove to include conversation in their own lives" (*Ideology and Fiction: Resisting Novels*, New York: Methuen, 1987, p. 162.)

[21] In *The Crisis in Criticism: Theory, Literature and Reform in English Studies* (Baltimore and London: The Johns Hopkins University Press, 1984), William Cain demonstrates how most "new and innovative critical meth-ods" within the field remain securely and centrally defined by New Critical assumptions. Writing today, he might be tempted to include a chapter on the "Bakhtin industry."

[22] In *Metafiction: The Theory and Practice of Self-Conscious Fiction* (New York: Methuen, 1984), she observes that "the metafictionist is highly conscious of a basic dilemma: if he or she sets out to 'represent' the world, he or she realizes fairly soon that the world, as such, cannot be 'represented.' In literary fiction it is, in fact, possible only to 'represent' the *discourses* of that world" (p. 3).

[23] In his essay "Achievement", written in 1939, Eisenstein remarks that "the cinema is that genuine and ultimate synthesis of all artistic mani-festations that fell to pieces after the peak of Greek culture." And cinema can make this claim because it "achieves the full embrace of the whole inner world of man, of a whole reproduction of the outer world" by means of the fact that in cinema "the desired image is directly mater-ialized in audio-visual perceptions" (*Film Sense* translated by Jay Leyda, New York: Harcourt Brace and Meridian, 1957, pp. 184–5.)

[24] *Ideology and the Image* (Bloomington: University of Indiana Press, 1981).

[25] This paper was presented at the 1983 conference sponsored by the So-ciety for Cinema Studies. Its present title is " 'Lounge Time': Post-War Crises and the Chronotopes of Film Noir."

[26] "Mikhail Bakhtin and the Dialogical Dimensions of the Novel," *Journal of Aesthetics and Art Criticism* 44 no. 2 (Winter 1985), p.136.

BAKHTINIAN TRANSLINGUISTICS: A POSTSCRIPTUM

Robert Stam

In the light of Bart Palmer's suggestive remarks in "Bakhtinian Translinguistics and Film Criticism: The Dialogical Image?" I would like to elaborate further on the possibilities opened up by a "translinguistics" of the cinema. The cine-semiology of Christian Metz, Bart Palmer and I agree, was both too linguistic and not linguistic enough. Based as it was on just one linguistic tradition, that of "abstract objectivism," cine-semiology gave us everything that that tradition could give us. "Translinguistics," while it would reject the Saussurean framework of cine-semiology, would at the same time highlight even more effectively the fundamental affinities linking "natural language" and cinematic utterance conceived as a discursive and communicative rather than a merely signifying practice. Cine-semiology, we agree, needs to become translinguistic. It badly needs key Bakhtinian notions such as the omnipresence of language in all cultural production, the transcendence of conventional ideas of mimesis, the fundamental dynamism and instability of the sign, and the attack on the notion of unitary language. I enthusiastically endorse Bart Palmer's call for the application of the Bakhtinian category of "speech genres" to the cinema, as well as his call for cinematic "discourse analysis." My only reservation has to do with some of the discourse analyses chosen: "text grammar" and "text linguistics," it seems to me, run the risk of "taking out" the very politics and history that the Bakhtinian model allowed us to put back in.

Bakhtin's approach, it is important to say at the outset, has a built-in "place" for film, since Bakhtin sees verbal language as part of a continuum of semioses sharing a common logic. He sees verbal language, furthermore, as ubiquitous in all social life and cultural production. "All the diverse areas of human activity," he writes in "The Problem of Speech Genres," "involve the use of language."[1] Yet it would be a mistake, for Bakhtin, to think that this pan-semiotic language-bathed reality can be "the subject of one science, linguistics, or that it can be understood through linguistic methods alone."[2] Whence the need for a "trans-" linguistics. A Bakhtinian "translinguistics," we are arguing, offers a more adequate basis for cine-semiotics, since it is capable of clarifying some of the theoretical confusions and ideological ambiguities generated by the Saussurean framework. Bakhtin's location of meaning not in petrified linguistic forms but rather in the use of language in action and communication (the utterance), his insistence that these meanings are generated and heard as social voices anticipating and answering one another (dialogism), and his recognition that these voices represent distinct socio-ideological positionings whose conflictual relation exists at the very heart of language change (heteroglossia), have immense importance for the theory, analysis and even the praxis of cinema.

Purely linguistic definitions of an artistic language and its elements, Bakhtin suggests in "The Problem of the Text," can serve only as "initial terms for description," for what is most important "is not described by them and does not reside within them."[3] A familiarity with Bakhtin's work might have saved the pioneer cine-semiologists in the Franco-Italian tradition considerable effort by warning them against undertaking what turned out to be a futile search for the cinematic equivalents of Saussure-derived entities such as *langue*, the arbitrary sign, minimal units and double articulation. (Metz deserves credit, of course, for recognizing the absence of such entities rather than trying to make forced comparisons.) It is not phonemes and morphemes that enter dialogism, but utterances, and it is as utterance that the cinematic "word" acquires relation to the spectator and to life.

While the written transcription of speech, whether in a trial, a novel, or a journalistic report, inevitably involves a certain loss of "accent," the sound film, as Palmer and others have pointed out, is virtually incapable of representing speech without an accent. Indeed, it was this very literalness of the "accentedness" of film speech that engendered difficulties in the period of the transition from silent to sound cinema. With sound, spectators were obliged to confront particular voices with particular accents. Greta Garbo, silent-film goers discovered, had an attractive Swedish accent, but John Gilbert's voice turned out to be irritatingly "reedy" and "unpleasant." (The effect of loss was analogous, in some respects, to that experienced by lovers of a novel when verbally-cued fantasized characters are incarnated by disappointingly specific actors with particular voices and physiognomies.) The sound film, then, comes inevitably equipped with "accent" and "intonation," even when that accent is false in terms of the diegetic social representation.

In "The Problem of Speech Genres," Bakhtin again provides extremely suggestive concepts susceptible to extrapolation for the analysis of cinema as the mise-en-scène of discursive situations. Bakhtin here calls attention to a wide gamut of "speech genres," both oral and written, simple and complex, which range all the way from "the short rejoinders of ordinary dialogue" through everyday narration, the military command, to all the literary genres (from the proverb to the multi-volume novel) and other "secondary (complex) speech genres" such as major types of social-cultural commentary and scientific research. The secondary complex genres draw from the primary ones of unmediated speech communion and influence them as well in a process of constant back-and-forth flow. A translinguistic approach to speech genres in the cinema would correlate the primary speech genres—familial conversation, dialogue among friends, chance encounters, boss–worker exchange, classroom discussion, cocktail party banter, military commands—with their secondary cinematic mediation. It would analyze the etiquette by which the classical Hollywood film, for example, deals with typical speech situations such as two-person dialogue (usually by the conventional ping-pong of shot/counter shot), dramatic confrontations (the verbal standoffs of the western and the gangster film,) as well as with the more avant-gardist subversions of that etiquette. Godard's entire career, for example, might be seen as a protracted attack on the conventional Hollywood decorum for handling discursive situations in the cinema, whence his refusal of the canonical alternation of over-the-shoulder shots for dialogue, substituting instead pendulum-like lateral tracks (*Le Mepris*), a "dialogue" of book covers (*Une Femme est une femme*), lengthy single-shot sequences (*Masculin, feminin*), and unorthodox positioning of the bodies of the interlocutors (for example, having one speaker's head block the view of the other, as in *Vivre sa Vie*).

A number of films can be seen as dealing quite consciously and reflexively with the question of primary speech genres and their cinematic mediation. The Brazilian avant-garde film *Bangue Bangue* (Bang, Bang, 1971), by Andrea Tonacci, performs a metalinguistic examination of the everyday speech genre called "greeting and exchange of trivialities." A man and a woman initiate, five times in succession, the same conversation, concluding, after considerable prolixity, that the word "Hi" should be systematically substituted for the usual sequence of "Good Morning," "How are you?" "I'm fine," and so forth. One of a number of reflexive mini-sequences in the film, the episode implicitly compares film itself to discourse, to conversation. It consists, more accurately, of metadiscourse, discourse on discourse, just as the film is metacinema. The apparent point of the discourse—the desirability of using as few words as possible—is contradicted by the discourse itself, which is wordy and redundant. What matters, the sequence suggests, is not the message but the articulation, or better the inseparable link between the two, a point further illustrated when the same conversation is played against different contextual sound elements, first with harsh ambient noise and then again with harp music, to completely different effect.

Japanese director Juzo Itami deals with a more specialized primary speech genre in *The Funeral*. The film covers three traumatic days in the lives of an upscale Japanese couple in the wake of the husband's father's death, from the day they receive the news till the day the corpse is cremated, the ashes buried and everyone can go home. The trauma consists not in the loss of the father, a cruel and whiny glutton, but rather in the discursive challenge of dealing with an unfamiliar speech situation. Somewhat out of touch both with the venerable Shinto traditions and contemporary funeral decorum,, the couple has to learn both for this special occasion. They do so with the help of a video-cassette entitled "The ABC's of the Funeral," thanks to which they can learn what formulaic phrases to expect—"our condolences on your tragic loss" . . . "what a blessing he didn't suffer long" . . . "he looks so peaceful in the coffin, as if he were asleep . . ." and so forth—and how to make equally formulaic responses —"he would have been so happy to know you were here"—and thus to become proficient in the tragic-loss-of-a-loved-one "speech genre."

Buñuel's *Exterminating Angel*(1962), similarly, can be seen as a comic deconstruction of the primary speech genre called "polite dinner conversation." The film's plot, revolving around the inexplicable entrapment of a pride of socialites at dinner, provides the point of departure for the critical dissection of the elaborate discursive rituals of the haute bourgeoisie. On one level, the film is a joke on everday social experience, the excruciatingly formal dinner where everyone is quite miserable but pretends to be having a marvelous time, and where everyone would prefer to leave but no one has the courage. The film also offers satiric variants of "speech subgenres," the "civil" discourse of individuals who detest one another but are constrained to be polite, the encounters of wives and lovers, quite aware of a triangular situation, who conveniently pretend not to know, and so forth. In a kind of *grammatica jocosa* of the language of social etiquette, Buñuel engenders absurd discursive encounters. A couple about to marry, for example, performs a kind of bureaucratized parody of the man-meets-woman-at-social-gathering genre, as she asks while they dance: "Name? Age? Profession? Marital status?" Or Buñuel mingles the polite and the impolite, the noble and the vulgar. "You smell like a hyena, Madame," one socialite tells another. A doctor confides to a friend that one of his patients will soon be "completely bald," (a Spanish expression roughly equivalent to "croak" or "kick the bucket"). As bourgeois etiquette disintegrates, Buñuel seems to be offering the linguistic-discursive evidence of grave ruptures in the fabric of a pathologically polite society.

The cinema is superbly equipped to present the extra-verbal aspects of linguistic discourse, precisely those subtle contextualizing factors evoked by what Bakhtin calls "tact." In the sound film, we not only hear the words, with their accent and intonation, but also witness the facial or corporeal expression which accompanies the words—the posture of arrogance or regignation, the raised eyebrow, the look of distrust, the ironic glance which modifies the ostensible meaning of an utterance—in short all those elements which discourse analysts have taught us to see as so terribly important to social communication. While a writer such as Proust can brilliantly evoke such discursive phenomena in sinuous prose, the cinema presents them, as it were, "intact." As a powerful condenser of unspoken social evaluations, film has the power to represent the complexities of verbal behavior. Words, for Bakhtin, are always "saturated" with "accents" and "intonations;" they carry with them the "aura" of a profession, a party, a generation. Film acting largely consists in getting these accents and intonations right, much as film directing has to do with contextualizing them. With its capacity for contexting words not only through mise-en-scène but also through its other tracks (music, noise, written materials), film is ideally suited for conveying what Bakhtin calls "contextual overtones." Film dramaturgy has its special tact, its ways of suggesting, through camera placement, framing and acting, such phenomena as intimacy or distance, camaraderie or domination, in short all the social and personal dynamics operating between interlocutors.

The discursive rules of "tact" operate not only in the fiction film—think for example of the evolving tact between master and servant in Losey's *The Servant*—but also even in the documentary. In countless documentaries (including those considered "progressive") about oppressed or colonized people, the off-screen voice of a narrator takes on intonations of domination and omniscience. Studio-protected, this voice speaks in regular and homogeneous rhythms, while the human subjects of the film speak hesitantly, in direct sound. The voice speaks of them confidently, in the third person, while they speak of themselves hesitantly, in the first. The narrator becomes the voice of knowledge and mastery, while the narratees are the voice of undiscriminating experience. The voice translates their "alien words" into the impersonal discourse of objective truth.

While Metz was highly successful in calling attention to the "specifically cinematic," he was less successful in linking the specific and the non-specific, the social and the cinematic, the textual and the contextual. In this context, it is worth comparing the Metzian and the Bakhtinian accounts of textual contradiction. There is a clear tension in *Language and Cinema*, as both Bart Palmer and I point out, between a static, taxonomic, structuralist-formalist view of textual systems, and a more dynamic view of text as productivity, displacement, and écriture. It is as if within Metz the structuralist there were a post-structuralist yearning to breathe free. It is this latter, less static view of the text as a "non-finalized" perpetual displacement that constitutes the more dynamic pole in *Language and Cinema* and the one most easily reconciled with a translinguistic approach. Bakhtin's formulations about the novelistic text, in fact, are at times strikingly anticipatory of Metz' formulations concerning the textual systems of films. The language of the novel, Bakhtin asserts in "Discourse in the

Novel," is "the system of its languages."[4] But even here there are differences. First, Metz' abstract objectivist presuppositions, as Bart Palmer points out, oblige him to speak of "codes," while for Bakhtin all utterances, including artistic utterances, are determined not by the systematicity of codes but by the always unique circumstances of the communication. More important, Metz never makes the crucial link between textual and social contradiction. In this sense, Bakhtin's critique of the Formalists can be extrapolated to the Metzian view of textual systems. As Graham Pechey points out, the Formalists described textual contradiction in terms redolent of social struggle. Shklovsky, for example, compared each new school of literature to a revolution, "something like the emergence of a new class,"[5] and the Formalists generally were fond of metaphors of combat, struggle, and conflict. But Shklovsky went on to downplay his own metaphor as "only an analogy," and literary contradiction remained in a hermetically sealed world of pure textuality. In *The Formal Method in Literary Scholarship*, Pechey argues, Bakhtin/Medvedev take the Formalist metaphors seriously—especially those terms which easily resonate with class and social struggle, terms such as "revolt," "conflict," "struggle" "destruction" and even "the dominant"—and make them apply equally to the text and to the social itself.[6]

What both Metz and the Formalists "need," then, is the Bakhtinian concept of "heteroglossia," i.e. a notion of competing languages and discourses which would apply equally to "text" and "hors-texte." Heteroglossia refers to the shifting stratifications of language into class dialects, professional jargons (lawyers, doctors, academics), generic discourses (melodrama, comedy), bureaucratic lingos, popular slangs, along with all the other specific languages generated by cultural praxis. The languages composing heteroglossia represent "bounded verbal-ideological belief systems," points of view on the world, forms for conceptualizing social experience, each marked by its own tonalities, meanings and values. A given linguistic community shares a common language, but different segments "live" that common language diversely. The role of the artistic text, be it a novel, a play, or a film, is not to represent real life "existents" but rather to stage the conflicts inherent in heteroglossia, the coincidences and competitions of languages and discourses.

A social semiotic of the cinema, then, would remain the Formalist and the Metzian notion of textual contradiction, but rethink it through heteroglossia. The languages of heteroglossia, Bakhtin argues in "Discourse in the Novel," may be "juxtaposed to one another, mutually supplement one another, contradict one another and be interrelated dialogically."[7] This formulation has a double advantage. First, it avoids the kind of referentialism that sometimes creeps into the Metzian account of cinematic representation even against Metz' best intentions. (The "grande syntagmatique," for example, premised on an impossible comparison between the putative time-space of the diegesis and the actual spatio-temporal articulation of the filmic discourse itself, at times seems to imply that some pre-existing anecdotal nucleus precedes the text, when in fact it is pure construct). By completely bracketing the question of the real, what Metz would call the "totality of pro-filmic elements," and instead emphasizing the representation of languages and discourses, Bakhtin relocates the question altogether. Secondly, the Bakhtinian formulation is especially appropriate to any number of post-modernist films which, rather than represent "real" humanly purposeful events according to an illusionistic aesthetic, simply stage the clash of languages and discourses. Here one could cite a wide spectrum of films and filmmakers, from Bruce Conner's avant-garde collages of pre-existing found footage, to the work of such filmmakers as Yvonne Rainer and Jean-Luc Godard. Rainer's *The Man Who Envied Women*, for example, horizontally juxtaposes or vertically superimposes a variety of discourses: newspaper advertisements, overheard snippets of conversation, nonsensical lectures, ironic paraphrases of Foucault and Lacan. Godard-Gorin's *Tout Va Bien*, similarly, is structured around a tripartite play of ideological languages: that of capital, that of the Communist Party, and that of the Maoists. Deploying dialogue consisting primarily of quotations from disparate policical sources, the film places languages in collision, thus generating a semantic richness beyond the reach of monological texts. Such films practice what Bakhtin called the "mutural illumination of languages," languages which intersect, collide, rub off on and relativize one another. And, as Bakhtin argued in regard to Dostoevsky, the fact that these languages are borrowed from the social atmosphere in no way detracts from the "deep-seated intentionality" and "overarching ideological conceptualization" of the work as a whole. "Dostoevsky astounds us with a wide diversity of types and varieties of discourse, but one still senses in his work the voice of a unified creative will." Filmmakers like Godard or Ruiz, similarly, offer a dizzying array of filmic and extra-filmic discourses, yet we never lose consciousness of the compositional *écriture* "behind" the discourses.

NOTES

[1] M.M. Bakhtin, *Speech Genres and Other Late Essays*, trans. Vern W. McGee (Austin: University of Texas Press,1986), p. 60.

[2] Ibid. p. 118.

[3] Ibid. p. 122.

[4] M.M. Bakhtin, *The Dialogical Imagination* (Austin: University of Texas Press, 1981), p. 416.

[5] This passage appeared in *Rozanov* (1921) and again in *Theory of prose* (1925) and is quoted in Graham Pechey, "Bakhtin, Marxism and Post-Structuralism," in Barker *et. al*, *Literature, Politics and Theory* (London: Methuen, 1986), pp. 113–114.

[6] Ibid. p. 115.

[7] M.M. Bakhtin, "Discourse in the Novel," in *The Dialogical Imagination*, p. 292.

RECEPTION STUDIES: THE DEATH OF THE READER

Janet Staiger

To subtitle an essay about reception studies "the death of the reader" may seem odd. The intertextual reference, however, should be obvious. In his 1968 essay, Roland Barthes postulates a set of themes which have become dominant in structuralist and post-structuralist media theory. These include that (1) authorship is a modern notion, relating to capitalist ideologies and projects; that (2) in an instance of writing, language speaks, destroying any possibility of locating the origin of "who" is speaking; that (3) these above two propositions "restore the place of the reader."[1]

Though Barthes' essay both influenced and served as a symptom of the last two decades' interest in the reader—or for film, the spectator—the final theme, I would suggest, requires qualification. For while the "place of the reader" now enters our discussions, certain tendencies of recent scholarship have been to restore the privilege of determining immanent meaning to the reading person. Where once the "author" reigned supreme in critical and biographical tomes, now the central hermeneutic figure is the reader with "his" or "her" response. The danger of such tendencies, it seems to me, is to forget the lessons of structuralism implied by Barthes' first two themes. For if Barthes' arguments about why scholars should assume that the "author" as conceived within liberal humanistics studies is—or should be—dead, then the "reader" ought to be as well. As Barthes writes, "language knows a 'subject', not a 'person', and this subject, empty outside the very enunciation which defines it, suffices to make lan-

guage 'hold together,' suffices, that is to say, to exhaust it" (P. 145).
I would add that *history* also knows a "subject."

These facts mark off reception studies from other theories and
critical methods, perhaps making an essay on reception studies as
much as anomaly within this volume of essays as one on "historical
poetics." For reception studies ought be neither a theory nor a textual
procedure—although it might fruitfully employ various theories or
critical insights. Neither should reception studies be considered a
grand theory "covering" other theories or textual methods, even
though it may at times have observations to make regarding the history
and organization of theories and textual analyses.

If reception studies ought not to include these scholarly practices,
what should its concerns be? I would like to see reception studies
attain somewhat the same position that feminist studies has held for
recent dominant theoretical work in film studies—that is, as a critical
tool or intervening practice which dislodges attempts at "centering"
and stabilizing theories and knowledges as privileged or "true" or
"hierarchical." As I envision its field of research in cinema (or other
media), its central questions would be: (1) What have been the receptions of cinema/genres/specific films/movements and (2) what explains these receptions? Such a notion of reception studies as an area
of research implicitly crosses almost all of the fields of research covered
in óther essays included in this volume. But where it marks out its
own angle of vision is in its constant assessment of the institutional-
izing, within history, of propositions: e.g., "textual meaning," "the
spectator," "the cinematic apparatus." Consequently, a reception
studies of this kind would be (1) historical; (2) comparative; and (3)
critical.

You may have noticed the use of a future tense in my writing. As
a phrase, "reception studies" has been current for several years, with
a number of essays and anthologies (mostly related to literary studies)
already devoted to surveying "reception aesthetics" or "reader-response" theory. A Methuen New Accents book provides a "critical
introduction" to one branch of work—that of the Constance School
which includes Wolfgang Iser and Hans Robert Jauss.[2] While almost
all of this work is valuable, I would prefer to distance my notion of
"reception studies" from it, suggesting that "reception studies" is not
yet an organized endeavor around which one might group a concerted
effort of research (although a number of essays might reasonably be

aligned with it). Perhaps this is for the best, and in proceeding in the following sections to lay out "reception studies" as a field of inquiry, I shall be arguing for something as I would like it to be, but not as it will necessarily become.

I

Yet the notion that the text is simply a ceaselessly self-signifying practice, without source or object, stands four square with the bourgeois mythology of individual freedom.[3]

Reception studies should first of all be historical. Among other points, structuralist and post-structuralist theories of language have emphasized that language is discourse—a speech act which is also a social utterance, understood through a social contract. Ferdinand de Saussure wanted to define semiology as "a science that studies the life of signs within society. . . . "[4] For one of the more influential predecessors of contemporary linguistics, the act of speaking is a historical, social act. Yet this postulate was somewhat set aside as scholars concentrated on various media as self-contained, synchronic semiotic systems. Consequently, in a large part for dominant literary and cinema semiotics, language theory moved through a phase of ahistorical, nonsocial idealism in which meanings were assumed decipherable from structured oppositions or decoded via other strategies of analyzing textual syntagmas and semantics. When applied to the reader, the result of this phase of semiotic research has been conceiving of the reader-text relation as the text "positioning" or "interpellating" the reader to occupy a single (although perhaps fluctuating) position. The consequence of studies of "readership" inflected by structuralist and semiotic research of the 1970s has been to locate "the reader in the text"—i.e., the reader hypothesized *by the critic* as that "intended" by the text or, with some slightly greater finesse, but in a manner no less idealistic, the reader that ought to have been. Both ideal readers and competent readers are almost always represented in the singular: this is the way the reader processes the text; this is the way the reader, if he[5] is doing what he ought to do, processes the text. Even phenomenological theories of reading, which might acknowledge the historical, social reader, often tend to construct idealized readers—modeled, for want of considering alternatives, after the critic's own reading-ego.

A most exemplary literary instance of the ideal reader might be Michael Riffaterre's superreader who is emptied of "idiosyncrasy-oriented responses (positive or negative according to the reader's culture, era, esthetics, personality) and goal-oriented responses (those of the reader with nonliterary intent, who may be using the poem as a historical document, for purposes of linguistic analysis, etc. . . .)."[6] Until recently in film studies almost everyone writing textual analysis about the spectator has proceeded along similar lines.

Feminist studies has been one of the major sites of opposition, attempting either to promote "resisting readers," or simply questioning reader theories based on "human" [that is, male] postulates. For instance, work derived from psychoanalytic studies of oedipal processes assume effects derived from constructs of a gendered male reader, a postulation criticized as discriminatory by feminists. However, often in addressing this idealizing activity, feminist studies in turn postulate "ideal" female or femininized readers, and gay and lesbian studies may end up doing this too. I know that those working in these areas of study would agree with my criticism: that historically real conditions of power and structures of domination need to be known as they exist. While it may be politically useful to use ideal notions of "female" or "feminized" or gay or lesbian readers to throw off retrograde representations of "the reader," none of these recent "idealized" readers can be allowed to stand, for they merely repeat—at perhaps a more discrete level—the errors of the "fathers."

The ideal reader is hypothesized from textual evidence by the astute critic. A notion of a competent reader suggests the possibility of variations among readings. In practice, however, critics tend to evaluate rather than explain such readings. Variations are "mistakes" or, at least, not pertinent to the research questions. In his earlier work, Jonathan Culler tends to such a position, most notably in his chapters on "Literary Competence" and "Convention and Naturalization" in *Structuralist Poetics*.[7] There you can find attitudes such as the following:

> None would deny that literary works, like most other objects of human attention, can be enjoyed for reasons that have little [to] do with understanding and mastery—that texts can be quite blatantly misunder-

stood and still be appreciated for a variety of personal reasons. But to reject the notion of misunderstanding as a legislative imposition is to leave unexplained the common experience of being shown where one went wrong, of grasping a mistake and seeing why it was a mistake (120–21).

In a recent attempt to expound a new explanation of film spectatorship, David Bordwell (who also has an essay in this volume) pursues something akin to the competent-reader approach. In *Narration in the Fiction Film*,[8] he counters other theories of narration (termed by him as "mimetic" and "diegetic") which imply particular epistemologies of spectatorship, for a procedure based on constructivist cognitive psychology. Thus the film viewer is "a hypothetical entity executing the operations relevant to constructing a story out of the film's representation" (p. 30). Bordwell particularly notes that his spectator is neither an ideal nor an empirical viewer. His spectator "acts according to the protocols of story comprehension which this and following chapters will spell out" and is "real" and "active." Proposing a model something like Iser's representation of the text as a constellation ("The 'stars' in a literary text are fixed; the lines that join them are variable"[9]), Bordwell continues: "the artwork is necessarily incomplete, needing to be unified and fleshed out by the active participation of the perceiver" (p. 32). Bordwell even suggests that films prescribe appropriate cognitive activities for the spectator: "In the romance plot, it is the viewer's duty to be alert for such heterogeneous categories" (p. 43).[10] But it is also quite apparent that for Bordwell, as for Culler, "empirical spectators can err" (p. 39).

I will not debate here whether "readings" other than those the critic claims are the readings solicited by the text are mistakes, whether "misreadings" are even possible, or whether Culler is correct in concluding that "if the distinction between understanding and misunderstanding were irrelevant . . . there would be little point to discussing and arguing about literary works and still less to writing about them" (p. 121). Rather, I would suggest that it is precisely at this point that reception studies begins asking its questions. That is, its area of inquiry is to describe and explain the consistencies *and the variations* of spectatorial activities and of readings, not to reconcile them or to judge them (which is not to suggest that reception studies withdraws overall from evaluation: more on this below). Reception studies might be interested in what critics think ought to be the way you and I read a text or view a film (because such observations can themselves become determinants in reading and viewing), but, as an area of inquiry, reception studies also recognizes that not everyone does what critics wish (or think films wish). Why this is so is just as important as why a lot of readers and spectators actually do behave as the critics suggest.

Actually, explaining either adherence to or deviation from notions of literary or cinematic competence requires us to turn to history and politics. If the reception theorist adopts an idealist position or something of a "consensus" historian's version of people in history, then the generalizing views evident in the ideal or competent versions of readers and spectators result logically.

However, if the historian understands individuals in social formations as in conflict or believes differences exist among social formations, then the focus of the research shifts to considering readings of texts or viewings of films as related to issues of political debates, dialogue among people in historical moments, and facts of discriminatory hierarchies among peoples.[11] The more recent use of the term "reading formations" attempts to reach toward this through acknowledging the heterogeneity of and conflict within and between societies and cultures. Consequently, specific readings and viewings by individuals can be organized into various abstract groupings as these readings/viewings gather around possible (and perhaps interrelated) categories such as gender, sexual orientation, race, ethnicity, class, and so forth. If the researcher of the reader or spectator cancels out as irrelevant that real, historical readers exist (as the idealist approach does) or that all readers do not end up with the *same* "unified" account (as the competent reader approach does), then the results of the research, while useful to some degree in our understanding of readers and spectators, answer only some questions but not every one. I would encourage the researcher to be sensitive to the history of struggles to end exploitation and domination as well as to the historically varied and not innate character of language or cognitive processing. Not every research question needs to end up involved with reception studies, but a researcher might wish to acknowledge the limits of claims of her/his research regarding readers and spectators.

Let me stress that the researcher's conception of history and her/his political orientation are among the most important bases for how readings and viewings are understood. Tony Bennett refers to this when he writes that "the study of 'literary phenomena within social reality' . . . . directs attention to the history of its use, of its perpetual remaking and transformation, in the light of its inscription into a variety of different material, social, institutional and ideological contexts."[12] Elegantly phrasing the potential determinants a reception studies researcher would need to consider, Bennett focuses on the uses to which texts and films have been put—by groups, "sub"-groups, and individuals. In fact, readings and viewings that do not conform to versions recognized by the academy are no less "real" or any less important within a history of audience consumption of literary and filmic fiction and non-fiction. " 'Untutored' readings are just as real and material in their effects as 'tutored' ones and may, indeed, be considerably more influential" (p. 9).

Let me take as an example of such an "untutored" reading a section of one undergraduate film student's interpretation of the Odessa Steps sequence in *Potemkin*. As related by the instructor, this student's interpretation was produced after the student heard a typical 50-minute lecture about the Soviet revolution, Eisenstein, and dialectical montage prior to seeing the film:

> In Eisenstein's *Potemkin* with reference to the 'Odessa Steps" clip, we see many aspects of mise-en-scene. Three which I believe are more obvious are the action of the baby carriage, the uniformity of the communists [sic] march and the boat scene, where all the Turks [sic] watch their people set out on sailboats.
>
> The function of the Soviets uniformally [sic] marching down the steps with the same foot and rate [sic], I believe function [sic] as a symbol for a communist country. Viewers see no individuality. The soldiers [sic] look, walk, and 'armswing' is [sic] the same throughout the line. I think Eisenstein is placing the soldiers in the marching line-up to show that in a communist country everything has a set form and no exception. This was manifested when the soldiers were marching down the stairs and there was a body lying there—the soldiers stepped on it to pass it. They didn't jump or move out of the way.
>
> Another instance of mise-en-scene is the placement of the baby in the carriage. I believe its function is to be a symbol of the future generations of independent Turkey. . . . [13]

Much could be said about this interpretation of *Potemkin*. For one thing, I would argue that the student has incorporated much of the critical apparatus and strategies taught in film analysis courses. The student observes "mise-en-scène" as potentially functioning to produce filmic meaning and, like Eisenstein, takes the blocking of soldiers' movements as operating for purposes beyond the mere evocation of realism. The "uniformity" of the movements signifies another uniformity. In addition, the student seeks several sites of mise-en-scène to find the interpretation through multiple areas of the film. On the other hand, of course, the student makes a major "mistake": the - soldiers "are not" communists. Now this "mis-reading" can be explained (e.g., the student's previous ideological formation has blocked a reading in which communists could be seen sympathetically; the student is uneducated in the history of the Soviet revolution, not realizing that Tsarist forces are in charge in 1905), but it is harder to explain a "mis-reading" that occurs *in spite of* class information to the contrary. Here inattention or fatigue might be explanatory, but given the student's duplication of standard procedures for critical interpretation it is difficult to assume that this student would be caught reading a newspaper or napping during the lecture. All that can be said is that in this instance the classroom material could not be integrated into or reconciled with the student's expectations for a film made by a great filmmaker.

Such a reading might lead one to assert that alternative approaches to ideal or competent readers are admitting to an absolute uniqueness to every reader or to a relativism of readings.[14] While these are possible positions to take, I would argue that they participate in the "bourgeois mythology of individual freedom" that disregards history and ideology. Just as the text is not "a ceaselessly self-signifying practice, without source or object," neither is the reader or spectator. The student's reading that people who move uniformly are communists did not fall from the heavens; it came from discourses circulating in the social formation in which the student lives. In a study of the film *Rear Window*, Jean Douchet describes the complexity of evaluating the spectator's attitude toward and identification with the L. B. Jeffries (James Stewart) character: "If the reader also remembers that Stewart is first the spectator, he [sic] can conclude that the hero 'invents his own cinema.' But is that not the very definition of a 'voyeur,' the very core of morose gratification?"[15] Whether you consider representing readings as unique or relative to be instances of a "bourgeois mythology" or a "morose gratification," in either case history and language are again neglected. For not all readings are possible at all times.

In the reception studies I would like to see developed, the reader or spectator is recognized as historical and as participating in the circulation of available meanings. *Which spheres of cultural intelligibility* are available to a particular spectator is part of the research area that recognizes the historical and dialogical nature of film viewing. This, then, is the province of reception studies: to describe and explain *historically* the reception of films, genres, movements, "auteurs," and so forth.

II

Elsewhere I have discussed the problems of actually doing historical research on reception without lapsing into empiricism or positivism.[16] Here I would like to argue briefly for a comparative approach as a potentially useful solution to certain difficulties in gathering and interpreting "evidence" of reception. Additionally, it might well be time to define "reception."

Quite frankly, I am not thrilled with the word "reception," but I have not been able to find a better one. "Consumption" smacks too much of merely an economic exchange in the spectator–film relation. Experiences of identification and pleasure (or lack thereof) seem underrepresented in "consumption." Nor is "reader-response research" satisfactory, since that term, because of its association with American criticism, tends to suggest an ideal or unique reader approach. On the other hand, "reception" evokes a well-mannered social function—something not always the case when a film and spectator get together. I have chosen to use it, however, because it already appears so much in the literature and its connections to Jauss's "reception aesthetics" research serve as an important critical link. Indeed, Jauss's seven theses in his "Literary History as a Challenge to Literary Theory" still seem the best jumping off point for what reception studies might become.[17]

Pluralizing the second word in this term seems significant to me as well. Reception studies is not given in the singular because reception studies is not about reading or viewing but reading*s*, institution*s*, historical spectator*s*, ideolog*ies*. The field is concerned with social formations and politics. Because it acknowledges history and considers discourses as social utterances, it cannot construct a theory which would cover all instances, the future having as yet not occurred.

Consequently, a comparative approach to studying receptions has two particular advantages. First of all, it requires actual instances of reception, keeping in touch with the historical and discursive criteria for the field of inquiry. Secondly, comparativist approaches illuminate through differences rather than hypothetical possibilities.[18] One of the major problems with reception studies is gathering "evidence." Every possible bit is tainted by its sources of production and even by the fact that it is still available in a form accessible to the historian. Take, for instance, one of my favorite sources—the film review. For the review to exist it has already acceded to innumerable moments of "secondary revision."[19] It certainly is no direct display of the reviewer's "response" to the film; it capitulates to norms of its genre; its function warps its material. Still, as a text it is as "readable" and available for analysis as any other text via the methods used by critics to study literary texts. In other words, if we can't read a review symptomatically, then we might as well give up the notion of reading any text. Furthermore, if a review is placed into a comparative relation with other reviews generated from analogous circumstances, certain similarities and differences begin to be observable and potentially pertinent.[20] In addition, across time, other characteristics become observable. For instance, norms and conventions of film reviewing become apparent, by contrast, when they are no longer accepted.

In just the briefest of examples, it strikes me as significant that socialist newspapers in the early 1920s reviewed the film *Foolish Wives* in much the same way that capitalist papers did.[21] Attention was given to a plot synopsis, evaluations of acting, questions of verisimilitude, and claims for production value. Any notions of ideological criticism were not yet operating in at least those sources I was able to examine. As a result, I now want to know when Marxist ideological analysis enters the range of possibilities for providing a conscious reading strategy that might promote a "counter" reading to the film's (hypothesized) "intent." Likewise, the very possibility of "resisting" readings or overtly feminist interpretations requires noting when such reading strategies become possible.

To have conscious alternative reading stategies, however, is a different issue from observing through textual analysis variant reactions and interpretations of texts or films, which may not be explainable by formalized alternative reading formations. In fact, oppressed groups may find substitute procedures for appropriating texts to their own purposes. A history of gay (or lesbian or ethnic or racial minority) reception of cinema might require a mixture of gay discourse about cinema which informs gay readings of films, a social subtext in which gay receptions of films operate, and a historical treatment of gay life within dominant or hegemonic culture. Such a history would necessitate treating gay "gossip" and submerged channels of communication as important institutions in constructing the potential for alternative readings.

I have suggested in these above examples at least two specific types of questions that I perceive as within the area of reception studies research: when and how have certain more-or-less formal reading and viewing strategies entered and operated within the sphere of cultural intelligibility, and when and how have oppressed groups understood, rejected, or appropriated texts or films directed at dominant or "mass" groups? In the latter question, instances of riots or cult followings become moments of conjuncture for the historian to analyze and explain. Why *Rock Around the Clock*? Why *Rocky Horror Picture Show*? Why *Chelsea Girls*? Why *Star Trek*?

Another type of question also requires a comparative historical approach. To what degree are receptions of films today comparable to those of earlier years or different cultures? Take, for instance, the five-minute 1905 Biograph film, "Interior N.Y. Subway, 14th Street to 42nd Street," in which angles and movement of the camera result in tricks of depth perception, providing a 1987 viewer with the odd experience of perceiving visual illusions of the depth shifting from three-dimensions to two. Having available modernist notions of surface as meaningful, today's spectator might well wish to place the experience of the film (if not the film itself) within some "visual pleasure" or avant-garde category. Yet was such a perception of visual illusion even possible in experiencing moving pictures in 1905? Was it "unperceivable"? Or if perceived, was it considered a "mistake"? Or perceived but understood as within the norms of cinematography's apparatus? All of these are different considerations of the event than that of a 1987 spectator who might seek such moments in these early films.

From a post-structuralist stance, of course, none of these possibilities is an "error" in perceiving, experiencing, interpreting or judging. Yet from a historical perspective, the researcher in reception studies might wish to make distinctions among these possibilities, particularly if she or he subsequently wishes to claim anything about "causality" for the development of the set of films known as Hollywood or the centering or decentering of a perceiving subject.

A comparative approach could consider "ideolects" of reception across nations (questions of social formations at a large scale); cultural groups (questions of perhaps reified, but socially real and effective, classifications such as race, ethnicity, and class); sexual differences (questions of gender, socialized masculinity and feminity, sexual orientation); political sympathies and beliefs; and popular versus academic procedures. Such a comparative approach would consider these questions diachronically through history as well.

III

I have tried to show why reception studies should be historical and comparative. It would gain much from being critical as well. By this I mean that every choice made in constructing the various versions of readers and spectators has consequences for promoting (or hindering) the possibility of progressive political action. One of my major complaints about the notion of an ideal reader (besides its lack of correspondence with the historical real) is that the effect of such a version of the reader–text or spectator–film relation is to freeze the text or film into having either a singular use-value for all people or a use-value only for its historical moment. In either case, aesthetic appeal and personal interpretation are anesthetized into appropriate, sanctioned versions of reader-response.

The case of the student who "misread" the Odessa Steps sequence is important because it implies pedagogical implications for our research. Reception studies has potential findings that may be useful in understanding how interpretations, value judgments, and ideologies circulate in social formations. The political economy of discourses is part of this research area. If certain moments or some groups evince progressively radical interpretative strategies, the question of what permitted this or supported it or hindered its continuation is one that matters.

Consequently, the researcher investigating questions of reception would do well to take a critical perspective on her or his work. As judgments about texts or films cannot but be made within ideologies, the need for a self-consciousness for reception studies is doubly significant. As an interpreter of interpretations of texts or films, the reception studies researcher can easily find herself or himself beginning to "stand above" it all when she or he is, through the very choice of doing reception studies, operating within the concerns of a historical moment, mobilized by the academy's recent (and privileging) attention to questions of readers. The reception studies researcher ought to remember that if the author is dead, the reception studies researcher as another idealized and free reader is dead as well. Hence a critical stance toward readings and toward reception studies as a field might be a good idea.

NOTES

[1] Roland Barthes, "The Death of the Author" [1968], in *Image-Music-Text*, trans. Stephen Heath (New York: Hill and Wang, 1977) 142–48.

[2] Robert C. Holub, *Reception Theory: A Critical Introduction* (London: Methuen, 1984). Also see: Jane P. Tompkins, ed., *Reader-Response Criticism: From Formalism to Post-Structuralism* (Baltimore: Johns Hopkins University Press, 1980) and Susan R.Suleiman and Inge Crosman, eds., *The Reader in the Text: Essays on Audience and Interpretation* (Princeton: Princeton University Press, 1980). Both anthologies contain excellent bibliographies of nearly everything that might possibly be considered within the range of this notion up to 1980. Since then, at least in the United States, this type of research has occasioned a spurt of publications.

[3] Terry Eagleton, *Criticism and Ideology* [1976] (London: Verso, 1978), 73.

[4] Ferdinand de Saussure, *Course in General Linguistics*, [1915], ed. by Charles Bally and Albert Sechehaye, trans. by Wade Baskin (rpt., New York: McGraw-Hill, 1966), 16. A newer translation results in a different meaning for this passage; however, it has been the Baskin version which would have influenced English-speaking readers. Cf. trans. Roy Harris (La Salle: Open Court, 1986), 15.

[5] Versions of the ideal reader run from some type of undifferentiated human being to a "perfect reader," to the reader of the text at the time of the text's production, to some "normative" reader based on hegemonic culture. This fourth reader might well be in the USA's academy

a male middle- to upper-class heterosexual well educated in western European canonized texts—hence the conscious choice of using "he" as a pronoun in this passage. For an expansion of these issues (and two reactions), see my "The Politics of Film Canons," *Cinema Journal*, 24, no. 3 (Spring 1985), 4–23; Dudley Andrew, "Of Canons and Quietism," *Cinema Journal*, 25, no. 1 (Fall 1985), 55–58; Gerald Mast, "Reply," 59–61; and my reply, 61–64.

[6] Michael Riffaterre, "Describing Poetic Structures: Two Approaches in Baudelaire's 'Les Chats'," [1966] rpt. in *Reader–Response Criticism*, ed. Tompkins, 37.

[7] Jonathan Culler, *Structuralist Poetics: Structuralism, Linguistics, and the Study of Literature* (Ithaca: Cornell University Press, 1975), 113–60.

[8] David Bordwell, *Narration in the Fiction Film* (Madison: University of Wisconsin Press, 1985).

[9] Wolfgang Iser, *The Implied Reader: Patterns of Communication in Prose Fiction from Bunyan to Beckett* [1972] (Baltimore: Johns Hopkins University Press, 1974), 282.

[10] Bordwell argues that he wishes to do away with excessive theoretical baggage, such as a necessary notion of a narrator: "Far better, I think, to give the narrational process the power to signal under certain circumstances that the spectator should construct a narrator. . . . Contrary to what the communication model implies, this sort of narrator does not create the narration; the narration, appealing to historical norms of viewing, creates the narrator" (p. 62). The result of this move is felt, however, in a rhetorical tendency to anthropomorphize the film or narration: "This pattern is set: this film [*Rear Window*] will encourage us to construct a story on the basis of visual information (objects, behavior) and then confirm or disconfirm that construction through verbal comment" (p. 41). "Here the narration's closer framings do not try to bamboozle us" (p. 45). Competent readers bow to the authority of the film (or figure out its tricks). "Every film trains its spectator" (p. 45).

[11] This emphasis on social and political formations is not meant to exclude the importance of psychic formations. Instead, that which permits observing and categorizing a set of material effects as a "social formation" surely includes the psychic, political, juridical, economic, and cultural.

[12] Tony Bennett, "Text and Social Process: The Case of James Bond," *Screen Education*, no. 41 (Winter/Spring 1982), 3.

[13] Unidentified student's exam paper quoted by Sara McLennan, "History/Culture/Ideology: The Reading Process and its Determinants," New York University Seminar paper, Fall 1984.

[14] In some ways this aligns with versions of deconstructionism without a radical politics.

15 Jean Douchet, "Hitch and His Public," (1960), trans. Verena Conley, rpt. in *A Hitchcock Reader*, ed. Marshall Deutelbaum and Leland Pogue (Ames: Iowa State University Press, 1986) 10.

16 See my " 'The Handmaiden of Villainy': Methods and Problems in Studying the Historical Reception of a Film," *Wide Angle*, 8, no. 1 (1986), 19–27, and "This Moving Image I Have Before me," in *The Historian and the Moving-Image*, ed. John O'Connor (forthcoming).

17 Hans Robert Jauss, "Literary History as a Challenge to Literary Theory," [1970], trans. Timothy Bahti, rpt. in *Toward an Aesthetic of Reception* (Minneapolis: University of Minnesota Press, 1982), 3–45. Jauss is particularly good in considering the historical development of the reception of texts but he only acknowledges in passing the possibility of variations among readers at any historical moment.

18 This should not be confused with the concept in structural linguistics of binary oppositions as constituting meaning, along with the dangers of such a static and idealist theory of semantics. Differences do not have to run to the number of two.

19 The use of this term should be understood both literally and figuratively. That is, I am assuming a review (as would any text) has been distorted by psychoanalytical processes. In addition, other subconscious and conscious factors have participated in its formation.

20 The issue of reference could be raised: that is, to what extent can any semiotic text refer to the historical real? Here I am merely going to assert that I believe that some representations are more politically progressive than others and, as long as those representations abide by currently agreed to versions of facts about the historical real, I prefer those representations. In other words, as long as the "facts" are not disputed, representations that work to outline exploitation and structures of power are prefered to those that do not. Scope and elegance of representation are also valued, but only secondarily.

21 " 'The Handmaiden of Villainy.' "

HISTORICAL POETICS OF CINEMA

David Bordwell

INTRODUCTION

The volume you hold in your hands belongs to a genre that came into currency during the postwar boom in college literary criticism. In the late 1940s, two major works, Wellek and Warren's *Theory of Literature* and Stanley Edgar Hyman's *The Armed Vision*, set forth the premise that literary studies played host to distinct "methods."[1] Intrinsic/ extrinsic; textual/ contextual; sociological/ psychological/ Marxist/ psychoanalytic/ archetypal/ formalist/ deconstructionist/ reader-responsiveness: as such categories have accumulated over the last forty years, many members of the literary institution have believed themselves to be moving beyond the doctrines of New Criticism. While the field was being carved up methodically, the "anthology of approaches" moved into the library and the classroom. The genre became a going concern in the 1950s and 1960s, and it continues to flourish.[2] The present book reminds us that film studies has, as part of its entry into the academy, come to subscribe to such critical Methodism—an affiliation testified to by the title of one of the most popular anthologies, *Movies and Methods*.[3] A recent collection of approaches to television criticism may signal the legitimation of TV studies under the same auspices.[4]

There would be much to remark on in this process, not least the extent to which film and television studies may seek to establish their seriousness by asserting that, whatever the intrinsic importance of the object of study, a set of up-to-date approaches constitutes adequate credentials. But I sketch this institutional background for another reason: to establish that historical poetics does not grow organically out of this history, and this for a very good reason. What I shall be discussing is not a method at all.

In film studies, as in its literary counterpart, "method" has been largely synonymous with "interpretive school." An interpretive school, I take it, consists chiefly of: (a) a semantic field with which particular theoretical concepts are associated; (b) a set of inferential procedures that render certain features of films salient and significant on *a priori* grounds; (c) one or more conceptual maps of textual progression across which salient features enact a transformation of the semantic field; (d) a set of characteristic rhetorical tactics for setting forth the writer's argument. For example, the psychoanalytic critic posits a semantic field (e.g., male/ female, or self/ other, or sadism/ masochism) with associated concepts (e.g., the deployment of power around sexual difference); concentrates on textual cues that can bear the weight of the semantic *differentiae* (e.g., narrative roles, the act of looking); traces a drama of semantic transformation (e.g., through condensation and displacement the subject finds identity in the Symbolic); and deploys a rhetoric that seeks to gain the reader's assent to the interpretation's conclusions (e.g., a rhetoric of demystification). Every recognized "method"—phenomenological, feminist, Marxist, or whatever—can be described along these lines. They all aim to produce interpretations—that is, the ascription of implicit or symptomatic meanings to texts.[5]

A historical poetics of cinema does not fit this description. It does not constitute a distinct critical school; it has no privileged semantic field, no core of procedures for identifying or interpreting textual features, no map of the flow of meaning, and no unique rhetorical tactics. It does not seek to produce interpretations. What, then, does it do?

I. POETICS AND HISTORICAL POETICS

Aristotle's fragmentary lecture notes, the *Poetics*, addressed what we nowadays recognize as drama and literature. Since his day we have had Stravinsky's *Poetics of Music*, Todorov's *Poetics of Prose*, a study of the poetics of architecture, and of course the Russian Formalists' *Poetics of the Cinema*.[6] Such extensions of the concept are plausible, since it need not be restricted to any particular medium. "Poetics" derives from the Greek word *poiêsis*, or *active making*. The poetics of any medium studies the finished work as the result of a process of construction—a process which includes a craft component (e.g., rules of thumb), the more general principles according to which the work is composed, and its functions, effects, and uses. Any inquiry into the fundamental principles by which a work in any representational medium is constructed can fall within the domain of poetics.

By adding the predicate "historical" I mean to narrow the field somewhat. Poetics of literature has long been the province of sterile taxonomies and dogmatic prescriptions. In the twentieth century, German-language art studies and Slavic literary theory laid the groundwork for a historical poetics. Heinrich Wölfflin, Alois Riegl, Erwin Panofsky, and later E. H. Gombrich showed how one could systematically describe forms and styles in painging and go on to explain their changes causally.[7] The Russian Formalists—most notably Viktor Shklovsky, Yuri Tynianov, Boris Eikhenbaum, and Roman Jakobson—and the Prague Structuralists—e.g., Jan Mukařovský and (again) Jakobson—proposed both concrete analyses of literary works and larger explanations for how they functioned in historical contexts.[8] This tradition has been alive in film studies as well, crossing periods and doctrinal schools and recently emerging as a significant force in academic work.

A historical poetics of cinema produces knowledge in answer to two broad questions:

1. What are the principles according to which films are constructed and by means of which they achieve particular effects?
2. How and why have these principles arisen and changed in particular empirical circumstances?

Historical poetics is thus characterized by the phenomena it studies—films' constructional principles and effects—and the questions it asks about those phenomena—their constitution, functions, consequences, and historical manifestations. Poetics does not put at the forefront of its activities phenomena such as the economic patterns of film distribution, the growth of the teenage audience, or the ideology of private property. The poetician may need to investigate such matters, and indeed many others, but they become relevant only in the light of more properly poetic issues. Underlying this hierarchy of significance is the assumption that, while in our world everything is connected to everything else, one can produce novel and precise knowledge only by making distinctions among core questions, peripheral questions, and irrelevant questions.[9]

André Bazin's "Evolution of the Language of the Cinema" can illustrate how a project within historical poetics works. The essay relies upon some fundamental conceptual distinctions, such as inter-shot effects vs. intra-shot effects, types of montage, distortion vs. fidelity, spatiotemporal unity vs. discontinuity, shallow space vs. depth. Bazin holds these to be principles determining the stylistic construction of any film whatsoever. They yield categories which permit the analyst to correlate devices with particular effects—e.g., a linearization of meaning with "visible" montage versus a more natural conveyance of meaning through Welles' or Wyler's depth of field. Furthermore, Bazin offers a historical account which employs these categories to trace the development of Western cinema from primitive filmmaking to Neorealism. Bazin argues for a dialectical movement whereby the struggle between a realistic style and a more distorted style reached a compromise in the Hollywood decoupage of the 1930s, and then was transcended by a new synthesis in the deep-focus style.

While Bazin's remains the most influential history of film style currently available, I am not here concerned with the persuasiveness of his argument; the point is to show how the essay exemplifies the possibilities of a poetics. For one thing, it self-consciously constructs its analytical categories while also referring to a range of data by which the arguments can be assessed. Bazin supplies concrete historical evidence that subjects his claims to revision or rejection. This appeal to empirical evidence, or "facts," does not make poetics an "empiricism," at least, in any interesting sense of that term. A poetics can be rationalist or empiricist, Kantian or phenomenological, deductivist or inductivist, idealist (as Bazin probably was) or positivist (as Barry Salt seems to be).[10] Insofar as a poetics seeks to explain historically existing works, whatever its ontology or epistemology or discovery procedures, it requires an appeal to intersubjectively accepted data which are in principle amenable to alternative explanation. Just as in the philosophy of language, a Chomskyan nativist must confront the fact that people seem to acquire significant aspects of language through experience, so even the post-structuralist film theorist must recognize the existence of apparent motion or characterization or editing. Every enterprise within film study necessarily draws upon facts in this sense. Whether such facts are "socially constructed" is an open question. (Indeed, it is partly an *empirical* question.)

Bazin's "Evolution" essay also illustrates the extent to which a poetics takes as its object a body of *conventions*. Conventions, in film as in other domains, lie at the intersection of logical distinctions and social customs. Admittedly, Bazin's realist aesthetic leads him to range stylistic devices along a continuum whereby some are less "conventional" than others. Nevertheless, he is studying constructive choices which have collectively recognized functions within definable contexts; editing and deep-focus, he argues, constitute reciprocal choices in the history of Western cinema.[11] These conventions can be regarded as leading to preferred choices—that is, norms or rules, two more concepts valuable for a poetics.

Bazin's essay exemplifies still other aspects of a cinematic poetics. He refuses a division of labor among theory, history, and criticism; the essay is all three at once. It mixes intensive scrutiny with extensive viewing. Bazin considers both "texts" and "contexts" (technology, genre). He offers descriptions, analyses, and explanations: he seeks to establish *what* happened, *how* it happened, and *why* it happened. Finally, Bazin presupposes that the phenomena he studies are the results of filmmakers' choices. (Welles could have cut *Citizen Kane* as if it had been *It Happened One Night*.) A historical poetics will thus often be concerned to reconstruct the options facing a filmmaker at a given historical juncture, assuming that the filmmaker chooses an option in order to achieve some end.

My initial questions and my exposition of Bazin should raise several questions. What, for example, is the status of the "principles" studied by poetics? At what level of generality are they pitched? Are they conceived as "specific" to cinema in some sense? My replies here must be brief. I would argue that the principles should be conceived as underlying concepts, constitutive and/or regulative, governing the sorts of material that can be used in a film and the possible ways in which it can be formed. The degree of generality will depend upon the questions asked and the phenomena to be studied. If you want to know what makes Hollywood narratives cohere, "personalized causality" may suffice as one constructive principle; if you want to know what distinguishes the Western from the musical, that principle will not do the job. For some poeticians, some principles are held to be "laws" on the model of covering laws in physical science; but one need not push this far. One could assert that a concept or category—e.g., intra-shot/ inter-shot relations—is conceptually stable, but that the constructive principles that utilize it are so historically variable that they constitute empirical generalizations or tendencies.

On the matter of specificity, suffice it to say that although certain poeticians have assumed a distinction between the cinematic and the non-cinematic, this is by no means constitutive of poetics as such. One could assume that any film could be studied by poetics, with no film lying any closer to the essence of the medium than others. One could, however, argue that the distinction is not a substantive but a functional one, to be filled out in different periods with different content. Or one could use the cinematic/ non-cinematic distinction in an explanation by seeking to show that in particular circumstances this pair of concepts entered into the norms of filmmaking practice.

Since poetics is often assumed to be merely a descriptive or classificatory enterprise, the range of explanations it offers also requires some elaboration. There is no need to assume any one model of causation and change. Bazin argues for a suprapersonal dialectic through which cinema evolves toward an ever more faithful capturing of phenomenal reality. This is a *teleological* explanation. One could also propose an *intentionalistic* model that centers on more localized acts of choice and avoidance. Two collaborators and I have argued for a *functionalist* model of explanation, whereby the institutional dynamics of filmmaking set up constraints and preferred options that fulfill overall systemic norms.[12]

Nor need poetics confine itself to "immanent" explanations that refuse to leave the field of cinema or art or signifying practice. Nothing prevents the poetician from arguing that economics, ideology, the class struggle, or inherent social or psychological dispositions operate as causes of constructional devices or effects. There is likewise no need to cast poetics as offering "scientific" explanations (although, again, some poeticians have done so). Poetics has the explanatory value of any empirical discipline, which always involves a degree of tentativeness about conclusions. On the other hand, one should not discard "scientific" pretensions too quickly, since there are many sorts of science, such as geography and meteorology, which are low in predictive power but high in *ex post facto* explanatory power. Poetics can, in short, be considered either as a science offering knowledge in some strict sense, or as a discipline that aims at *Verstehen*, or "understanding."

Finally, explanation in poetics does not confine itself to issues of what films mean. Of course, meaning in one (very general) sense comprises a big part of what poetics describes, analyzes, and explains; but meaning in the more specific sense that is the product of film interpretation ("readings") can be considered only one domain of inquiry. Films produce many effects, ranging from perceptual ones (e.g., the phenomenon of apparent motion, the perception of color or shape) to conceptual ones (e.g., how we know that X is the protagonist) that film interpretation never seeks to explain. Historical poetics offers *explanations*, not *explications*. In the modern critical institution, of course, explications need explaining.

II. DOMAINS AND TENDENCIES

The core questions of poetics have led to the formulation of distinct domains and tendencies within the field. Traditional poetics distinguishes among three objects of study:

A. *Thematics* considers subject matter and theme as components of the constructive process. Not every study of such matters qualifies as a contribution to poetics, since many such studies are unconcerned with films' constructive principles; the film may be ransacked for discrete items of "content" (e.g., the representation of social stereotypes) which are then used to answer questions about, say, the film industry or cultural values. Thematics would study motifs, iconography, and themes as materials, as constructive principles, or as effects of constructive principles. For example, several scholars have revealed how genres present recurring imagery, myths, and themes, while other writers, inspired by art-historical research, have shown the importance of iconography in popular cinema.[13]

B. *Constructional form.* We lack a term for those trans-media architectonic principles that govern the shape and dynamics of a film. The most prominent research domain here is the theory and analysis of narrative, which is a fundamental constructive principle in films.[14] Current interest in this subject should not, however, lead to a neglect of other compositional principles, such as argumentative form, categorical form, associational form, and abstract form.[15]

C. *Stylistics* deals with the materials and patterning of the film medium as components of the constructive process. Bazin's "Evolution" essay is a model of stylistic history.

We could carve up the domain of historical poetics in still other ways. Following R. S. Crane, we could distinguish studies of *precompositional* factors (sources, influences, clichés, received forms) from *compositional* ones (normalized principles of combination and transformation within works) and from *postcompositional* ones (effects, reception, varying responses in different contexts).[16] For example, Noël Burch's *To the Distant Observer* treats Japanese cinema as the legatee of stylistic practices from earlier centuries, while Vance Kepley's *In the Service of the State*, using a different precompositional focus, traces more proximate influences on Dovzhenko's films.[17] The work of Charles Musser, Tom Gunning, and André Gaudreault has demonstrated that pre-1915 films obey coherent compositional norms.[18] And recent work in reception by Janet Staiger (also represented in this volume) has revealed how audiences' varying construals of the same film presuppose historically variable viewing conventions.[19] In my own studies of Dreyer and Ozu, I have tried to relate the three domains by suggesting historically determinate gaps among them. In the works of Ozu, for instance, source material and contemporary conventions are transformed by specific compositional procedures, but the results have been appropriated differently by various audiences.[20]

Recognizing that linguistic analogies are notoriously shaky in film studies, I will risk one more mapping of the field. Like linguistics, film poetics has its "semantics," the study of how meaning is produced. It has its "syntactics," the study of rules for selecting and combining units (with respect to style, Raymond Bellour's microanalyses; with respect to compositional form, Thierry Kuntzel's study of openings, Peter Wollen's applications of Propp, or Rick Altman's "dual-focus" narrative).[21] And poetics has its "pragmatics," the study of how relations between viewer and text develop in the process of the film's unfolding (e.g., accounts of narration or of filmic "enunciation").[22] Meaning, structure, and process—these three aspects of any representational system are also central to poetics.

These equable mappings of the terrain conceal, of course, how much territory is in dispute. I have already suggested several issues about which poeticians wrangle; two more divergences seem to me worth brief discussion.

Across history, poetics has had to steer a course between strictly "immanent" accounts and strictly "subsumptive" ones. Few poeticians have been willing to accept the consequences of an utterly intrinsic account of constructional processes; even Wölfflin, mistakenly treated as the model of the pure formalist, explained changes in artistic styles partly by changes in a culture's visual habits.[23] On the other side, very few poeticians have sought to account for every phenomenon by appeal to processes in other social domains; even the Zhdanovite recognizes some special quality in art. For most poeticians, the constructional principles studied are not self-sealed, but they are also not in every respect subsumable to other principles. Assuming that the escape hatch of "relative autonomy" is of no help, we can distinguish two tendencies within poetics. One tendency hypothesizes that the phenomenon we study has a considerable degree of self-regulated coherence. The early Shklovsky seems to hold this view; he seeks to explain the laws of fairy tale composition by purely poetic principles like repetition, retardation, and so forth.[24] He gives *theoretical* priority to such factors. In film poetics, perhaps Burch's *Theory of Film Practice* approaches this position. The second tendency, articulated by the later Russian Formalists and the Prague Structuralists, gives immanent factors only a *methodological* priority. For example, as Tynianov and Jakobson point out, even if the immanent evolution of literature can explain the direction of change, it cannot explain *timing*, which must be governed by extra-literary causes.[25] A comparable position is taken by Staiger, Thompson, and myself in studying the history of the classical Hollywood cinema.[26] Here the analyst looks first to the "immanent" factors that might be the most proximate and pertinent causal factors, but also assumes that virtually every explanatory task will require moving to those mediations that lie in "adjacent" domains.

To continue the geographical metaphor, poetics is less a field with distinct boundaries than a kind of Alsace-Lorraine constantly being claimed by interested neighbors. On one side is Aesthetics, which, in the eighteenth century, replaced the study of poetic *praxis* with a concern for the philosophical problems involved in the creation and appreciation of beauty. On another side lies Semiotics, which seeks to subsume poetics into a general theory of the production of meaning. Interestingly, poeticians have been drafted into both camps. Aristotle, the Russian Formalists, and the Prague Structuralists can play roles in the history of aesthetics, as in Beardsley's survey history, or they can be promoted to the rank of proto-semioticians, as with Peter Steiner.[27]

In my view, the tension between semiotic approach and the aesthetic one has been immensely fruitful. There remains, however, a core of questions and issues that cannot be wholly absorbed into the adjacent areas. It is useful to differentiate between the *practical theory* of an art and the *philosophy* of it. The "practical theory" of music or poetry, for instance rests upon *a posteriori* questions, involving empirical generalizations about conventions and practices in these arts. From this perspective, film poetics is a systematizing of theoretical inquiry into cinematic practices as they have existed. The philosophy of an art, on the other hand, inquires into its *a priori* aspects; it involves conceptual analysis of the art's logical nature and functions. On the whole, aesthetics concentrates upon such matters.[28] As for semiotics, it concentrates on matters of meaning, which is only part of the effects for which a poetics seeks to account; on the other hand, if semiotics seeks to explain "the life of signs in society," it encompasses far more than any poetics can. Yet one should not discourage border crossings; if Barthes' *S/Z* offers a semiotics and Goodman's *Languages of Art* offers an aesthetics, both are splendid contributions to poetics.

III. NEOFORMALISM

One trend within the domain of historical poetics has been dubbed by Kristin Thompson "neoformalism." It is associated with research she and I have done over the past dozen years or so. The trend derives principally from Slavic poetics, particular the Russian and Czech thinkers, but it is also influenced by the more or less oblique "return to Slavic theory" one finds in Todorov, Genette, the 1966–1970 Barthes, and contemporary Israeli poeticians like Meir Sternberg. It draws heavily upon the writings of Bazin, the Soviet filmmakers, and Burch, without being committed to a "phenomenological" or "materialist" or "serialist" theory of film. In fact, neoformalism is not a theory of film at all, if we take that to consist of a set of propositions explaining the fundamental nature and function of all cinematic phenomena.

Neoformalism has even less in common with what has been called "Grand Theory," that development in the humanities that has embraced ever more wide-ranging intellectual programs.[29] Under these auspices, the study of film has become "only a part" of the theory of ideology or of sexual difference or, most abstractly, of "the human subject." The principal issue here is not whether there is something "inherently filmic" that must be addressed, for, as mentioned above, the specificity of cinema may be conceived as more social and functional than substantive. The point is that concepts constructed at this level of generality and abstraction are not well suited to answering questions pitched at lower levels. Neoformalism, which addresses the latter sort of questions, is thus not a general theory of film, let alone a Grand one.

Nor is it, once again, a method. It is a set of assumptions, an angle of heuristic approach, and a way of asking questions.[30] It is frankly empirical and places great emphasis on the discovery of facts about films. Since recent film theory usually claps the word "fact" within sneer-quotes, my claim is apt to seem a recourse to naive empiricism; but this conclusion, already jumped to by one writer,[31] is itself naive. As I indicated above, any poetics—indeed, any descriptive or explanatory project—is committed to some grounding in intersubjective data. Furthermore, one can consider a fact to be an accepted claim about what there is in the world, *including theoretical or unobservable entities*—something that positivism rules out. Moreover, there is no question of letting the facts speak for themselves. Neoformalism presumes that one cannot discover factual answers to questions about films' construction without carefully devising analytical concepts appropriate to these questions. But it also assumes that not all concepts are equally precise, coherent, or pertinent, and so we may evaluate competing conceptual schemes; it also assumes that not all concepts explain the data with equal clarity, richness, and economy; and, crucially, it assumes that we are not complete prisoners of our conceptual schemes, that we may so construct them that anomalous and exceptional phenomena are not invisible but actually leap to our notice. In sum, neoformalist poetics makes theoretically defined, open-ended, corrigible, and falsifiable claims.

This is a direct result of its not being a general theory of film. If

I am bent on substantiating the belief that every film constructs an ongoing process of "subject positioning" for the spectator, nothing I find in a film will disconfirm it. Given the roomy interpretive procedures of film criticism, I can treat every cut or camera movement, every line of dialogue or piece of character behavior, as a reinforcement of subject positioning. The theory thus becomes vacuous, since any theory that explains every phenomenon by the same mechanism explains nothing. On the other hand, I can ask how Hollywood films secure unity among successive scenes, and answer with something more concrete—say, that one scene often ends with an unresolved causal sub-chain that is soon resolved in the following scene. Here I have said something that is informative: it is not self-evident, it is not discoverable by deduction from a set of premises, and it is fruitful, leading to further questions. (Does this suggest some hypotheses about the nature of narrational norms in Hollywood? Do films in other filmmaking traditions utilize more self-contained episodes?) Most important, the answer I supply is empirically disconfirmable. If it *is* disconfirmed, I need to rethink the data and indeed, the question itself. Shklovsky's counsel of skepticism should be our guide: "If the facts destroy the theory—so much the better for the theory. It is created by us, not entrusted to us for safekeeping."[32] Neoformalism's hypotheses are grounded in a theoretical *activity* rather than a fixed theory. This theorizing moves across various levels of generality and deploys various concepts and categories. It does not presume global propositions to which the researcher pledges unswerving allegiance and which automatically block our noticing recalcitrant data.

In being question-centered and focused on particular phenomena, neoformalism does resemble the practices of science as many theorists are coming to understand them. Stephen Jay Gould writes:

> Progress in science, paradoxically by the layman's criterion, often demands that we back away from cosmic questions of greatest scope (anyone with half a brain can formulate 'big' questions in his armchair, so why heap kudos on such a pleasant and pedestrian activity?). Great scientists have an instinct for the fruitful and the doable, particularly for smaller questions that lead on and eventually transform the grand issues from speculation to action. . . . Great theories must sink a huge anchor in details.[33]

This is not to grant neoformalism the status of a science, only to suggest that, as compared with Grand Theory, its approach and spirit are closer to certain scientific practices. It is in this frame of reference we can best understand Boris Eikhenbaum's defense of the Russian Formalist group:

> In our studies we value a theory only as a working hypothesis to help us discover and interpret facts; that is, we determine the validity of the facts and use them as the material of our research. We are not concerned with definitions, for which the late-comers thirst; nor do we build general theories, which so delight eclectics. We posit specific principles and adhere to them insofar as the material justifies them. If the material demands their refinement or change, we change or refine them.[34]

With no set point of arrival, committed to no *a priori* conclusions, seeking to answer precisely posed question with concepts that will be refined through encounter with data, neoformalism deploys "hollow" categories. While the "Oedipal trajectory" and "looking equals power" carry interpretable meaning whenever they appear, other concepts mark out fundamental constructive principles that have effects but not *a priori* meanings. An instance of such a "hollow" principle is that of norms. The neoformalist assumes that every film may be placed in relation to sets of transtextual norms. These operate at various levels of generality and possess various degrees of coherence. For instance, in most studio-made narrative films, the credits sequence characteristically occurs before the first scene, but it may also, as a lesser option, occur after a "pre-credits sequence." Such norms, while "codified," are not reducible to *codes* in the semiotic sense, since there is no fixed meaning attached to one choice rather than the other. And no particular meaning automatically proceeds from Godard's decision, in *Détective*, to salt the credits throughout the first several scenes.

A great deal of theorizing about norms remains to be done. (Are there, for instance, fruitful distinctions among convention, norm, and rule?) But even at this stage neoformalist poetics has put forward fairly detailed and comprehensive accounts of norms of narration and style in Hollywood cinema, "art cinema," Soviet montage cinema, and other modes.[35] These are not definitive analyses; they are attempts to chart the range of constructional options open to filmmakers at various historical conjunctures, and the results are always open to revision. At this point, however, several analytical concepts seem well founded. For example, Neoformalist poetics has established the usefulness of distinguishing between stylistic or narrative *devices* (e.g., the cut or the motif) and *systems* (e.g., spatial continuity or narrative causality) within which they achieve various *functions*. Establishing a unified locale is a function which different devices and different systems have fulfilled in various ways across history. But even this function is not historically invariant. (Some norms do not make unity of locale a salient feature.) In practical research terms, neoformalism's emphasis on historically changing norms, devices, systems, and functions requires that the analyst complement the scrutiny of single films with the study of a wide range of films.

An orientation toward transtextual norms allows the analyst to be sensitive to the abnormal. Neoformalist poetics has been especially interested in how, against a background of conventions, a film or a director's work stands out. Kristin Thompson has been concerned to demonstrate how the works of Eisenstein, Ozu, Tati, Godard, Renoir, and others provide not wayward deviations from norms but rather systematic innovations in thematic, stylistic, and narrative construction. Neoformalism balances a concern for revealing the tacit conventions governing the ordinary film with a keen interest in the bizarre film that, subtly or flagrantly, challenges them. Accordingly, new concepts will often have to be forged. To account for Ozu's editing, Thompson and I had to propose the concept of the "graphic match" and to spell out how Ozu's across-the-line shot/ reverse- shots do not sporadically transgress rules but rather achieve perceptual functions within a larger, idiosyncratic system of 360-degree space.[36]

The construction of concepts in accord with empirical data leads to historical explanations for the phenomena in question. Neoformalist poetics has relied upon three explanatory schemes, adjusted to cases at hand: a *rational-agent* model, an *institutional* model, and a *perceptual-cognitive* model. The first follows from the concept of the filmmaker's choosing among constructional options. Here the task becomes that of reconstructing, on the basis of whatever historical data one can find, the choice situation which the filmmaker confronts. This is not to say, however, that the filmmaker becomes the sole source of the film's construction and effects.

The institutional dimension—most proximately, the social and economic system of filmmaking, involving tacit aesthetic assumptions, the division of labor, and technological procedures—forms the horizon of what is permitted or encouraged at particular moments. It is not just that the filmmaker's choices are *constrained*; they are actively constituted in large part by socially structured factors. In the Hollywood studio system of the 1920s and 1930s, for instance, the continuity script not only became a way to rationalize production but also encouraged workers to think of a film as assemblage out of discrete bits (shots, scenes), and the individual filmmaker found choices and opportunities structured accordingly.[37] By the same token, an institution-centered conception would seem the most promising basis for the study of how spectators use appropriate films in different historical contexts (though I would argue that the "microfoundations" of such a study would have to include some rational-agent assumptions).

Most recently, a perceptual-cognitive model has been used to describe and explain the effects of various constructional tactics. I have proposed that a Constructivist theory of psychological activity yields the most discriminating and detailed explanation of such narrational principles as syuzhet/fabula construction and such stylistic processes as continuity editing.[38] In a work in progress, I consider how the routine practices of film interpretation can be partly explained through principles of inference and problem-solving set forth by cognitive theory. In all cases, the models are not absolute; the neoformalist poetician does not treat individual phenomena as instantiating laws but rather as demanding an inferential argument "to the best explanation," which always remains in principle corrigible.

Some discussions of Godard's *Sauve qui peut (la vie)* provide a convenient contrast with advantages offered by the neoformalist approach. For example, in his review of the film, Colin MacCabe follows the conventional journalistic format: teaser (description of the notorious "sex-machine" scene), one-paragraph plot synopsis, background on Godard's career (over a page), mention of themes (town vs. country, prostitution, masculine vs. feminine), discussion of "form" (the image track dominates the soundtrack), reflections on the author as person (Godard's dissatisfaction with the familiar "economic and aesthetic constraints," as confided to MacCabe), and a final, unexplained invocation of "the exhilaration of actually watching the movie."[39] As in his contemporaneous book on Godard, MacCabe's discussion relies upon a straightforward thematics (Godard's fetishization of woman) and an "empty" formalism (e.g., the celebration, in all contexts, of moments when sound dominates image).

Or, to take a more substantial example, consider the articles on

Sauve qui peut (la vie) gathered in *Camera Obscura*. Although more detailed than MacCabe's, they are plagued by errors of description; several also make some questionable assumptions (e.g., that the protagonist Paul Godard stands for the director, or that all cuts "cannot be seen"[40]). One essay, by perhaps the most influential textual analyst, describes the film's editing this way:

> The images seem to hit each other, musically, pictorially, striking each other admirably and thus making impossible any continuity of movement which would produce, the moment it is a question of bodies and of the sexes, an imaginary ideality that has simply ceased to exist.[41]

It must be recalled that 1970s film theory never tired of attacking exactly such writing as "impressionistic."

In its commitment to explaining difficult films precisely, neoformalist poetics offers signal advantages. Kristin Thompson's lengthy analysis of *Sauve qui peut (la vie)*[42] sets out to answer some specific questions: what makes the film so complex, and how and why have critics made it seem far simpler than it is? She situates the film within an institutional context, that of the promotion of a new, apolitical, "accessible" Godard. She goes on to show how the recurrence of characteristic themes (e.g., prostitution) and attitudes (e.g., misogyny) lent the film an easy recognition along the lines that MacCabe in fact took. She argues that Godard deliberately solicits art-cinema comprehension strategies, of exactly the kind that the *Camera Obscura* writers employ (without displaying any awareness of those *as* normalized strategies). Thompson goes on to reveal how gaps and dislocations in the syuzhet prompt such thematizing. In place of MacCabe's hackneyed country/ city opposition, Thompson shows that the film employs a continuum of settings: a city, a town, a village, a farm, and the countryside. Instead of a plot synopsis, Thompson offers a segmentation that points up the temporal construction of the syuzhet. Rather than positing a form and a content, Thompson argues that the film transforms its thematic material by means of an overall organization of parallel parts which compare different characters. Having established all these macrostructural factors, Thompson is able to explain functionally what most critics ignore or interpret atomistically: the stop-motion sequences that interrupt the film and (contra MacCabe) the insistent and ambiguous organization of sounds. It is not just that Thompson's analysis of narrative, narration, and style has a finesse not approached by any other discussion. The real point is the range and depth of the conceptual scheme she employs. Neo-formalist poetics, while concentrating on historical context, narrative form, and cinematic style, does not exclude thematic interpretations. It absorbs them into a dynamic system—here, one that reveals why discrete meanings can be the bait at which critics will snap, and how a clever filmmaker has set the trap for them. Historical poetics, in its concern for constructional effects, thereby comes to include the study of the conventions of film criticism itself.

IV. GRAND THEORY, SLAB THEORY, AND POETICS

Although Grand Theory and historical poetics operate at different levels of generality, they invite comparison, if only because most people studying film have been influenced by one particular version of the former. This version treats cinema study as an instance of the study of the "human subject," employing tenets based upon Saussurean semiotics, Lacanian psychoanalysis, Althusserian Marxism, and Barthesian textual theory. I shall therefore call this version, acronymically and a little acrimoniously, SLAB theory.[43] SLAB theory is most clearly identified with the main current of work in *Cahiers du cinéma* during the early 1970s and *Screen* later in the decade. It is handily codified in Rosalind Coward and John Ellis' *Language and Materialism*. Most subsequent survey texts, such as Dudley Andrew's *Concepts of Film Theory* and Kaja Silverman's *Subject of Semiotics*, treat this trend as central to contemporary film studies. Although SLAB theory is subject to internal revision,[44] and although it now seems close to a skirmish on its left flank with the burgeoning area called "cultural studies," I shall treat it as the mainstream position within film theory at present. I am not here concerned with laying out conceptual problems in SLAB theory as such, only with contrasting its intellectual *modus operandi*—its methods, if you like—with the aims of a historical poetics.

A. Whereas poetics is problem- and question-centered, SLAB theory is doctrine-centered.

SLAB theorists assume that they possess a general theory of social and psychic life which can subsume cinematic phenomena under broader laws. But this theory constitutes an *ad hoc* assemblage of pieces from various thinkers' works: some chunks of Lacan, a little of Althusser, etc. Hence Jonathan Rée's description—the *nouveau mélange*.[45] The effect is most clearly seen in those syntheses or textbooks that cut up pieces of doctrine and then provide an exposition that patches them together.

Likewise, SLAB theory changes by adding on new pieces of doctrine. The fact that one bit of any thinker's work can always be linked, somehow, with a bit of any other's underwrites the project of theory as *bricolage*. The absorption of a few terms from the Christian, anti-Freudian, and neo-Kantian Mikhail Bakhtin into psychoanalytic, feminist, culturalist, and orthodox lit-crit "methods" is only the most recent example.[46] Even a single word can trigger the bricolage impulse. Teresa de Lauretis finds that both the physiologist Colin Blakemore and the semiotician Umberto Eco use the term "mapping." She concludes from this that both theorists' works support the idea that "perception and signification are neither direct or simple reproduction (copy, mimesis, reflection) nor inevitably predetermined by biology, anatomy, or destiny; though they are socially determined and overdetermined."[47] This is an unwarranted inference from Blakemore's discussion, which stresses physiological invariants and evolutionary adaptation; a commitment to the social over-determination of perception is hard to square with Blakemore's assertion: "Human perception depends ultimately on activity within the nerve centers of the brain."[48] De Lauretis might reply that even if Blakemore does not believe in the social construction of perception, his evidence supports it. But then one could counter that he has marshalled the bulk of his evidence, which she does not examine, to demonstrate exactly the opposite position, which she denounces but does not attempt to refute.

It is thus not surprising that challenges to SLAB theory are typically cast in the form "My Continental thinker can lick yours": Deleuze against Lacan, Benjamin against Althusser, Frankfurt versus Paris. Since doctrines age faster than ideas, there emerges an urge to stay on the cutting edge. How the SLAB theorist does so is, again, most clearly seen in the summarizing texts. Here the author functions as a tipster, assuming that having the most recent word in a debate means having the last word on the subject. In a review of *Language and Materialism*, Rée described many kindred efforts:

In fact most of Coward and Ellis' fallacies are of a slightly different kind: they involve not so much referring to a particular authority, as watching the ways in which the currents of opinion are flowing: a kind of punting on what future authorities will say, based on ideas of what can be "seen" and seen "only now."[49]

In its grim determination to keep abreast, SLAB theory reveals its only open-ended side: almost anything may become grist for the doctrinal mill.

B. Poetics, in its contemporary form, conducts systematic research; SLAB theory does not.

Systematic research consists of posing questions, reflecting on the historical factors that lead to the questions' becoming salient, broaching alternative answers, and weighing them in the light of evidence; it also presents arguments that seek to demonstrate that some answers are better than others. By these canons, SLAB theory does not constitute systematic research.

As a rule, SLAB theory does not ask particular questions and reason out possible answers, rejecting and refining them and weighing the comparative advantages of competing explanatory frameworks. The writer instead starts with a doctrinal abstraction and draws on cinematic phenomena as *illustrative examples*. Thus Silverman's *Subject of Semiotics* employs filmic and literary texts as audio-visual aids in laying out claims about the Oedipus complex or condensation and displacement; she does not, by and large, cite evidence that would establish the claims as holding good about general human phenomena of the sort that the theory aspires to explain.[50] Nor does she consider how the same cinematic processes might be explained by rival theories. Nor does she consider counterexamples that might challenge her premises or inferences. The point is important because any belief, including astrology and a trust in dowsing rods, can be *illustrated* by particular phenomena. Marshall Edelson calls this "enumerative inductivism," the notion that adducing instances of a hypothesis will support it; in fact, such a notion is vacuous because any number of hypotheses can be supported by a set of instances. The real test involves "eliminative inductivism": "No conjecture about the world is in and of itself confirmed by evidence. It is always evaluated relative to some rival. The degree of its acceptance is simply the extent to which at any particular time it is considered better than its comparable rivals."[51]

The focus upon doctrine can blind one to the most obvious counterinstances. Instead of asking what the everyday ideology of vision might be, John Ellis starts from the premise that the cinematic institution necessarily imitates a phenomenological model. So he informs us that projection in a movie theatre "exactly parallels" our ideology of vision, "one that thinks of the eyes as projecting a beam of light, like a torch-beam, that illuminates what we look at, making it visible and perceptible."[52] Ellis' commitment to SLAB theory has apparently made him oblivious to people's habit of switching on the lights when they enter a darkened room.

If SLAB theory is largely uninterested in posing questions and examining a range of evidence, it is no more keen on doing homework in the history of its concepts. Its canonical texts arrive untainted by any larger context (save perhaps that of "1920s Soviet culture" or "Paris after 1968"). Freud is not situated within the history of psychology, nor Saussure in the history of linguistics; Lacan's ties to Surrealism are passed over, as is Althusser's complicated relation to the French Communist Party.[53] In the endless exposition of these texts, the writer has license to remake history. One can skip from a schematic account of Descartes' conception of the "subject" to an account of Freud's, as if everyone in the intervening centuries, including minor thinkers like Hume, Kant, and Hegel, were blundering about in rationalist darkness.[54] To read SLAB theory, one would never know that such books as Sebastiano Timpanaro's *Freudian Slip* or B. A. Farrell's *Standing of Psychoanalysis* or G. A. Cohen's *Karl Marx's Theory of History: A Defence* exist.[55]

Such provincialism cripples SLAB theory as an intellectual endeavor. Any theorist who really wanted to pose questions about language would grapple with the work of Locke, Humboldt, Sapir, Whorf, Wittgenstein, Quine, Chomsky, Montague, Grice, Putnam, Kripke, Davidson, Dummett, Searle, Katz, and Sperber. Any theorist claiming an interest in psychology would certainly need to consider the contending ideas of Piaget, the Russian reflexologists, Vygotsky, Bruner, Fodor, et al. Any theorist seeking the sociopolitical functions of cinema cannot ignore Weber, Durkheim, Mauss, Parsons, Elster, and Giddens. A theorist who pronounces upon whether semiotics or psychoanalysis is a science ought to be familiar with the history and philosophy of the sciences. Yet inspection of current "theoretical" texts in our field reveals an embarrassing ignorance on all these scores. As it stands, SLAB theory constitutes a convenient way of not knowing a lot of things. Paradoxically, a movement that makes novelty its chief appeal seems unaware of recent developments in the fields to which it lays claim. SLAB theory wants to be new without being current.[56]

The rhetoric of SLAB theory can be seen as a strategic concealment of the conceptual problems I have noted. Despite its persistent use of the phrase "X argues," SLAB theory does not characteristically offer arguments. Argument presupposes a dialectical confrontation with potential or actual opponents. Assuming that s/he writes for a skeptical reader, the writer anticipates objections, refutes antagonists, and advances her/his thesis as the most plausible candidate. SLAB theory is instead largely expository, summarizing and synthesizing claims made by previous theorists. There was a short flurry of pseudo-scientific rigor in the early 1970s, but this, which enraged so many opponents, now emerges as a momentary vogue. Once Barthes rejected his pre-*S/Z* work as tainted by "scientificity,"[57] he ratified a movement back to the intuitive belletrism we have already seen in the *Sauve qui peut (la vie)* discussions and which comes virtually second nature to people of literary training.

SLAB theory has found its most comfortable rhetorical mode in a form of commentary whose components include the following: exegesis through quotation and paraphrase, the rectification of this or that point in the light of recent developments (Rée's "only now can we see" syndrome), the extrapolation of other points on the basis of conceptual or terminological association (e.g., de Lauretis on "mapping"), the interpretation of illustrative examples from films, and above all the striking of a stance that means business. The essay, chapter, or book is likely to end with some tough talk, when the writer invokes something new and dangerous: a recently translated book demanding to be assimilated, a just-finished film to be interpreted, or a new mode of filmmaking.

What the exposition-rumination-illustrations format blocks, of course, are the massive critiques that have been launched at SLAB theory and its cinematic adherents. Reading SLAB work, one could not learn that there are standard arguments against Saussure, Lacan, Althusser, and Barthes, for no SLAB theorist bothers to defend these thinkers' ideas in any engaged way.[58] One would scarcely know that many writers have pointed out conceptual difficulties in SLAB arguments about film.[59] Unlike Shklovksy, SLAB expositors usually regard theory as entrusted to them for long-term safekeeping. Still, if one holds some power, as SLAB theory does, ignoring all opponents, however complacent it may seem, is the safest rhetorical recourse.

C. Whereas poetics uses concepts to construct explanatory propositions, SLAB theory uses concepts to construct interpretive narratives.

If SLAB theorists are uninterested in debating their views within wider contexts, it is for the very practical reason that theorizing seldom lies at the center of their concerns. Theory becomes not explanation but a guide for explication. As applied to cinema, SLAB theory *tells stories.* Or rather, a story with few variants—the tale of stable personal identity, lost and (perhaps) found (but differently). This is a perennially popular tale among humanist academics, and SLAB theory draws upon psychoanalysis (that trove of great stories) in order to deck it out in different costumes. By means of traditional interpretive tactics, such as analogy and personification, any aspect of a film (setting, camera position, editing) can be assigned a meaning within this drama of subjectivity. SLAB theory yields a scheme for interpreting films that is close enough to traditional semantic fields (order/ disorder, identity/ loss of identity, self/ other, male/ female) to seem comfortable but also new enough in its particular working out to rejuvenate thematic criticism (as when the Mirror Stage underwrites critics' penchant for looking for reflections and doublings). SLAB theory *as* theory can escape scrutiny because it is made to be used, to let the critic come to the desired conclusions about this text's conventionality or that text's transgressiveness.

Historical poetics needs no such stories to guide its work. It offers explanations, not the recasting of films into the form of a master narrative; and insofar as metacriticism is part of its purview, it may take as part of its business the study of how SLAB theory has become geared toward interpretation.

As SLAB theory has incorporated many diverse ideas into its bricolage, so has it included historical poetics. Characteristically, however, the evidence mobilized by the Soviet filmmakers, the Russian

Formalists, Arnheim, Bazin, and more recent poeticians have become, in the hands of SLAB theorists, yet more illustrations of the same received doctrines.[60] True, the theorist often gets it wrong—shot/ reverse shot and point-of-view editing seem surprisingly difficult to grasp[61]—but even in the muddles, there is a recognition that if SLAB doctrine is to be mapped onto cinema, it needs at least the vocabulary and concepts provided by some poetics.

In light of these points, I conclude that contemporary film studies, thought to be dominated by abstract theory, is actually quite untheo-retical—if theory is understood not as the routine exposition of cryptic doctrines but as an active, open-ended enterprise that poses clearly defined questions, seeks empirical evidence that will help decide them, analyzes alternative explanations of that evidence, and systematically argues for the best answer. Film theory, I take it, demands wide reading, constant reflection, intimate acquaintance with the history of the problems posed, and a degree of skepticism that compels the researcher to seek out difficult challenges, either in the data or in the form of opposing arguments. But these qualities are not characteristic of SLAB theory. Its doctrinaire quality has led to dogmatism; its inadequate research has made it blinkered; and its streamlined sche-matism has rendered it simply another method for interpreting films. Unfortunately, this *modus operandi* is encouraged by several institu-tional factors, most recently those publication ventures which reward academics for dashing off homogenized summaries of Grand Theory aimed at student consumption. This might be called the Methueni-zation of the humanities.

SLAB theorists commonly counterpose "theory" to "history," as if historical research could not also be theoretical. I propose a more informative opposition. SLAB theory and its offshoots, in their deep-est assumptions and their concrete practices, have consolidated a new *scholasticism*, a ceaseless commentary on authoritative sources.[62] Po-etics, on the other hand, frankly offers *scholarship*—an open-ended, corrigible inquiry that respects the reciprocal claims of conceptual coherence and empirical adequacy. Lacking a substantive doctrine, it does not have the answers ready before anyone has asked the ques-tions.

To commit oneself to scholarship is, at this point in history, openly to commit oneself to academic institutions. Although SLAB theorists have been reluctant to acknowledge it, their theory depends crucially upon the university; indeed, Saussure, Lacan et al. produced most of their work in academic circumstances which were, by contemporary American or English standards, leisurely. Historical poetics can succeed only if colleges, universities, and archives give the researcher the resources to work steadily on questions that cannot be answered from the depths of the armchair.

I am certainly not recommending that we embrace a cozy professionalism. What matters now is that we exploit the academicization of film study for scholarly ends. If we recall that Bazin and the Formalists produced brilliant insights within academic conditions we would consider materially barren, we can appreciate the enormous opportunity which most Grand Theorists of film neglect. We can, for the first time in history, study cinema according to the stringent demands of scholarly inquiry. We have the time to fight with each other about ideas and enthusiastically pursue answers to truly demanding questions. We can do this best, I think, by transcending that Methodist division of labor initiated in Hyman's and Wellek and Warren's time. In this respect, historical poetics becomes not one method but a model of basic research into cinema. It offers the best current hope for setting high intellectual standards for film study.

NOTES

[1] René Wellek and Austin Warren, *Theory of Literature* (New York: Harcourt, Brace, 1949); Stanley Edgar Hyman, *The Armed Vision: A Study in the Methods of Modern Literary Criticism* (New York: Knopf, 1948).

[2] See, for example, such collections as Hyman's *The Critical Performance* (New York: Vintage, 1956) and Sheldon P. Zittner's *Practices of Modern Literary Scholarship* (Glenview, Illinois: Scott, Foresman, 1966). A more recent example is Mary Ann Caws, ed., *Textual Analysis: Some Readers Reading* (New York: Modern Language Association, 1986).

[3] Bill Nichols, ed., *Movies and Methods: An Anthology*, vol. 1 (Berkeley: University of California Press, 1976); vol. 2 (Berkeley: University of California Press, 1985).

[4] Robert C. Allen, ed., *Channels of Discourse: Television and Contemporary Criticism* (Chapel Hill: University of North Carolina Press, 1987).

[5] This paragraph rests upon arguments set forth in greater detail in a work in progress on the logic and rhetoric of film interpetation.

6 Igor Stravinsky, *Poetics of Music in the Form of Six Lessons* (New York: Vintage, 1956); Alexander Tzonis and Liane Lefaivre, *Classical Architecture: The Poetics of Order* (Cambridge: MIT Press, 1987); Herbert Eagle, ed. and trans., *Russian Formalist Film Theory* (Ann Arbor: Michigan Slavic Publications, 1981); and Richard Taylor, ed., *The Poetics of the Cinema, Russian Poetics in Translation* 9 (1982).

7 For survey accounts, see Michael Podro, *The Critical Historians of Art* (New Haven: Yale University Press, 1982); Michael Ann Holly, *Panofsky and the Foundations of Art History* (Ithaca: Cornell University Press, 1984).

8 See, for comprehensive surveys, Victor Erlich, *Russian Formalism: History, Doctrine*, third ed. (The Hague: Mouton, 1969); F. W. Galan, *Historic Structures: The Prague School Project 1928–1946* (Austin: University of Texas Press, 1985).

9 Some researchers of a post-Structuralist bent will find drawing any such boundaries repugnant, but in practice these writers often presuppose distinctions of their own, without signaling them explicitly.

10 See David Bordwell and Kristin Thompson, "Toward a Scientific Film History?" *Quarterly Review of Film Studies* 10, 3 (Summer 1985): 224–237.

11 I do not think that Bazin is right on this point, especially as regards Japanese directors of the 1930s and Soviet filmmakers of the 1920s and early 1930s. For discussion, see "Mizoguchi and the Evolution of Film Language," in *Language and Cinema*, ed. Stephen Heath and Patricia Mellencamp (Washington: University Publications of America, 1983), pp. 107–117; and *Narration in the Fiction Film* (Madison: University of Wisconsin Press, 1985), pp. 235–268.

12 David Bordwell, Janet Staiger, and Kristin Thompson, *The Classical Hollywood Cinema: Film Style and Mode of Production to 1960* (New York: Columbia University Press, 1985), pp. 3–11, 70–84, 87–112, 243–261. Noël Carroll argues at a more abstract level for such a model in "Film History and Film Theory: An Outline for an Institutional Theory of Film," *Film Reader* no. 4 (1979): 81–96.

13 See Rick Altman, ed., *Genre: The Musical* (London: Routledge and Kegan Paul, 1981), and Donald Crafton, "Animation Iconography: The Hand of the Artist," *Quarterly Review of Film Studies* 4, 3 (Fall 1979): 409–428.

14 See Seymour Chatman, *Story and Discourse: Narrative Structure in Fiction and Film* (Ithaca: Cornell University Press, 1978); Nick Browne, *The Rhetoric of Filmic Narration* (Ann Arbor: UMI Research Press, 1982); Edward R. Branigan, *Point of View in the Cinema: A Theory of Narration and Subjectivity in Classical Film* (The Hague: Mouton, 1984).

[15] For discussion of these non-narrative constructive principles, see David Bordwell and Kristin Thompson, *Film Art: An Introduction* (New York: Knopf, 1985), pp. 44–81.

[16] R. S. Crane, "Critical and Historical Principles of Literary History," in *The Idea of the Humanities* vol. 2 (University of Chicago Press, 1967), pp. 45–156.

[17] Noël Burch, *To the Distant Observer: Form and Meaning in Japanese Cinema* (Berkeley: University of California Press, 1979), pp. 25–74, and Vance Kepley, Jr., *In the Service of the State: The Cinema of Alexander Dovzhenko* (Madison: University of Wisconsin Press, 1986), pp. 63–74.

[18] See, for examples, Charles Musser, "The Early Cinema of Edwin Porter," *Cinema Journal* 19, 1 (1979): 1–35; Charles Musser, "The Nickelodeon Era Begins: Establishing the Framework for Hollywood's Mode of Representation," *Framework* nos. 22–23 (1983): 4–11; André Gaudreault, "Detours in Film Narrative: The Development of Cross-Cutting." *Cinema Journal* 19, 1 (1979): 39–59; Tom Gunning, "The Cinema of Attraction: Early Film, Its Spectator and the Avant-Garde," *Wide Angle* 8, 3–4 (1986): 63–70; "Archives, Document, Fiction: Film before 1907," *Iris* 2, 1 (1984).

[19] Janet Staiger, " 'The Handmaiden of Villainy': Methods and Problems in Studying the Historical Reception of a Film," *Wide Angle* 8, 1 (1986): 19–27.

[20] *Ozu and the Poetics of Cinema* (Princeton: Princeton University Press, 1988). See also *The Films of Carl-Theodor Dreyer* (Berkeley: University of California Press, 1981).

[21] See Raymond Bellour, *L'analyse du Film* (Paris: Albatros, 191979); Thierry Kuntzel, "The Film-Work, 2," *Camera Obscura* 5 (1980): 7–68; Peter Wollen, "*North by Northwest*: A Morphological Analysis," in *Readings and Writings: Semiotic Counter-Strategies* (London: Verso, 1982), pp. 18–33; Rick Altman, *The American Film Musical* (Bloomington: Indiana University Press, 1987), pp. 16–58.

[22] See, for example, "Enonciation et cinéma," *Communications* no. 38 (1983); Bordwell, *Narration in the Fiction Film*, pp. 16–62.

[23] See Heinrich Wölfflin, *Principles of Art History*, trans. M. D. Hottinger (New York: Dover, 1950), pp. 1–17, 226–237.

[24] Viktor Shklovsky, "On the Connection between Devices of *Syuzhet* Construction and General Stylistic Devices," *Twentieth Century Studies* nos. 7/8 (December 1972): 48–72.

[25] Jurij Tynjanov and Roman Jakobson, "Problems in the Study of Literature and Language," in *Readings in Russian Poetics*, ed. Ladislav Matejka and Krystyna Pomorska (Cambridge: MIT Press, 1971), pp. 80–81.

26 Bordwell et al., *Classical Hollywood Cinema*, pp. 247–251.

27 Monroe C. Beardsley, *Aesthetics from Classical Greece to the Present: A Short History* (University, Alabama: University of Alabama Press, 1966); Peter Steiner, *Russian Formalism: A Metapoetics* (Ithaca: Cornell University Press, 1984).

28 I am indebted to Noël Carroll for this distinction, and for many other suggestions which have improved this essay.

29 See Quentin Skinner, ed., *The Return of Grand Theory in the Human Sciences* (Cambridge: Cambridge University Press, 1985).

30 Noël Carroll discusses the virtues of a question-centered approach to theorizing in the last section of *Mystifying Movies: Fads and Fallacies of Contemporary Film Theory* (New York: Columbia University Press, 1988).

31 See E. Ann Kaplan, review of Dudley Andrew, *Concepts in Film Theory*, *Wide Angle* 6, 2 (1984): 78.

32 "In Defence of the Sociological Method," *Russian Poetics in Translation* 4 (1977): 94.

33 Stephen Jay Gould, "Cardboard Darwinism," *New York Review of Books* (25 September 1986): 47.

34 Boris Eichenbaum, "The Theory of the 'Formal Method,' " in *Russian Formalist Criticism: Four Essays*, trans. and ed. Lee T. Lemon and Marion J. Reis (Lincoln: University of Nebraska Press, 1965), p. 103.

35 See Bordwell et al., *Classical Hollywood Cinema*; Bordwell, *Narration*, Part Three; Kristin Thompson, *Breaking the Glass Armor: Neoformalist Film Analysis* (Princeton: Princeton University Press, 1988).

36 Kristin Thompson and David Bordwell, "Space and Narrative in the Films of Ozu," *Screen* 17, 2 (Summer 1976: 55–64, 66–70; Thompson, *Glass Armor*, Chapter 12; Bordwell, *Ozu and the Poetics of Cinema*, Chapters 5–7.

37 See Bordwell et al., *Classical Hollywood Cinema*, 125–127, 137–139.

38 *Narration*, pp. 31–47.

39 Colin MacCabe, "*Slow Motion*," *Screen* 21, 3 (1980): 111–114.

40 Janet Bergstrom, "Violence and Enunciation," *Camera Obscura* no. 8–9–10 (Fall 1982): 24.

41 Raymond Bellour, " 'I Am an Image'," *Camera Obscura* no. 8–9–10 (Fall 1982): 121.

42 Thompson, *Glass Armor*, Chapter 10.

43 To take notice of the theory's commitment to a binarist conception of meaning and of the theory's textual-analytical practice, one should also include Lévi-Strauss; to allow for Saussurean accounts of pragmatics, one should include Benveniste; to be wholly up to date, one should add

Foucault. But Messrs. S, L, A, and B still seem to me to remain at the core of the theories' concerns.

[44] Lea Jacobs suggests to me that virtually no one currently holds SLAB theory as an intellectual position. I do not agree, as my citations in this section try to show. But even if SLAB theory is moribund, I would argue that (a) No equally coherent and pervasive frame of reference has replaced it, and so it remains the point of reference for those who would move beyond it; and (b) The successors to SLAB theorists exemplify the same *modus operandi* that I criticize here. Changing theoretical views does not entail changing one's reasoning routines.

[45] Jonathan Rée, "Marxist Modes," in *Radical Philosophy Reader* (London: Verso, 1985), p. 338.

[46] See, for an account of Bakhtin's views, Katerina Clark and Michael Holquist, *Mikhail Bakhtin* (Cambridge: Harvard University Press, 1984).

[47] Teresa de Lauretis, *Alice Doesn't: Feminism, Semiotics, Cinema* (Bloomington: Indiana University Press, 1984), p. 55.

[48] Colin Blakemore, "The Baffled Brain," in *Illusion in Nature and Art*, ed. R. L. Gregory and E. H. Gombrich (London: Duckworth, 1973), p. 19. Elsewhere Blakemore asserts: "The mechanisms of constant perception are built into our brains. . . . Every child discovers a pictorial version of the physical laws of the universe in his own perceptions." (*Mechanics of the Mind* [Cambridge: Cambridge University Press, 1977], p. 70.) A more formal and up-to-date discussion of the topological basis of neural "mapping" can be found in Lynn Nadel et al., "The Neurobiology of Mental Representation," in *The Representation of Knowledge and Belief*, ed. Myles Brand and Robert M. Harnish (Tucson: University of Arizona Press, 1986), pp. 219–257.

[49] Rée, "Marxist Modes," p. 357.

[50] Kaja Silverman, *The Subject of Semiotics* (New York: Oxford University Press, 1983); see especially pp. 89–109, 153–193.

[51] Marshall Edelson, *Hypothesis and Evidence in Psychoanalysis*, quoted in Frederick Crews, *Skeptical Engagements* (New York: Oxford University Press, 1986), p. 80.

[52] John Ellis, *Visible Fictions: Cinema, Television, Video* (London: Routledge and Kegan Paul), p. 41.

[53] For a sampling of such works, see Frank J. Sulloway, *Freud: Biologist of the Mind* (London: Fontana, 1979); Henri F. Ellenberger, *The Discovery of the Unconscious* (New York: Basic Books, 1970); Hans Aarsleff, *From Locke to Saussure: Essays on the Study of Language and Intellectual History* (Minneapolis: University of Minnesota Press, 1982), pp. 356–371; David Macey, "Fragments of an Analysis: Lacan in Context," *Radical*

Philosophy no. 35 (Autumn 1983): 1–9; Arthur Hirsh, *The French New Left: An Intellectual History from Sartre to Gorz* (Boston: South End Press, 1981), pp. 170; and, for a recent overview, R. W. Johnson, "The Intelligentsia Goes Pop," *Times Literary Supplement* (31 July 1987): 811–812.

54 Silverman, *Subject of Semiotics*, pp. 126–132.
55 See Sebastiano Timpanaro, *The Freudian Slip: Psychoanalysis and Textual Criticism*, trans. Kate Soper (London: New Left Books, 1974); B. A. Farrell, *The Standing of Psychoanalysis* (New York: Oxford University Press, 1981); G. A. Cohen, *Karl Marx's Theory of History: A Defence* (Princeton: Princeton University Press, 1978).
56 The issue of being up-to-date gets discussed in Eric Griffiths, "What Was New," *London Review of Books* (19 December 1985): 9–10, which may be the most excoriating analysis of SLAB theory yet to appear.
57 On Barthes' rejection of "scientificity," see "Interview: A Conversation with Roland Barthes," in *The Grain of the Voice* (New York: Hill and Wang, 1985), pp. 128–130.
58 A condensed summary of difficulties with a Saussurean model is in Michael Devitt and Kim Sterelny, *Language and Reality: An Introduction to the Philosophy of Language* (Cambridge: MIT Press, 1987), pp. 210–221. On Lacan, see Richard Wollheim, "The Cabinet of Dr. Lacan," *New York Review of Books* 25, nos. 21–22 (25 January 1979): 96–105; David Archard, *Consciousness and the Unconscious* (LaSalle, Illinois: Open Court, 1984), especially pp. 56–103; Adolf Grünbaum, *The Foundations of Psychoanalysis: A Philosophical Critique* (Berkeley: University of California Press, 1984). Early critical discussions of Althusser in English are Norman Geras, "Althusser's Marxism: An Account and Assessment," *New Left Review* no. 71 (January–February 1972): 57–86; Paul Hirst, "Althusser and the Theory of Ideology," *Economy and Society* 5, 4 (November 1976): 385–412; Mark Poster, *Existential Marxism in Postwar France: From Sartre to Althusser* (Princeton: Princeton University Press, 1975), pp. 306–360; Sebastian Timpanaro, *On Materialism*, trans. Lawrence Garner (London: New Left Books, 1975), pp. 135–219; E. P. Thompson, *The Poverty of Theory and Other Essays* (London: Merlin, 1978). See also Simon Clarke et al., *One-Dimensional Marxism: Althusser and the Politics of Culture* (London: Alison and Busby, 1980); Norman Geras, *Marx and Human Nature: Refutation of a Legend* (London: Verso, 1983); Michael Kelly, *Modern French Marxism* (Baltimore: Johns Hopkins University Press, 1982), pp. 118–144, 175–191; Alex Calinnicos, *Althusser's Marxism* (London: Pluto, 1979); Nicholas Abercrombie, Stephen Hill, and Bryan S. Turner, *The Dominant Ideology Thesis* (London: Allen and Unwin, 1980); Ted Benton, *The Rise*

and Fall of Structural Marxism: Althusser and His Influence (London: Macmillan, 1984). Kate Soper's *Humanism and Anti-Humanism* (LaSalle, Illinois: Open Court, 1986), Frederick Crews' *Skeptical Engagements*, and J. G. Merquior's *From Prague to Paris: A Critique of Structuralist and Post-Structuralist Thought* (London: Verso, 1986) are wide-ranging critiques of many aspects of Grand Theory generally and SLAB theory in particular.

59 Andrew Britton, "The Ideology of *Screen*," *Movie* no. 26 (Winter 1978/79): 1–28; Anonymous [Andrew Britton?], "*Pursued*: A Reply to Paul Willemen," *Framework* no. 4 (Autumn 1976): 4–15; Kevin McDonnell and Kevin Robbins, "Marxist Cultural Theory: The Althusserian Smokescreen," in Clarke et al., *One-Dimensional Marxism*, pp. 157–231; Noël Carroll, "Address to the Heathen," *October* no. 23 (Winter 1982): 89–163.

60 This formalistic foreplay is evident in those books that begin with a schematic summary of the "invisible style" of Hollywood cinema before passing quickly to "reading." An example is Robert Ray, *A Certain Tendency of the Hollywood Cinema, 1930–1980* (Princeton: Princeton University Press, 1985), pp. 32–55.

61 Examples of inaccurate explanations of such stylistic procedures can be found in Silverman, *Subject*, pp. 201–202; Colin MacCabe, *Godard: Images, Sounds, Politics* (Bloomington: Indiana University Press, 1980), pp. 68–69.

62 Michel Charles' description of medieval scholasticism has an eerily contemporary ring: "Scholasticism would be a mode of thought and expression in which all knowledge must be authorized by a text, however fluid or variable it becomes; an intellectual world in which the renewal of knowledge must come through the rereading of a text; a system in which, necessarily, nothing new can be produced outside the discovery of a new text (which can, of course, include the rereading of a canonical text) . . . " See *L'Arbre et la source* (Paris: Seuil, 1985), p. 126. The book is one of the best analyses of the logic of literary criticism I have seen.

SELECTED BIBLIOGRAPHY
R. Barton Palmer

Aarsleff, Hans. *From Locke to Saussure: Essays on the Study of Language and Intellectual History*. Minneapolis: University of Minnesota Press, 1982.

Abercrombie, Nicholas; Stephen Hill; and Bryan S. Turner. *The Dominant Ideology Thesis*. London: Allen and Unwin, 1980.

Affron, Charles. *Star Acting: Gish, Garbo and Davis*. New York: Dutton, 1977.

Agel, Henri. *Poétique du cinéma: manifeste essentialiste*. Paris: Éditions du Signe, 1973.

Allen, Robert C., ed. *Channels of Discourse: Television and Contemporary Criticism*. Chapel Hill: University of North Carolina Press, 1987.

Allen, Robert C. and Douglas Gomery. *Film History:Theory and Practice*. New York: Knopf, 1985.

Altman, Rick, ed. *Genre: The Musical*. London: Routledge and Kegan Paul, 1981.

Altman, Rick. *The American Film Musical*. Bloomington: Indiana University Press, 1987.

Andrew, Dudley. *Concepts in Film Theory*. New York: Oxford University Press, 1984.

Andrew, Dudley. "Of Canons and Quietism." *Cinema Journal* 25 no. 1 (Fall 1985).

Anon. "*Pursued*: A Reply to Paul Willemen." *Framework* no. 4 (Autumn 1976).

Aranda, Francisco. *Luis Buñuel: A Critical Biography*. New York: Da Capo Press, 1976.

Archard, David. *Consciousness and the Unconsciousness*. La Salle, Illinois: Open Court, 1984.

Armes, Roy. *Patterns of Realism*. New York: A.S. Barnes, 1971.

Armes, Roy. "Peckinpah and the Changing West." *London Magazine* 9 (March 1970).

Auden, W.H. *The Dyer's Hand and Other Essays*. New York: Vintage Books, 1968.

Auerbach, Erich. *Mimesis: The Representation of Reality in Western Literature*. Trans. William Trask. Princeton: Princeton University Press, 1953.

Bakhtin, Mikhail. *Rabelais and his World*. Trans. Helen Iswolsky. Cambridge: MIT Press, 1968.

Bakhtin, Mikhail. *Speech Genres and Other Late Essays*. Trans. Vern W. McGee, ed. Caryl Emerson and Michael Holquist. Austin: University of Texas Press, 1986.

Bakhtin, Mikhail. *The Dialogic Imagination: Four Essays by M. M. Bakhtin*. Trans. Michael Holquist, ed. Caryl Emerson and Michael Holquist. Austin: University of Texas Press, 1981.

Bakhtin, Mikhail and P.M. Medvedev. *The Formal Method in Literary Scholarship*. Trans. Albert J. Wehrle. Cambridge: Harvard University Press, 1985.

Balazs, Bela. *Theory of the Film: Character and Growth of a New Art*. Trans. Edith Bone. New York: Arno Press, 1972.

Baldelli, Pio. "Résistance, néoréalisme et leçons des anciens." *Image et Son* 195 (Juin 1966).

Barthes, Roland. *Image—Music—Text*. Trans. Stephen Heath. New York: Hill and Wang, 1977.

Barthes, Roland. *Le Degré zero de l'écriture*. Paris: Seuil, 1953.

Barthes, Roland. *The Grain of the Voice*. New York: Hill and Wang, 1985.

Barthes, Roland. *S/Z*. Trans. Richard Miller. New York: Hill and Wang, 1974.

Bataille, Georges, *Story of the Eye*. New York: Urizen, 1977.

Baudry, Jean-Louis, "Ideological Effects of the Basic Cinematographic Apparatus." *Film Quarterly* 28 no. 2 (Winter 1974/5).

Beardsley, Monroe C. *Aesthetics from Classical Greece to the Present: A Short History*. University, Alabama: Alabama University Press, 1966.

Beattie, James. *The Philosophical and Critical Works*. Hildesheim and New York: Georg Olms, 1975.

Bellour, Raymond. " 'I Am an Image.' " *Camera Obscura* 8/9/10 (Fall 1982).

Bellour, Raymond. *L'Analyse du film*. Paris: Albatros, 1979.

Bennett, Tony. "Text and Social Process: The Case of James Bond." *Screen Education* no. 41 (Winter/Spring 1982).

Benton, Ted. *The Rise and Fall of Structural Marxism: Althusser and His Influence*. London: Macmillan, 1984.

Bergstrom, Janet. "Alternation, Segmentation, Hypnosis: Interview with Raymond Bellour." Trans. Susan Suleiman. *Camera Obscura* 3/4 (1979)

Bergstrom, Janet. "Violence and Enunciation." *Camera Obscura* 8/9/10 (Fall 1982.

Bogdanovich, Peter. *The Cinema of Alfred Hitchcock*. New York: Museum of Modern Art, 1962.

Bordwell, David and Kristin Thompson. *Film Art: An Introduction*. New York: Knopf, 1985.

Bordwell, David. "Mizoguchi and the Evolution of Film Language." In *Language and Cinema*, ed. Stephen Heath and Patricia Mellencamp. Washington: University Publications of America, 1983.

Bordwell, David, *Narration in the Fiction Film*. Madison: University of Wisconsin Press, 1985.

Bordwell, David. *Ozu and the Poetics of Cinema*. Princeton: Princeton University Press, 1988.

Bordwell, David. "Textual Analysis, etc." *Enclitic* 5 no. 2/ 6 no. 1 (Fall 1981/Spring 1982).

Bordwell, David; Janet Staiger; and Kristin Thompson. *The Classical Hollywood Cinema: Film Style and Mode of Production to 1960*. New York: Columbia University Press, 1985.

Bordwell, David. *The Films of Carl-Theodor Dreyer*. Berkeley: University of California Press, 1981.

Bordwell, David and Kristin Thompson. "Toward a Scientific Film History?" *Quarterly Review of Film Studies* 10 no. 3 (Summer 1985).

Borrelli, Armando. *Neorealismo e Marxismo*. Avellino: Edizioni di Cinemasud, 1966.

Brand, Myle and Robert M. Harnish. eds. *The Representation of Knowledge and Belief*. Tucson: University of Arizona Press, 1986.

Branigan, Edward R. *Point of View in the Cinema: A Theory of Narration and Subjectivity in Classical Film*. The Hague: Mouton, 1984.

Braudy, Leo. *The World in a Frame: What We See in Films*. Garden City, N.Y.: Doubleday, 1975.

Brecht, Bertolt. *Brecht on Theater*. Trans. John Willett. New York: Hill and Wang, 1964.

Britton, Andrew. "The Ideology of *Screen*." *Movie* no. 26 (Winter 1978/9).

Brown, Gillian and George Yule. *Discourse Analysis*. Cambridge: Cambridge University Press, 1983.

Browne, Nick. *The Rhetoric of Filmic Narration*. Ann Arbor: UMI Research Press, 1982.

Brunette, Peter. "Rossellini and Cinematic Realism." *Cinema Journal* 25 no. 1 (Fall 1985).

Bruno, Giuliano and Maria Nadotti. eds. *Women and Film in Italy*. London: Methuen, 1986.

Buache, Freddy. *Le cinéma Italien d' Antonioni à Rosi*. Yverdon, Switzerland: Le Thiele, 1969.

Budgen, Suzanne. *Fellini*. London: BFI, 1966.

Buñuel, Luis and Jean-Claude Carrière. *My Last Sigh*. Trans. Abagail Israel. New York: Vintage, 1984.

Burch, Noël. "Propositions." *Afterimage* 5 (Spring 1974).

Burch, Nöel. *To the Distant Observer: Form and Meaning in Japanese Cinema*. Berkeley: University of California Press, 1979.

Burke, Kenneth. *A Grammar of Motives*. Los Angeles: University of California Press, 1969.

Butler, Terence. *Crucified Heroes: The Films of Sam Peckinpah*. London: Gordon Fraser, 1979.

Cain, William. *The Crisis in Criticism: Literature and Reform in English Studies*. Baltimore and London: The Johns Hopkins University Press, 1984.

Calinnicos, Alex. *Althusser's Marxism*. London: Plato, 1979.

Carroll, John M. "A Program for Film Theory." *Journal of Aesthetics and Art Criticism* 35 no. 3 (Fall 1977).

Carroll, Noël. Address to the Heathen." *October* no. 23 (Winter 1982).

Carroll, Nöel. "Film History and Film Theory: An Outline for an Institutional Theory of Film." *Film Reader* 4 (1979).

Carroll, Nöel. *Mystifying Movies: Fads and Fallacies of Contemporary Film Theory*. New York: Columbia University Press, 1988.

Carroll, Nöel. "The Power of Movies." *Daedalus* 114 (Autumn 1985).

Cawelti, John. "Myths of Violence in American Popular Culture." *Critical Inquiry* 1 no. 3 (March 1975).

Caws, Mary Ann. *Textual Analysis: Some Readers Reading*. New York: Modern Language Association, 1986.

Charles, Michel. *L'arbre et la source*. Paris: Seuil, 1985.

Chatman, Seymour. *Story and Discourse: Narrative Structure in Fiction and Film*. Ithaca: Cornell University Press, 1978.

Clark, Katerina and Holquist, Michael. *Mikhail Bakhtin*. Cambridge: Harvard University Press, 1984.

Clarke, Simon et al. *One-Dimensional Marxism: Althusser and the Politics of Culture*. London: Alison and Busby, 1980.

Cohen, G.A. *Karl Marx's Theory of History: A Defense*. Princeton: Princeton University Press, 1978.

Colin, Michel. *Langue, film, discours; prolégomenes à une sémiologie génerative du film*. Paris: Klincksieck, 1985.

Copland, Aaron. "Tip to Moviegoers: Take off Those Ear Muffs." *New York Times* November 6, 1949, section six, p. 28.

Courtade, Francis. *Les Maledictions du cinéma francais*. Paris: Alain Moreau, 1978.

Crafton, Donald. "Animation Iconography: The Hand of the Artist." *Quarterly Review of Film Studies* 4 no. 3 (Fall 1979).

Crane, R.S. *The Idea of the Humanities*, volume 2. Chicago: University of Chicago Press, 1967.

Crews, Frederick. *Skeptical Engagements*. New York: Oxford University Press, 1986.

Culler, Jonathan. *Structuralist Poetics: Structuralism, Linguistics, and the Study of Language*. Ithaca: Cornell University Press, 1975.

Davis, Lennard. *Ideology and Fiction: Resisting Novels*. New York: Methuen, 1987.

Davis, Robert Con and Ronald Schleifer. eds. *Deconstruction at Yale*. Norman: University of Oklahoma Press, 1985.

De Beaugrande, Robert and Wolfgang Dressler. *Introduction to Text Linguistics*. London: Longman, 1981.

De Lauretis, Teresa. *Alice Doesn't: Feminism, Semiotics, Cinema*. Bloomington: Indiana University Press, 1984.

De Lauretis, Teresa. "Oedipus Interruptus." *Wide Angle* 7 nos. 1/2 (Spring 1985).

Deleuze, Gilles. *L'Image mouvement*. Paris: Minuit, 1983.

Derriday, Jacques. *La Verité en peinture*. Paris: Flammarion, 1978.

Derrida, Jacques. *Of Grammatology*. Baltimore: Johns Hopkins University Press, 1976.

Derrida, Jacques. *Positions*. Trans. Alan Bass. Chicago: University of Chicago Press, 1981.

Derrida, Jacques. "The Principle of Reason: The University in the Eyes of Its Pupils." *Diacritics* (Fall 1983).

Derrida, Jacques. *Writing and Difference*. Trans. Alan Bass. Chicago: University of Chicago Press, 1978.

De Rougemont, Denis. *Love in the Western World*. New York: Harper and Row, 1977.

De Saussure, Ferdinand. *Course in General Linguistics (1915)*. Ed. Charles Bally and Albert Sechehaye. Trans. Wade Baskins. New York: McGraw-Hill, 1966.

Devitt, Michael and Kim Sterelny. *Language and Reality: An Introduction to the Philosophy of Language*. Cambridge: MIT Press, 1987.

Doane, Mary Ann. "Woman's Stake in Representation: Filming the Female Body." *October* 17 (1981).

Douchet, Jean. "Hitch and his Public." Trans. Verena Conley. In *A Hitchcock Reader*. Ed. Marshall Deutelbaum and Leland Pogue. Ames: Iowa State University Press, 1986.

Dupont-Roc, Roselyne and Jean Callot. eds. and trans. *Aristote: La Poétique* Paris: Éditions du Seuil, 1980.

Durgnat, Raymond. "Film Theory: From Narrative to Description." *Quarterly Review of Film Studies* 7 no. 2 (Spring 1982).

Dyer, Richard. *The Stars*. London: Macmillan Press, 1983.

Eagle, Herbert, ed. and trans. *Russian Formalist Film Theory*. Ann Arbor: Michigan Slavic Publications, 1981.

Eagleton, Terry. "Brecht on Rhetoric." *New Literary History* 16 no. 3 (Spring 1985).

Eagleton, Terry. *Criticism and Ideology*. London: Verso, 1978.

Eichenbaum, Boris. "The Theory of the 'Formal Method.' " In *Russian Formalist Criticism: Four Essays*. Trans. and eds. Lee T. Lemon and Marion J. Reis. Lincoln: University of Nebraska Press, 1985.

Eisenstein, Sergei. *Film Sense*. Trans. Jay Leyda. New York: Harcourt Brace and Meridian, 1957.

Eisner, Lotte. *The Haunted Screen*. Berkeley: University of California Press, 1969.

Ellenberger, Henri F. *The Discovery of the Unconscious*. New York: Basic Books, 1970.

Ellis, John. *Visible Fictions: Cinema, Television, Video*. London: Routledge and Kegan Paul, 1982.

Erlich, Victor. *Russian Formalism: History, Doctrine*. The Hague: Mouton, 1969.

Farber, Stephen, "Coppola and *The Godfather*." *Sight and Sound* 41 no. 4 (Autumn 1974).

Farber, Stephen. "*Straw Dogs*." *Cinema* 7 (Spring 1972).

Farrell, B.A. *The Standing of Psychoanalysis*. New York: Oxford University Press, 1981.

Faure, Élie. "Un Nouveau film de Jean Vigo." *Pour Vous* 283 (May 31 1934).

Feuer, Jane. *The Hollywood Musical*. Bloomington: Indiana University Press, 1982.

Freeman, David. "The Last Days of Alfred Hitchcock." *Esquire* 97 no. 4 (April 1982).

Freud, Sigmund, *Three Case Histories*. Ed. Philip Rieff. New York: Collier Books, 1963.

Galan, F.W. *Historic Structures: The Prague School Project 1928–1946*. Austin: University of Texas Press, 1985.

Garçon, Francois. *De Blum à Petain*. Paris: Cerf, 1984.

Gaudreault, André. "Detours in Film Narrative: The Development of Cross-Cutting." *Cinema Journal* 19 no. 1 (Spring 1979).

Genette, Gérard. *Figures*. Paris: Éditions du Seuil, 1966.

Genette, Gérard. *Narrative Discourse: An Essay in Method*. Trans. Jane E. Lewin. Ithaca: Cornell University Press, 1980.

Geras, Norman. "Althusser's Marxism: An Account and Assessment." *New Left Review* no. 7. (January/February 1972).

Geras, Norman. *Marx and Human Nature: Refutation of a Legend.* London: Verso, 1983

Gleason, H.A. *Linguistics and English Grammar.* New York: Holt, Rinehart, and Winston, 1965.

Gledhill, Christine. "Recent Developments in Feminist Film Criticism." *Quarterly Review of Film Studies* 3 no. 4 (Fall 1977).

Goffman, Erving. *Frame Analysis.* New York: Harper, 1974.

Goffman, Erving. *The Presentation of Self in Everyday Life.* New York: Doubleday, 1959.

Gombrich, E. H. *The Image and the Eye.* Ithaca: Phaidon Books, 1982.

Goodman, Nelson. *Ways of Worldmaking.* Indianapolis: Hackett, 1978.

Gould, Stephen Jay. "Cardboard Darwinism." *New York Review of Books* (25 September 1986).

Graff, Gerald. *Literature Against Itself: Literary Ideas in Modern Society.* Chicago: University of Chicago Press, 1979.

Gregory, R.L. and E.H. Gombrich. *Illusion in Nature and Art.* London: Duckworth, 1973.

Grey, Harry. *The Hoods.* New York: Crown Publishers, 1952.

Griffiths, Eric. "What Was New." *London Review of Books* (19 December 1985).

Grünbaum, Adolf. *The Foundations of Psychoanalysis: A Philosophical Critique.* Berkeley: University of California Press, 1984.

Gunn, Giles. "The Semiotics of Culture and the Interpretation of Literature: Clifford Geertz and the Moral Imagination." *Studies In the Literary Imagination* 12 no. 1 (Spring 1979).

Gunning, Tom. "Archives, Document, Fiction: Film Before 1907." *Iris* 2 no. 1 (Spring 1984).

Gunning, Tom. "The Cinema of Attraction: Early Film, Its Spectator, and the Avant-Garde." *Wide Angle* 8 nos. 3–4 (Summer/Winter 1986).

Gutwinski, Waldemar. *Cohesion in Literary Texts.* The Hague: Mouton, 1976.

Hagenauer, Fedor and James W. Hamilton. "*Straw Dogs*: Aggression and Violence in Modern Film." *American Imago* 30 (Fall 1973).

Halliday, M.A.K. and Ihab Hassan. *Cohesion in English.* London: Longman, 1976.

Halliday, M.A.K. "Language Structure and Language Function." In J. Lyons, ed., *New Horizons in Linguistics* Harmondsworth: Penguin, 1970.

Hanslick, Edward. *The Beautiful in Music.* Trans. Gustav Cohen. New York: Liberal Arts Press, 1957.

Heath, Stephen. "Film and System: Terms of Analysis." *Screen* 16 no. 1 (Spring 1975); 16 no. 2 (Summer 1975); 17 no. 1 (Spring 1976); and *Enclitic* 5 no. 2 (Fall 1981); 6 no. 1 (Spring 1982).

Heath, Stephen and Teresa De Lauretis. eds. *The Cinematic Apparatus.* (London: Macmillan, 1980).

Higginboth, Virginia. *Luis Buñuel.* New York: G.K. Hall, 1979.

Hiller, Johann Adam. "Abhandlung von der Nachahmung der Natur in der Musik." In *Historisch-Kritische Beyträge.* Ed. F.W. Marpurg. Berlin, 1754.

Hirsh, Arthur. *The French New Left: An Intellectual History from Sartre to Gorz.* Boston: South End Press, 1981.

Hirst, Paul. "Althusser and the Theory of Ideology." *Economy and Society* 5 no. 4 (November 1976).

Holly, Michael Ann. *Panofsky and the Foundations of Art History.* Ithaca: Cornell University Press, 1984.

Holub, Robert C. *Reception Theory: A Critical Introduction.* London: Methuen, 1984.

Honeycutt, Kirk. "Milius the Barbarian." *American Film* 7 (May 1982).

Hyman, Stanley Edgar. *The Armed Vision: A Study in the Methods of Modern Literary Criticism.* New York: Knopf, 1948

Hyman, Stanley Edgar. *The Critical Performance.* New York: Vintage, 1956

Isaacs, Neil D. "Lubitsch and the Filmed Play Syndrome." *Literature/Film Quarterly* 3 (Fall 1975).

Iser, Wolfgang. *The Act of Reading: A Theory of Aesthetic Response.* Baltimore: Johns Hopkins University Press, 1978.

Iser, Wolfgang. *The Implied Reader: Patterns of Communication in Prose Fiction from Bunyan to Beckett.* Baltimore: Johns Hopkins University Press, 1974.

Jameson, Fredric. *The Political Unconscious.* Ithaca: Cornell University Press, 1981.

Jameson, Fredric. "The Symbolic Inference: or Kenneth Burke and Ideological Analysis." *Critical Inquiry* 4 no. 2 (Spring 1978).

Jauss, Hans Robert. *Toward an Aesthetic of Reception.* Trans. Timothy Bakhti. Minneapolis: University of Minnesota Press, 1982.

Jeancolas, Jean-Pierre. *Le Cinémathèque québecoise.* Montreal, 1976.

Jeancolas, Jean-Pierre. *Les 15 ans des années trentes.* Paris: Stock, 1983.

Johnson, Barbara. *The Critical Difference.* Baltimore: Johns Hopkins University Press, 1980.

Johnson, R. W. "The Intelligentsia Goes Pop." *Times Literary Supplement* (31 July 1987).

Johnson, Robert K. *Francis Ford Coppola.* Boston: Twayne Publishers, 1977.

Kaplan, E. Ann. "Aspects of British Feminist Film Theory." *Jump Cut* nos. 12–13 (1976).

Kaplan, E. Ann. *Motherhood and Representation.* London and New York: Methuen, 1987.

Kaplan, E. Ann. Reply to Linda Williams. *Cinema Journal* 24 no. 2 (Winter 1985).

Kaplan, E. Ann. Review of Dudley Andrew's *Concepts in Film Theory. Wide Angle* 6 no. 2 (Summer 1984).

Kaplan, E. Ann. *Rocking Around the Clock: Advertising, Pastiche and Schizophrenia in Music Television.* London and New York: Methuen, 1986.

Kelly, Michael. *Modern French Marxism.* Baltimore: Johns Hopkins University Press, 1982.

Kenny, Anthony. *Action, Emotion and Will.* London: Routledge and Kegan Paul, 1963.

Kepley, Vance, Jr. *In the Service of the State: The Cinema of Alexander Dovzhenko.* Madison: University of Wisconsin Press, 1986.

Kivy, Peter. *Sound and Semblance.* Princeton: Princeton University Press, 1984.

Kivy, Peter. *The Corded Shell.* Princeton: Princeton University Press, 1980.

Kolker, Robert Philip. *A Cinema of Loneliness: Penn, Kubrick, Coppola, Scorsese, Altman.* New York: Oxford University Press, 1980.

Kracauer, Siegfried. *History: The Last Things Before the Last.* New York: Oxford University Press, 1969.

Kracauer, Siegfried. *Theory of Film: The Redemption of Physical Reality.* New York: Oxford University Press, 1960.

Krupnik, Mark. *Displacement: Derrida and After.* Bloomington: Indiana University Press, 1983.

Kuntzel, Thierry. "The Film-Work, 2." *Camera Obscura* 5 (1980).

Lapierre, Marcel. *Anthologie du cinéma.* Paris: La Nouvelle Édition, 1946.

Lawton, Ben. "Italian Neo-Realism: A Mirror Constructed by Reality." *Film Criticism* 3 no. 2 (Winter 1979).

Lentricchia, Frank. *Criticism and Social Change.* Chicago: University of Chicago Press, 1983.

L'Herbier, Marcel. *Intelligence du cinématographe.* Paris: Éd. Correa, 1946.

L'Herminier, Pierre. *L'Art du cinéma.* Paris: Seghers, 1960.

MacCabe, Colin. *Godard: Images, Sounds, Politics.* Bloomington: Indiana University Press, 1980.

MacCabe, Colin. *"Slow Motion." Screen* 21 no. 3 (Autumn 1980).

Macey, David. "Fragments of an Analysis: Lacan in Context." *Radical Philosophy* no. 35 (Autumn 1983).

Martin, Marcel. *Le langage cinématographique.* Paris: Cerf, 1955.

Mast, Gerald. "Reply." *Cinema Journal* 25 no. 1 (Fall 1985).

Matejka, Ladislav and Krystyna Pomorska. eds. *Readings in Russian Poetics.* Cambridge: MIT Press, 1971.

Mathews, J.H. *Surrealism and Film.* Ann Arbor: University of Michigan Press, 1971.

Mayne, Judith. "Feminist Film Theory and Criticism: A Review Essay." *Signs* 11 no. 1 (Autumn 1985).

McGee, Rex. "All That Jazz . . . Swing . . . Pop . . . and Rock." *American Film* 5 (July–August 1980).

Mechini, Piero and Roberto Salvatore. eds. *Rossellini, Antonioni, and Buñuel.* Venice: Marsilio Editore, 1973.

Mellen, Joan. *The World of Luis Buñuel.* New York: Oxford University Press, 1978.

Mellencamp, Pat, Mary Ann Doane; and Linda Williams, eds. *Re-Vision: Essays in Feminist Film Criticism.* Los Angeles: American Film Institute, 1983.

Merleau-Ponty, Maurice. *Sense and Non-Sense.* Trans. L. Huber and Patricia Allen Dreyfus. Evanston: Northwestern University Press, 1964.

Merquior, J.G. *From Prague to Paris: A Critique of Structuralist and Poststructuralist Thought.* London: Verso, 1986.

Metz, Christian. *Film Language.* Trans. Michael Taylor. New York: Oxford University Press, 1974.

Metz, Christian. *Language and Cinema.* Trans. Donna Jean Umiker-Sebeok. The Hague: Mouton, 1974.

Metz, Christian. *The Imaginary Signifier.* Bloomington: Indiana University Press, 1981.

Mitchell, Juliet. *Psychoanalysis and Feminism: Freud, Reich, Laing and Women.* New York: Vintage Books, 1975.

Mitry, Jean. *Esthétique et psychologie du cinéma.* Paris: Éd. Univérsitaires, 1963.

Modleski, Tania. *Loving with a Vengeance: Mass-Produced Fantasies for Women.* New York: Methuen, 1982.

Morson, Gary Saul, ed. *Bakhtin: Essays and Dialogues on his Work.* Chicago: University of Chicago Press, 1986.

Mulvey, Laura. "Afterthoughts on 'Visual Pleasure and the Narrative Cinema' Inspired by *Duel in the Sun* (Vidor, 1946)." *Framework* 15/16/17 (Summer 1981).

Mulvey, Laura. "Visual Pleasure and Narrative Cinema." *Screen* 16 no. 3 (August 1975).

Musser, Charles. "The Early Cinema of Edwin Porter." *Cinema Journal* 19 no. 1 (Spring 1979).

Musser, Charles. "The Nickelodeon Era Begins: Establishing the Framework for Hollywood's Mode of Representation." *Framework* nos. 22–23 (1983).

Nichols, Bill. *Ideology and the Image.* Bloomington: University of Indiana Press, 1981.

Nichols, Bill, ed. *Movies and Methods: An Anthology*, volume 1. Berkeley:

University of California Press, 1976; volume 2. Berkeley: University of California Press, 1985.

Nietzsche, Friedrich. *The Birth of Tragedy and the Case of Wagner*. Trans. Walter Kaufman. New York: Random House, 1967.

Palmer, R. Barton. "The Successful Failure of Therapy in *Now, Voyager*: The Woman's Picture as Unresponsive Symptom," *Wide Angle* 8 no. 1 (Spring 1986).

Patterson, David. "Mikhail Bakhtin and the Dialogical Dimensions of the Novel." *Journal of Aesthetics and Art Criticism* 44 no. 2 (Winter 1985).

Petro, Patrice; Cathy Flinn; and E. Ann Kaplan. Reply to Linda Williams. *Cinema Journal* 25 no. 1 (Fall 1985).

Perkins, V.F. *Film as Film: Understanding and Judging Movies*. Harmondsworth: Penguin, 1972.

Podro, Michael. *The Critical History of Art*. New Haven: Yale University Press, 1982.

Poster, Mark. *Existential Marxism in Postwar France: From Sartre to Althusser*. Princeton: Princeton University Press, 1975.

Prendergast, Roy M. *Film Technique and Film Acting*. Trans. Ivor Montagu. New York: Bonanza Books, 1949.

Ray, Robert. *A Certain Tendency of the Hollywood Cinema, 1930–1980*. Princeton: Princeton University Press, 1985.

Rée, Jonathan. "Marxist Modes." In *Radical Philosophy Reader*. London: Verso, 1985.

Ricoeur, Paul. *Interpretation Theory: Discourse and the Surplus of Meaning*. Fort Worth: Texas Christian University Press, 1977.

Riffaterre, Michael. "Describing Poetic Structures: Two Approaches in Baudelaire's 'Les Chats.' " In Tompkins, ed., *Reader-Response Criticism*.

Rondi, Gian Luigi. *Cinema italiano oggi*. Roma: Carlo Bestetti, 1966.

Ropars-Wuilleumier, Marie-Claire. *Le Texte divisé*. Paris: Presses Universitaires de France, 1981.

Rose, Jacqueline. "Paranoia and the Film System." *Screen* 17 no. 4 (Winter 1976/7).

Ryan, Michael. *Marxism and Deconstruction: A Critical Articulation*. Baltimore: Johns Hopkins University Press, 1982.

Sadoul, Georges. *Le Cinéma francais*. Paris: Flammarion, 1962.

Schefer, Jean-Louis. *L'Homme ordinaire du cinéma*. Paris: Gallimard, 1981.

Schlesinger, Tom. "Putting People Together: An Interview with John Sayles." *Film Quarterly* 34 no. 3 (Summer 1981).

Seydor, Paul. *Peckinpah: The Western Films*. Urbana: University of Illinois Press, 1980.

Shaffer, Lawrence. "Reflections on the Face in Film." *Film Quarterly* 31 no. 2 (Winter 1977/8).

Shklovsky, Viktor. "On the Connection Between Devices of *Syuzhet* Construction and General Stylistic Devices." *Twentieth Century Studies* nos. 7/8 (December 1971).

Silverman, Kaja. *The Subject of Semiotics*. New York: Oxford University Press, 1983.

Siska, William C. "Metacinema: A Modern Necessity." *Literature/Film Quarterly* 7 (1979).

Skinner, Quentin, ed. *The Return of Grand Theory in the Human Sciences*. Cambridge: Cambridge University Press, 1985.

Spigel, Lynn. "Detours in the Search for Tomorrow." *Camera Obscura* 13/14 (1985).

Staiger, Janet, "Reply." *Cinema Journal* 25 no. 1 (Fall 1985).

Staiger, Janet, " 'The Handmaiden of Villainy': Methods and Problems in Studying the Historical Reception of a Film." *Wide Angle* 8 no. 1 (Spring 1986).

Staiger, Janet, "The Politics of Film Canons." *Cinema Journal* 24 no. 3 (Spring 1985).

Staiger, Janet. "This Moving Image I Have Before Me." In John O'Connor, ed. *The Historian and the Moving-Image* (forthcoming).

Stam, Robert. "On the Carnivalesque." *Wedge* no. 1 (Summer 1982).

Stam, Robert, *Reflexivity in Film and Literature: From Don Quixote to Jean-Luc Godard*. Ann Arbor: UMI Research Press, 1985.

Stanislavski, Konstantin. *My Life in Art*. Trans. J.J. Robbins. New York: Theater Arts, 1948.

Steiner, Peter. *Russian Formalism: A Metapoetics*. Ithaca: Cornell University Press, 1984.

Stravinsky, Igor. *Poetics of Music in the Form of Six Lessons*. New York: Vintage, 1956.

Suleiman, Susan R. and Inge Crosman, eds. *The Reader in the Text: Essays on Audience and Interpretation*. Princeton: Princeton University Press, 1980.

Sulloway, Frank J. *Freud: Biologist of the Mind*. London: Fontana, 1979.

Soper, Kate. *Humanism and Anti-Humanism*. La Salle, Illinois: Open Court, 1986.

Taylor, John Russell. *Hitch: the Life and Times of Alfred Hitchcock*. New York: Pantheon, 1978.

Taylor, Richard, ed. *The Poetics of the Cinema, Russian Poetics in Translation* 9 (1982).

Therborn, Goran. *The Ideology of Power and the Power of Ideology*. London: Verso, 1980.

Thompson, E.P. *The Poverty of Theory and Other Essays*. London: Merlin, 1978.

Thompson, Kristin. *Breaking the Glass Armor: Neoformalist Film Analysis.* Princeton: Princeton University Press, 1988.

Thompson, Kristin and David Bordwell. "Space and Narrative in the Films of Ozu." *Screen* 17 no. 2 (Summer 1976).

Timpanaro, Sebastiano. *The Freudian Slip: Psychoanalysis and Textual Criticism.* Trans. Kate Soper. London: Verso, 1974.

Timpanaro, Sebastiano. *On Materialism.* Trans. Lawrence Garner. London: New Left Books, 1975.

Todorov, Tzvetan. *Littérature et réalité.* Paris: Éditions du Seuil, 1982.

Todorov, Tzvetan. *Mikhail Bakhtin: The Dialogical Principle.* Trans. Wlad Godzich. Minneapolis: University of Minnesota Press, 1984.

Tompkins, Jane P., ed. *Reader-Response Criticism: From Formalism to Poststructuralism.* Baltimore: Johns Hopkins University Press, 1980.

Trauner, Alexander. "Interview." *Positif* 223 (October 1979).

Truffaut, Francois. *Hitchcock.* New York: Simon and Schuster, 1967.

Taul, Denise. *Le temps devore.* Paris: Fayard, 1980.

Tzonis, Alexander and Liane Lefaivre. *Classical Architecture: The Poetics of Order.* Cambridge: MIT Press, 1987.

Vidal, Jean. Review of *L'Atalante. Pour Vous* 305 (September 20 1934).

Volosinov, V.N. *Freudianism: A Marxist Critique.* Trans. I.R. Titunik and edited in collaboration with Neal H. Bruis. New York: Academic Press, 1976.

Volosinov, V.N. *Marxism and the Philosophy of Language.* Trans. Ladislav Matejka and I.R. Titunik. Cambridge: Harvard University Press, 1976.

Warshow, Robert. *The Immediate Experience.* New York: Atheneum, 1971.

Waugh, Patricia. *Metafiction: The Theory and Practice of Self-Conscious Fiction.* New York: Methuen, 1984.

Wellek, René and Warren, Austin. *Theory of Literature.* New York: Harcourt, Brace, World, 1949.

White, Allon. "Bakhtin, Sociolinguistics, and Deconstruction." In Frank Gloversmith, ed. *The Theory of Reading.* New Jersey: Barnes and Noble Books, 1984.

Wilbur, Ken. *No Boundary.* Boulder and London: Shambala, 1979.

Williams, Christopher, ed. *Realism and the Cinema.* London: Routledge and Kegan Paul, 1980.

Williams, Gordon M. *The Siege of Trencher's Farm.* New York: Dell, 1972.

Williams, Linda. *Figures of Desire: A Theory and Analysis of Surrealist Film.* Urbana: University of Illinois Press, 1981.

Williams, Linda. " 'Something Else Besides a Mother': Stella Dallas and the Maternal Melodrama." *Cinema Journal* 24 no. 1 (Fall 1984).

Wolff, Janet. *The Social Production of Art.* New York: St. Martin's Press, 1981.

Wölfflin, Heinrich. *Principles of Art History.* Trans. M.D. Huttinger. New York: Dover, 1950.

Wollen, Peter. *Readings and Writings: Semiotic Counter Strategies.* London: Verso, 1982.

Wollheim, Richard. "The Cabinet of Dr. Lacan." *New York Review of Books* 25, nos. 21–22 (25 January 1979).

Wood, Robin. *Hollywood from Vietnam to Reagan.* New York: Columbia University Press, 1986.

Wright, Will. *Six Guns and Society: A Structural Study of the Western.* Berkeley: University of California Press, 1975.

Zittner, Sheldon P. *Practices of Modern Literary Scholarship.* Glenview, Illinois: Scott, Foresman, 1966.

INDEX

413